XCON TO ICON

The Kali Muscle Story

Kali Muscle

1st WORLD
PUBLISHING

XCON TO ICON

Kali Muscle

Copyright © Kali Muscle 2013

Published by 1st World Publishing
P.O. Box 2211, Fairfield, Iowa 52556
tel: 641-209-5000 • fax: 866-440-5234
web: www.1stworldpublishing.com

First Edition

LCCN: 2013919509
SoftCover ISBN: 978-1-4218-8676-3
HardCover ISBN: 978-1-4218-8677-0

Acknowledgments

To my beautiful loving wife Dvyne, thank you for staying by my side through thick and thin, through broke times and rich times. If it weren't for you and God, I wouldn't have achieved the things in life that I have. Everything I do is to make you and my children happy without any stress. I also want to say thank you to my mother, my mother in-law, and my best friend Tre for helping me when times were tough. You were there spiritually and financially; you will definitely be blessed.

Introduction

When you look at me what do you see? Do you see a man with a successful rising career, someone with a body of art, a man with a beautiful wife? Well it hasn't always been like that for me. Born into the deep streets of East Oakland, I had to learn how to survive. I was the second born to a single mother on welfare trying to maintain two young men on her own.

Reading this you will see my story, feel my pain and understand my journey of losing my brother and uncle. You will hear about my journey through bodybuilding, see my rise and fall of a promising football career, and walk along with me while I do prison time, drug deals, pimping, stripping, and gang affiliation. You will see my transition to Godly principles, meet my soul mate and experience my new success.

You think you know me, well come along with me on this roller coaster ride and see if you can relate to my struggles of learning what true love is really about, something I didn't know anything about until God put my wife in my life. I never knew what love was growing up because all the love during my childhood was given to my younger brother.

I can say now that I have found my place in life and I am where I need to be and fulfilling my dreams.

Step into my world!

"Wipper Snapper"

I was given the birth name Chuck Kirkendall Jr. because of my biological father's name. I remember being five years old and living in an apartment complex on 76th and Ney Street in Oakland California with my mother and my brother Archie. My mother was the most beautiful woman I had ever laid my eyes on at that young age. Being that my mother was born and raised in Oakland California, she was as vicious as a pit bull on steroids. She didn't take any mess from anybody. In her mind the world was hers and she was going to get what was owed to her. I think this was why I never saw any men at our house. Most people thought that Archie and I had the same father because we looked so much alike, but in reality we didn't, and our mother was currently with neither Archie's father nor my own. I don't think that any man would be able to deal with my mother, not to mention me. I was like a wild silver back gorilla when it came down to protecting her.

My mother had two siblings, Uncle Butch and Aunt Fee. Years later I found out that my mother had an identical twin that died at birth and she also had an older brother that died by drowning.

My mother's brother Doyle (Uncle Butch) was a husky man (what we call buff now). He had muscles on top of muscles and I had never seen anybody else with the stature that he had until years later in my life. Uncle Butch was the same skin complexion as me and he had the same hair texture as I did too. He carried himself like a man should and he didn't mess around. He had fun when it was time to have fun, but he was serious when it was time to be serious. My mother and Uncle Butch were extremely close to one another and Uncle Butch would come and check on her daily to make sure that she hadn't hurt anyone.

Uncle Butch was like my father. He did all the things with me that a father would typically do. He used to take Doyle Jr. and me to the park to teach us to play basketball, football, baseball, running, wrestling, and boxing. He was teaching us how to be men, and I loved him for it.

Then there was my gorgeous Aunt Jeanette or, as everyone called her, Fee. Aunt Fee was darker in color than my mother, though they had the same proportions and were only 4 years apart – my mother being the older of the two and Uncle Butch being the oldest of them all.

Out of my mother and her siblings, Aunt Fee was the loudest, wildest, and most care-free. Aunt Fee just didn't give a damn about what anybody thought about her and her straight forward approach to life. Aunt Fee treated me like she was also my mother and catered to me as if she had given birth to me herself. This caused me to love her more so than I loved my own mother at the time, because Aunt Fee didn't discipline me. I just couldn't do any wrong in her eyes.

My brother Archie was 4 years older than me and he would always let it be known that he was the man of the house, even though he was only nine years old at the time. Archie was darker than me in complexion and though his hair was a different texture than mine, it was almost the same. Archie was wise beyond his years. Even though he was only nine years old, it seemed as though he may have been 18 years old instead. It was almost as if Archie had been here before. He was a sharp dresser, even in his young age, and he always knew how to coordinate the clothes he had put together perfectly. Archie always kept his things in an orderly fashion. He was a neat freak. His hair had to be perfect, his clothes had to be perfect, his shoes had to be spotless – everything that had something to do with him just had to be on a level of perfection. I admired my brother to the upmost. He exuded the air of a king and we got along good except when I didn't do what he told me to. We, of course, as little brother and big brother would have our sibling spats, and of course, because Archie was bigger than I was he would easily win the brotherly battles.

As a young kid I remember living a life every kid should live at five years old – going to school and playing a lot. I went to Stonehurst elementary school on 103rd and E Street in east Oakland CA, as did Archie. I was always superior to the other kids my age, probably because

I had an older brother that was so damn mature. I had fun going to Stonehurst because having an older brother attending the same school makes a huge difference in status. Archie was loved by the teachers as well as by the students, so this elevated my status beyond my understanding. Archie always got straight A's on his report cards, while I struggled to get above average. I didn't understand why Archie was so much smarter I was, but it was probably because I always wanted to be the class clown and be rebellious, not to mention I had a tremendous amount of energy and I didn't know how to control what came out of my mouth.

I was loved by my classmates, but I was hated by the teachers because I would blurt out nasty things about them, especially if they were ugly and had a raggedy car or wore glasses or whatever else I could conjure up that would hurt the teacher's feelings. I certainly got suspended from school quite a bit. I remember getting suspended once because I was showing playboy magazines in the class.

There were railroad tracks about 400 yards from the school's play ground that the students would have to cross to get to school. These railroad tracks were always a place where high jackers would rob the trains and drop a lot of the goods that they had looted from them.

As we would cross the trains to get to school, we would always come across merchandise. A lot of the times we would find candy, potato chips, and magazines, much the way I had on this particular day. I, being the attention getter that I was, took a stack of around 10 magazines that I had found on the railroad tracks and took them to class with me. It was time to silently read to ourselves in class when I decided to show the class some nice ass that was strategically placed on the pages of Playboy magazine. I had one of those desks that you can pull up the top to and I was blocking the teacher from seeing what I was so sneakily doing. What I didn't realize then was that I was sitting right in front of the teacher. Duh! Right! So as everybody started giggling and shuffling about, the teacher looked up and asked me what I was doing and, lying, I told her I was reading my book. The teacher walked around to my desk and pulled the top up, revealing all those magazines I had been trying to hide. She asked me where I got them from and I told her I found them, which I did. Mrs. Teacher grabbed both me and the magazines, and escorted us to the principal's office. The principal asked me what I was doing showing that junk in class and I lied and said I wasn't showing it to anyone.

The principle knew I was lying and picked up the phone. I asked him what he was doing and he said, "I'm calling your mother."

I begged him to please not call that witch, I mean my mother, but he went ahead and called her anyway.

"Yes! Mrs. Kirkendall we seem to have an issue with Chuck!" he said, "He was in class showing his classmates pornography while he was supposed to be silently reading, so we will be sending him home for the rest of the day."

The principle said, "Alright we will be waiting for you. See you soon!"

I, at that moment, felt like bolting out of that office and running away forever, because my mother was relentless when it came to ass whooping. Her whippings' were on the borderline of torture. As I sat there nervous, sweating, pouting, shaking un-controllably, it seemed as though I had telekinesis powers, because I could feel my mother as she was walking down that hallway. At that point I think I peed and boo booed my pants. When she entered the principal's office she resembled the pictures I used to see of what the devil looked like. I saw horns coming out of her head and she was red as a lobster. She kindly told the principal thank you, but her kindness quickly disappeared as soon as she looked at me.

"Let's go!" She said evilly, and as soon as I walked out of the principal's office, she slapped me so hard I think I boo booed a tad bit more in my already boo booey draws.

"It's on when we get to the house!" my mother said to me, and I knew she was serious.

The drive to the house seemed as though it took one second. I didn't even have time to prepare for the ass whooping, which really I should be calling a body whooping, because you never knew where that thick leather belt would be landing on your body.

After my treacherous body whooping, Archie came home from school and asked me what happened. As I was telling him, Meany came back in and told Archie not to talk to me. This was only one of the many treacherous body whoopings I would encounter before I became a teenager.

Life was going good! I was going through my usual suspensions from school and my usual body whooping. My mother would let me and Archie spend the weekends with our father's side of the family, meaning that we were split up most of the time. From Friday to Sunday, Archie would go to his father's side of the family and I would go to my father's side of the family. I remember the first time my mother chose to split us up in this manner. I didn't like it at all and I wouldn't talk during the entire weekend I was at whomevers house it was I was visiting.

But after about the fourth time of me being split up from Archie, I was comfortable with the weekend separations and grew an unexpected love for Fridays, mainly because I knew that I would get the chance to be away from Meany!

Everything was going good and I was getting bigger. Archie had already grown a mustache so he was definitely growing fast. Things couldn't get any better. Then one day my mother broke the news that she was pregnant by her boyfriend Wallace.

Wallace was a man with class, who had a thick afro and was just a little lighter than myself. He had one of the hottest auto-body shops in east Oakland, so he was usually bringing in a lot of money. I, being the protector of the family, didn't like the fact that my mother was seeing a dude, period. Therefore, I gave Wallace hell. I liked to come in between Wallace and my mother when they would hug and give him the meanest look I had to offer, just in an attempt to try and scare him away. It didn't take me long to see that he wasn't going anywhere and I finally embraced Wallace as my step-father. Wallace, not wanting my mother to live in an apartment with his son, opted to buy a house for his soon-to-be baby mama, her two sons, and his son on the way. The house that they decided to buy was Wallace's brother's house that was in foreclosure. Wallace bought the house, which was a hellified mess, and so my mother and I would go by the house to clean it – and I mean this was the nastiest house I had ever encountered in my life up till that point. I guess Wallace's relatives had had dogs living in the house with them, because dog shit was all on the floors and the house smelled of death. I know there must have been a dead body hidden somewhere around in that house. On top of that, the filth was pretty horrible as well. I will never forget that moment in my life. I remember sweeping the floor in the room that would eventually be my bedroom and I decided that I was going to see what was in the only closet in the room. As I twisted the door knob, and slowly pulled the door open, I instantly heard my mother screaming, "No! Don't open that door!" But it was too late.

I had opened the door to the home of a billion cockroaches and before I could get the door shut again about a thousand of them had made their way up the walls and into the cracks. Pure filth! Yuck!

I remember my mother getting the house prepared for her new son to come and how we worked on it day-in-day out for months.

Uncle Butch did all the electrical work in the house, him being an electrician and all, which saved Wallace and my mother a lot of money, because Wallace's relatives were living there with no lights or running water. Savages! As I remember, my mother was about eight months pregnant when the house was finally completed It went from the most disastrous house on the block to the most luxurious.

I would have never thought that that house could have looked the way it did as a finished project. My mother, Archie, and I moved all of our things from the apartment on Ney Street, to the house on E Street, with the help of Uncle Butch and Wallace. I was happy to be moving into a house and away from that crime ridden apartment building we were living in.

When I moved to E Street I made friends fast. There were a lot of kids on E Street. My best friends ended up being my next door neighbors, Derrick and Darold. Their mother's name was Alfreta, and their older brother was named Darrin. Alfreta was another one of those no bullshit type of women. She was a single mother and proud of it. She had a good job and always said, "She don't need no stanking man for nothing." She still says this to this day.

Derrick was one year younger than me, Darold was 4 years younger than me, and Darrin was 10 years older than me. Derrick and Darold were more like crime partners. They did everything together. They were the first ones that tried me in the neighborhood. Derrick was a chubby kid that was always hesitant to do things that a young boy normally wouldn't be hesitant to do, but Darold, on the other hand, wasn't hesitant to do anything. He was like a torpedo, and he was up for any challenge. I also had another best friend on the block whose name was Justin. He was half black, half-white, but he looked more white than anything else.

He had a little brother named Jason, who was weird to me so we didn't let Jason hang out with us too often. Justin's mother was also a single parent raising two sons. Justin was like my hype man, better yet, he was my yes man. Justin did whatever I told him to do, and he was definitely a follower. Then you had my associates that lived down the street. They were what you would call ghetto. They sold dope, smoked dope, drank dope, and it seemed as though they had no hope, but I loved the adrenaline rush when I snuck down the street to hang out with them. We would shoot dice, play football and baseball in the streets, and do wheelies on our bikes. The hoodlums were my type of people.

My mother was going into labor and Wallace had to rush her to the hospital while Archie and I stayed at home anticipating another brother. We were nervous because we didn't know what to expect on dealing with a new-born baby.

Later that night, or I should say early morning, we were awakened by our mother telling us that she was home with our baby brother. Archie and I ran to go see him. He was red like his skin was irritated or something. He had a water head, as the doctors called it. His head was abnormally large and my mother told us that we couldn't touch it due to him having soft spots. We said o.k. but I didn't understand. Of course, Mr. Genius Archie always understood everything. Our new brother was a loud crying ass baby! He wouldn't stop crying until his parents would come running to his beck and call to hold him, feed him, or change him. He was a unique baby, and he already knew that the house was his and everyone in it was his slave. I'm telling you that that baby was put into our family to cause pure hell.

My mother didn't stay home long. She was a nurse and had gotten used to making that money, so she mapped out a baby-sitting schedule for Archie and me. Wallace couldn't baby sit because he had to run his automotive business, which left Archie and me as the only option to watch the kid sent from hell. When my mother told us about this plan, I almost fainted. I just couldn't fathom having to watch that spoiled infant every day of the week.

My summer vacation after fifth grade was a summer that I'll never forget for the rest of my life. It started off good. Aunt Fee had a baby girl she named Erica. She was the most beautiful baby I had ever laid my eyes on and I'm not just saying that, because not all babies are pretty. Erica had hazel eyes that turned all sorts of colors. It was the first time I had ever seen a black baby with hazel eyes. I didn't think that she was even Aunt Fee's baby. I thought that maybe they had had an accidental baby switch in the hospital.

Erica actually looked like a white baby, because she didn't look like she had any melanin in her skin. Everybody kept saying she would darken up, but Aunt Fee was just happy that she had a baby, and I was happy for her. During the summer I would go over her house any chance I could get just so I could help watch Ms. Hazel Eyes.

When I wasn't spending time at Aunt Fee's house, I was spending all day at the boys club on 85th. I loved the boys club and the scandalous people that frequented it. I met a lot of friends at that club and it helped in molding me into the person I am today. You had to be physically and mentally strong to be a member at the 85th boys club, simple as that.

Fourth of July rolled around fast and my mother was throwing a huge family gathering at our house. All the family would be there and I couldn't wait to see everybody. Uncle Butch bought me and Archie a ton of fireworks and we were pretty excited. He showed us how to light the fireworks and how to run once they were lit. The day was going great. Everyone was partying and all of us kids were in the front yard popping our firecrackers, having a blast. I mean, we had everybody at that house; Alfreta was there with Derrick, Darold and Darrin. Justin and Jason were there too and even some of the hoodlums from down the street were there. Everyone was having a jolly old time. Archie came up to me at one point and told me to give him my cigarette lighter because he had lost his. I said to him, "No! Go get you another one. I need mines." He then hoodwinked me and asked if he could use it right quick to light his bottle-rocket, so being my brother I gave him the lighter not thinking that he would trick me.

After Archie lit his bottle-rocket I asked him for my lighter back and he told me that it was his now. I don't know what had gotten into my brother on that particular day to cause him to try and bully me out of what was mine, but I asked him to give me my lighter and he once again told me no! I grabbed him and tried to wrestle the lighter out of his hand, but he had a lock on it and I couldn't get it away from him. I told him that if he didn't give me my lighter that I was going to stab him, so I pulled out my buck knife that I carried with me all day everyday for protection. I asked him one more time to give me my lighter and he laughed at me and began riding his bike down the street at full speed. I chased him down and when I caught up to him I cocked my arm back and I stabbed my brother in the back. He yelled out in shear pain! Owwww!

I felt bad at that point, but it was something that God put in me not to let anyone get the better of me or bully me. Archie dropped the bike and ran to the house crying that I had stabbed him. Everyone came running to see what had happened and I was more scared than a snitch at a gangster party. Meany told me to go to my room until she told me otherwise, but Uncle Butch, being the mediator, he found out exactly what had happened. From there he told my mother not to give me a whooping because Archie was bullying me and that Archie had gotten what he deserved.

"He won't be bullying him anymore, I bet you that." Those were Uncle Butch's exact words to my mother!

Archie got home that night from getting a few stitches and he told me that he didn't want me to feel bad, that he was glad I didn't let him or no one else punk me. This would be the last altercation Archie and I ever had.

My mother didn't come and say anything to me, and for some odd reason I didn't feel like she loved me at all. She treated me like a foster child or something, but Wallace came in and told me that I did what I had to do and not to feel bad about it. Everyone knew that I loved my brother as I loved myself and that I didn't want to intentionally hurt him in that manner. But it happened and I had to move forward.

My first day at Highland was something that I wasn't used too. Out of all the faces, I knew only a few people. Justin and his brother Jason went there, so that was a relief. At least I knew somebody, which was cool. I made friends extremely fast, mostly because I was a pure athlete – basketball, football, baseball, you name it, I could play it. I gained a lot of respect, and fast, because of my athleticism. I'll never forget the class that I was placed in. It seemed as though the kids in that particular class were slow, and I didn't understand why I was placed in there with them. It wasn't long before God answered my prayers though and my class was closed down due to remodeling, causing all the kids to be split up and sent to different classes. When the teacher called my name and said that I would be going to Mr. Tolbert's class, I yelled out like an ignorant buffoon. I was so excited. Mr. Tolbert's class was for the gifted kids of the school. If you were in there you were taught everything from math to acting. His was the class to be in, because not only was Mr. Tolbert cool, but the prettiest girls in the school were in there, so I had struck gold. Mr. Tolbert was unbelievable. I never thought that I would enjoy learning until being in his class. Mr. Tolbert made it cool to be smart.

During the era I grew up in in Oakland, smart kids were bullied and harassed on a daily basis, so no one wanted to seem smart, but everyone in this class was smart.

I loved school. I never thought that I would ever have that sort of reaction towards learning, and I even started to think I was getting weird or something. Every day that I went home to babysit Spoiled, all I thought about was school and getting back to Mr. Tolbert's class. I hated watching Spoiled. He was the worst of the worst. Wallace and my mom made a huge mistake bringing that demon into the world.

"Death Comes"

I'll never forget the day that I lost my Uncle Butch. I was ten years old at the time, and Uncle Butch had told me and Archie that he was going to buy us a huge television for our bedroom. Archie and I could hardly contain the excitement we felt over having our own television, and we stayed up waiting on Uncle Butch for two hours past the time that he said he would be back. We thought maybe he would bring it the next day instead, so we went to sleep only to be woken up with my mother screaming.

"No! Not my only brother! Why God? Why?" She cried.

I had never, in all my life, seen my mother that hysterical. Wallace was trying his best to comfort her while Archie and I looked on helplessly, trying to figure out what was going on. I knew something had happened to my uncle, but nobody told us one way or the other. My mother cried herself to sleep that night.

Eventually Wallace told Archie and me what had happened. He explained to us that Uncle Butch had just picked up our television set, and that as he was on his way to bring it back, when he tried to pull to the far exit lane and evidentially he couldn't dodge the 18 wheeler that was parked in the median. Uncle Butch ended up under the 18 wheeler with his chest caved in from the steering wheel. He was pronounced dead at the hospital.

I told Wallace he was lying about my Uncle Butch. "He was too buff to die," I said, "You lying Wallace!"

My mother took me to see for myself the next day. I don't know the reason why she took me to see my Uncle Butch's truck. It was horrifying to see it crushed in the way it was, like a soda can. Blood was everywhere, thick blood, and when I looked in the bed of his truck and saw the television set, I immediately started blaming myself for what had happened. I told myself that if Uncle Butch hadn't got that television he would still be alive. That truck, that truck! What a memory! Uncle Butch's funeral was one of many that I would attend as a young man.

The wake for my Uncle was held at the infamous C.P. Bannon. Everyone that I knew who had died had either their wake or funeral there. My mother was a mess then. She couldn't even stand up. At the time, I didn't understand what was wrong with my mother. I had never seen her like that before. Wallace and a lot of our family members were busy trying to take care of her and keep her calm, while Archie and I struggled to hold ourselves together as best as we could. Funerals have never been my thing though. That was the only time that I would cry was at a funeral. I started crying when I looked into the casket and realized that Uncle Butch was actually in it. He looked as if he could just wake up and step up out of that coffin of his. It was hard to imagine that he was never coming back. My brother and I were having a hard time, of course, but when my mother looked up and saw her brother's face, she totally lost it. She fainted, right then and there, and the ambulance had to be called to come take her to the hospital.

Wallace told me and Archie that everything was going to be alright, and for some reason whenever Wallace said something was going to be alright, I knew he was telling the truth. Archie and I stayed by each other's side the entire day and since Wallace had Spoiled , we didn't have to baby sit at the funeral. Afterwards I went and hugged Uncle Butch's son, Doyle, and told him how sorry I was for what had happened. He told me he was sorry too, being that Uncle Butch loved me as if I were his son as well.

Even though my mother and I weren't very fond of one another, I couldn't help but be concerned about her. When we finally got home after the burial, it was such a surreal experience. I couldn't imagine Uncle Butch being gone and never seeing him again. For years it was difficult on my entire family, particularly my mother, who was never quite the same person after losing her brother.

My school year at Highland was good, but it would have been even better if Uncle Butch had still been alive. I learned more in that single school year at Highland than I ever did in the five I spent at Stonehurst. For graduation, Mr. Tolbert's class gave a musical, and I was the human beat box. I beat boxed to whatever song was being sung and it was great. After the graduation we had a dinner dance for all those that were graduating. During that time everyone was making dates with the girl or boy that they liked most, but because I didn't like any of the girls – they were too mouthy and all of them had that ghetto mama attitude that I despised – so I was planning on being my own date.

Just as I was thinking about what I was going to wear to the dinner dance, my nemesis, Dahlia – a girl in the sixth grade who looked as though she was supposed to be a senior in high school – came up to me. The first thing I thought was that Dahlia probably heard that I was talking about her, because her and I used to go at it like cats and dogs, and that she was coming to confront me about it. She called me Shaka Zulu and I asked her how many times she flunked the sixth grade. Those were the types of things that we threw at one another constantly. As I watched Dahlia walk towards me, she had a smile I had never seen her wear before and I immediately became suspicious, however, when she approached me I couldn't have been more surprised.

"You know we be talking about each other all the time and you may think that I don't like you, but in fact I have always liked you, I just didn't know how to express it," she said to me.

Well she was certainly right about one thing. I didn't think she liked me. In fact, the whole situation was absolutely unbelievable. I mean, me and that girl would have probably killed one another if we thought we could get away with it, and suddenly she was telling me that she liked me. Crazy!

Dahlia asked me if I would go to the dinner dance with her and out of bewilderment I said of course I would go. None of my friends could believe that the black widow (as we called her)asked me to go with her to the dinner dance. For an entire year that girl and I seemed as if we hated each other. I mean, we got into heated arguments where we would have to go to the principal's office to settle the dispute, and it was serious! And here everyone would see us dancing the night away as if none of that had ever happened. Life has so many different turns and scenic routes. We don't have any idea what will lie ahead of us.

The dinner dance was fun. Dahlia and I danced all night long. She kept those huge knockers of hers all in my face and we even kissed later. That was weird but I just went with the flow. Afterwards, we all said our goodbyes, even though most of us would see each other again once school started back up. People like Dahlia I haven't seen since that dance though – which was around 20 years ago – and we used to live just a few miles away.

The summer following my graduation from Highland was similar to my last summer. I went to the boys club every day, and after I left the boys club I usually went by pop's shop (Archie and I called Wallace pops now) to clean up and make a few dollars. Ever since I can remember I was a money hungry kid. I was always looking up ways to make money somehow. I call it a money addiction, which is the worst kind of addiction to have because a money addict will do anything, and I mean anything, to get some money in their pocket. A money addict is truly worse than a heroin, meth, or crack addict. Pops used to give me a few dollars every day for cleaning up the shop and, of course, I would use it to buy junk food. I continued to do that for the duration of the summer and I was pretty happy with my life at that point. I could play all day, go make a few dollars, and eat the best junk food around. What more could a kid ask for?

Towards the end of that summer, my mother took Archie and me shopping for the school clothes we would need for the year. Because Archie had his own stores in mind that he wanted to shop at, my mother just gave him the money he needed and let him do his own thing. He wouldn't even let me know where these stores of his were. Like I told you, Archie was serious about whatever he did in life, especially when it came to his clothes. Clothes were his addiction, though I guess they were mine too, because I was always competing with Archie in one way or another. He was way more GQ than me though. Archie wore boots, sweaters, and tailored pants, while I wore tennis shoes, button up shirts, and jeans.

On the first day of school I was so excited I was shaking. Like with everything else in Archie's life, he didn't mess around when it came to school and so he left early. I got dressed fast and made sure that my waves were in place, that my teeth were clean, and that I was smelling good. On my way out the door I told my mother I would see her later and she handed me the two dollars that I would need for lunch that day. I looked at that measly two bucks thinking, what am I supposed to do with this? She read the expression on my face right away.

"Shit boy that's enough, what you thought you were getting, ten dollars or something? Two dollars is more than enough," she said to me.

I didn't argue with her. I said thank you and I rushed out the door without even saying bye to Spoiled.

"Make sure yo ass is here before 4'o clock, I have to go to work," she yelled out at me.

That meant that I had to rush home after school to babysit Spoiled. Oh well, there goes hanging out after school. On my way to class, Boogie (this was Justin's nickname then) met me outside and we walked to school together. I noticed that he didn't have on spiffy clothes like me and I asked him if he went clothes shopping. He said he had to wait on his father to give his mother some money to take them shopping. I was thinking, damn! I got it made! I saw the jealousy in Boogie's eyes and I asked him how much money he had on him, but he said none.

"Damn! How you going to eat player?" I said to him.

He told me that his mother signed him up for free lunches. Now I don't know about you, but when I grew up, free lunches were a definite no, no! Boogie didn't have any shame in his game though; I think he was used to these conditions in his life. I knew I had to make sure that Boogie wasn't labeled as my friend anymore, being that he was broke and all. Sorry, but that's just how it was in Oakland. You couldn't let the world see that you were broke, even if you were.

My first day back at school was very eventful. I met a lot of people, good and bad, and I found out about all the different blocks (sets that people claimed). You had 98th, (where I was supposed to be from) 100th, 85th, 77th, 72nd, dag, Brookfield, and the most notorious at that time - Sobrante Park. I claimed I was from 77th because Aunt Fee lived over there and I stayed at her house a lot. I knew everyone from 77th and that was the block I knew the most about in general. I didn't know all the people on my block yet, but when I finally did feel like E Street was mine, which was in about a two month time period, I dropped 77th for E Street.

Elmhurst was a school I felt like I could conquer pretty easily. Granted, there were a lot of kids there that thought they were ballers – wearing their Fila sweat suits, big donkey chains, and Cazal glasses – but I also knew a lot of those kids were being raised with a silver spoon in their mouths. I knew they couldn't fight. Fighting was a necessity in the hood; if people knew you could fight you would get the upmost respect.

I took my time to analyze the entire campus. I watched people and I didn't talk much, because I had to get comfortable with the new atmosphere. I saw who the bullies were, who were scary, who had the money and the girls.

I'll never forget the first time that I went to the food court on campus. It was like a restaurant. You could order hot dogs, hamburgers, nachos, and even chili cheese fries. I immediately rushed over and asked for the chili cheese fries, but they told me it would cost three dollars and I knew that I didn't have that. I didn't let on that I was lacking the money though. I just told them that I had changed my mind and not to worry about it. I was embarrassed, not because anyone had seen, but because of my financial situation – of only having that two stanking dollars. I vowed then that I would never go through an experience like that again.

After that day at the food court, I asked my mother if I could get around four dollars a day.

"Hell no!" she said to me.

She told me she was on a budget and she could only give me two dollars. At that moment of her saying "hell no", I knew that I had to do something to put money in my pockets fast.

I remember seeing the hoodlums at the green apartments shooting dice and having a wad of cash in their hands and pockets, talking loud and cussing and calling out numbers. It was very intriguing to me, so I snuck down there one day and asked them if they could teach me how to shoot dice.

"No problem" they said, "You will learn in five minutes!"

They weren't lying. I learned how to shoot dice in five minutes and in an hour I had one hundred dollars. I couldn't believe that it was so easy to make money. I decided then that shooting dice was going to be my new job. I went home with that money and went into the bathroom and counted out one hundred and nine dollars. I couldn't believe it. That was the first time I had ever made that much money and since I was only 11 years old at the time, that one hundred dollars was a lot.

I wanted to tell somebody but at that point in my life I wasn't fond of trusting people at all. I couldn't even tell Archie, because there was no telling what he would do. Instead I kept my new found job all to myself.

The next day I went to school with my head held high and with a big bulge of one dollar bills protruding from my pockets. I used to play basketball every day on campus and I remember seeing a crowd of guys bending down while some other people watched out for campus police. I knew that was the dice shooting crowd, so instead of going to play basketball that day, I decided to go see what was going on with them. It blew me away what I saw. Those junior high kids were shooting one hundred dollar bills, while I was shooting one dollar bills and I thought that was a lot. That's when I realized just how baller some of these kids at Elmhurst were. There was over twenty thousand dollars lying on the ground of a junior high school, more than the teachers were making, which was crazy.

I was standing there a while, trying to get a feel for the game, when someone blurted out, "I bet he hit for $20."

I don't know what had gotten into me, but I said, "He don't hit" (meaning that the guy shooting the dice won't hit his point).

I counted out $20 and dropped it on the ground and the guy said, "Bet." I was nervous as hell; I didn't want to lose my hard earned money! The guy's point was eight, the best number to have while you are shooting dice. The guy rolled a nine; he started doing a lot of talking saying, "come on baby eight a skate, hit".

The dice rolled in slow motion and I saw the four stop while the next dice kept spinning uncontrollably.

"Come on baby!" the guy kept saying.

The dice started slowing down, slow, slow, slow, until it stopped on the three. Four and three is seven, so the guy lost and I won. I couldn't believe I just won twenty dollars in one minute. It was incredible. I snatched up my money, and walked off.

"Do you want to bet again?" the guy asked as I walked away, but I told him I couldn't, because I had to go to class.

I was walking with my head held up even higher after that, with pride in having money in my pockets and not just two measly dollars that I couldn't even get a complete lunch with. Ha! I was going to show everybody that I was a money making machine.

Once I discovered my new job of shooting dice, my grades started lacking because I used to cut classes to meet up with the boys in the back of the school and try to win myself some money. My pockets were fat but everything else was caving in on me. I had to babysit Spoiled from the moment I got home from school until Wallace or Meany got home later that night. I knew ever since we were kids that Spoiled and I would never be the close brothers that Archie and I were. There was just something about that kid that wasn't right.

Spoiled lied a lot, made up fairy tale type stories, and threw tantrums constantly, – all the things that weren't tolerated by Archie and me. Spoiled was pop's so called "golden child" because pops had him at 50 years old. I think pops was too old to have Spoiled, because he wasn't playing with a full deck. I was also upset that I had to babysit Spoiled because that meant I could never do anything after school, like play football, basketball or baseball. Elmhurst coaches were always asking me if I wanted to play for the Elmhurst Eagles, and of course I wanted to, but I would get laughed at if I told the coaches that I couldn't play because I had to babysit. Instead I would tell the coaches that I would play next year, just to get them off my back.

"Lies Will Kill"

My school year became tragic for me when, during this one particular day while watching Spoiled, things got eerie. Something wasn't right about this particular day, and I strongly felt like something bad was going to happen. I remember Spoiled throwing a lot of tantrums and demanding me to get him this and get him that. He was telling me that he was going to get me in trouble. I just couldn't understand that demon. Meany came home early with a messed up attitude, so I hurried up and went in my room to play my video games and get some peace. That was when I overheard my mother asking Spoiled, "He touched you where?"

"Down there on my private!" Spoiled told her.

"What! He touched my baby!" Meany said, furious.

I went in the room and asked my mother what was wrong and I saw a look from her that I had never seen before; she really looked like a demon then. She was beet red and crying, her veins popping out of her head like she was about to explode.

"You touched my baby you motherfucker you! You not going to turn my son into no faggot! I'm about to kill yo black ass!" she screamed at me.

I yelled back at her that I didn't touch him, "He lying!" I said to her, and then I turned towards Spoiled, "You better tell her you are lying boy!" I shouted at him.

As I was talking, I saw my mother reaching for her gun, a .38 snub nose Saturday night special that she kept in her closet in a shoe box. I pleaded with her that I didn't touch him, that I was in my room all day playing my video games, but she wasn't hearing what I was saying. She had her mind made up that she was going to kill me that day, and that was the only time in my life that I felt as if I were about to die.

I was frightened, sitting nervously on the bed in my room and wondering how this could be real. She searched through the box in her closet until she found what she was looking for and then appeared out of nowhere in my room. She looked like a gargoyle ready to kill. She slowly raised her gun and pointed it at me.

"You touched my baby! I'm about to kill your black ass!" she said to me, crying.

I hurriedly tucked and rolled under my bed and no sooner had I done that than the telephone rang. I was peeking out from under the bed and when I looked at Meany's eyes it seemed as though she had just snapped out of a trance. She went and answered the phone and that was when I made a mad dash for the front door, bolting out barefoot into the streets and running like Kunta Kinte from a slave plantation. Everyone was outside and watching me as I flew past them on my way to my friend Julius' house. When I got to his house I knocked on the door and Julius' mother answered.

"Can I help you?" She said to me.

I told her I was a friend of Julius, so she called Julius' name and told him that someone was outside to see him. Julius was a plump, high yellow cat that acted like he was full grown, despite the fact that he was only 11 years old at the time. For being so young, Julius looked like he must have been around 20 years old, but then again the kid already had a beard by 11.

"What's up boy? What's wrong with you, you been crying?" Julius said to me.

I told him what had happened and asked him if I could stay at his house. He said he had to ask his mother, but when he asked her, she told me that she would have to call my mother to inform her that I was at her house first, and that's exactly what she did. I heard my mother saying she was going to be right over to get me. I started shaking uncontrollably, crying and stuttering all at the same time, trying to explain to Julius' mother that my own mother was going to kill me. Julius' mother looked pretty doubtful.

"She might give yo ass a whooping but she ain't going kill you," she said to me. Little did she know!

Meany pulled up and honked the horn for me to come out, but I didn't budge. Julius' mom told me to go ahead and I told them both that if I never saw them again that it was their fault. I went to the car and opened the door and Meany told me to get in the back seat because she didn't want to see my face. I got in the back seat quietly. The house wasn't even a mile from Julius' house, yet that was the longest ride I think I I've ever taken in my life.

When we reached the house I got out of the car, knees shaking, and I walked inside. Archie was home by that point and I looked at him and gave a quick nod. Archie seemed to know right off the bat that I was in a shit load of trouble, and he looked at me with obvious solace in his eyes. I went into my room and got under the covers reluctantly, not knowing whether or not it was safe for me to live in that house any longer. I drifted off to sleep, and as soon as I started dreaming, I felt the covers snatched back. My hands were in my pants in order to keep my hands warm and Meany snatched them out and told me that she never wanted to see my hands in my pants again or she would chop off my little dick. She reached back like she was a lumberjack about to chop some wood, and she violently came across my face with a vicious extension cord. My mother kept going until she was tired, and I was bruised and battered up.

"Bet not never hear about you touching my son again, I will kill you!" she yelled.

I lived a life of fear after that day because of Spoiled and Meany. It seemed as though they were put on Earth to make my life a living hell, and they were doing a damn good job. The weirdest part of it all was that I still had to babysit Spoiled every day after school. I would have thought that if someone would have touched your child that you wouldn't have continued to let that person watch them anymore, but that's not what happened. I still had full babysitting responsibilities. The only difference now was that Spoiled had to stay in my mother's room and I had to stay in mine. That was a method that I had been doing anyway, even on that dreadful day when Spoiled lied about me the way he did.

My mother used to call every 30 minutes and Spoiled would answer the phone at four years old and tell her what was going on. He used to call me "Blacky" and would say stuff like, "Blacky in there playing the video game" or "Blacky in there watching television."

This went on for a few more months until one day my babysitting responsibilities came to an abrupt stop.

"One Less in the Nest"

Dice shooting continued and it even got so serious that me and some of my friends from the block used to catch the bus during school hours and head to Union City to buy an assortment of different dice. This place had all colors, shapes and sizes. I loved the dice store. I used to get so excited when I walked in there and asked what was new. If you were a real dice shooter you always kept at least two pairs of dice on you at all times. I was labeled a dice specialist at that point, and I had the pocket bulge to prove it.

One day I was at school shooting dice during fifth period and I didn't realize that we were shooting dice right outside the window of Mrs. Lassiter's class. She heard all the commotion outside and looked out her window to see me counting over two hundred dollars in one dollar bills, so that stack was humongous. She yelled out for all of us to get to class, except for me, who she specifically told to come to her class. All I could think about was her trying to take my money.

I had already programmed myself to never let anyone take anything away from me, and I meant never. I went to Mrs. Lassiter's class and she continued with her lesson, but as she talked all I could do was watch the clock anxiously and hope that class would be over with immediately.

When the school bell rang, Mrs. Lassiter told me to have a seat. She said that we were going to the principal's office to call my mother and see if she knew about all that money I had. Mrs. Lassiter said I had enough money to choke a horse. That was the first time I had heard someone say that.

The principal called my mother to the school and it's as if I felt my mother's spirit when she was near. My body seemed to heat up whenever Meany was around. I heard her footsteps walking towards the principal's office, when she appeared out of nowhere like a magician or something. Mrs. Lassiter told my mother what she had seen, and my mother told her thank you regretfully. The principal pulled out the dice that they had confiscated from me and showed my mother, who was dumb founded. My mother asked the principal what they were and the principal told her that they were my fancy dice that I had in my pocket. Then the principal took out my wad of cash, over two hundred dollars, and handed it to my mother.

"What in the world is that?" my mother asked, her eyes huge.

"That's your son's money," the principal replied.

My mother grabbed the money and told the principle thank you. Meany then grabbed me by my ear and pushed me outside the principal's office and slapped me in front of the entire school. She looked at me evilly and that's when I lost it. I ran out of that school as fast as I could without ever once looking back. I ran, crying, with no money, and not knowing where I was going to go. It hit me fast to go to the Skinners house. The Skinners were my cousins through marriage. My Aunt Fee had married a Skinner, but she was divorced from him by then.

The Skinners were a reputable family in Oakland, so they were my extended family that I stayed in contact with. I ran from 98th to 85th in no time. The Skinners were used to seeing me quite often so they didn't even question why I was there; they just let me in and told me that Brian was downstairs. Brian was the youngest skinner boy. He was a cocky, flamboyant sort of kid, and tough too. Brian and I had a weird type of friendship. We fought a lot and, though I didn't know why at the time, he always bought me stuff and cooked for me.

By the time night rolled around, Brian told me it was getting dark and that I better get home before my mother started tripping. I asked him if I could stay at his house, because my mother was already tripping and didn't want to live at the house with her anymore.

Brian told me that I could stay with him as long as I needed to, and he didn't even ask his mother, unlike Julius. Brian was the youngest boy but he ran the house like he was the father of it instead.

I actually got a good night's sleep for a change; I didn't have to worry about someone coming and ripping my covers back and whooping me with an extension cord.

I woke up the next morning and I didn't know what I was going to wear to school. When I asked Brian if he had something for me to wear, he told me to go in the walk-in closet and get whatever I wanted.

"Anything?" I asked Brian.

"Anything," he said, "You are my brother now, whatever we got you got."

That house had love in it and I never wanted to leave.

School was going good while I was on the run from Meany and Spoiled. I was back to shooting dice a little, but I wasn't cutting class the way I used to and I even started playing on the school basketball team. I thought to myself that I should have run away from that house of mine a long time ago.

I was still living with the Skinners for three weeks and life was going good, I tell you. Brian was the first person I ever saw to cook French fries with the skin still on them. Those things were good as hell. Just about every day we ate hamburgers and French fries, and I loved it. I was around people that respected me and I respected them. That was the way a house was supposed to be. I had almost been living with my new family for one month, when out of nowhere Aunt Fee was driving down 85th one day and saw me at the Skinner's house.

Aunt Fee calmly parked her car and walked towards me with her huge belly. She was pregnant with her second baby at the time.

"Boy, where you been for almost a month?" She said to me.

"I been right here, Aunt Fee, at my new family house," I told her.

"Well, go get your stuff. I am going to take you to my house," she said

"Alright everybody, I'm about to go with my Aunt Fee. I want to thank you all for putting up with me for the time I was here. Thank you for everything. I love you guys!" I said.

A tear wanted to roll down my eyes but I wouldn't let it. I knew I couldn't let the Skinners see me cry or they would definitely be bullying me from there on out! I went and got in the car with Aunt Fee and she just couldn't believe that I had been at the Skinner's house that entire time. She said that she passed that house every day and didn't see me out there. That was because I was in hiding, I thought. I didn't play outside so I wouldn't get captured.

We got to Aunt Fee's house on Renwick Street and she asked me if I was hungry, but I was too nervous to eat because I knew that she was going to call my mother. No sooner had I thought it, than Aunt Fee picked up her phone. I asked her who she was calling and she whispered, "Your mother."

"Hello!" Aunt Fee said to my mother.

I heard my mother respond with a dry "Hello" on the other end of the line. Her voice was always dry when she spoke to Aunt Fee, mainly because of issues involving Aunt Fee wanting to be my mother. Seriously, Aunt Fee wanted to adopt me as her own son because she loved me as her own, not to mention she had lost her baby son to crib death. Ever since then, Aunt Fee would ask my mother to let me live with her. After that, the relationship between the two of them was severed a little more than it already was. To make matters worse, my mother knew I loved Aunt Fee tremendously more than I loved her.

"Girl you ain't going to believe this, I got your son ass over here!" Aunt Fee told my mother.

I could hear Meany ranting angrily on the other end of the line.

"Bitch you had him over there all this damn time? I'm about to call the police right now!" I could hear her saying.

Aunt Fee tried to explain what had happened to my mother, but Meany wouldn't listen and she hung up the phone. I never thought in a million years that my mother would call the police, because I thought that she hated the police, but I guess I was wrong, because before I knew it, I heard someone banging on Aunt Fee's door saying, "Oakland police! Open up!"

I thought, damn that bitch actually called the police. They asked my aunt what had happened and she told them what was going on. They told me to come with them, because they had to take me to a group home until the issue was resolved.

Sitting in the back of that police car was the first time out of many more that I would be sitting in the back of a police car, sweating and nervous. The police escorted me into what looked like a house and then into an office where the house counselor was.

"Hello!" the counselor said.

"What's up?" I replied.

I didn't know where I was, so when the police left I was pretty nervous. The counselor asked me a lot of questions, and all I kept telling him was that that bitch had pulled a gun out on me and that I never wanted to go back to that house ever again.

"Who pulled a gun out on you?" he asked.

"That damn demon lady that you would probably call my mother," I said.

The counselor didn't seem to know how to respond. Rather than ask any more questions, he just sighed and went over the mandatory house rules with me: mind your business, clean up your room, take showers, brush your teeth, and be respectful to everyone in the house.

I joined all the kids in the pool room – which was made out of a garage. I liked shooting pool so I would be spending a lot of time in that room if I were going to stay. I greeted everybody inside, which was around eight kids, and they all looked well rested and healthy. My time at the group home was short though. I only stayed three days, and on that dreaded morning of my departure from the group home I had to tell all my new friends that I was leaving and for everyone to take care of themselves. They all said their goodbyes, and I headed off in a police car in the back seat. I didn't want to sit in the front of the police car; no one was going to say I was snitching!

The police took me to a building not far from Elmhurst. I was escorted by the cop to an office that Meany and I were supposedly having our counseling session at. The guy inside the office was a middle-aged black guy who was friendly, I could tell that. He also had a smoothness about his approach when it came to dealing with disgruntled people.

"What's the problem with you and your mom?" He asked me.

"Spoiled," I replied simply, "He came into the family and broke it to pieces. We were a happy family until Spoiled came into existence, and then my world was turned upside down."

"How did your brother coming into the family mess it up?" The counselor asked calmly.

I told him a list of things that Spoiled did to split the family up and the counselor was astounded to hear them.

At that moment Meany walked in the office and spoke to me but I didn't say a word in response. I was disgusted at the sight of her. I felt nauseous every time my mother was around and I sincerely hated everything about her during that time. She sat down and the counselor went over everything I said. He asked her if she had anything to say about what had been discussed, but she refused to talk.

Her silence must have given me some sort of boost in confidence, because at that point I started acting like I was on some crazy medication. "I am not going home with this bitch!" I yelled.

That was the first time I had ever cussed at my mom to her face. I felt suddenly empowered; I was a new kid that wasn't taking any shit from anybody, not even from Meany.

"You ain't going to talk disrespectful to me nigga!" she said, rising to her feet.

"Fuck you bitch!" I said to her, and then I turned to the counselor, "Counselor, I'm not going to this bitch house so she can kill me with her .38 snub nose Saturday night special."

My mom and I were both standing up at that time, the counselor trying desperately to calm us down. Finally he got us calm so that we could talk and try to resolve the situation. He asked me how I could make the situation better and I told him that I didn't want to make it better.

"She can have her Spoiled and they can live happily ever after without me," I said.

The counselor asked Meany how she could make the situation better and, her being the stubborn person she was, she told the counselor that it might not work.

The counselor went into the chapters of his psychology books and started quoting things that neither one of us understood. Finally, my mother said that she would try to show me more love, and that she would not believe the things that Spoiled said about me. I still had my mean mug on because, truthfully, I didn't want to live back at that house anyway. I thought the house was haunted and, on top of that, I didn't want to have to worry about my covers being snatched off of me at three o'clock in the morning and being whipped like a slave. I said I would go back though as long as I could play on the basketball team at school, and I didn't have to watch Spoiled anymore. Meany agreed to everything I said, and then I agreed to go back home.

I will never forget the first day I spent back in that house after being gone for so long. It was such an eerie feeling as I walked in. Archie was at work so it was just me and Meany there. I didn't have a doubt in my mind that I would kill her before she had the opportunity to kill me. It was sad that I had thoughts like that at such a young age, but that the way I had to think. From the day she pulled that .38 on me, I vowed that I wouldn't let anyone get to their gun before I got to mine.

The first day I spent back home was uneventful. I took a bath, went to my room and then watched television. My favorite thing on television back then was the ten o'clock news. Sounds weird that a 12 year old boy would enjoy watching the news every single night, but believe it or not I had a purpose. I watched the news so that I could learn how to get away with crimes, however, studying the ten o'clock news didn't make me a good criminal, it just made me a stupid jailbird.

On my first night back home, I couldn't believe that I actually got a good night's sleep. I wasn't awakened to my covers being pulled off of me onto the floor or getting whopped like I stole something.

That morning I talked to Archie for a while before the both of us had to get to school. I remember him telling me that I was the strongest person in our family and that I was going to be somebody famous one day. I didn't really listen to him at the time; I heard him but I didn't listen, not until years later.

"Time for School"

Aunt Fee gave birth to a beautiful baby girl that she named Arnetta. Arnetta was beautiful. She had curly black hair and brown eyes. I could tell when Arnetta was a baby that she was going to be smart because she was doing things as a baby that I didn't see Erica doing. Aunt Fee was happy, and I promised her that I would come over to her house as much as possible to help her out. I didn't mind helping Aunt Fee the way I minded helping my mom, because I loved my cousins more than I loved my own brother, which is sad. Erica made things a lot easier for Aunt Fee though because Erica was four going on twenty and she damn near knew how to take care of Arnetta better than my aunt did.

School was going good. I was still shooting dice periodically, but because I was on the school basketball team I couldn't cut class or get caught shooting dice, otherwise I would be kicked off.

I enjoyed playing basketball, but there was a lot of favoritism going on with the team, which is understandable, but I just didn't see the logic in doing all that practicing and working out just to ride the bench. After the second game of me not playing a full minute, I handed Mr. Ross, our basketball coach, his uniform and told him thanks, but that the team wasn't for me. I was a warrior and I wasn't going to be sitting on the bench warming that thing up every game. The coach understood where I was coming from though, and he actually respected me for it. I still had to see coach every day because he was my physical education teacher.

Once I was no longer on the basketball team, I realized that there was going to be a flag football tryout, and so I went to try out and I made the team. I was happy about that. The only person I told was Archie though and he didn't care because he didn't even like sports.

"That's nice," Archie said to me, "Keep up the nice work." I could tell he was happy for me but at the same time it just didn't mean the same to him as it did to me.

During this time in Archie's life, all he cared about was school, work, clothes, shoes, girls, and driving.

Archie was getting ready to go to college soon, and I didn't want him to leave me alone with the house full of demons. I knew that we had to leave the nest sometime in our life, but it seemed as though that time was coming up way too fast.

The rest of the school year went good. I did well on the flag football team and I finished the year off with a 3.0 grade average which was excellent for me. Another hectic year down and it was time for to graduate junior high and go to high school. I was, of course, going to Castlemont High School to take over where Archie left off.

Once graduation time came around, Archie and I started planning our graduation out, of course, since Archie was graduating from high school, his graduation was a much bigger deal than mine. Meany, Spoiled, Pops and I all piled up in the truck and went to Archie's graduation. Archie carried himself like a man of class. Not only was Archie senior class president, but he was also valedictorian, meaning that he was the number one smartest person in his graduating class. I was proud to be Archie's brother and I vowed then that I would follow his footsteps to success and greatness one day. My brother gave a touching speech and he was witty in his approach with words. I loved my brother so much. Archie was grown and on his way to Poly College in San Luis Obispo ca.

My graduation wasn't as eventful as Archie's, but I was glad to move up to high school so that I could one day go to college like Archie.

The summer after graduation was the first summer that I was kind of sad, because I knew that Archie was going to college and I wouldn't see him as much anymore. Even though I worked a summer job at the youth center on 85th in East Oakland, I always thought about Archie going to college, and what a major impact it was going to have on my life.

My job with the kids at the youth center was fun. Despite the fact that I was only a few years older than they were, they thought I was a grown up and so I enjoyed telling them what to do. I used to take the kids outside to play basketball and baseball, and I would even get them to read books and do assignments. It was like I was a teacher, only I was getting way less money for it.

My job with the youth center was the first real job I'd had, and so I enjoyed making some real money that summer. I even opened up my own bank account because I was ballin in my own right.

I already knew what I was going to do with my money. I was going to buy the best clothes and be the flyest cat at Castlemont.

Archie was packing all of his things, getting ready to head off to college. I was very sad at that point, but he was happy as hell to get out of that haunted house with Spoiled and Meany, and I couldn't really blame him. Archie had himself a U-Haul and a trailer to pull his car with. The U-Haul was packed all up and he started saying his farewells to me and our family. I told him that as soon as he got settled out there I wanted to visit him, and he said ok. My mother and I seemed the most upset out of everyone. A tear rolled down our face, but Spoiled and Wallace didn't seem to care, which didn't surprise me. I was sad but to be truthful, Archie and I didn't spend a lot of time together once he got in high school anyway because of school, work, and all those damn extracurricular activities he had going on. I loved my brother though, that was the bottom line. It was going to be weird not seeing him in his room so I could go harass him like I always did. We all waved to Archie as he drove the U-Haul down E Street.

Damn! Life was getting real now, I thought. That was the first day in my life that I knew things were getting serious. The night Archie left, I felt super lonely. Even though we didn't hang out much, I just missed him being close around. I knew that night that I had to man up and handle my business so I could go to college just like Archie did.

Archie went to college a couple of weeks before school started to get his living arrangements together and to get a feel of the school. Whenever he called home he was always excited about being in college. I could tell that he was having a good time in just those two short weeks he was there. He and I never stayed on the telephone too long; we would talk to each other about four times a week though. I knew he would do well in college and be a successful electrical engineer. Archie even got himself an academic scholarship for school.

It was the night before my first day of high school and I had just finished creasing up my clothes to a tee. I was a pro at using an iron by then and I was pretty proud of my skills. I laid all my clothes out and looked at them thinking, damn, I'm going to be fly tomorrow.

I had plans on playing football for Castlemont and I knew I would be the top player in the bay area. I went to double day practices in the summer and that's when I realized that I was skinny as hell. The football team looked like grown ass men compared to me; I mean, those dudes were weighing in at 300 lbs and the running backs looked like they played for the Oakland raiders. I couldn't believe that those guys were in high school. Luckily, I made the team, but I barely made the cut because of only weighing in at 99 lbs. Coach Green said that I would have to gain one pound to make the team, so all summer I ate a lot of McDonalds and the day of the weigh-in I weighed in at 101 pounds. I made the weight and I was happy to be a part of a team.

On the first day of school I was excited as hell. I was fitted to a tee in my creased down outfit and my hair was so wavy that you would have thought that I had a perm in it but really my hair was wavy like it was because of brushing it around six to eight hours a day, and laying it down with a wave cap. When I was growing up, whomever had the best waves in their head were the ones with major status.

My first day of class I didn't want to walk or catch the bus, so I asked Pops to take me and he said he would. I got in his black-on-black Chevy truck with the 350 engine that would bark when you hit the gas, and at the time I felt like I was riding in a top of the line vehicle. On the way to school I had Pops pick up Corey. Corey was my closest friend during that time and everybody that didn't know us thought we were brothers because we were together so much. Chuck, Corey and Marlon – the three amigos is what all of our peers called us. We later named ourselves the "us" click, because we planned on it only being "us" three friends for the remainder of our lives.

Cory and I met up with Marlon at the front entrance of Castlemont High School. I couldn't believe that I had finally made it to high school. Out of the three of us, I was definitely the best dressed and it was clear on the first day of school. Marlon greeted me and Corey with our famous hand shake and we went inside to get our paper with our classes on them. We all prayed that we would get some classes together since we were together all the time. Cory and I ended up getting three classes together; Marlon and I had one class together. The first day of school was an experience I'll never forget. I met a lot of Archie's friends that he had left behind, and they treated me with a lot of favoritism because of my brother. I learned quickly to ride on Archie's name to get what I wanted, and it worked magnificently. Everybody loved me, both the students and teachers alike.

Lunch time was the best time of the day at Castlemont because I got to see everybody and what they were wearing to school, and how they carried themselves. There would always be rap and singing battles that almost always lead to fights, which were always exciting. Cory, Marlon and I would always meet up at our designated spot for lunch time to determine if we were going to eat on or off campus. We would switch it up and later learned that it was safer to eat on campus than to go to the ghetto stores in the neighborhood. We basically always got the same things for lunch. If we ate on campus we would eat chili cheese fries or chili cheese nachos; if we went off campus we would get either a sub sandwich or a burrito, with potato chips and a soda.

First day of football practice was hectic because Coach Green was not one to mess with. If anyone made him mad, the entire team would have to run until he was tired of looking at us run. We were definitely in shape with this type of regiment, but Coach Green had a weird philosophy about football. He thought that a team in better shape would win games, but I found out later just how full of shit his philosophy was.

I was made a cornerback on defense and a running back on offense. I quickly learned that I was fearless and I preferred to play defense because I liked hurting people. I didn't like playing running back as much because I never wanted to get hit. I knew right off the bat that I had to get bigger and faster to compete at that level. Those guys all wanted a way out of the ghetto, and mostly everyone knew that their only way out the ghetto would be through football. Everyone on Castlemont's football team was serious about what they were doing. Not only did we run a lot, but we also did a lot of hitting drills. For only being 100 pounds, the coaches were impressed by my heart.

Practices were always tough at Castlemont. I knew that I had to get stronger in order to compete in football, so I started working out a little in the weight room after practice. I didn't know what I was doing so I just did basic bench presses, curls, and squats. I was usually too tired to do much after practice because Coach Green would run us to death. We had a coach named Coach Barnett that was the strength coach, and he was also the track coach, and he would always take time out to help me because he said he saw a lot of potential in me. All the older players didn't seem to take Coach Barnett seriously, but I had a feeling that he knew what he was talking about, so I always gave him the upmost respect. Coach Barnett wanted me to join the track team but I didn't have any desire to run track at that time, so I told him that I would think about it.

"Dice shooting Gambler"

I loved Castlemont because there was something going on every single day. There were even some shootings that occurred in the court yard during lunch time. Castlemont was a school full of action; you never knew what to expect there. Being the money hungry kid that I was, I saw an opportunity to make some money by shooting dice with the gamblers. I did well at the dice games, and I rarely lost. The few times that I did lose, I remember it was the worst feeling I had ever encountered at that time. When I lost, I couldn't function again until I was able to get more money and try my luck again. I always picked fourth period to shoot dice because we would be able to shoot dice up until lunch was over with. Meeting up with Corey and Marlon during lunch time ended pretty quickly once I got back into shooting dice. They knew where I was though and if someone asked them where I was at they would tell them, "Back there shooting dice!" Dice shooting had become a serious problem for me because I started missing a lot more classes and my grades were beginning to show it. I dropped from a 3.0 to a 2.5 and everybody was concerned. At that time I didn't care though, because I had pockets full of money and I was addicted to keeping that money coming.

Castlemont's football team was garbage and I was glad once the season was over. We had coaches fighting the players, and the players doing whatever they wanted when they were on the field. There was no true order because the football players didn't respect the coaches. By the end of the season I was pissed, because in all ten games we had, I had only played one. I was furious! After that football season I went to the weight room everyday and pounded them weights like I was a mad man. I promised myself after that season that I would not be ridiculed like that ever again in my life.

I continued shooting dice during school and after school. Once football season was over, I didn't care about anything other than making money, but unfortunately my time at hustling dice was about to be over.

I remember the day like it was yesterday. There were around 20 kids in the back of the apartments behind Castlemont and everybody – being super into the game – had their heads down watching the money and the dice intently. There had been some dice games a few weeks past that had been robbed, so everyone was on pins and needles because of that.

I had a lot of money down on the ground that day, around one hundred dollars in bets, and I remember looking out of the corner of my eyes and seeing the cat who had been robbing the dice games walking up.

"Run! It's Man!" I shouted, grabbing my money in a mad dash.

Man was the dude who had been robbing all Castlemont's students of their money and starter jackets. Man was going to get a rude awakening that day though. I ran off and as I was running I saw a guy pulling out his Dirty Harry revolver. All I heard next was that huge gun barking off (boom, boom).

"You won't rob me again punk," I heard the kid yelling.

Come to find out, Man had robbed that cat like two previous times. That was my last day shooting dice at school. I vowed that I would never again put myself in a situation that I had no control over.

"School back priority"

Once I stopped shooting dice at school, my grades went dramatically back up. Cory, Marlon and I started hanging out again like we used to and as far as my school life went, things were finally getting back to normal. However, after school I used to go to dice games on the street where I lived. I had to make money somehow, since my mother was only giving me three dollars a day, and shooting dice was the best way I knew how to do that.

I quickly learned all the hip sayings and dice etiquette that went with dice games. There were thousands of dollars in these games, but I only wanted to win $100. Once I got that $100 I would act like I had to go home because when you won in a dice game the people losing usually wanted the chance to win their money back. Most the time, I acted like my mother or pops called me though.

"They didn't call you, you lying!" the players would say to me.

But I would insist that they did call me and tell them that I'd see them tomorrow. Of course, they would get mad at me for leaving, but they knew they would have a chance to win their money back the next day.

My first year in high school was definitely an experience I'll never forget. At one point I got to see Archie during the holidays and he told us all about how much he loved college. Hearing about how much he loved it made me excited to the point where I couldn't wait to go there myself. I even wanted to go to Cal Poly with Archie when I graduated high school.

Archie had a job with an athletic company called Hines, and he was doing well for himself. I was happy for him and my life at home was better than it had ever been growing up there before.

The summer after my freshman year I was focused on gaining weight and, of course, making some of that money that I loved so much. I got a job at Domino's Pizza with Corey and Marlon. I loved my job there because we would get free pizza after we delivered flyers all around the bay area, but we did a lot of walking and I knew that it wasn't the type of job that I planned on having for long. I took full advantage of eating all the free pizza I could get though so that I could gain weight, and once it was time for school to start, Corey, Marlon and I quit Domino's.

Overall, the summer wasn't too eventful, except for the fact that, during that summer, there was pure chaos in Oakland. Four people ended up getting killed on E street, and all involving drugs.

All the older guys on E Street encouraged me to continue doing the positive things that I was doing because they knew that the life they were living at the time would only have them ending up dead or in jail. I took heed to what they told me, because I was better dressed and had just about the same amount of money as them, so I didn't even see the benefit in selling drugs at that time.

There was one older cat in particular on E Street that took a liking to me and he became like my big brother. His name was Anthony, but everyone called him Ant. Ant had the most respect on E Street because he had been to youth authority and he was the swolest cat I had ever seen besides Uncle Butch. Not only that, but Ant was serious about getting money, just like me. Ant would tell me that if I ever had any problems in the streets, that he would handle it for me. He said he wanted me to stay on the positive path of going to school and playing sports.

"Migraine headaches"

At the start of my sophomore year I was not only excited for school, I was excited for football too. I was anxious to show off my 140 lbs of muscle. At double days in the summer I was annihilating anyone that came up against me. I came and took charge of the Castlemont Knights. Everybody was in awe of my ripped physique, and everyone started saying that I was on drugs because they couldn't understand how I got so ripped in such a short period of time. I told them that I didn't take drugs, that I just ate around five thousand calories a day and worked out, but they still didn't believe me.

I had impressed Coach Green so much during that summer that he moved me to play starting corner-back on varsity. I was ecstatic because it was just last year that they hadn't let me play but one down the last season, and all of a sudden I was on varsity. That was a huge achievement for me.

Marlon and I were on varsity together, but Corey was left behind on junior varsity because they needed him to stay on the team for leadership.

Everything was going good with practices except for when it came to this one coach named Denny. He was a dick towards me and I didn't know why. I gave him the same respect that I gave all the other coaches, and yet it seemed as though he had a personal vendetta against me. Coach Denny would critique my every move, as well as yell at me a lot. At that point in my life, I was not one to mess with. I had a lot of built up anger in me from my childhood and when it exploded it exploded. During this one particular day at practice, Coach Denny yelled at me and I ran up on him, ready to fight, and the coaches and my teammates had to get us off one another. Right then I told Coach Green that it would be better for me if I stayed away from that clown, and I would prefer to go back on junior varsity with Corey anyways. Coach Green understood and granted my request. Corey was happy as hell that we were back together. I was made the captain of the junior varsity team, as well as Corey. We dominated together but it seemed as though it was me and Corey all alone because the rest of our team sucked. I never came off the field when we played other teams. On defense I was safety, on offense I was running back. It was tough but I was in amazing shape.

There was one particular day at football practice that I won't ever forget. It was a tough day of practice, and a lot of guys were fucking up, which caused the team to have to do a lot of unnecessary running. I noticed that my vision was getting blurry, but I just tried to shake it off. Luckily practice was over by the time I was hardly able to see. I didn't know what was wrong with me. My mouth went numb and I couldn't even talk, then the left side of my body went numb too. I went in the locker room and laid on the bench, while Corey and Marlon were asking me if I was alright, and I told them no. My head was thumping hard, I couldn't see or talk and the left side of my body was numb. I was lying down on that bench for about an hour, when all of a sudden I had the urge to throw up. I ran to a garbage can as fast as I could and started throwing up all the food I had eaten at lunch. I still remember that moment to this day. I had gone to the liquor store at lunch time and got a taco dog, which was something I had never eaten in my life. At the time I thought that the taco dog was the reason I was so sick. I promised myself I wouldn't eat another taco dog in my life. When I made it home to an empty house, my head was still killing me so I just laid in the hallway on the floor rolling around and moaning. My mother came in the house and saw I was on the floor moaning, and asked what was wrong with me. I told her what had happened and what I had eaten and she wrote it off as food poisoning. The day after that terrible experience, I was still somewhat off balance, but I knew I had to pull it together for football practice.

"Wrestle"

Just like last season, my next sophomore season of football sucked. I As far as I can remember, I don't think we won but a single game out of the ten games that we played. I was happy to get the MVP award though, which was an accomplishment from the previous year. All I cared about at that point was getting good grades, getting bigger, and preparing to go to college. One of the football coaches named Coach Dave was also the wrestling coach and he told me that I should wrestle for him. I told him that I wasn't interested because of the one piece uniforms the wrestlers had to wear, but he told me that I would be great at it and that I should consider it. I gave the idea a lot of thought and finally I asked Corey, Marlon and the rest of my peers what they thought and they all agreed that it would be a good idea that I wrestled too. I told Coach Dave that I would wrestle for him and he was pretty happy about my decision.

Wrestling practices were ten times worse than football practices. We had to run hills and stairs before we even sparred. It was the toughest thing I had ever done in my life. The situation that happened to me at football practice happened to me again after a tough wrestling practice. Once again my mother walked in the house and heard me moaning and rolling around on the floor. I told her that I was experiencing the same thing that had happened to me before. I told her my symptoms and, she, being a nurse, said that it sounded like a mild stroke I was having. My mother took me to the hospital for a checkup and the doctor didn't find any problems, but from that point on I started having those headaches much more frequently.

I was good at wrestling and I had my favorite moves like the head-and-arm. I lived by that head-and-arm, and because of it most of my matches didn't last more than ten seconds. Firstly, I had 19 inch arms at 140 lbs, so my arms made the opponent think I was bigger than I actually was, so they would get intimidated as soon as they laid eyes on me; not to mention I had abnormal strength for a guy that weighed only 140 lbs. It didn't take long before all my peers started coming out to my matches so they could cheer me on too, which also gave me an edge over my competition. I didn't know until years later that all the girls used to come to the matches just so they could see me in my one piece uniform, which they could see my dick showing through. My entire first year I only lost one time and it was to the top guy at the state meet. I got MVP on the wrestling team and I received my first all-city honor.

I was happy as hell when I got my pins to put on my school jacket from wrestling. School was going good then and my grades were above 3.5 at that point so I was the big man on campus. Everyone loved me and I loved everyone back.

"Hunger for Speed"

Word was out on campus that Man was roaming around again, robbing the students for their money and starter jackets. I had two starter jackets of my own that I was not going to get robbed for, so I went and told Ant about the situation and told him that I needed a gun to protect myself. Ant didn't ask any questions; he told me he would be right back. Ant ran in his house and came out in the blink of an eye, and handed me a brown paper bag.

"This is yours to keep, and if anybody ask you where you got it, you didn't get it from me" he said.

I thanked him and told him that we don't do no snitching! I rushed home to an empty house and immediately opened the brown paper bag. In it was a pretty 22 revolver which was enough to blow a man's brains out. I felt powerful then and I vowed I would kill Man if he tried anything with me.

After wrestling season was over, Coach Barnett said I should join the track team to build my speed for football and I didn't second guess Coach Barnett's request. I would do whatever I had to do to get better for football, because iI knew that football was my ticket to college. Corey and Marlon also joined the track team and the "US" click was at it again. Track practices were tough and I was having migraines very often and I noticed I would have them when I over-exerted my body.

I knew that I would always get them after a strenuous practice or workout, so I would hurry up and get to a place where I could lie down and let it pass.

I loved track because it was a challenge and it was very competitive and I needed a lot of practice because I only had average speed at the time.

Coach Barnett said that he was going to get me fast, so he started picking me and some of the veteran runners up at 5:00 a.m. to go and run Lake Merritt. I respected Coach Barnett highly for his help, because he didn't have to go these extra miles to help me or the other kids, but he did. Gradually, my speed increased and I got good enough to be put on the 4*100 relay team as well as the 110 high hurdles and the 300 yard hurdles. Track season went fantastic. The "US" click was on our way to the state track meet in Los Angeles California. I was going to run the 4*100 relay, Corey was doing the shot-put and discus, and Marlon was doing the 100 yard dash and the 4*100 relay. We had a hell of a time in Los Angeles. That was the first time I saw Marion Jones run, and her speed was unreal. My high school did alright at the state meet; some of the seniors that ran long distance did their thing. But as far as the 100, 200, 400, and hurdles we didn't have a chance. I don't know what the hell these kids were taking, but we were far out of our league. I felt good that I had made it to the state track meet, not to mention I received another honor of first team all-city in track and field. I was turning into a true athlete and Coach Barnett promised me that he was going to work with me during the summer so that I would be the top athlete in the bay area.

The rest of the school year went good. I had one brush with Man on campus and I walked right up to him with my starter jacket on and said, "What's up?", while my finger was on the trigger of my gun. He replied with a simple "nothing" and kept on walking. I have to tell you that I felt like the Incredible Hulk at that present moment. All I could think to myself was that I punked the bully, and it truly felt amazing. After the run in with Man, I feared nothing in life.

"Turning into a Man"

Another school year down and I would be in the 11th grade when school started. High school was moving along quite fast. My summer vacation was no different than any of the others except that I went to visit Archie in San Luis Obispo California. I rode with his girlfriend Cynthia to see him and I was excited to see how my brother was living. When Cynthia and I arrived at Archie's house, Archie ran outside and gave me a brotherly hug.

"What's up with my little big brother?" He said to me.

At that time I was around 165 lbs of raw ripped muscle, and I looked like a weighed more than I actually did. Archie introduced me to his soft college geek roommates. They all wanted to know how I got so cut, and I told them by working out. My stay with my brother was great; I didn't want to leave. I even told him that I should transfer out there to finish high school, but Archie told me that it would probably be best to just finish my schooling at Castlemont where everyone loves me and I agreed.

I said my goodbyes to Archie and his roommates, and told them that I would see them soon. I hated to leave my brother because I felt like I was on earth to protect him. Cynthia and I got into her car and drove back to Oakland. I was sad the entire trip because I didn't want to be apart from my brother.

Double days for the football team started the end of July and I was more than ready for them because I had been working out and running all summer long, so I was prepared to bring the "hat", as we called it in football. I now weighed around 175 pounds of cut muscle and I felt superior to everyone. I was varsity's head captain and I got the respect as such. Everyone knew that I was a mean character and that I turned into Mr. Hyde when I touched that football field. The migraines were still coming but I just had to press through them. I couldn't understand how I never got a migraine after an actual football game, because I never got any rest on the field.

When my junior year of school started, I was fitted to a tee as usual. The past two years I received best dressed in school and I, of course, was shooting to be best dressed my junior year as well. I was labeled as Mr. Castlemont and I knew everybody knew me. One day I noticed that there was a bulletin up in the school hallway that McDonalds was hiring all Castlemont students to open up a brand new McDonalds. I filled out an application in hopes to work there so I could eat up all those damn big Macs, which were my favorite food at that time.

A week after I'd submitted my application to McDonalds, I got notice that I'd been hired. I was happy as hell. Me and the rest of the students that got hired at McDonalds had to go through extensive training to learn the ins-and-outs of the McDonalds franchise. Training lasted an entire month, and I liked it because I was able to eat and gain weight. After that month long training, Castlemont students were cleared to open the new McDonalds. I went to work after football practice, from 6:00 p.m. to midnight.

Football season was the usual and we beat our all time record by winning three whole football games. Corey and I were holding things together but Marlon dropped out of school to make money to help his mother pay the bills. We were still close but not as close as Cory and I were.

I received another MVP title, as well as another first team all-city award. My teammates that graduated high school before me told me to send out my football footage to colleges so that they would start scouting me. I did exactly what they told me to do and I started having colleges interested in me coming to their college to play football. That was the best feeling in the world for me, because I wanted to play college football so bad. There was Texas A&M, Oregon, Idaho, San Jose State, Fresno state, Cal Berkeley, Chico State and Laney! I was confused on where to go, but I had a year to sleep on it so I didn't panic.

I chose to pass on wrestling the rest of my high school stint because I truly didn't see me pursuing wrestling after high school. All the girls were mad I didn't wrestle anymore, because they couldn't come out and watch me like they used to. Coach Dave understood that I wanted to focus on football and track only though.

Things were going good at school and at my McDonalds job. I was getting a 3.83 grade average in school, and I was making money and eating a ton of McDonald's food. Life was awesome. I think I had worked at McDonalds for around three months when another job opportunity presented itself at Archie's old telemarketing job for the San Francisco chronicle. The reason this job sparked my interest was because I remember Archie making a ton of money working there. I felt like I had ran my course at McDonalds, plus I started feeling like a poot butt working at McDonalds. I submitted an application to Archie's old job and used him as a reference and I was hired immediately. Now I would be making the big bucks. I told McDonalds that I was moving on and I started working for the San Francisco chronicle soon after. I liked working at the chronicle because it was exciting to call strangers and get them to buy the newspaper from you. There was also a lot of competition going on to see who would get the most sales, and I liked competition. I was making more money at that job than I had made all my life. I didn't have to shoot dice anymore and I had a pocket full of money from calling strangers.

Being a junior in high school was kind of nerve racking because you knew that in a few months you would be a senior and that was when all the real problems would come. Problems like figuring out what college you were going to, if you would even make it into college, getting ready to take the SAT exam, senior prom, grad night, and a host of other nerve racking things. Junior year went smoothly for me though – my money was up, my grades were up, and my body was up. I had been working at the San Francisco chronicle for two short months, when one of my old teammates (Bobby) – who had graduated three years ahead of me – knew I was serious about working out so he asked me if I wanted a job with him at the gym, 24 Hour Nautilus (24 Hour Fitness now). I couldn't believe my ears. I knew it would feel like I was in heaven to be working in a gym, and I would get a free membership, so of course I told Bobby, "Hell yeah!"

After two months of working at the San Francisco Chronicle, I moved on to 24 Hour Nautilus and I was as happy as ever. I started working as a porter, cleaning up the gym, and fixing the machines when they broke. I loved my job and I tried to work every single day. I went to work after school until 11 p.m. at night. I knew everyone at the gym and they all knew me to be the youngster that was getting ready to go play college football soon. I rarely saw anyone at home, because by the time I got back everyone was asleep, and then in the mornings I beat everyone out of the house. I had a great schedule that kept me busy.

Once I started working at the gym, I gained some more weight. I was weighing 180 pounds at the time and I wore tight shirts so that people could see my huge arms and wide shoulders. Everyone thought I was taking something at that point, but I wasn't.

It was towards the beginning of track season and I'll never forget how Coach Barnett told me that I would have to stop working-out because I was getting too big to run track. That was the first time in three years I had lost some respect for Coach Barnett. I felt like he was trying to stagnate my growth as a football player. Football was the ultimate reason why I was even running track in the first place. I laughed off what Coach Barnett said to me and I actually started working out more. I noticed that I was faster and stronger than I'd ever been before, but I was getting migraines quite frequently too. I knew I was working out like a crazed maniac, but I figured if I died from working out then at least I would die happy.

After track practice I went to work and I'd go in my office and lie down until I'd throw up from having those treacherous migraines of mine. Once I threw up I started my daily duties at the gym. All the hard work I had been putting in was paying off.

"Fellowship of Christian Athletes"

My junior year went by fast because of the three different jobs I'd had and the excitement of working at the gym. I ended the year off with another 3.83 grade point average. The only reason I hadn't achieved a 4.0 was because of the trouble I had with math.

My summer after my junior year was off the hook! Firstly, I was awarded a scholarship to go to Fellowship of Christian Athletes Football Camp for the top football players in the state.

I packed up my things to go to the football camp and I couldn't wait to see what was going on there. I had to catch the Greyhound bus from West Oakland California to Thousand Oaks California. It was my first time riding the Greyhound and I didn't like it one bit. The bus ride seemed like it took forever because of how much it stunk, and I was relieved when I finally made it to my destination and was able to smell some fresh air again.

I was picked up by one of the counselors, and as we rode to the camp site – which ended up being the enormous college campus, Cal Lutheran in Thousand Aaks' California – the counselor explained all the rules, times to eat, times to practice, time to wake, and time to sleep. I was all for it and I couldn't wait to show off my defensive skills. There were tons of kids running around the campus, both girls and boys. There was every sport imaginable at that camp, not just football. I was escorted to my room by the counselor and he told me that I had one hour to be in the auditorium for orientation. Me and the other boys in my room went outside to mingle with all the other kids. The camp looked just like Disneyland at the college with the way all us campus kids were running around and playing everywhere. The orientation was long and to the point and everybody at the camp had an extensive routine. There was no down time except when you were sleeping. We had to get up at 5:30 in the morning to do a cardio session, then we would go to breakfast, and then we would go straight to practice. Practices were intense but I didn't get one migraine my entire trip, which was a blessing.

I was too strong for the kids at the camp. They all thought I was older than I was because of my stature and me, being from Oakland's football league, my number one thing was aggressiveness, which I had an enormous amount of. When I guarded the other kids, they weren't even able to pass me. I was in a league of my own. The seven day camp was amazing, and it went by extremely fast. I was awarded with the honors of fellowship of Christian athletes' most valuable defensive player. That was pretty over the top for me. There were at least one thousand football players at that camp, and for me to receive the award I did was a huge deal. I thanked everyone at the camp for giving me an opportunity to be a part of the camp, and that it truly was beneficial to me.

When I returned home I was so excited and I showed mom and pops my award as soon as I saw them. They were happy for me, and they told me that they knew I would eventually get it together, meaning that they knew I would get my life in order so that good things would happen. I felt like the camp had elevated me to a higher height.

I went back to work the Monday after I got back from camp and I took my award into work to show it off to everybody. They were all happy for me. Once I learned all the different techniques at the camp that I did, I was ready to get on that football field and use them. I ran a lot and worked out hard the rest of the summer, all the way to double days. I had reached a weight of around 185 pounds, which made me look like I weighed around 200 pounds to everybody else. My body had definitely matured since being the scrawny, 100 pound kid I used to be in the ninth grade, the one that didn't play but one down his entire freshman year of football.

"Senior year"

I won't ever forget the first day of double days my senior year.

I showed everybody the award that I got at the Fellowship of Christian Athletes Camp. Everyone was happy that I represented Castlemont well, but nobody could believe how buff I had become. At that point my teammates and coaches wanted to get on my workout regiment and I told them that all they had to do was come to my job and I would put them through my workouts. Being that that was my last year in high school, it was very stressful because I knew I had to handle my business on and off the football field.

The Castlemont Knight's football team was looking the best I had ever seen it. We had some new guys that were really talented, so I saw us having a good football season. All of the coaches let me basically run the team because they realized that I knew what I was doing by that point. Double days went the best ever since being at Castlemont.

We had a few hot heads that we would have to simmer down here and there, but things were looking promising for my senior year.

The first day of my senior year was yet another exciting day and of course I was fitted and my waves dipping. As soon as Corey and I entered Castlemont's main entrance to the school, I saw a bulletin stating that anybody who wanted to be the senior class president should enter their names, because election would start in two weeks. I entered my name, and I knew I was popular and all, but I was also going up against two of the most popular girls at Castlemont. I knew that it was going to be a battle. I started my campaign early by talking to all of my peers and telling them what I was going to do to help our senior class be the greatest class ever in Castlemont's history. I noticed that I had a lot of supporters, and I also knew that the two girls running against me had some enemies amongst our peers. When the election started, I had a speech put together so well that it amazed the entire school at how articulate I truly was. That's what ultimately gave me such a land slide of a win over the two other girls. I was definitely following in Archie's footsteps, because he was also senior class president. I called Archie that night to tell him I won the election and that I was shadowing his every move. He was glad for me and told me to keep up the good work. We never talked to long on the phone because of long distance charges.

Football season was going good and after the fifth game I had around 60 tackles and two interceptions, and a touchdown. I was doing my thing and all the hard work was paying off. The college recruits were interested in me and I knew it, and that's what made me play all that much harder. We ended the football season winning an all-time high of four games. I couldn't complain. That was the best year in all my four years of playing at Castlemont. I once again received MVP honors and I was first team all city once again – yet another medal to put on my letterman jacket. At the banquet I gave a farewell speech that touched everyone.

The rest of the school year went good but as senior class president I had a lot of responsibilities. I had to go to meetings off campus for the grad night trip to Los Angeles and I had to meet the people that did our year books. It was hectic but I loved being busy like that. After going to the meetings for a month for grad night, I was finally able to start collecting everyone's money for grad night trip. I had to keep a receipt book with me at all times because I needed to be ready to take checks from my peers when they gave them too me, which could be at any point when they saw me on campus. Not only did I have to keep the receipts but I also had to keep documentation of each person and how much they paid. The total for the trip was three hundred dollars per student.

Because I was the senior class president and had to do all the hard work, my fee was waived. While I was busy getting everything for grad night taken care of, I also had to get our senior year book together. I had to get all my peer's input on how they wanted the year book to go.

After I got a majority rule, I submitted the outline of our yearbook to the yearbook people. Once I had grad night and the year book going, I had to get the arrangements together for prom, which was another headache altogether, but I let my vice president get everything in order for that and then confirm with me once it was done.

Senior year was surreal! Everything was going amazingly well, and track season was about to start. I was in incredible shape. In fact, I was so ripped that during track practice I used to wear biker shorts with no shirt and all the girls would come and watch me practice. I didn't have a girlfriend during my entire time at Castlemont, because I was too damn picky. None of those girls caught my eye, and the ones who did were gold diggers and I was a stingy dude that wasn't giving up a dime. I knew that senior prom was nearing and I was going to have to ask somebody if they wanted to go with me to the prom, but I figured I would let someone ask me instead. A few girls actually did ask me to go, but I refused because they weren't my type, then one day a girl I had never seen before came up and started a conversation with me. She asked me who I was taking to the senior prom and I told her I wasn't taking anyone.

"Who are you taking?" I asked her.

She told me she wasn't taking anyone either and that we should go to the prom together. I told her I would let her know in a day or so. Her name was Sin, and Sin she was! She had big, round brown eyes that were mesmerizing, but other than that she looked kind of weird to me. Being the picky person I was, I didn't particularly like her look. The only thing, other than her eyes, that drew me to her was her gigantic titties. She only weighed about 100 pounds but she had tits the size of Dolly Parton's. I went and told Corey about Sin, and I asked him if he knew anything about her. He said he heard that she was a freak in the sheets. At that time, I had only had sex once before with a girl that was ugly as hell and I still considered myself a virgin at that point, so I wasn't too concerned with her being a freak. I was focused on going to college and playing football, everything else was meaningless to me.

I dodged Sin for a few days. I just wasn't sure about her; she gave me weird vibes, and hearing about her being a freak kind of threw me for a loop. I finally gave in and told her that we could go to the prom together, and she was happy as hell that Mr. Castlemont was taking her. I wasn't that excited about it though. That girl just wasn't my type. She was beyond ghetto and I saw it more and more with each passing day.

I caught Sin smoking weed once, which was a definite no for me. I didn't want anyone that did any type of drugs being affiliated with me. I went and told Sin that I didn't think that I was going to be able to take her to the prom anymore, and she started crying and asking me why. I told her that I saw her smoking and I wasn't into that type of behavior. She promised she wouldn't do it again, and that she wanted to go with me to the prom more than anything. I felt sorry for the pathetic looking girl and told her that we could still go to the prom.

My senior year was mellow as far as my classes were concerned. I only had to take four classes so that meant that I was done with school by lunch time. The rest of the school day I went to everyone else's classes and made sure everybody was doing alright.

Once Christmas vacation drew closer, there were all types of festivities that I had to orchestrate at the school. We had a winter ball at which I was crowned Mr. Castlemont, another foot step followed by me that Archie had lead the way of. I was on top of the world my senior year. I couldn't wait until Christmas break because Archie was coming home for a week.

When Christmas week arrived, Archie came home looking his debonair self. He was full of energy and spunky. I'll never forget when I picked him up in the black truck at the Greyhound bus station and the surprise on his face at seeing that it was me. He got in the truck and told me that he was proud of me. It was a touching moment that I'll never forget in my life. I took Archie home to E Street and everyone was happy to see him. We hadn't seen Archie in quite some time, so we had a lot of catching up to do, but Archie had to make a few runs to see some of his old girlfriends. I was disappointed that Archie was leaving, but I knew I had to suck it up. I missed my brother and I wanted to hang out with him, but I didn't see Archie much during the entire Christmas vacation. I wanted to hang with Archie more than he wanted to hang with me. I finally came to terms with it all and I knew that we were growing up and apart.

Archie's stay went by too fast and the next thing I knew we were saying our goodbyes once again. Archie and Cynthia drove back together in her car, but it didn't seem like they had the best relationship. There was a lot of arguing going on between the both of them, and I could tell their relationship was almost over.

Sin was my first real sex partner and I didn't know what I was doing at all, but truthfully, I wasn't all that into the sex thing. I backed away from Sin when she asked me to lick her pussy and I told her, "Bitch, I aint never licking no broad pussy so don't ever get at me like that again in life."

When school started back up, it was back to planning all of the events of grad night, senior prom and graduation. I finally decided that I was going to Fresno State after I graduated, because of their winning football team – not to mention it wasn't that far from Oakland, but it just far enough away too.

It was around Archie's birthday when I tried to call him but I couldn't reach him. My mother tried to call him too but she wasn't able to reach him either. It had been a week since we had talked to Archie, and in all his four years of being in college we talked to him a few times a week every week. For Archie not to call was totally out of the ordinary for him. My mother finally contacted Archie's roommate and asked where Archie was, and he said he didn't know. He said that he had just gotten home from out of town and that Archie's room was locked. My mother called San Luis Obispo Police to go and open Archie's room door. I didn't know what was going on really because my mother kept everything so secretive.

I'll never forget that night at 1:00 a.m. when there was a knock at our door. The knock was terrifying and I called mom and pops, who got their pistols and walked to the door and asked who it was. They said it was the Oakland police, and immediately I wondered why they were there, because we hadn't seen or heard anything to give them reason to be outside our door. My mother opened the door to two police officers, who she nervously let in the house. I'll never forget the look those police officers had on their face – It was a look of regret and my mother could see it too.

"What's going on?" I heard my mother ask.

"We regretfully have bad news to tell you about your son, Archie Coles –" The white officer started, but my mother had started screaming before he even finished.

"Not my son!" she cried.

"Ma'am, your son was found dead inside his room with a single shot gun blast to his chest. It looks as if it was a possible suicide," they explained to her.

I ran in my room and beat my bed until I got too tired to beat it anymore. I didn't want anybody saying anything to me. Mom and pops knew how much I loved my brother, and that that moment would have a negative impact on my whole life.

I thought to myself that it all had to be a bad dream. Not my Archie! He would never kill himself; we both were strong. I had a lot of mixed emotions at that time and I didn't know what to believe. I didn't talk for two whole days or go to school. My mother sat me down and told me that she understood what I was going through, because she had lost both of her brothers. She told me that sitting at home would only make me more depressed and that I needed to go to school and be around people. I took her advice because she was a good example of staying busy.

When I finally went to school, I had to explain to everyone why I was absent. Everyone gave their condolences, but it didn't really help. I felt like a zombie just floating around while Corey and Marlon were by my side every day. I'll never forget one day at lunch time in the cafeteria, when Marlon, Corey, and I decided to stay on campus to eat because I was still so down and depressed. We were eating our food when a dude kept calling my name and Corey and Marlon told him to leave me alone because I wasn't feeling good. The guy kept on calling my name though, and before I knew it I had politely walked over him and started beating him into a bloody pulp. Everyone on campus heard what had happened, and they said that's what he gets, because everyone on campus knew my situation.

I had to go to the principal's office to explain what happened and the principle agreed with what I did and told me that I should have whipped his ass.

Archie's funeral was very hard for me and I understood then what my mother must have felt like at my Uncle Butch's funeral. I couldn't breathe. It was unreal that my brother of only 21 years was in a fucking casket. What was this life really about? I was confused and I asked God why he would do this to me. The loss of my brother was a pain that I had never felt before. It was a lot more intense than when I lost Uncle Butch. My mother and I cried on each other at the funeral that day, and I didn't talk to anyone. Everyone knew to leave me alone.

I put all my energy into running track, working out and finishing up my business with the prom and grad night. It took time, but I slowly started getting my spirit back and I wore Archie's class ring in remembrance of him. I had my own class ring on one hand and his ring on the other.

Track season went well, and I clocked in my best times ever. Prom and graduation went alright but I missed my brother dearly and I wasn't able to enjoy the ending of my senior year of high school the way most of the people in my class were.

"Graduating to the Real World"

On the day of graduation I was nervous to be moving on to college. My mother didn't want me to go to Fresno State because of Archie's death. She wanted me to stay in Oakland and go to Laney Junior College for two years then transfer to a four year college. I was adamant about getting out of Oakland though, because at the time violence was at an all-time high there. There were 175 murders my graduation year.

Being the senior class president, I was supposed to give the farewell speech at graduation, but because I showed immaturity at the senior prom by not dancing with Miss Castlemont – I thought she was ugly – I couldn't give my speech anymore.

Since it was my vice president that I refused to dance with at the senior prom, she did the honors of saying the speech at graduation instead. The ceremony was sad because we all knew that we may never see each other again, and that we were adults and life was truly about to start. We all said our farewells and everyone vowed not to lose contact with one another.

After graduation I continued working at the gym until July. July was the month that I would be going to Fresno State bridge program. It was a program that let upcoming freshmen take classes to get familiar with college life, and each student would have older students as their mentors to teach them the ins-and-outs of college life.

July came around fast and I had to say my farewells to everyone at my job. The owner of 24 Hour Nautilus told me that I would always have a job with his company (which eventually took the fitness world by storm). I hated saying goodbye to people because usually when I said goodbye to someone, it meant that I would never see them again.

My mother took me to the Greyhound bus station to catch the bus to Fresno State. I kissed her on the cheek and told her I would see her in three weeks. My mother and I were in a better place once I was older and handling my business, but deep inside I still held a grudge about my childhood.

"Bridge program"

The ride to Fresno was terrible as usual. I hated riding the Greyhound buses because they stunk and you could never get comfortable on them. I tried to sleep to pass some time, but I woke up every ten minutes looking around. That was the most uncomfortable ride imaginable, but I finally made it to Fresno and I was happy to get off that damn bus. My student mentors picked me up from the bus station right on time. Their names were Damon and Pretty Boy. Both of those cats were pretty boys – Damon looked like a cross between will smith and the singer Ginuwine and Pretty Boy had his own look that seemed as though he was mixed with something.

They both asked me a lot of questions on the way up to my room, trying to get to know me. I wasn't too keen on talking a lot at that point in my life. I knew people feared silence though, and so I only talked when it was absolutely necessary. When Damon and Pretty Boy showed me my room, I put my bags down and told them thanks for their help. They gave me their phone number and room number so if I had any questions I could contact them. They left and I started putting my things away when, to my surprise, a white boy had walked in the room asking me if I was his roommate. I told him I guess so. I had never been around white people much except at the fellowship of Christian athlete camp, and I knew that our conversation would be awkward. I automatically didn't like the guy because I felt like he was weird, and I didn't want anyone in my room with me anyhow. I was very territorial and I let it be known. I could tell that that white kid was intimidated of me and he was very uncomfortable in the room with me, and I was glad he was uncomfortable because I was hoping he would request a room change.

I put up all my things and plugged my boom box in that I had brought with me. I started playing some hard core rap and it sounded like a club was in my room, so people started coming to my room to see who I was and I quickly made a lot of friends. My roommate and I didn't talk too much the rest of the night; we both went to bed around midnight.

The next morning I woke up at the crack of dawn and immediately started blasting my boom box again. My roommate was still sleeping, but the sound of Tupac startled him awake. He looked around wanting to say something, but I gave him a look as if to say, "I wish you would say something!" He didn't say anything to me except "Good morning", and I ironed my clothes and got dressed. I couldn't wait to see if there were some pretty girls in the bridge program.

Once I was dressed I rushed outside to see what was going on. I already had a following of guys that wanted to hang with me, so we walked to the student cafeteria to get our eat on. The cafeteria was huge and it reminded me of Home Town Buffet. There was a ton of food to select from and at that stage in my life I got hungry every hour so I packed the food on my plate, and if I didn't eat it all I would take some back to my room.

While eating I spotted a few cute girls but I wasn't the type to go up to a girl and start rambling off.

I was the type of dude that liked to get introduced to the girl. I don't know why but I was always more comfortable with being introduced. I scanned the room for cute girls and I saw the ones that I wanted to talk to. There were a few girls that graduated with me at Castlemont that came with me to the bridge program too.

Breakfast was good and I was stuffed, so I got a box and put my left overs in it for later. The campus cafeteria only fed the students three times a day, and I ate around five to six times a day so I always needed food nearby. After breakfast we had to go to the college introductory meeting that lasted quite some time, something like two hours, which was entirely too long for hyper teenagers. I made it through the boring meeting though and I had my eyes on this gorgeous girl that the girls from Castlemont were friends with. I inched my way towards them and immediately said hi to all of the girls, who gave a hi back. I didn't waste any time in asking the gorgeous girl what her name was, and she said some name I couldn't pronounce at the time. Honestly, it sounded as if she could barely pronounce her own damn name. She repeated her name three times to me before I finally got it. I decided that I would go with her nickname Sara, which was much simpler for me. Sara and I had a good vibe with one another. She was a girly girl, but she had a competitive side to her that stole some of her femininity away. Come to find out she graduated from Berkeley High, which was also in the bay area. She was an athlete that was going to run track at Fresno State. That was the first girl that I had truly ever had a connection with. I was a happy camper at the bridge now because I found a girl that I could hang out with.

The days at the bridge program went by fast now that I had an entire room to myself. My roommate requested a room change because I was too rowdy for him, which is exactly what I wanted anyhow.

Sara and I spent all of our free time together. If I wasn't working out, running, in class, or studying, I was with Sara. It seemed like the ten days that we'd known each other was more like 10 years. We went out at night and sat on the bleachers, just talking about anything there was to talk about. I was still more of a listener than a talker. Sara had a lot to talk about. She was very expressive about her feelings, and I would gladly just listen. By listening to her talk, I knew that she was more advanced than me sexually, because she was talking about getting her pussy ate out, and I didn't even want to talk about that subject because I was against licking pussy. It just seemed gross to me at my young age.

Bridge program had run its 21 day course and I was glad to have been a part of the program. It definitely gave me an edge on what to expect when college started the next month. Damon and Pretty Boy told me to stay in touch with them and that if I needed anything that they would be there for me. I let them know that they were great mentors and I couldn't wait to get back to college so we could kick it.

Once I got back to Oakland after the bridge program, all I did was work out every day at 24 Hour Nautilus. I didn't even bother working there anymore because I was going to Fresno state in a couple of weeks, so I wanted a little vacation.

The couple of weeks that I was back home, Sara and I saw each other quite a bit. I would either go to her house or she would come to mine. I remember the first time she came to my house on E Street; she was shocked that I lived in such a nice home. My mother was definitely a perfectionist. She liked the best of things in life and, truthfully, I – had all of the same characteristics my mother had, and it irked me that I was so much like her. When Sara got to the house no one was there but me. We went in the T.V. room and she immediately started kissing on me and in my mind I was thinking, here we go again with the teasing. As Sara was kissing me she straddled across my legs and she started un-buckling my pants. I was nervous as hell because I knew that someone was going to be coming home at any second.

Sara continued pulling down my pants and I remember telling her that it wasn't a good time or place to have our first sexual encounter, but she was persistent and she said that she needed it. I had never seen her like that before; she seemed like a possessed, sex crazed lunatic. My pants were around my ankles and Sara was straddling me as she pulled her panties to the side.

"Hold on, we don't have a condom," I said to her, but Sara, being her seductive self, put me at ease by telling me that we were both clean, and then she slid down my pulsating dick. It was unbelievable, but I tried to think about all types of other things so that I wouldn't prematurely cum too fast. She was riding me like a cow girl on one of those me-chanical bulls. I felt my loins brewing for an explosion, and at that very moment pops walked in the house asking who was there. I nervously told him that I was, and that I had company. Sara and I rushed to get ourselves together and as soon as I zipped up my fly, pops walked in the T.V. room and I introduced him to Sara. I can't lie, that was about the best excitement I had ever had with a girl. The entire two weeks in Oakland Sara and I had a couple of more sex sessions, but she would always piss me off with asking me to lick her pussy, and I just wasn't into all of that.

"Off to College"

The day arrived when Sara and I were leaving for college. I went and got the U-Haul truck early that morning and then I went to Sara's house in Berkeley and loaded all of her stuff in the truck.

Sara and I touched down in Fresno in about three and a half hours. The ride was uncomfortable in that damn U-Haul, but we made it and I was happy. That was the longest distance I had ever driven. It was definitely a step towards adulthood. When we got to Fresno, Sara and I immediately went to the college campus to find out what dorm we would be living in. Sara had received her room assignment but there was a mix up in my dorm room assignment.

Actually there wasn't any documentation on me receiving a dorm room. I couldn't believe it and I didn't know what to do. I took all of Sara's things to her room as I thought about what I would do, and it hit me to call Damon and Pretty Boy. I gave them a call and Damon picked up the phone.

"What's up Damon, this your swole patna from Oakland," I said to him. Swole dude from Oakland was a moniker that stuck with me in college.

Damon asked me what was going on and I told him that I didn't have a dorm room because there was some sort of mix up with my paper work. Damon cut me off and told me to say no more. Damon told me to bring my stuff to his apartment and I could live with him and Pretty Boy. I was truly thankful to Damon for looking out for me. If it weren't for Damon helping me out, I don't know what would have taken place. I got to Damon's apartment and he greeted me outside with a brotherly hug and said not to even worry about a dorm room because I could stay with him and Pretty Boy as long as I wanted to. That was truly a blessing from above. As I unpacked all of my things, Damon told me that Pretty Boy was out of town, and that he was on his way out of town for a few days. He was going home to Los Angeles to see his family. He told me that I would have the entire house to myself, and to make sure that I didn't mess up his sheets, if you get my drift. Damon said that if I did mess up his sheets, to make sure that I washed them. That was all of Damon's house rules. He was cool as hell. I finished unpacking and Damon showed me where I could put my stuff; he told me that he would see me in a few days and to take good care of our house. I told him how much I appreciated him, and Damon said not to worry about it.

I was on cloud nine because I didn't have to live in the dorm room, and Damon told me that when he got back we would talk about our living arrangements. I knew he was talking about me paying my way which I didn't have a problem with at all. Once I got settled into my new apartment, I called Sara and asked her how everything was coming along, and she told me that she had unpacked all of her things and that she wanted to come and stay with me. I got in the U-Haul truck and went to pick up Sara at her dorm room. When I got there, a geeky white girl opened the door and I said hello. Sara told me that the white girl was her roommate and I told the girl it was nice to meet her.

Sara and I left out the dorms and got in the U-Haul and rode to my new apartment. The apartment was super nice. It had a fitness center, swimming pool, basketball courts, tennis courts, and hot tubs. It couldn't get any better for an 18 year old kid. I remember Sara and I ordered a pizza from rRund Table, which was just 100 yards from my apartment. We walked and picked up the pizza and went back to the apartment and ate. We watched a few movies and Sara, being Sara, wanted to get nasty, so we did, in Damon's bed on his sheets. Oh well I would just have to wash them. We had two more days before school actually started so we just hung out until Sunday night at the apartment. Sunday was when pretty boy got back so I introduced him to Sara, and Pretty Boy had a gorgeous girlfriend that he introduced to me and Sara as well. As we were all getting to know each other better, Damon came home, and we all greeted Damon. I introduced Damon to Sara and, though I wasn't sure why, I knew they didn't have good vibes with one another from the jump.

I had to sit out my first year of playing football but I was allowed to go to the football team gym and work out. At that time in my life, I was a workout fanatic. Every chance I got I was working out because I wanted to dominate on the football field when I stepped on it. I caught the eyes of all the coaches for the Bulldogs, because they knew by my work ethic that I would be a force on the field. I not only worked out at the football stadium, but I also had a free membership to Clovis athletic gym. Clovis was the city over from Fresno and from my apartment it was a seven minute walk, so I either walked or rode my bike to the gym before I got my car. I got a free membership at Clovis athletic because they gave every student athlete at Fresno state a free membership.

Damon and I had become like brothers and I respected him to the upmost for giving me a place to stay. Damon was trying to get big like me, so he would come and work out with me when he had time, which wasn't too often, maybe once or twice a week. At that point in my life I was working out six days a week, Sundays being my only off day. I had become a hell of a cook because I had too. I ate all the damn time and I didn't have the money to be going out to fast food restaurants every time I got hungry. I guess cooking was somewhat of a hobby of mine. My favorite thing to cook was spaghetti, so I cooked it a lot. I also cooked lasagna, steak, and chicken, and I cooked pancakes practically every morning. I knew I wanted to get bigger so I ate like a beast.

Damon and Sara couldn't stand one another but I was thinking that they really liked each other and they were putting on a front that they didn't like one another. My antennas were up with those two because they argued more than Sara and I did. The arguments mostly ended up being about Sara eating up Damon's personal stuff that he had bought, which I did understand. Sara was a feisty girl that did what she wanted to though, and when she wanted to do something she did it. Damon eventually sat me down to talk about the issue with him and Sara. The only solution I came up with was that Sara would have to come over less. Sara didn't like the dorms, so she came to my apartment and ended up acting like she owned the place. Damon and Pretty Boy felt uncomfortable around Sara because she had a mean spirit and, reluctantly, I had to tell her about the way that Damon and Pretty Boy felt. I told her that she would only be able to come over a few times out of the week and Sara immediately went into a rant, saying that I paid rent there too, and that I should be able to have whoever I wanted over at the apartment when I wanted them over. I felt where she was coming from, but I was in a messed up position because those two gentlemen let me move in with them. It was final; Sara would only come over a few times out of the week, mainly on the weekend.

Since Sara was banned from the apartment, things were more at ease at there. Damon, Pretty Boy and I had become like real brothers and I would do anything for them and they knew it.

One night Damon told me that he wanted me to go to his fraternity party with him and I was reluctant because I was somewhat of a hermit at that point. I didn't like the party settings and plus I didn't dance or drink, so I didn't think I would have a good time. Damon was adamant about me going with him though so that he could introduce me to all of his fraternity brothers. I told him that I would go with him, but I still had reservations about going to this party. I never liked parties very much because, in Oakland, at least one person was killed at every single party, which deterred me from that sort of environment. I told Sara where I was going that night and she was pissed. Sara felt as if Damon was a bad influence on me.

"Funk season"

I'll never forget what I wore that particular night at the fraternity party with Damon. I wore black jeans, a coke white tank top, black vest and black shoes. I was buff already so I liked to show off what I worked so hard to achieve. Damon and I pulled up to the club in his shiny black maximum with a sound system like none I had heard before. We got out of the car and went to the clubs entrance and Damon was greeted by his fraternity brothers, and he introduced me to everybody.

Damon was the host of the party, so he was there to work because it was an alpha phi alpha party and whenever alphas threw parties all of the members had to work. Once Damon introduced me to everyone, I went and sat down at a table by myself and watched everybody. I didn't smile or talk much; I guess I was still in mourning over the loss of my brother, not to mention I was in an unfamiliar place. I stayed to myself and said hello to girls here and there, but something was weird about that night. I kept having the feeling that I needed to watch Damon's movements the whole night, so that's exactly what I did. Damon was at the front door collecting the entrance fees from people when a crowd of dudes pushed up to the front of the line and said that they didn't have to pay. Damon stepped up to the loud mouth dude in the front and asked him who he was to think that he didn't have to pay.

"I'm Carl Ray sucka, you better ask your frat brothers about me," Carl Ray said to him.

Damon told Carl Ray that he knew who he was and that he still had to pay like everyone else. Loud Mouth began ranting off about not having to pay, that he was Fresno State and he didn't pay to get into parties.

"No pay, no entrance," Damon said calmly.

Carl Ray took a wad of money out of his pockets and threw the money for him and his crew in Damon's face. Damon handled himself like a real gentleman but I was pissed that my best friend had to deal with that sort of treatment. An hour went by since Carl Ray and his crew came in the club, and all of a sudden I saw a group of people cheering on a fight. I immediately got up and ran over to where the commotion was and I saw Damon and Carl Ray throwing blow for blow. Damon was entirely too fast for Carl Ray. Damon was 6' 3" 175 pounds, and Carl ray was 6' 7" 240 lbs, but size didn't matter here because Damon was giving this loud mouth what he deserved. Damon kept hitting Carl Ray and then he kicked him in the chest, in which Carl Ray ended up outside the club.

Damon kept putting the three pieces on that boy and when Carl Ray couldn't take any more, he rushed Damon and grabbed him and threw him on top of a car. That's when I became enraged and ran over to Carl Ray and started beating him senseless. I didn't stop until one of the alpha cats started shooting in the air. That was when everyone dispersed. Damon and I met up at his car, and sped off to our apartment that was only a mile away. Once we got to the house we joked around about what went down, but Damon had concerns because Carl Ray was a known gang member in Fresno and Damon feared there would be retaliation. At that point I got nervous because I didn't want to be going to college and having to watch my back.

Damon and I were talking about the situation when our house phone rang. Damon picked it up and it was his frat brothers saying that Carl Ray wanted to talk to Damon and me about what had just happened. We were going to meet up at Sam's house – who was the top alpha. Sam and I had similar physiques but he was a little bigger than I was. Sam was also the starting safety at Fresno state.

Damon and I drove over to Sam's house and I was ready for whatever was going to happen. My adrenaline was pumping hard, and I was ready to kill. Damon and I walked inside Sam's house and it was dark inside so my eyes had to get adjusted to the darkness. Once my eyes got adjusted I saw that Carl Ray was standing right across from me and that boy was jacked up. It was the first time I'd seen the after effects of my handy work. Carl Ray started talking about how that situation wasn't right in the way it went down. As he was talking, I saw one of my classmates, Darnell, standing by that clown's side. I was enraged that Darnell would hang with a sucka like that. I didn't do any talking though, I just let Carl Ray and Damon speak their peace. I just stood there looking vicious. The meeting ended up non-violent, but I overheard Carl Ray saying that this shit wasn't cool. He kept repeating that over and over, and so my antennas were up. When Carl Ray and his crew left, Sam came over to me and Damon and got our side of the story. Sam told Damon that the fraternity was backing us up 100%.

A few days after the brawl, I went to Sara's dorm room and she told me that the word was out and that I better cancel Christmas. That was the first time I had ever heard that saying and it stuck in my head. Sara said that a few of her friends told her that Carl Ray had said specifically that the buff cat from Oakland can cancel Christmas. I played it cool with Sara, but I was steaming on the inside. I hung out with Sara at her dorm room that night, all the while contemplating what my next move would be. I finally decided that I would get me a gun and blow Carl Ray's brains out before he got to me.

The next day I went and called up a few of my friends in Oakland. I told them the situation and they wanted to come to Fresno to take care of it for me, but I refused to let them come. I had made my bed so I was going to lie in it. I was going to take care of my own business. I became a different person after the fight. I was too serious all the time – I was always paranoid and snappy. I wouldn't be at peace until I dealt with Carl Ray. I went on a mission to find a gun. I was asking Damon's fraternity brothers if they knew anyone selling guns, and I got directed to one of the dorm rooms on campus. I knocked on the door and gave the password and I was let into the room. When I walked inside there were boxes of brand new guns all over the place. The two teenagers asked me how much I wanted to spend and I told them I had $150. They directed me to the guns they had at that price. I spotted my new bodyguard immediately. She was a shiny ass chrome with a little black strip on the handles. As soon as I grabbed that gun I felt a surge of energy dispense throughout my body and I knew that gun would change my life forever. I walked out of the dorm room feeling like I was ten feet tall. The cats that sold me the gun gave me some bullets and an extra clip, so I was ready.

Once I had my personal bodyguard, I was ready for whatever. I started going to all the college functions on campus with my gun and Sara always by my side. Sara didn't know I had the gun, and I couldn't let her know because she talked a lot. I went to parties that I felt like Carl Ray would go to so I could shoot him, but God never let me run into him in that manner.

Christmas vacation rolled around fast, and the reason it went by so fast was because I was in funk season. Sara and I had been having a lot of unprotected sex and I was worried because she was sick and throwing up all the time. I was praying she wasn't pregnant, not only for my sake, but for hers as well. She was on a track and field scholarship and she couldn't afford to lose that.

Sara and I drove to the bay area in a 1975 Toyota I had bought. It was one of those ugly yellow turtle looking Toyotas. It wasn't pretty but it got the job done. The Turtle, as I called it, was a stick shift and when I bought it I didn't even know how to drive it, but I learned quickly. The Turtle wasn't the ideal car to be proud of, but I had bought it on my own accord.

When we reached the bay area, I dropped Sara off at her mother's house and I went to my own mom's house to be with my family. Everyone was happy to see me but everybody was asking me if they had me on steroids in college or something because they wanted to know how I had gotten so big in 4 months. I told them what I had told them before – that I worked out a lot and ate a lot that was the reason I had gotten big. At that time I weighed 190 lbs, but it looked like I weighed 240 lbs.

During Christmas vacation, Sara went to the doctor's office and found out that she was pregnant. We were both a nervous wreck, so we sat down and talked about what we should do and we came to the conclusion that she would have to get an abortion, which I would need to fork over some cash for her to get. As we waited for Sara's abortion day, we had only seen each other a few times. I was hanging out with Corey and Marlon quite a bit.

The rest of the Christmas vacation I spent all my time with Sara because she was recovering from the abortion and I wanted to be there for her. Sara and I drove back to Fresno in the turtle and it ran like a champ. We made it back in two and a half hours this time. It wasn't as bad as the U-Haul drive. We got back to college feeling refreshed and ready to finish out the school year. I did the same thing day in day out. Eat, go to school, work out, hang out with Sara, and look for Carl Ray because that situation was still unfinished business to me. I had noticed that Sara and I's relationship was kind of drifting. I didn't know if it had to do with the abortion or what, but we just weren't the same as we used to be. That didn't stop us from humping like rabbits though, and I was scared of her getting pregnant all the while. There came a point where I didn't even want to have sex with her anymore because we were both too fertile to be messing around without protection, however, we foolishly kept doing the nasty like we didn't care.

The school year was going by tremendously fast. Spring had arrived and I'd gotten the opportunity to start practicing with the football team. I was excited about being a part of the team and I was going to prove to the coaches that I was a top notch football player. I was a defensive back so I practiced with them all the time. We went over drills, coverage's, and techniques. I loved going to practice and working out. I knew that was the life for me. After a few practices, I found out that Carl Ray brother, Lee, was a wide receiver for Fresno state. When I first heard about him I was glad he was a wide receiver so I could try to kill him at practice.

When I first saw Lee, I mean mugged him and asked him, "what's up?" He was a laid back sort of guy and just responded with a simple, "nothing." I was surely looking forward to getting in a rumble with Lee, but I guess he wasn't tripping on me. I kept an eye on him anyway though.

College football was no joke. Once you were on the football team you were a slave. My schedule was mapped out for me and I couldn't do the things I was doing the previous winter semester. I had to change my workout time from night time to after class at 1 p.m. , and as soon as I was done working out, I would eat a hamburger from Wendy's and go to sleep for a hour or two in the locker room. Life had definitely gotten hectic fast. Sara and I were seeing less and less of one another, which was fine with me because I was always tired during that time anyways. I wasn't having the migraines the way I used to, but I would get them at least twice a month after hard workouts. Once Sara started track, she became pretty tired too, so we basically just hung out on the weekends.

Spring football practice was one hell of an experience and I learned things that I wish I would have learned in high school. The coaches loved my work ethic. I never showed weakness and I always ran full speed in everything I did on that football field. Coach used to call me in his office and ask me if I was taking something, and I said no, why do you think that? He said that he had never seen one of his football players work out before practice then come to practice and run around like a mad man. I told him that I took naps and that's how I had so much energy.

"Well we will be drug testing you mister," Coach said to me. The idea that I would be tested didn't faze me a bit. I didn't have anything to hide.

"Great, is that all?" I asked him.

"That's all for now," he said, "Just keep up your amazing work on the field."

One particular day at practice I was on fire. I was defending the top wide receivers to the point that they couldn't even catch the balls thrown to them. All the wide receivers wanted a shot at the title and I just kept shutting them down one by one. That's when I heard someone call my name, and I found that it was Joe Broussard from the Fellowship of Christian Athletes. He was happy to see me and asked if I wanted to be a coach / mentor at the camps in Thousand Oaks and Arizona, and I immediately said I would love to be a part of the camp. Joe gave me all the details of what I had to do to be a coach / mentor at the camp, and I told him thanks for the opportunity, and that I wouldn't let him down.

Spring camp went good and the school year had almost ended when a few friends and I decided that we were going to pledge Alpha Phi Alpha the next school year. I knew that I couldn't live with Damon if I were to pledge. I would be his personal slave if I lived in the same house as him during that time, since he would be one of the ones pledging me. Quell and I decided that we would move in together and it was great that Quell already had a two bedroom apartment and he was living there by himself. I told Damon about the move and he said that it was a good idea, because he agreed that I would be his slave if I stayed with him.

Moving in with Quell was different for me because Quell always had a house full of people just hanging out. When I came home I wanted peace and quiet, so Quell and I bumped heads a little about him having all those damn people over all the time. I loved my privacy; I didn't like people to be around me every day all day.

Quell was a strange looking fellow. He had a spine condition that made his neck and head look deformed, but you would have thought that he was the prettiest motherfucker you had ever seen judging by his personality. Quell was a ladies' man who had the ability to charm any girl out of their panties. Quell was a true socialite. I kind of envied his chipper personality because I was so uptight all the damn time. I didn't know how to loosen up.

Quell and I argued a lot, not only because of the way people were always at the house, but because of the bills being due and the lack of cleanliness I had to deal with. Quell was a nasty motherfucker, who seemed to be allergic to cleaning up. I was a neat freak so that shit bothered the hell out of me.

"Summer of 1994"

Summer had arrived and it was time for me to get ready for the Fellowship of Christian Athletes Camp. I had to take a two month extensive coach / mentor course before I was qualified to work with the youth. Quell had already left days before me and I was glad to have to the apartment to myself for a few days. Sara came over a few times but we were growing apart. She was going back to Berkeley for the summer break, so I wasn't going to see her for about a month or two because I was going to Arizona and Thousand Oaks for a total of 21 days. After that, I had to start triple day football practice. I drove Sara to the train station and gave her a hug and said that I would see her soon. Something just didn't seem right with Sara and a few days before I was set to leave for camp, Sara called me and said that she was pregnant again. I couldn't believe it, not again. She was crying, saying that she would have to get another abortion and that this time she would have to go by herself because I was going out of town. It was disturbing to me to know that she had to mess up her insides for a second time. I was heartbroken. I hated that Sara had to go through all of that by herself. She told me not worry and that she would take care of it.

When the day finally arrived for me to meet up with the rest of the mentors / coaches so we could make our way to Arizona, I was shocked to see who was going to be driving us there. – It was Trent Dilfer, one of the best quarterbacks in Fresno State history.

The ride from Fresno to Arizona wasn't as bad as those Greyhound rides I took in the past, but I still couldn't wait to get out of that truck. When we finally got to Arizona, we were happy as hell that we made it in one piece. Once we arrived in Flagstaff, Arizona, Trent took all of us to a house that belonged to one of his relatives, and waiting there was a huge feast for us. I felt like a king at that point, because I wasn't in just any ordinary house; I was in a mansion. I had never been in a mansion until then. We had a ball eating, drinking (soda of course), and laughing. Time zipped by and before we knew it, it was time for us to go to the Northern Arizona University campus where the camp would be.

The ride to the university only took about ten minutes and the college campus was huge. The first thing Trent wanted to show me was the gym at the school. When I walked inside I thought I was in heaven. It was unbelievable that college students had such an elaborate place to work out. That gym was better than any gym I had ever set foot in. I messed around with some of the machines to show off my abnormal strength while everyone watched in awe. After that we went to meet up with the rest of the staff and everything was quite organized. We had our itineraries of what each day's schedule would be and the names of the kids that we were responsible for. The staff came a day before the kids, which was perfect, because then we could get our things in order before all the chaos started.

I got a good night's sleep and woke up early to take myself on an early morning run, because I wanted to be ruthless when I went to triple day practices. I didn't realize that the Arizona altitude was totally different from California's altitude. When I started my run, my chest went on fire immediately. I didn't know what was wrong with me, but I kept on running anyway. I ran, thinking that eventually I would feel better, I but I just couldn't manage to get my breathing in order. Eventually I saw someone else running and I asked them what was wrong with the air. They told me that we were in a high altitude area, so the air was thinner and my body would have to get used to it. I cut my run short and tried to gain my composer.

After my brief run, I went and took a shower, got dressed and ate breakfast because the kids were going to be there shortly. When the kids came, they came by the bus loads. The other mentor's and I had to keep all those loud kids in order, but it was pretty difficult because it was obvious that they were ready to let loose.

Once all the kids were there, each mentor called out their kid's names and the kids would go stand by them. It took about 45 minutes just to go through all the names, and once we finished we had to let them know what their room assignment was. After that was all taken care of, we showed them to their room and told them to meet back with their mentor in one hour.

My group of kids were good and they were amazed at how buff I was. I was only a few years older than them, but they said they had never seen anyone as buff as me. After the group talk and prayer, I sent all of them to bed because the next morning it was going to be treacherous.

Once again I got another good night of sleep, and I was beginning to think it must have been the thin air that made me sleep so good. I woke up early and took an early morning run, but unlike last time I took things slower and didn't do all the hard sprinting that I was used to doing. I had a lot of respect for Arizona's thin air. After my run I went and took a shower and went to wake up my kids. Those kids hated waking up. Wake up time was seven o'clock and they despised it, but I got them to get up by threatening them with having to do crabs if they were late. Everyone that has played football knows that crabs are one of the worst exercises invented. They hurt pretty bad, so once I said crabs they all hopped up and got dressed to go eat breakfast. After breakfast it was time to see who was who in my group.

It was easy to determine who would be best for what. My group of kids were amazingly good and I felt deep down in my heart that they would be the champs at the camp. There were 15 teams and whoever won first place got a trophy and their bragging rights. I knew my team had it in them to win it all. We did drills all morning, and at the second practice that evening we went over plays. My group wanted to win the championship badly, and I did too so we were working hard to be the best.

Fellowship of Christian Athletes in Northern Arizona went superb. I got the best coach award and my team won the championship title, which I was flabbergasted about. I was amazed at how wonderfully I had managed to coach my group.

The morning after the championship game, the kids were set to leave, so we all hugged and said our goodbyes to one another. It was sad to see the kids leave so soon. I hated bonding with people like that and then having to say goodbye to them. I think that's why I didn't like meeting a lot of new people. After all the kids left, the staff started getting their things in order because the following morning we would be going to Thousand Oaks California.

The next morning I didn't go for a run because we were set to leave the camp pretty early. All of the staff met up in the cafeteria and ate and planned our ride to Thousand Oaks. We were on our way and Trent was doing the driving while everyone else was getting their sleep on, well, everyone except for me – I was watching Trent like a hawk the entire time, because I had a phobia of other people driving me. We kept each other company on the eight hour drive to Thousand Oaks instead.

When we made it to Thousand Oaks around 8:00 p.m., we went through the same staff meeting that we had at Northern Arizona, but unlike Arizona, Cal Lutheran's camp was a lot bigger because of the variety of different sports they were going to be playing there. There were a lot more staff than there had been at the previous camp, due to the projected turn out of kids. We were briefed on what was going on and given our itineraries and we all dispersed to our assigned rooms.

After I put all my things away I took a shower and went to sleep.

I slept well in Thousand Oaks California too. I guess I was sleeping so well because I was getting worn out. Just like the Arizona camp, the kids came in by the bus loads. They were just as rowdy as the Arizona kids, maybe even more so because now you had girls running around too. Each mentor called out there group and this took around two hours at Cal Lutheran because there were so many kids.

Once I called my group, I looked all my kids over to see which ones would end up being a problem for me. They were all amazed and wanted to feel my arms, just like the kids in Arizona. I guess the muscles were good for something, because at least I got respect from the kids. The Cal Lutheran camp was more intense than the Arizona camp because it had some of the most elite athletes of California, and they were very competitive.

I ran my program the same way I did in Arizona, but I was much more hyper because there was a lot of good competition and I wanted my kids to do and be their best. The days at Cal Lutheran flew by and my team was honored with the most improved trophy because in the beginning of the camp we were getting killed, but then I sat them down and talked to them like adults and they quickly pulled it together. Along with the team trophy, I received another honor of best coach/mentor. It meant a lot to me to receive my second best coach award and I was honored. After the ceremony everyone went to the cafeteria where there was a huge feast for the staff and kids and we all had a blast.

The next morning I was a little sluggish getting up. I guess I ate the wrong thing or something, because I was feeling queasy. I took a shower and got dressed so that I could say my goodbyes to all of the kids. I was like a rock star at that camp because of my muscles. After saying goodbye to everyone it was time for the drive back to Fresno and I couldn't wait to get back to my apartment. I was also pretty happy that I would be getting $1,500 for the work I did at both camps, and I knew I was going to use that money to buy myself some clothes. Some things hadn't changed, and my addiction to clothes was one of those things.

After making it back to Fresno, I had one week to get ready for triple days football practice. I heard that triple days were grueling, especially because of the dry heat in Fresno. I hadn't had a migraine my entire summer so I was scared of what was going to happen at triple days.

Triple days came fast and they were more grueling than I had heard they were. I had a migraine practically every day; I was losing weight because of the heat and because of throwing up. It felt like those coaches were trying to kill us. Morning practice consisted of drills, and when I say drills, I mean drills. I was moved by the coaches from corner back to running back because Coach Sweeny felt like I would be a perfect addition to them. I was upset with the move at first because I liked to hit people and not get hit, but college was another animal altogether because it didn't matter if you were on offense or defense there was going to be a lot of hitting going on.

Once I got into the groove of the running back position, I grew to love it. Afternoon practice consisted of running special team drills, so that meant that it was a tremendous amount of running, but I didn't care because my whole objective was to impress those coaches even if it killed me. I had set out to be the best, and the coaches ended up loving me because I out ran and out hustled everybody there.

The migraines were terrible and I used to just want to get rid of them somehow. They were fucking up my life and I was having head pain the entire three weeks of triple days. I couldn't wait for it to be over.

Triple days were over but once the school year started up again it was time for me to pledge in the fraternity. I was nervous about pledging because of the horrific things I'd heard about it. One thing about me was that I was immune to pain, so the wood paddles didn't pump fear in me at all; it was more of the unknown that had me shook up.

"Hazing"

At the start of the new school year, mine and Sara's relationship was next to nothing. After her second abortion she was a different person. If I tried to kiss her she'd turn her face away from me and be like, "Nuh uh!"

I basically wrote our relationship off after that. I didn't have time for relationship problems anyway, because I was about to start pledging and I had football practice every day at that point.

The pledging had started and those guys were lunatics. They named me buckwheat and every time one of the big brothers called my name I had to say "Oooootay" like buckwheat used to do. It was over the top funny. Quell also pledged and his name was rat boy. When the big brothers called his name, he had to say, "rat boy rat boy" and do his mouth like a rat, saying, "I need cheese, I need cheese." The first time Quell had to do that chant, I was on the ground cracking up. I don't remember ever laughing that hard in my life and the big brothers didn't find my humor in the situation funny at all. They told me to assume the position and I knew I was about to get the first dose of that thick ass wood paddle with the suction holes in it. I assumed the position and the number one defensive end for Fresno State, Earl, started giggling. He told me that I was going to be the first one to get a taste of the super paddle that had taken him a week to make. That paddle was humongous, so humongous that he was able to grab it with both hands like a baseball bat. I stayed in the "cut", as the big brothers called it, and when I looked out my peripheral vision I saw Earl cocking that paddle of his back and from that point on I couldn't watch anymore and closed my eyes. I felt that board come across my ass so hard that it knocked me a couple of steps forward but, to my surprise, that super-paddle broke in half. My line brothers were happy about that.

The first night of pledging was something unthinkable. The big brothers had a big jug of peanut butter and we were like, what are they going to do with that? That's when the big brothers opened the jug and handed it to Quell. They told us that we had to eat all of the peanut butter in the jug, and that they wanted to see the jug spotless when we were through. Quell dipped his hand inside and then passed it to me; I dipped my hand inside and then passed it to the next person. I chewed on that scoop of peanut butter, which was horrendous and felt like a glob of glue in my mouth, for what felt like an eternity. There were seven of us at the time, so we kept at that jug of peanut butter, and after around 30 minutes we had finally completed that stepping stone. Our reward was a single can of beer for the seven of us to share to un-glue our mouths. The first night was painful because all of our asses were purple from all of the paddles we took that night.

We got paddled for any and every reason at all. If you looked at a big brother in the eye, if you didn't respond like they wanted you too, if you were too slow at doing something – the list goes on and on.

The next morning I had to go to class, which was weird because I couldn't sit down because my ass cheeks were swollen beyond swollen. When I went to my class, the professor told me to have a seat, but I told him that I couldn't and everyone in the room seemed to understand.

Along with going to school, I had football practice, I had to pledge at night and I had to memorize a lot of material for the big brothers. Life was crazy, but at the same time it was exciting.

We had to do a lot of different things while we were pledging. We had to get up early in the morning, every Saturday, and go to the homeless shelter to feed the homeless, which the brothers made us do in order to teach us to give back to the community and to volunteer when we could. We also had to raise money for the fraternity. I remember one particular fundraiser like it was yesterday. The big brothers made up flyers that they were throwing a stripper party for all the ladies on campus to come to at five dollars a piece. When I saw those flyers, I knew the big brothers couldn't possibly expect me to dance, because I was too cool to dance. My line brothers and I were made to pass out all of those flyers to every girl we saw for an entire week. Friday had arrived and my brothers and I were at our big brother Art's house. Art was always trying to break me while I was pledging, because Carl Ray was his cousin. Art knew that I wasn't one to be fucked with though.

When the day arrived, the big brothers finally told us our order – we would be stripping and I told them to let me go first. The big brothers laughed at me and told me that I was going to be last because I was the main attraction. All the ladies were coming to see me. We were all nervous as hell. All my brothers went out before me, then Art gave the announcement that the main attraction was coming out. All I was wearing was a white robe and some white Speedos. I'll never forget the music I had on. I danced to 12 Play by R. Kelly and all the girls that were packed into that apartment were going crazy. I was thinking, damn, I didn't know I had this effect on women. I teased the women a lot and they all loved me and gave me a standing ovation when I was done. I was shocked because that was my first time trying to dance in years. That fundraiser brought Alpha Phi Alpha a shit load of money, and that was my first strip show ever.

The hardest thing about pledging was memorizing all the different poems and history of Alpha Phi Alpha. The thing with memorizing all the material was that you may know everything, but if your brother didn't know it we were all punished.

I'll never forget the last night of pledging, because it was outright heinous. We were whipped relentlessly, especially me because I was the "rock" which meant that I was the most mentally and physically strong out of my line brothers. I was the one that, when my brothers couldn't take anymore paddles, I would jump in and take their paddles for them. Being the rock, I had to endure a lot of pain and I didn't mind, in fact, I actually welcomed the pain. After we were whipped, we were blindfolded and forced to crawl on our hands and knees for what seemed liked miles upon miles. My body was over exerted to the point that I got a migraine in the middle of being pledged. My mouth was paralyzed and I wasn't able to talk, but luckily we didn't have to recite anything at that point, otherwise I don't know what I would have done. My line brothers and I made it into Alpha Phi Alpha and we were happy as hell to be done with that chapter of our lives. Once we were big brothers, we were able to bring pain to other people the way our brothers had brought it to us.

Pledging for Alpha Phi Alpha lasted three long ass months and, during that three month period, I hung out with Sara a few times but we didn't have a sexual relationship with each other anymore. We were more like friends at that point. Sara expressed her disapproval of me being in Alpha Phi Alpha because she said that I would be fucking all types of different girls, but what she didn't realize was that fucking girls was the last thing on my mind. Sara and I couldn't be in one another's presence after I'd made it into Alpha Phi Alpha and so we stopped all communication between us after that.

"Good Guy turned Bad Guy"

Things were going good at school and the football field. I was still under redshirt status because the coaches said they were saving me for the following year to make my mark. At that time there was Reggie brown, Michael Pittman, and Greg Elliot that were the go to running backs. I still practiced with the team as if I were playing in the upcoming game.

After pledging I moved back in with Damon. Pretty Boy had moved into a place with his girlfriend, so Damon and I were back to doing our thing and it was actually better than it was before because Sara wasn't coming around with her negative spirit.

Since making it into the fraternity, my status on campus had elevated, Sara was right about that. The girls were trying to throw themselves at me, but I was still too paranoid about diseases.

I was looking to buy a new car and so I put the Turtle up for sale, and someone bought it within a few days. I put in for a loan at school for $1,200 dollars and it was granted to me. I was paying $300 a month in rent and $200 for food a month. I was living off my scholarships that I got in high school and my mother helped me out a little too.

Once I picked up my check from the school, I went and cashed it and went car shopping. I went to a few car lots to no avail. I told myself I was going to go look at one more car lot and if I didn't find what I wanted I was going home. The last car lot of the day was a success and I bought a Chevy Chevelle Laguna. It was immaculate. The car was a tan color with chrome rims. I did all the paperwork for the car and I drove off in my new stylish vehicle. When I got home I told Damon to come outside to check out my new ride. Damon was happy for me and told me that the car was nice. I told Damon that I was going to put a bumping sound system in it like the system Damon had in his car. I was on the top of the world with my new car, especially after I put a sound system in that baby. You couldn't tell me anything.

Spoiled birthday was coming up so I used that as an excuse to drive my new car home and show it off to everybody. I was driving the Laguna to Oakland when I noticed the oil light on but, I just thought it was something minor and didn't think any more of it.

All weekend I hung out with Spoiled, Derrick and Darold. We were going everywhere in my new car and I even took Spoiled shopping with some stolen credit cards I had. I had been charging stuff on those cards for six months straight, so I let Spoiled get whatever he wanted to on someone else's expense.

When that Sunday came around, I wanted to get home early in the day so I left my mother's house around ten that Sunday morning. Everyone saw that I was doing well for myself, and they all were proud of me.

On my way to Fresno I kept noticing the red oil light on in my car and I prayed that it wasn't anything serious. I kept my foot heavy on the gas pedal though and the music was so loud that my ears were hurting. I'll never forget what I was listening to in that moment; I was listening to Slick Rick's "Children Story", and I was bobbing my head to the beat. All of a sudden I felt the Laguna slowing down. The car came to a complete stop and I got out and popped the hood as if I knew what I was doing. I looked the car over and I tried to start it to no avail. I was super pissed. I had just bought that car and it was fucked up already. I was in Pleasanton at the time, so I had to walk a few miles to the gas station to call my mother and tell her what had happened, and she sent a tow truck out to tow the car to Fresno. As I was waiting on the shoulder of the freeway for the tow truck, some of my friends from Fresno State spotted me and asked me if I wanted to ride back with them. The tow truck had just showed up around the time that they saw me, so I rode back to Fresno with my friends.

Once I returned to Fresno I waited about 20 minutes and the tow truck pulled into the apartment complex with my fucked up car. I was fucking pissed off, and I didn't know how I was going to pay for the Laguna to get fixed. My money was low and I didn't have any extra to spare. Luckily I had also bought Quell's old car for a couple of hundred dollars, so I still had transportation but I didn't like the Pontiac I bought from him too much because it needed some work done to it.

Monday came and I called up the dealership that I had bought the Laguna from and the owner told me that he would send a truck to pick up the car and see what was wrong with it. All of Monday passed and I finally got a call from the dealership on Tuesday saying that a rod had busted in the engine, and because of that my car would need a new engine put in it. When I asked him how much that would cost he told me an even $500. I told him to start on the work and he told me it would be ready in about a week or two. I was desperate for money at that point. I loved the Laguna and I knew I had to get it back by any means necessary.

My first attempt for help was to ask Coach Sweeney, so I walked into his office and sat down. When Coach Sweeney looked at me and asked me what the problem was, I told him that I was hard up for money and I needed some help. I remember he looked at me and said, "Kirkendall, a man got to do what a man got to do to survive in this world." I looked at the coach with pure hate that day, and I gave him a simple thank you and went to practice.

My mind was all screwed up at that point and I didn't know who I could turn to for help. I even went to Sara and asked her if she had any money that I could borrow, but she looked at me like I was an alien from Mars. My last hope was my mother and I just knew she would help me. I called her and told her about the situation and how I needed her help, but she told me that she didn't have any extra money to spare at that time. At that point the devil must have taken control over my mind, because I found myself thinking that the obvious solution to my problem was to go and do some robberies. I had heard that some of my fraternity brothers were doing robberies and they were doing well with it. I talked to them about it and they said I could surely come and get down with them. A day later my fraternity brother called me and said to get ready because they were going to come and pick me up in an hour. I got dressed in all black, I cleaned my gun and loaded it, and

I sat waiting patiently. Then my house phone rang and my fraternity brother told me that the robbery was a no go and that something had come up. I was disappointed because I was hoping to make some money that night, but I decided I was full of adrenaline and that I didn't need anyone to get down with me. I made it up in my mind that I was going to commit some robberies that night on my own. I got up and started walking outside towards the Pontiac when Damon came walking towards me.

"What's up, bra?" Damon said eying me suspiciously.

I snapped at him that nothing was wrong and Damon instantly picked up by my tone that something wasn't right. He tried to look me in the eyes but I avoided eye contact with him altogether and kept on walking. I knew that if I looked at him I wouldn't be able to go and do what I was planning to do.

"Bro! Don't do anything stupid," Damon said to me calmly.

I just kept on walking and got in the Pontiac and smashed off. I drove around for nearly an hour looking for my victim. I hadn't seen anyone slipping so I had about decided to go home when all of a sudden I looked to my left and saw a man at an ATM machine. I quickly made a U-turn and parked around the corner from where he was parked. I got out of the car and ran to where he was standing at the ATM and quietly put the gun to his head. I told the man to withdrawal all the money he could and to give me his pin code. I told him that if he lied to me I would kill him on the spot. The man gave me the pin code and I snatched the card out of his hand and trotted back to the Pontiac and sped off.

As soon as I drove past the ATM, the guy saw me in the car and started chasing me down the street and writing down the license plate number. I was like, fuck, this motherfucka probably got the license, but then realized that the car wasn't in my name anyway, so I should be cool and not get caught. I stopped at a few different ATMs and made withdrawals from the guy's account. I had a good $600 after it was all said and done, so I went home. I parked the Pontiac on the street outside my apartment complex. It was a weird night because I locked the damn keys inside the car and I had to get my neighbor to give me a hanger so I could fish the keys out. It took me all of 15 minutes to get that car door open and get the keys. Once I finally got them out, I went into my apartment and started going through all the money and the possessions that I had. Luckily Damon wasn't at the house that night. He was at one of his girlfriend's houses. As I was counting the money out, my house telephone rang and for some odd reason my spirit told me that was the police, so I didn't answer it.

The phone rang a few more times and all of a sudden someone started banging on the door yelling, "Police! Open up!"

I was scared shitless but I knew for some reason that they couldn't have gotten a search warrant at 2:00 a.m. I stayed calm and took all the stolen property and hid it, just in case the police did in fact barge into the apartment. After the banging on the door stopped, I laid down and fell asleep for around two hours. I woke up and knew I was in trouble, so I gathered all the stolen property I had and some clothes. After I packed everything I needed, I climbed out my bedroom window and ran to where I thought the car was parked, but unfortunately the police had towed it as evidence. I began walking frantically to Quell's house – the same apartment I used to live in with him – and when I got there he opened the door and asked me what was wrong. I told him everything that had happened and he called the rest of our brothers to the house so they could figure out what to do.

I was a nervous wreck thinking about having to go to jail. Thankfully some of our sorority sisters wanted us to drive up to San Jose State to kick it with them, so we did. All five of us piled up in Jeremy's old ass BMW and made our way to San Jose California. Once we arrived to San Jose, the girls kept asking me if I was alright, and I told them I was cool, but I definitely wasn't cool and it was obvious that I had a ton of shit on my mind. I was glad that I wasn't in Fresno because the police were hunting for my ass. I couldn't figure out how they knew to come to my address and I kept dwelling on that over and over, until it finally came to me that I tried to switch the car in my name with my address. Damn I was fucked.

The couple of days in San Jose flew by. I didn't want to go back to Fresno, but I did want to see what was going on. When the five of us returned to Fresno our brothers were pledging some girls that wanted to be our sisters so we all showed up to the location that the girls were getting pledged at. As soon as we walked inside, everyone stopped and looked at me as if they had seen a ghost.

"What's up yall? Why you looking like that?" I said, confused.

Damon pulled me to the side and said to me, "Bro, they are looking for you something fierce. It's not cool for you to be in Fresno right now."

Damon said that the police had come and ransacked our apartment along with some of the other brother's apartments looking for me. I was definitely a nervous wreck. I walked off from the brothers and over to Sara's apartment, which wasn't too far from where the brothers were pledging the girls, and when I got to her house it was clear she didn't want me around. She had a stank attitude towards me from the moment she opened the door and asked me why I came to her house. I told her I was in trouble and I didn't know what to do.

"Oh well! You can't stay here!" she said to me.

I called my mother and told her I was in trouble and she told me to get on the Greyhound and come home. I called a cab to come get me from Sara's house and what I didn't know then was that that would be the last time I saw her again for an entire decade. The cab came and picked me up and took me to the Greyhound station. Lucky for me, I arrived there just in time to catch the last bus headed to Oakland that night. I bought myself a few snacks out of the vending machine for the long ride back home – much of which would be spent sleeping because I was so overly exhausted.

The bus ride home I was dozing in and out of sleep and thinking about the outcome of my situation. During that entire time of being on the run, I'd never thought about the possibility of jail, which is weird looking back on it. I guess in my mind I was going to get away with it, but that didn't work out so well.

When I arrived at the Oakland Greyhound at 6:00 a.m., I immediately hopped in a cab because I knew nobody was up going to come and pick me up. Once I got back to my mother's house, I rang the doorbell and my mother came and let me in the house. All she said was to get some rest and that we would talk later. I slept for a few hours and then got up, brushed my teeth and went into the kitchen where mom and pops were. That was the first time in my life I told my parents the evil I had done. They listened attentively, like they were listening to a story teller, and I had them hanging on my every word. After I was finished, pops told me that I could either be on the run for the rest of my life, or I could deal with the consequences of what I'd done while I was still young. I was confused and didn't think the Fresno police had enough evidence pointing at me to convict me for my crime. My face was covered up so how would I get identified? I gave mom and pops the same explanation and they agreed that the police probably didn't have enough evidence to convict me, but they also said that I should face the situation regardless. I agreed reluctantly. We decided that the next day they would drive me to Fresno.

"Fresno county Jail"

The ride to Fresno was a weird one. My spirit knew that nothing good was going to come from the evil act of violence I had committed. No one talked the entire drive. I guess mom and pops felt that something bad was going to happen to me too.

When we arrived to Fresno, mom and pops took me straight to the police station and I went to the front desk and told the officer that I was being sought after by the Fresno police. The police ran my name and two officers immediately handcuffed me and I told mom and pops goodbye. It would be a long time before we were together as a family again after they dropped me off at that police station.

The police placed me in a room that was empty when I got in there. Around 20 minutes later, "Ebony" and "Ivory" – a black and white cop – came inside. The black cop was doing all the talking.

"Why did you rob that man at the ATM?" He said to me.

I was never scared of the police, so they didn't intimidate me. I knew that they only human beings and could be killed just like anybody else.

"I don't know what you're talking about. Get me a lawyer," I replied calmly.

I learned that phrase watching television and I hated snitches so I definitely wasn't going to tell on myself.

They got fed up with me being quiet.

"You don't want to talk? Well, I guess we will also add a stolen property charge onto your robbery charge," the black officer said, "We found a woman's purse in your apartment closet and you are going to be taking the wrap for that too if you don't start talking."

"I need an attorney!" I said.

"We got a wise ass here," one of the cops said, and they both walked out the room.

After another 30 minutes of just sitting in that cold room, a cop walked in and told me that I was going to get booked into the jail for the crimes of armed robbery and receiving stolen property. I stayed quiet and the cop took me to get processed in the jail.

When I got into the processing room, there were people all over the fucking floor and it smelled like someone shit their pants. It was repugnant and I wanted to kill whoever was funky like that. The lady at the processing window told me to hand her all of my clothes and whatever else I had in my possession. I handed her everything I had on me and was left standing there butt booty naked in front of all those strangers. Once she had all my things, the lady handed me a two piece jump suit and some black karate shoes. I tried to put that jumpsuit on, but it ripped as I was pulling the top over my massive arms.

"Oh you're a big guy, you need a larger size," the lady said looking at me.

I told her thanks a lot because that wouldn't have looked right in jail. Once I got my jumpsuit on I was moved to another room and given a bag lunch. I wasn't that hungry at the time, especially once I looked inside the bag and saw those two, dry ass peanut butter sandwiches, a baby sized bag of lays potato chips, a chocolate chip cookie wrapped in plastic, and a milk. I didn't know at the time, but I would later learn to love that sack lunch.

While I and a ton of other people sat in that room of concrete walls for about four long hours, I tried to keep myself calm. I was furious I was in there for so long with a group of homeless vagrants. Finally, an officer came in and called my name and told me to go see the nurse. When I got to the nurse's window, she rudely asked me if I had any diseases or illness. I replied with a simple, "No ma'am." She then told me to place my arm in the window so that she could give me my TB shot. I was like, what is a TB shot? She explained to me that TB was tuberculosis.

I had never even heard of tuberculosis before that day. I asked the nurse what would happen if I refused, and she told me if I did that I would be placed in solitary confinement. I said "oh well", and stuck my arm in the window for my TB shot. After I was finished, the nurse told me to go back to the room I was in before.

After another long three hours in that room with those stank ass people, a cop came and called my name and said that I would be getting placed into a housing area now. The officer told me to grab one of the blankets that were in a huge bin. The blanket were an ugly gray color and wool like the blankets the military have. Inside of the blanket there were two sheets and a pillow case.

The cop walked me down a long ass corridor and we had to get buzzed into the housing area from an officer that was in the tower. The tower is where the police basically control the jail with the touch of buttons. Once I was buzzed into the area where I was supposed to be, I had to go and talk to another officer to see where my bed was. Once the officer told me all the house rules and gave me my bed assignment, I went straight to my bed. That particular housing area had two levels. All the whites were practically down stairs and all the blacks, Mexicans, and other nationalities were up on the second floor.

Once I got situated in my bed, a few guys came over and introduced themselves and they told me that they had seen a news clip about me on the news. I was a star already. The guys and I talked for a while getting to know each other and they wanted to know if they could work out with me when I worked out cause they said they wanted to get buff like me. I said "sure".

The first night in jail was tough because the beds were slabs of metal that didn't move, so my back was killing me. On top of that, I had never slept with a wool blanket like that before and that shit was causing me to itch like crazy. Then it was the thing with the lights. They didn't turn them off, and I was sleeping on a top bunk until I got seniority in the "pod" as everyone called the housing area. Then there were people up all fucking night walking around talking; it was crazy. It was weird for me because I didn't feel out of place when I got to jail. I wasn't nervous or anything. I don't know if it had something to do with my scheduled lifestyle that I lived before I went to jail or what, but I felt like I belonged there. It sounds weird but it's how I felt.

The next morning everybody was woken up by the c.o.'s (correctional officers) at three thirty in the fucking morning. I had just fallen to sleep and here they were waking me up already. I knew that jail shit was going to be one hell of an experience for me; I already felt it. Once everybody was up, about 30 people had to share a bathroom with only two toilets, two showers, and two sinks. It was chaos. I waited my turn for a sink so that I could brush my teeth with the baby sized tooth brush that I was given by the guards. Once everybody on the bottom tier and the top tier were ready, the guards told the bottom tier to grab a tray from the inmate at the pod door that was handing out the food. Once everybody from the bottom tier got their tray of food, the guard then instructed the top tier to get a tray. Everyone walked sluggishly to the inmate server and grabbed a tray. Once everyone had their tray we all walked back up the stairs to the second tier. Once up the tier I uncovered the tray to see what breakfast in jail was like, and I was in awe of what I saw.

There were some green scrambled eggs (I didn't know there were green eggs until then), some beans, two stale burrito shells, and a baby sized apple juice. Being my first breakfast in jail, I didn't know how to schedule how I ate. I quickly ate everything but the beans, since beans messed my stomach up. I saw everyone looking at me like I had done something wrong by eating that food. I asked my new jail house Patna Psycho what was the problem.

He said to me, "Bro! Its only 3:30 in the morning. We don't get our lunch until 11:00 a.m. and you haven't gone to the store yet for food, so that means that you'll be starving come seven or eight o'clock."

I saw his point; it was a pretty valid explanation. I looked around and almost everyone had a plastic bowl that they put their breakfast in to save for later. After breakfast people started getting called for court, but my name wasn't called, so all my new jail house friends were telling me that if I didn't go to court within 72 hours I would get out of jail. I prayed at the moment to God that I had learned my lesson in hopes that I would get out of jail.

After everyone that was going to court got called, a lot of the guys went back to sleep (I learned that sleep was a means of escape while incarcerated). I tried to go to sleep too, but that damn bunk was so uncomfortable that I couldn't find a comfortable spot to lie on. If I lay on my side, my shoulder went to sleep, and if I lay on my back – which everyone in jail did – my damn butt went to sleep, so there was a lot of tossing and turning on that metal slab of mine.

A few hours had passed and a guard yelled over the intercom that it was yard time, and whoever wanted to go should line up at the pods door. (Yard time was when inmates could work out, play basketball etc.) All my jailhouse friends were going and they said I should go too because there would be a weight machine I could use. That sparked my interest so I quickly got dressed and went to the pods front door to wait to go to the yard. After standing at the door for five minutes, a guard met us at the pod door and escorted us to the yard. The recreation room looked like a quarter of a high school basketball court. It was tiny! There was a weight machine that had a leg press, bench press, and a lat pull. It wasn't much, but it was enough to get the job done. There was also a basketball court and a deflated ball. First, my jailhouse friends and I played basketball, which had me exhausted and hungry, then they wanted to see how strong I was on the weight machine. Like I said earlier, I was a lot stronger than anyone I have ever met my age. I took off the top of my jumpsuit and everybody was like, "Damn your buff". I showed my jailhouse friends how to get big like me, and though they all had a long ways to go, they tried to keep up with me as best as they could. After being in recreation for two hours we were all ready to go back to the pod and prepare for our lunch because everybody was starving. The guard came and got us after two hours and ten minutes, and lunch was to be at the pod in about 20 minutes.

Once I was back in the pod, I went to take a shower because I was sweaty and stinky as hell. All I had was a piece of soap that looked like one of those soaps you get at a hotel. It was tiny and I learned fast that I had to preserve everything during my time in jail.

When I got in the shower, it was disgusting. When I looked in the drains of the shower it was obvious that people had been jacking off like crazy because I could see where they had left their babies covering all the drain holes. Luckily one of my jail house friends let me use an extra pair of shower thongs he had, because if I didn't wear any shower thongs in that shower my feet would have fallen off from an unknown disease. I hurried up and got out of that shower as quickly as I could and didn't want to go back in it ever again.

After my shower it was time for our bag lunches, so just like with breakfast the guards called the bottom tier then the top tier. I got my bag lunch and looked inside only to find that it was the same dry peanut butter sandwiches, chips, cookie and juice that they had given me the day before. I was starving though and I ate that shit up, though only sparsely because I understood that I couldn't eat anymore to get full; I had to eat to get rid of the hunger pangs. It didn't take me long to learn the system of eating in jail. After lunch everyone went to sleep again and I tried to go to sleep too but it was me against that metal slab.

There was about five more hours before I could have dinner and my stomach started growling like an hour after I had eaten half my lunch. I hopped off my bunk and went into my assigned drawer under the bunk and grabbed the remainder of what lunch I had left and ate the rest of it. Eating the peanut butter sandwich and cookie killed my hunger pangs so I got back on my bunk and fought with the slab of metal again, because there was still four hours until dinner would be served. I quickly saw that jail life was going to be about eating and sleeping.

The jail intercom blasted off, "Dinner will be served in 15 minutes so get up, wash your faces and brush yo stankin ass mouths!" The intercom had actually startled me to the point that I had almost fallen off my bunk. The first time I'm able to get a little sleep and I'm startled by a loud mouth guard.

Same as breakfast and lunch, dinner went the same way – bottom tier, and then top tier. Once I made it to the top tier I couldn't wait to see what we were getting fed that day. When I opened the tray there were two burritos like we used to get in elementary, corn, salsa, Jell-O pudding and milk. I didn't understand why we were getting fed so much Mexican food, I mean, damn it's like that's all they knew how to cook. I couldn't be picky at all though; either I ate what I was given or

I starved. I chose to eat one burrito and some corn, and then I saved one other burrito for later.

The next morning was the same 3:30 a.m. morning routine of getting what they called "chow" (eat time), and after chow was court. Once again I didn't get called to go to court, so all my jailhouse friends were telling me that if I didn't get called the next day that I was going to be a free man. I wanted to get out, but at the same time I didn't care if I did or not. I guess I felt like there wasn't anything in society for me at that time. Life on the streets was tough. I hated not having the amount of money that I wanted. I hated the stress of worrying about how I would pay for this and that. In jail, I didn't have to struggle financially like I did on the streets.

I hadn't called mom and pops since I'd been in jail. I was planning on calling them when I found out what was going on with the case.

I was starting to get comfortable around all the criminals. Most of the men in there were super soft to me, especially a lot of the white boys. They were always acting gay, saying gay things, and always touching one another. It was a weird thing to see. Most everyone in my pod was a non-violent offender. I was the only one I knew of with a violent case, which had a lot to do with the respect I got in the pod. I'm sure it helped that I looked like a competitive bodybuilder at 19 years old too. In jail, muscles meant you got a ton of respect from inmates, as well as correctional officers.

The next day came around and it was the usual bottom tier, top tier feeding schedule. It was the moment I had been waiting for: day number three. If I didn't get called that day I was going to be set free. I listened closely to the names that were called and I didn't hear my name once again. Everybody was telling me I would be getting out. They said that I wouldn't be charged within my 72 hour grace period. I started asking the guards if they saw my name on the release papers and they kept telling me no. Once 12 p.m. rolled around, I wasn't even hungry, so I put my lunch in my drawer. Right after that I heard the intercom pop on and my name called. "Kirkendall" the man on the intercom announced, and my heart skipped a beat. All I could think about in that moment was being on the streets again.

"Kirkendall, you have court!" the guards said to me.

I couldn't believe it. Those bastards called me at a special court time. I went down to the pod door where a guard met me and then walked me down a super long corridor. It took us 15 minutes to walk to our destination. Ultimately we reached a wooden door and the guard I was with knocked on it. Another guard opened the door and I was escorted to a podium. A public defender came up to me and gave me her card and said she was my appointed attorney. My attorney was an average looking Hispanic woman, about 150 lbs, at 5'7". The judge ranted off some shit I didn't understand and my public defender told me that this was called an arraignment and that all I had to do that day was say not guilty and that the judge would give me another court date. She told me to say not guilty, and so that's exactly what I did. After that the judge said that they would be setting my bail at $25,000 dollars, and that there had been a request of a line up, so they would be setting this manner for two weeks after the lineup had been done.

Once I was outside the court room, I was like, damn, I don't go back to court for two weeks. At the time two weeks was forever to me, but later on down the line two weeks was like two hours to me.

Once I returned to the pod from court, everyone ran up to me and asked what happened and I told them every detail.

"Your bail is only $25,000?" Psych said to me, astonished.

"*Only* $25,000? That's a lot of money," I said in response.

Psycho just started laughing. "All your people would have to pay is $2,500, which is ten percent of $25,000."

I immediately went to the phone to call my mother to let her know what was going on. The phone picked up in two rings and my mother was happy to hear from me. She asked me what was going on with the case, and I told her that I didn't go back to court for two more weeks, that I had to do a line up, but that my bail was only $2,500.

"You want us to bail you out?" My mother quickly responded, but I said no because if I got some time in my days would be accounted for.

But what I didn't realize at that time was that if I got bailed out then I had more probability of beating a case. Listening to the jailhouse special- ist, my mind was brain washed into believing that I should just stay in jail and do my time like a man. My mother asked me if I was sure, and

I told her I was because there was no need in wasting money. I did ask her to send me some money so I could buy some food though, because I was starving in that jail and I also asked her to call the shop where my Laguna was, but my mother told me that I had bigger things to worry about other than a car.

The weeks leading to my court day were action packed and I had become the head honcho on the top tier. I had a crew of young cats ready to do anything when I said too. I had finally made it to the store so I wasn't as hungry all the damn time, and once I was eating more I had more energy. I had so much energy now that I could work out twice a day, doing pushups, dips, and curls. My crew and I weren't ones to be fucked with, because we were all young and crazy.

I'll never forget this one particular incident where a white guy was placed on the top tier with me and my crew,. All the guards knew that it was a no-no to put white boys with us because we would fuck them over relentlessly. The white guy was alright until store night, when he spent the max at the store. I managed my money to a tee, because I knew that if I bought a lot of stuff I would eat a lot of stuff and my money would run out fast. The white guy walked up the stairs to the top tier with his bag of food thrown over his shoulder like he Santa Claus was coming to drop off some presents. My crew and I had our eyes locked on his bag. I mean, this guy had over twenty Snickers bars, five bags of potato chips, dip for the chips, and all type of good ole' stuff. I called the crew over to my bunk and told them that we would be taking all that white boy's food when he went to sleep. They were all amped up and couldn't wait to pull a 211 in jail (211 is the police code for robbery.) The white guy didn't look like he was going to sleep any time soon. He ate that Snickers bar like it was his last fucking meal on earth, and he was smacking uncontrollably. Everyone felt as if he were being a show off because he spent so much money at the store. The crew and I didn't like it at all. Finally around 2:00 a.m. he went to sleep, and I mean this guy was snoring up a storm. He had a bunky but we told the bunky to play sleep, and if he said anything we would kill him. We pulled the guy's drawer open quietly, then Psycho grabbed all of the goodies and put them in a bag and we went to Psycho's bunk in the corner of the pod and issued out all of the white guy's food to the crew. I had around ten Snickers, two bags of chips, toothpaste, and some other miscellaneous stuff, and this stuff was on top of the stuff that I had bought at the store before, so I was jail house balling. I was eating one of the guy's Snickers when all of a sudden I heard a loud scream.

It was the white guy and he was yelling that whoever took his food was a cock sucking bitch, and that he would whoop whoever's ass it was that took it. The crew and I started busting out laughing. I politely asked him what happened and he said to me, "You know what happened! Somebody stole my entire canteen."

"Hey, look here white boy, you better roll yourself out this pod before something happens to you," I said as I took another bite out of one of his Snickers.

The white boy roared up like he was ready for some action and that's exactly what he got. I finished eating my Snickers and then walked over to the white boy.

"Is there a problem?" I asked, and as soon as that boy went to say something I cocked my fist back and hit him so hard in the face that he fell stone cold to the ground. The crew and I went back to our bunks laughing about what had happened and as we were laughing about the incident an alarm went off and a ton of guards ran into the pod and got the guy and asked him what had happened to him. He said he didn't know and they escorted him out of the pod.

The other guards started searching the pod for whatever they could find that was illegal for us to have. The police asked the pod what had happened, and everybody said the white guy had a seizure, and the police believed us and walked out.

After the pod robbery my status was elevated to the point that I was like the god of the pod. If there was a problem between people, they had to come to me to get approval from me if they wanted to fight. Things were going smooth for me while I was in jail. I went to my line up and I was tricked to do the line up without my attorney present. What that means is that the police could have easily told the victim that I was the one locked up for the crime, and in my mind that's what happened. The reason I say this is because the victim had never seen my face, because I had a hoodie over my head, so how was he able to pick me out of a line-up?

Once I had been identified as the robber, I had to go back to court for a pre-preliminary hearing. On this court day the judge read off the results of the line up and said that I was indeed picked out in the line-up and I would have to prove my innocence or be punished. The judge told me that he was setting my preliminary hearing two months from that day. I walked out of the court room very angry. I was like, two fucking months, fuck!

I got back to the pod and everyone could tell that court didn't go well for me. Psycho asked me what happened and I told him I went to my prelim in two months. "Damn! Two months!" he said.

"Yeah, that's a long ass time for someone that has never been locked up before," I said.

Once I went back to court, it would be almost three months that I'd been in jail. Well, I decided I would just cause havoc until then. That was my mind frame.

My time in Fresno County Jail was action packed, and I mean it. There was something going on every single day. If there wasn't a fight, there was about to be a fight. There was this one day when Psycho had gotten into an argument with a white boy that was placed on the top tier with us. Psycho was on the phone and the white boy walked up to Psycho and said that he needed to use it, now! I guess if no one had warned the white boy about how we got down on the upper tier, he would have to learn the hard way.

Psycho kept arguing with the white boy and I calmly walked over to where they were and cold cocked the boy in the face. He was out before he hit the ground. Psycho wanted to get a piece of the white boy too, so he started kicking him relentlessly. I told Psycho that that was enough, that the police were coming but Psycho kept on kicking the guy until the guard came in the pod and rushed Psycho to the ground. Everyone from the top and bottom tier was quiet. You could hear a pin drop, that's how quiet it was. The guard took the white guy and Psycho out of the pod, and told everyone to get on their bunks. An hour had passed that we were confined to our bunks and then I heard my name blast across the intercom, "Kirkendall, come down to the pod door. The Sergeant wants to talk to you."

I was thinking, fuck, I hope no one ratted me out! Once I got in the sergeant's office he looked at me and said, "We don't have any evidence that you did anything in this incident, but we have been watching you and you seem to be the pod's shot caller and everyone respects you. So what we are going to do is place you in another building where I know you belong."

"Where do I belong?" I asked him.

"In maximum security," he replied simply.

A guard escorted me back to the pod and I told everyone that I was being moved to maximum security. My crew was sad but everyone else had a look of satisfaction on their faces because they knew that their major threat was getting moved away from them.

"Maximum Security"

Maximum security was totally different from minimum security. There weren't any bunks out the way there had been in minimum security. There were two man cells and there were 15 cells in each pod. Therefore, there were about 30 people in the pod. Maximum security was where the killers, robbers, rapists, and hard core criminals resided. When I walked in the pod the dorm area was empty and everyone was locked in their cells. The tower buzzed the door of the cell I was placed in and there was an older black cat that looked to be in his late 40's early 50's. He said to me, "How are you doing young brother.

"Cool," I replied. I didn't know this old dude so I would see what he was about before I got friendly with him. My celly (the person that lives with you in a cell) said his name was Pete and we shook hands. Pete and I talked the night away getting to know one another. Pete seemed like an alright dude but you could never let your guard down in jail. Pete was an old school pimp that was in jail for pimping and pandering. When he told me why he was in jail, I asked him what kind of charge he got.

"Youngster, these crackers trying to give me 20 years because an old ass prostitute said that I was her pimp and she told the police she wanted to press charges against me, and here I been for a whole damn year because of what a lying, stanking bitch done lied on me about," he said.

"Damn! You been in here that long?" I said.

He explained to me that yes, he had, but that there were people in the pod that had been in there a lot longer than him. In my mind a fucking year was a long ass time and I definitely didn't want to stay in jail that long.

Chow came and it was at 3:30 a.m. again but the process of feeding the pod was a lot faster than it was in minimum security because there was only one tier to feed. After I got my tray, I went and sat down at the table with Pete and two more guys. I said, "What's up" to everybody at the table and they all spoke back. The maximum security pod was 90 percent black, and this was an eye opener for me. Everybody in the pod seemed as though they were a family, and there wasn't any form of segregation like there was in the minimum security portion of the jail. Everyone was cordial with everyone and everybody came to my table and introduced themselves. I felt like this was the type of environment I belonged in. After everyone greeted everyone, we started heading back to our cells to go back to sleep until it was time to go to pod.

I was startled when the guard started talking on the intercom because the intercoms were right in our cell by the door, so that shit was entirely too loud. The guard said that it was time for pod and yard so everyone's door would be opening in ten minutes if they wanted to go to either one.

Ten minutes came fast and Pete told me to close the door behind me because he wasn't coming out. I grabbed my shower things so I could take a shower after I worked out. A guard was standing at the pod's door and said everybody that wants to go to yard lets go. I followed all the inmates to the yard, which was actually the roof top of the jail. There was a basketball court, and a weight machine like the one in minimum security. I went over to the weight machine and started bench pressing the entire stack of weights. All of the inmates were impressed and told me I was strong as hell, something I already knew. After I did a few sets on the machine, I took off my shirt and everyone looked at me in amazement and kept saying the same thing to me I had heard a million times before – "Damn you big!"

One inmate asked me if I just came from youth authority or something, and I replied that I'd just came from the streets almost three months ago. After two long hours outside everyone was ready to go in, so the guard came to escort us back to the pod. It was cool getting some fresh air considering it had been three months since I'd smelled it.

Once back in the pod, everyone that didn't go to yard was watching television, playing chess, or playing dominoes. I didn't watch television because it was the number one thing in jail that got people hurt, and I never trusted people walking behind me when I was sitting down. The people that always watched television would be so into what they were watching that they would forget where they were and get caught slipping all the time. Personally, the thing I loved to do most was play chess. Ever since I learned in Mr. Tolbert's class, I loved to play chess because in my eyes it was a game for smart people. I was good at chess but it was all the old guys in the pod that were the chess masters. I studied the older guys and how they played the game, and I probably watched the O.G.'s (old gangster/ original gangster) play one another for an entire week before I decided I was ready to compete with them. My celly, Pete, was the best chess player in the pod. He didn't play for free though, he only played for canteen. He was no joke when it came down to chess and I watched him beat everybody in the pod, and I vowed to myself then that I would eventually beat Pete.

Pete and I started playing chess in our cell and Pete always played to win, which I was glad of because it made me an amazing chess player. We played like 50 games and I didn't even come close to beating Pete once, but I knew that one day that would change.

My court date had finally come and I was anxious to see what had been going on with the case. After breakfast I was escorted with a group of other inmates down the corridor to the court house where we had to sit from 5:00 a.m. until 9:00 a.m. My ass was numb from sitting on the concrete slabs for so long. 9:00 a.m. finally came around and my public defender called me out of the bull-pen (that's the room where inmates were held) to talk to me. I had never had the opportunity to talk to my public defender until that day. She asked for a brief background of myself and I told her that I was 19 years old and from Oakland California. I also told her I was going to Fresno state at the time that I was arrested and that I played football. The public defender said that she was going to let the district attorney know my age and that I was going to college to try to get the most leniencies as possible. Then she told me that the judge would more than likely give me another court day in a few weeks to see if the case could get resolved.

I was cool with everything the public defender and I talked about. I was escorted into the court room and the judge immediately started talking about some mumbo jumbo that I didn't understand, but all of the attorneys and public defenders seemed to understand the judge just fine. All I could comprehend was that they would be seeing me next month. The next time I go to court, I'll have been in jail for almost five months.

Maximum security was laid back and everyone had their own unique program and the way they did things. A few of the inmates and I became jail house friends, but I didn't get close to people because usually when you got close to someone they would end up getting out of jail or they would go to prison. I basically made sure that I only stayed cordial with everyone and I didn't talk a lot. All I did at that point was work out, play chess, and read. I only called my mother about twice a month, just to let her know I was alright. There hadn't been any fights in the pod I was in, but some of the other pods were rocking and rolling. My pod was mostly full of O.G.'s looking at doing a lot of time and they minded their own business. From observing the other pods, it was more youngsters that didn't know how to mind their own business so that's why they always got into fights.

My next court date took its time getting here but it eventually arrived and I was full of adrenaline. It was always the same timing on everything in jail. I ate, then got escorted to the court house to sit and wait for four hours. Once nine o'clock hit, people started shuffling around outside the "bullpen" door. We couldn't see outside the door because it was solid steel.

A guard opened the door and called my name and I responded, "I'm right here!"

He told me to come with him, because my public defender wanted to talk to me before I went to court. The guard escorted me to a room where my public defender was and she was smiling hard as she said hello to me.

"I have some great news for you, but before I tell you, I need to let you know that your mother and father are here today and some of your fraternity brothers," she said to me.

I was shocked that moms, pops and some Alpha Phi Alpha cats came. I didn't think my frat brothers would come because I sent them all death threats via mail because I felt that they left me for dead.

I hurriedly asked my public defender what was going on, and Maria (my public defender) told me that there was a deal on the table for me. I asked Maria what it was, she said that the D.A. offered me a two year joint suspension (which is the same as 2 year probation) and that they would let me out today on my own recognizance and I asked her where I needed to sign. It was a great deal. I would be able to go back to school and continue on with my life. After I signed I was told to go back in the bullpen and wait until I was called out to court. I sat in that bullpen for what felt like eternity, anxious to get out of jail. I waited one hour before I was called out to court. When I walked in the courtroom, I saw moms and pops first, then I saw about five Alpha cats with their fraternity jackets on. I was excited. I gave everyone a thumbs up to show my enthusiasm. I could never forget what happened next in that court room. As my attorney read off the deal that was supposedly given to me by the D.A. (district attorney), the black D.A. lady stopped Maria middle sentence and said that she objected to the deal and that she would have to verify it with her boss. So, the judge ordered a one hour recess to get down to the bottom of things. As I waited in that bullpen, I was full of anxiety. I knew in my spirit that I wasn't going to get out that day and many more after it.

After the hour long wait, I was called back to the court room and Maria wasn't smiling anymore. The black D.A. bitch came into the court room with her head held high and a smirk on her face. She looked like a demon walking in and I knew I was in trouble.

The D.A. stood up, "Your honor, there was a mix up in Mr. Kirkendall's plea agreement. The plea that he had signed was voided out, and the present deal is five years in C.Y.A. (California Youth Authority) because he was going to college and since he is only 19 years old, he can finish his schooling in C.Y.A. That's the state of California's deal, your honor," she said.

I was furious. "We going to trial then!" I shouted angrily.

Maria tried to shut me up, but I kept ranting off until the bailiff had to escort me out the courtroom. I knew that fucking first deal was too good to be true, and I also knew at that point that I had to go to trial.

The walk back to the pod was stressful. Everyone in the pod was having high hopes that I would be getting out, but in jail you learn to read facial expressions and when everyone saw me walking in the pod they started shaking their heads. They understood what had happened without me saying a word. I went to the table that Pete and I had claimed as ours and explained to the whole pod what went down. Everybody said that they had never heard of anyone going through what I just had. I knew I would have to start studying my case in depth to find some loop holes. I wasn't too much worried about the time because my next court date was a month away for pre-trial and I would have been here six months and done some good time. I knew that the max time I could get on my case was seven years, so with half time off of seven years a person would do three and a half years and with my time in I figured I would have to do two more years at the max.

My pre-trial took what seemed like forever and I was cellmates with a cat that acted like a 16 year old kid that threw fits when he didn't get his way. I couldn't wait to get away from that clown.

At court, Maria told me that if I didn't take the five years that the court was offering me, then I would be facing seven years if I lost at trial. I told her to tell the D.A. to shove it and that I would see them at trial. She asked me if I was sure and I lost it.

"Yeah I'm sure! Shit, you working with them or something?" I screamed at her.

Public defenders got a bad rap from inmates because they didn't show that they had a desire to defend their clients, and everyone knew that the DA's and the public defenders hung out together and made bets on which inmate would take what deals, things of that nature. After I yelled at Maria, I was called out to the court room and the judge talked to me personally this time.

He said to me, "Mr. Kirkendall, I hear that you are not going to take the five year deal offered to you, is that right?"

I replied to him that, yes, that was right. The judge then went on to say that if in fact I went to trial and lost I would be facing a maximum of seven years in the state penitentiary. He asked me if I was sure I wanted to go to trial, and I said, "Yes your honor, I want to go to trial." And so it was set in stone that I would start my trial in two months.

The two months leading up to my trial I studied my case relentlessly for hours every single day. I knew my case verbatim, word for word. If I wasn't studying my case, I was working out. I didn't play chess during this period because there was just too much on my mind. I had gained about 15 pounds since being in jail. I guess it was all the rest I was getting, not to mention the pushups, curls and pull-ups I was doing. I didn't realize that my bodybuilder physique would end up being one of the reasons for my down fall in my case.

"Guilty until proven innocent"

The day of my trial had come and my mother had put some clothes on my property so that I would look decent going to trial. Going to trial was a little different from going to regular court because when you go to trial you have to go to the property room to change into your personal clothes. When people went to trial, all the other inmates would give a look of encouragement because everybody knew that if someone was going to trial that they were looking at getting a lot of years in prison if they lost. All the inmates that saw me told me good luck and I would say thanks to them. I must say, that was the most nervous I had ever been in my life, but no one knew it because I kept myself poised and with my mean mug on at all times. I learned that you could never show weakness, never.

When I was called into the court, the judge ranted off some more shit I didn't comprehend. Then I saw a group of people walk in and sit down in what was called the jury box. Today was going to be the first day of jury selection.

First day of jury selection was fairly simple. My attorney and I weeded out the people we didn't think would be best suited to understand me and my circumstance. But of course, the district attorney was able to pick who they thought would convict me. I picked six people I thought would be in my best interest and the district attorney picked who they knew was in their best interest, and then we also had to pick an alternate in case a juror got sick or had an emergency to attend to.

My jury selection only took one day, and I felt confident that my attorney and I had picked the best people for my sake. After I picked the jury, I went back to the pod and nobody in the pod said a word to me. They tried reading my expression to see if it was wise to say anything to me, and finally an o.g. () asked how everything went at trial that day and I told him that I picked my jury so it was on and cracking from this point. It was funny because I wasn't scared at all of getting convicted. I knew that I could only get a seven year maximum term and I had already been in Fresno County Jail for about a year, so that time would get deducted from my sentence and I would only have to do half of the seven years. Therefore, I projected I would only have to do two more years at the most if I were convicted.

I didn't talk much to anyone at this point. I was engulfed in studying my case to find loopholes and mistakes that the police and victim had made in their statements.

The next morning I was woke up at three am, which was the wake-up time for people going to trial. I was already prepared because I didn't get much sleep anyhow. The nervousness of going to trial was enough to drive a weakling to the crazy house. I got dressed in my clothes that my mother had sent to me. The only problem with the clothes was that they were tighter than they were before. I had been incarcerated so everyone was able to see the bodybuilder frame that I carried, which would hurt me in my case. After I got dressed, I was taken to a cell where I would have to wait for about four hours to go to court. Fortunately, I was put in a cell by myself because the correctional officers knew that people going to trial didn't have patience with people that weren't. I studied the entire four hours in that cell. I was confident that I would be found not guilty. Finally, when I was called to go to court, I said a quick prayer and made my way to the courtroom. I'll never forget that courtroom in my life. Once inside, I was seated next to my attorney and handcuffed. Usually people that go to trial get their handcuffs taken off but mine were left on because of my muscular build and the intimidation factor that I had. After I was seated and given instructions by the judge and my attorney on what I could and couldn't do, the jury was brought in to get the day started. I gave all the jurors a slight smile as they were seated. I didn't smile at all so I did the best I could with it under the circumstances.

After everyone was giving their instructions on how the court proceedings would be handled, which took half of the day, the judge told everyone that we would be coming back the next day to start with witness testimony.

The next day came fast and this was when my nerves really took a turn for the worst. Like I said, I wasn't afraid to do the time but it was just the anxiety of not knowing what was going to happen in that courtroom that had me shook up. On the outside looking in, people only saw a tough, young, buff criminal that showed no fear. I may not have been afraid of much, but I did have a fear of the unknown.

Once inside the courtroom I spoke with my attorney for a while and then all the jurors were brought in. I gave them the best smile I had to offer, and once they were seated the judge read off the court proceedings for that day. First person on the stand was the crooked police that tried to interrogate me when I was booked in the jail. The black Uncle Tom got on the stand lying profusely about the entire situation, and he even added that when the Fresno police raided my apartment they found a girls purse in my closet that I had stolen. I held my composure through it all though because I didn't want the jury to see me make any outburst that could possibly harm my case. I just sat there emotionless about all the lies. After the bitch police got off the stand, another cop got on the stand and said that he was the officer that conducted the line up and that the victim picked me out with no problems.

That's when I had my attorney object to the statement, but the judge asked why we were objecting and my attorney stated that the officer conducted an illegal line up. The judge asked what my attorney meant by an illegal line up. My attorney then told the judge that I didn't have any representation at the line up to verify that the lineup was held in the right fashion. The judge quickly denied the objection. As soon as the judge denied that objection, I knew that I was doomed because that issue was one of the main ones that I thought would set me free. After the second police got on stand, the judge called to the stand someone I had never seen in my life. She was of the Indian descent and one of the most beautiful women I had seen in my young life. I asked my attorney who she was and my attorney explained to me that it was the lady whose purse was in my apartment. The district attorney started asking the lady questions about whether she knew who I was, and she quickly said that she had never seen me before. The district attorney started probing at the lady like, "Are you sure ,miss, that you have never seen this gentleman before?" Once again, she claimed that she had never seen me. The district attorney then said that he was turning the questioning over to my attorney, but she already knew that there wasn't any reason to cross examine this lady because there wasn't any evidence on me that I stole her purse. My attorney declined cross examination. I looked at her like, what the fuck are you doing? She reassured me that she knew what she was doing though. The Indian lady looked at me and gave a huge smile and waved at me like she was flirting. After the Indian girl got off the stand, the judge said that we would continue the next day. My attorney and I talked about our strategy for the remainder of the trial and she reassured me that should would do her best to get me free.

As I walked into the courtroom for my fourth day of trial, I saw my fraternity brother, Damon, and my teammate Leroy. I asked my attorney what they were doing there and she said that the district attorney got a court order for them to be there. I asked her if they were testifying against me, because why else would they have been called by the district attorney if they weren't? My attorney shrugged her shoulders as if she didn't have a clue. Once the court room was situated, the district attorney called up Leroy, my teammate on the football team, as well as my neighbor at where I lived. The district attorney didn't hold back with the questioning. The district attorney started off with, "How do you know the defendant?" Leroy told the court that we were on the same football team and we were neighbors. The district attorney then asked Leroy about the night the robbery happened, where he was and what took place. Leroy told them that he was at home when he heard a knock at the door and when he answered the door I asked him for a hanger because I had locked my keys inside the car. Leroy said that he gave me a hanger and helped me retrieve the keys out of the car, and he went inside his apartment. The district attorney then asked Leroy if he knew anything about the robbery and Leroy told them that he didn't. The district attorney said that he rested his case with Leroy and once again my attorney declined to cross examine. As Leroy walked off the stand he gave me a thumbs up, and I gave him a nod. I got into a spat with my attorney afterwards because she didn't cross examine Leroy with the questions that I had written down for her to ask him. I was fuming and I didn't care who saw it this time.

After Leroy got off the stand, the district attorney called my fraternity brother and roommate Damon. He gave me a nod as he took a seat on the stand. After Damon vowed he wouldn't lie, the district attorney started an extensive bout of questioning. He asked things like: how did he know me? Did Damon think I was a good person? Did he know about the robbery? Did he know about the purse in the closet? Did he think I was capable of doing the robbery? Fortunately, Damon said everything in my favor, and he didn't say one thing that could have harmed my case. Once again, my attorney didn't see the need in cross examining Damon. I was alright with it this time because I didn't see the need in questioning Damon any further either. I gave a thumbs up to Damon as he left the stand and he gave me thumbs up as well. After Damon left the stand, the judge let everyone go to a recess for an hour. As everyone was leaving the courtroom, my attorney told me that the last and final witness was going to be the robbery victim and I immediately started sweating with nervousness. I was then escorted to a cell to wait until the hour recess was over. That was one of the fastest hours in my life. I guess because I didn't want to face the victim and hear all the terrible things that I knew would be said. As the bailiff escorted me back to the court room, I felt my legs feeling shaky as I was seated next to my attorney. She was not a top of the line attorney in my eyes because she let the district attorney do what he wanted to do. She had her tail tucked the majority of the trial. Once everyone was seated in the court room, the district attorney said he was calling his final witness to the stand, Yeager, a name that I will never forget. Yeager was a skinny white guy in his mid to late fourties. He was very pale and wore glasses. As he took his seat on the stand, he gave me an evil glare that I actually laughed at.

It appeared that he felt empowered that I was in jail and he would make sure of it with his testimony. The district attorney approached where Yeager was and in a soft voice asked him if he saw the person that robbed him at gun point in the court room, and Yeager said, "Yes I do." The district attorney then told him to point to the person that robbed him and Yeager pointed at me with a stiff finger, and if I could I would have tried to dodge that finger that ultimately sent me to the big house. After Yeager pointed at me, the district attorney went into a frantic dialogue with the jury. He started off by telling me to stand, but

I refused. The judge then told me that I would have to stand via request of the district attorney. I asked my attorney if I had to and she said I did. I already knew the reasoning that the district attorney wanted me to stand and it wasn't a good reason.

As I stood, I started hearing the jurors whispering to one another, "Look at his muscle!"

As I was standing, the district attorney started with, "Jury, look at this guy and his huge muscles, could you imagine this huge guy holding a gun to your head at midnight when you are all alone trying to get some money out of an ATM? It would be devastating wouldn't it? Well that's what Mr. Yeager had to experience."

As the district attorney made me look like a monster, I stood emotionless and said nothing and didn't flinch. The judge then told me that I could be seated. The district attorney then asked Yeager questions like, how did you feel when you were being held at gunpoint? Did you think you were going to die? Do you have nightmares of that incident? How has this affected your life? Every answer the victim gave was digging me a deeper ditch. All I could do was put down questions that I wanted my attorney to ask. After the district attorney was done barbecuing me, I handed the questions I wanted my attorney to ask Yeager. My attorney then attempted to cross examine Yeager but she was not asking the things I wanted her to. It seemed as though she was on the prosecutions side, and I was furious. I yelled at her to ask the questions that I had given her to ask, but she ignored me and did what she wanted to do. At that point I knew it was over for me because nothing was going my way. After my so called attorney finished, I moved my chair over so I wouldn't have to be so close to her. I was so mad that I probably would have done something crazy to that attorney if I had had the chance for her sending me down the river the way she was. After Yeager was told he could leave, the judge told the court that we would continue with deliberation on Monday. I walked out of the courtroom with a look of pure evil on my face, because I knew that my attorney was going to be the cause of my demise.

All weekend in the pod, all I did was push-ups and thought about my case. Everyone gave me my space because they all knew that I was a walking time bomb waiting to explode. I actually stayed in my cell most of those two days waiting the day of deliberation. I didn't even talk to my cellmate much and he understood.

Monday came quick. I guess when you want time to slow down it speeds up, and when you want time to speed up it slows down. The correctional officer came for me at the usual time of three am, and I was already up, dressed and ready to face the day that would change my life forever. Everyone in the pod told me good luck, and I knew I was going to need it because it was going to take God to get me out of this situation.

Once in the holding cell waiting to find out my verdict, I prayed to God that he would save me from the wrath of the penal system and I told him that I was sorry for making the decisions I did in my 19 years of living. When I was praying, I thought about Archie and Uncle Butch. They were all young when they lost their lives and now I would lose mine in another fashion if I were convicted of this violent crime. That was the first time I had thought of the men in my family being cursed. It was plain to see that something was definitely not right with us. I prayed to God and I didn't stop until hours later when the bailiff came and unlocked the door to my cell. He said that a verdict has been reached. All I could think was, "Damn, that was super fast!" It was so fast that I couldn't decipher if I was going to be found guilty or not. As I walked to the court room, my heart felt as if it were about to explode. It was beating faster than I had ever experienced it. I started sweating profusely and when I went inside the courtroom I read everyone's facial expressions and it wasn't good. What gave away my verdict was the bailiff snapping the safety button off his gun. That simple act right there was my indication that I was going away for a while. As the judge reached the podium, he told everyone to stand. As I stood, I watched the faces of the jurors and none of them looked at me, which was enough to let me know that the verdict wasn't good.

Once all the jurors were inside, the head juror said, "We the people of Fresno County find the defendant guilty of first degree armed robbery, and not guilty of receiving stolen property."

I held my head up because I didn't want anyone to know that the verdict had affected me in any type of fashion. The judge then said that he was setting the sentencing for a month away, but at that time I didn't care about anything other than the fact that I was going to prison. I walked out of the courtroom feeling numb, as if I were in a bad dream, only it was reality. When I got to the pod I yelled out to everyone that I was found guilty and they all held their heads down as if they were defeated as well. I called my mother to let her know the news so that she could come to my sentencing and hopefully say something positive about her convicted, armed robber son. My mother was sad but I told her that I had made my bed so I had to lie in it. I reassured her that I would be alright.

For the month awaiting my sentencing I engulfed myself into working out and reading. I didn't have much patience for chess at this point. The month kind of dragged along slowly, but I had gained another five pounds of muscle within that time period.

The day of my cursed future had arrived and I was emotionless. It felt as though I wasn't even alive. It seemed as if I were going to wake up at any moment but I never did. I didn't even get dressed in my clothes because there wasn't any point in getting dressed up to get seven years.

Once in court, I saw my mother and step-father, who both smiled at me and I gave them a nod. They could tell that I wasn't happy because my face said it all for them,. When the judge arrived to the courtroom he immediately called my mother to the stand. It was hard seeing my mother while I was in jail.

Even though we didn't have the best mother-son relationship, I still hated seeing her sad. My mother said what she could in my defense, but it didn't matter at this time because the bad definitely outweighed the good. After my mother was done speaking, the victim said why he felt I should be put away for a very long time. Yeager grabbed the attention of the judge, and I could see that the judge was in his corner all the way.

After everyone said what they had to say, the judge said, "The Court of Fresno County hereby sentences the defendant to seven years in the state of California correctional department. The defendant has credit for 12 months off good time that will be deducted from the seven years."

My mother started crying and I even saw a tear drop from my step-father's face, which I had never seen before in my life. I stood strong like a Mandingo slave taking his whipping. After the judge was finished ranting off, I waved to my mother and step-father and gestured that I would call them.

When I reached the pod, I had to tell everyone that I was given seven years and they tried to make me feel better by saying that I only had to do two more years and that when I got to prison the time was going to fly by. I started thinking how I wasn't missing anything on the streets anyway, which made me feel a little better.

While waiting to get transferred to state prison, I immersed myself into working-out and studying Islam. I started going to Jummah (Islamic day of worship) every Friday and I read the Quran instead of the Bible because I felt that the Bible had let me down. I fell in love with Islam and the discipline that it instilled in its followers. I felt at peace once I started practicing Islam and I took my Shahada (oath to practice Islam) in Fresno County Jail. About a week after I took my Shahada, my name was called over the cell intercom at 2:30 a.m. telling me that I was getting transferred to the California Department of Corrections. I hopped out of my bunk happy as if I were going home. I packed all of my things quickly and told my celly so long. I was escorted by the deputy to a holding cell where there were around 30 other inmates getting transferred as well. I didn't socialize much with the other inmates, because I was thinking a lot about what was to come. About an hour after sitting in the cell with the other inmates, some police came in with some uniforms I had never seen before. The uniforms were pitch black and these police or whatever they were had an entirely different aura about themselves from the deputies I was used to seeing. These police were in shape and it looked like they worked out, even the women. They demanded respect and everyone gave it to them. The older guys in the cell were telling me not to mess with them or they would kill me without thinking. I definitely wasn't going to be a casualty in jail and I vowed to myself that I was going to make it back to the streets.

The police in black came into the cell and started putting shackles on everyone's ankles, and a chain around our waist with the handcuffs connected. Then we were locked in at the feet and hands, with the hands locked onto the chain around our waist. They made sure that the inmates couldn't harm them or anyone else in any form or fashion.

"Off to the Big House"

Once everyone was handcuffed and chained up, we were escorted to the prison bus. Once everyone was inside , the no nonsense police gave out harsh instructions and told us that if we didn't comply with them that it would resort in injury. Everyone was tight lipped because these police in black were not messing around. They were serious and everyone felt it. The bus ride took about two and a half hours to reach our destination of Wasco State Prison. Wasco was a regular prison but it was also a prison that held people until they were shipped off to other prisons, so it was called a reception center.

It was a gloomy day and it felt as if I were entering a place of pure evil. Once the bus stopped on the prison yard, it seemed as if a million guards had come to see who the new inmates were, and to let us know that they were here in full effect. Each inmate was called by their last name to exit off the bus and then they were put into a single file line. When my name was called, I exited the bus and the guard immediately took notice of me.

"Damn you're buff! Where you came from, youth authority?" He said to me. I told him no, that I was in college before I came to jail.

"Are you that football player from Fresno State that I saw on the news?" The guard asked.

"Yep, that's me," I said reluctantly.

"Damn, you done fucked up your life," the guard said, shaking his head.

I reciprocated, "I ain't fucked up my life, I'm still young and I will be young when I get out."

The guard had nothing else to say after that and I was escorted to the cell that I would be in for the next 90 days.

When the cell door opened, there was a middle aged, heavy set, black cat that sat up when I entered and said his name was "D". I told him my name was Khalid, which was my new Muslim name that I had acquired.

We hit things off fast. He was a cool O.G. and he played chess, which was the best time killer for me. My first week was kind of hectic at Wasco because I didn't have the amount of food that I was used to consuming on a daily basis. I had to eat half of whatever I got from the prison at a time. So at breakfast I would eat half of whatever it was I had at the time and I would eat the other half in the late afternoon. I tried to sleep as long as possible to kill the time in between. Then I would do my daily workout of pushups, curls, calve raises, and triceps extensions. My routine had me swollen like a bodybuilder. People couldn't understand how I was able to get so big and at times neither did I. After I would do my daily workout, I would eat the dinner the prison served. Just like with my breakfast, I would save half of it for later that night my celly and I stayed up till about 1:00 or 2:00 in the morning playing chess. My first week at Wasco went by very fast because I was learning the ropes of the prison as well as the do's and don'ts of it. During the first week, there was a lot of movement for me. I had to take a physical, I had to talk to some doctors, and I was able to go to the store to buy some food and hygiene stuff.

After my first week at Wasco, time started to slow down because I was moving less and I was in the cell practically all day every day, except for two days a week when everyone was allowed to go to the yard and work out or do whatever they felt like doing. For me, I was always at the pull-up bars when we were allowed to go to the yard.

I'll never forget my first day on that yard. It was both exciting and nerve racking at the same time. I saw some people I knew that I never thought I would see in prison. Everyone wanted to be my friend because I was the buffest young cat in the prison system. It was as if I were a personal trainer in prison. I was always answering questions about fitness and how to get buff. I enjoyed all the attention I was getting in a positive light. The first day on the yard was very eventful. It started off with me taking over the pull-up bars and everyone watching me and telling me how swollen I was. After me doing about 20 sets of pull-ups, I heard a loud ass alarm go off and the guards started yelling for everyone to get flat on their stomachs. I had gotten down on one knee but everyone else was flat on their stomachs and the other inmates started telling me that I needed to get all the way down before the guards started shooting their guns. I hated being on the ground and I've never been fond of getting dirty, but I got down anyway. As I was on that dirty ass ground, I was thinking, "What have I gotten myself into?" That's when the guards started running around like they were possessed mad men. There were guards up in the towers pointing their assault rifles at us in case they had to kill somebody. This shit was serious, and one false move and I could die in prison. I immediately became like a warrior that was in battle. My mind was made up that I wouldn't let myself die in prison. After the alarm was cut off, the guards told everyone to resume normal activity, and everyone continued to do what they were doing as if nothing had ever happened. I became accustomed to prison life very fast as if I had been there all my life.

The next morning, after my first experience with a prison alarm, I was awakened by a guard at six o'clock in the morning talking about how I had to go and take my physical. I told the guard that I had already taken my physical, but he told me that I had to go again because I was on the list. I kept telling the guard that I had already taken it, but he kept saying I had to go and that they would see when I got there if I had already done it or not. I reluctantly got dressed and went to the damn physical. At this point in my life, my body was accustomed to eating at a certain time every day and if I didn't eat at that certain time my body would start to shut down. Once all the inmates and I were escorted to the prison hospital (infirmary), the guards were told by the prison nurse that I had already taken my physical so I was placed in a cell with other inmates that were waiting to get sent back to their cells. After an hour of sitting in that cell, I got irritated and started knocking on the door for a guard to take us back to our cells so we could eat. It was two hours past my feeding time and I got super grouchy, mean and somewhat delirious when I was hungry. As I was banging on the cell door, a guard asked what was wrong and I told him that we hadn't eaten yet and that we were waiting to get escorted back to our cells.

The guard said that he would take all of us back in just a short while. I waited patiently for another whole hour and at that point I was ready to get out of that cell at all cost. I started kicking the door as hard as I could to get someone's attention. I had been kicking that door for about two whole minutes when a tall, white, middle aged guard rushed to the cell door and unlocked it frantically, telling me to step out of the cell with my hands behind my back.

Once out of the cell with my hands behind my back, the guard grabbed my hands as my fingers were interlocked behind me and he said angrily, "I am tired of your shit boy! You been causing me hell all morning and I'm tired of your shit."

As he was talking to me he was walking me towards an area full of empty cells that looked deserted. The guard led me towards one empty cell in particular, and he opened it and told me to step inside. As soon as I got my left foot inside, the guard again grabbed my interlocked hands and rammed me into the cell wall.

"Look here boy, when a guard tell you to wait you wait, you been giving me hell and I am going to give you hell!" he spat angrily at me.

"This is unnecessary and you would want to let me go," I said calmly.

"What boy? I better let you go or what?" he said.

That's when I snapped. I spun from the guard's grasp and caught him with a solid hook to the jaw. He was out cold, snoring on the ground. At that point I was scared as hell because I knew what guards did to inmates that harmed another guard. I prepared for battle by rolling down my one piece jumpsuit to my waist and tying the arms together like a belt so that the one piece would stay in place while I was in combat. I started throwing punches to warm up for the rest of the guards that I knew were going to ambush me for knocking out one of their own. After about five minutes, a guard walked by the cell and saw his co-worker on the ground asleep. He immediately pressed his alarm button and asked me what I'd done to his co-worker. I bounced up and down in silence waiting for the clan of men to try and attempt to lynch me.

As the guard pulled his co-worker out of the cell, it seemed as though a million guards had come. I thought they were coming to harm me, but the guards looked at me in awe of my muscular physique and they closed the cell door and looked some more. I was very intriguing to the guards because they didn't understand how I had so much muscle on my young body. After three hours of preparing myself for war in that cell, a guard came over and I instantly started roaring up like a lion. The guard said that he was coming in peace. I looked in the guard's eyes and I knew he was telling the truth. I realized that he was very intimidated and that I didn't have anything to worry about.

I asked him, "What's up?"

"The captain wants to talk to you," he told me. He then explained that he had to handcuff me, but I was reluctant and the guard reassured me that he wasn't there to trick me. He even said that the guard I punched got what he deserved and that no one was mad at me.

I was still on my toes though, because I could never trust a guard. I was then escorted to the captain's office and to my surprise the captain was a young, pretty black lady. I was shocked, because Wasco State Prison was known to be a prison of the Klu Klux Klan, and to see a young black lady was a miracle.

Once inside the captain's office, she told the other guards to leave us alone. My antennas immediately went up because I knew that that wasn't typical prison protocol for a violent inmate to be left alone with a correctional officer, especially a young, pretty one.

The captain surprised me by starting off with, "Dang boy, you are buff! Let me see your arms!"

I reluctantly pulled up my sleeve to show her my arm.

"Damn! Where did you come from, Y.A. or something?" she asked me.

"No," I told her, "I came from college playing football."

"Why did you knock that white boy out?" the captain asked, referring to the guard I had knocked out.

I shrugged my shoulders as if I were a child getting scolded by his mother.

"You lucked out today with me being here because if I weren't here, a white captain would have had nasty things done to you, and on top of that you would have been put in the hole and charges would have been filed on you as well!" she went on.

She waited briefly before continuing, "That asshole that you knocked out deserved it because he is a known racist that has been treating all black inmates bad, so you did what you had to do and you won't be punished for it by me. You are free to go!"

I gave her a smile and told her thank you, and I was escorted back to my cell. Hours had gone by and I hadn't eaten, but I guess I was fed with my adrenaline because I wasn't hungry at all until hours later. I told my celly what had happened and he couldn't believe that they didn't beat me up and send me to the hole. He said God was definitely watching over me and I agreed.

The next day was a day of bad news for me when I went to classification. The top dogs of the prison would all be at the inmates classification to let each inmate know how much time they had to do, what level prison they would go to, and what prison they would go to. Well, as classification was reading off my charges, they said that my release date was October 2000. I immediately said that date couldn't be right because I was told that I was getting half time. The top dog at the meeting looked at the court documents and said that I wasn't given half time because it wasn't documented by the courts.

Therefore, with the seriousness of my charges, and under the new law that was implemented in October 1994 (The same month and year I was caught), my case fell under the law demanding I do 85% of my time. I was in disbelief. All I could think about was how everyone had been saying that the world was going to end in the year 2000. I was like, "Damn. I'm going to die in jail after all!"

My classification hearing didn't go in my favor at all. I was told that I would be getting transferred to a level three prison, which is one level below the highest level an inmate can go. The highest level an inmate can go in prison is level four. I was somewhat nervous about going to a level three prison, because an inmate's ideal level was either a level one or two. Anything above a level two and you were looking at being in a violent prison. I sucked it up and dealt the cards I was given though. I did write to the courts and to my attorney about getting the issue resolved of me doing 85% of my time as opposed to 50% of my time.

My 90 days at Wasco State Prison went by fast and the next thing I knew I was getting transferred to Delano State Prison. I went through the same process I did when I left Fresno County Jail. Handcuffed, shackled, and locked in at the waist. The no holds, barred transportation guards were the same type of guards that I experienced the first time I was transferred. They didn't mess around and they guaranteed they would shoot to kill. The bus ride to Delano State Prison was fairly short, since it only took about an hour and a half to get there. Once there, the inmates were greeted by one of the prison's guards to tell us the policies of the prison and that if anyone failed to comply, disciplinary actions would take forth. Each inmate was then given a jumpsuit and karate shoes to put on.

I immediately told the officer that I was supposed to go to the level three yard of the prison. The guard told me that I was on the list of people going to the reception center and all I could think in that moment was, "Here we go again with the mix ups." I repetitively told the guards that I had just been sent from Wasco Reception Center to Delano mainline, and all of the guards told me the same thing. I would have to go to classification (inmate informed of status) to get the situation panned out.

Ten days had gone by waiting to go to classification, and it was a hard ten days because I didn't have any extra food, therefore I had to save my food like I did when I went to Wasco State Prison. I was literally starving because my body had become so accustomed to eating a vast amount of food each day, and now I was only eating half of that. As soon as I walked into the classification room, the head honcho asked his staff what I was doing there and told them that I was supposed to be on the mainline. They apologized to me for the mix-up and told me that I would be on the mainline in a couple of hours. I was then escorted to my cell so that I could pack my things in order to get sent to the mainline of Delano State Prison. I was excited to see what the mainline was like and to get a package from home. Getting a package in prison is the most exciting time for prisoners.

Once I was escorted onto the mainline, everyone on the prison yard came to see who was coming to the yard. I didn't know anyone at the prison, because practically everyone at the prison was from the Los

Angeles area. Later on I found out that there were a few guys from the bay area there though. Once on the main yard, I was escorted to a cell that I had to stay confined to for ten days. Prison and ten days went hand-in-hand! The ten day isolation was for the prison to figure out what they would do with the inmate. Either they would send the inmate to school or to work. During my ten day wait to find out what job I would get, everyone that was into working out came to my cell to introduce themselves to me because they had heard that a super buff youngster was on the yard. Later on I found out that everyone knew me because they saw my case on the news and I was a celebrity to them.

I'll never forget the day I was let free from my ten day isolation. As soon as I was told I was released to the main yard, I went to the cell I was given and put my possessions up and made my bed. I then went straight to the weight pile. I went crazy on the weights like a kid at a candy store. I mean, I didn't know when to stop and everybody on the weight pile was asking to work out with me. Because I didn't know any of the other inmates very well, I told them that I worked legs and the reason I told them that was because in jail no one liked to do legs, they just wanted a huge upper body without concern of having huge legs. Everyone at that point was like, "I'm cool. I don't do legs!" Eventually I was told by the guards that the weight pile was closed, and I left disappointed. As soon as I walked from the weight pile, my vision got blurry and I knew that I was about to have a treacherous migraine headache. I rushed to the cell I was assigned to and spoke to my celly and told him that I was having a migraine headache so I would be sleeping it off. I think this was the only time I had ever missed going to get my food at the prison chow hall.

The day following my migraine, I was still a little off but I was able to function at 80% of my usual self. I was called into the counselor's office and she told me the projected date of my release if I stayed out of trouble. She told me that my release date was October 2000. When she said it I got somewhat hostile with her and told her she was wrong, that that wasn't my date because I was supposed to be getting half time. She told me that as of now, that was my release date until the courts said otherwise. The counselor then asked me what type of job I wanted in the prison. All the other inmates told me that being a porter was the easiest kick back job in the prison system so I told her that I would like to be a porter in the building my cell was in. She said that she would document the job I requested but that there were no guarantees that I would get any one in particular.

As I was working out on the weight pile doing arm curls, I looked across to the other side of the weight pile and I saw some big mother-fuckers working out. They had a whole crew of dudes and they weren't messing around. After about my fifth set of curls, I took off my shirt to show everybody that the new buff youngster had hit the yard and I was coming to embarrass anyone who thought they were big and strong. As I was doing my sixth set of curls, a huge motherfucker walked towards me and I swear he looked like a silver back gorilla. He was dressed in the famous prison garbs, blue jeans and a blue jean jacket, but he was so massive that you could see his matured, buffed muscles popping out of the biggest jacket the prison had to offer. He walked over as I was setting the curl bar down and said, "What's up bro, my name is Ken. I see you know what you are doing with these weights and I would love to be your workout partner."

At the time I was cautious because this dude was the biggest I had ever seen with my own two eyes, and he wanted to work out with me? The first thing I said was that I do legs, and to my surprise Ken said that he would do whatever I did. I told Ken alright, that we could start the next day and Ken said, "Cool, I'll see you tomorrow."

I was still mind boggled on why the biggest dude on the prison yard wanted to work out with me and do what I told him to do. I hadn't seen what I looked like in over a year so, so I wasn't able to see what everybody else did in my physique. I didn't realize that I was the biggest, most cut dude on the yard, but everyone else knew it and that's why Ken wanted to work out with me.

After getting settled in for a few days, I went to Jummah service on Friday and introduced myself to everyone as Khalid. I was already known on the prison yard as the buff cat from Oakland, so I didn't have to say much. I was welcomed with open arms to the Muslim community. I was given a new Quran and a ton of literature to read. I felt as if I was a part of a brotherhood now, not to mention the Muslim community at Delano was the strongest organization on that prison yard, and we demanded the upmost respect from the inmates and guards.

A week had past when a guard came to my cell and called my name and slid a piece of paper through the door that had my job assignment on it. I had lucked out and got a porter job in the building my cell was in. I was happy as ever because I didn't want to work in the kitchen where all the chaos was. I was able to concentrate on my studies and working out. I was still fighting my case in court through the appeals process so I wanted to be free at all times to either go to the law library or the weight pile, and being a porter it was as if I had no job because I could come and go as I pleased.

Everything was going good for the sake of being in prison. I was getting packages that my mother was sending me, I was going to the prison store monthly, I was learning a ton of knowledge and wisdom through Islam, and Ken and I were killing the weight pile. I had gained about ten pounds in a month and everyone on the prison yard took notice. Everyone was trying to work out with me and Ken but we vowed that it would just be us until the wheels fell off and we stood by our vow to one another. Ken and I worked out seven days a week. We were lunatics on the weight pile. We would work out in the rain, sleet, or snow. A lot of the times we would be the only two people on the weight pile and we loved it. It showed everyone the reason why we were the biggest, baddest dudes on the yard, because we did what everyone else wouldn't do.

The Islamic month of Ramadan (fasting) had come and I was nervous about the fasting thing because I didn't know how my body would react to not eating for hours and hours throughout the day. I knew that the fasting would be a hard thing for me, but I did it anyways because it was ordained for Muslims to fast during the month and I have never been one to rebel against something I was a part of. I had moved in with the top inmate Muslim on the yard, whose name was Amir, and he was the inmate imam (preacher). He was a cool cat and he taught me the ins and outs of Islam. We prayed together as well as studied the religion together. I loved learning and it made the time fly by at a fast pace, not to mention Amir played chess and he was considered a master of the game just like I was.

The month of Ramadan was tough on my body and I was grouchy as hell during the day until the sunset and I was able to eat. Afterwards the Muslim brothers and I would break our fast and I would rush to the weight pile to get mine and ken's weights for our workout session. Ken and I had our schedule down so that we were always on the weight pile first to get our weights. My strength was down a tad bit while I was fasting and I hated it. Fasting was one of the things that I didn't like about Islam, and I knew that it was contradictory to my bodybuilding lifestyle but I persevered through the month. It was tough but I did it. Right after the month of Ramadan, I gained like ten pounds in a month and I had gotten super swole. Everyone on the yard was amazed at the muscle I held on my young body. Ken told me that I was even bigger than he was and I didn't believe him, so Ken said that we should take a picture when the weekend came so that I could see what he said was true.

The weekend came and the inmate camera man was on the yard taking pictures so Ken and I did us a few pushups and pull-ups to get a good pump. Once we were pumped up, we went to the camera man and took our picture. As the picture was developing, Ken was saying, "Watch. What did I tell you youngster? You got me beat. You are way more cut than me!" I just couldn't believe that what Ken was saying was true. When the Polaroid finally developed, I looked at it in amazement. I couldn't believe that I was actually bigger and more cut than he was. I was now officially the biggest, most cut dude on the prison yard. Ken was right.

"I told you!" ken said simply. After Ken and I took that picture on the yard, I started working out more than ever. When I got tired of the weights I would go to the pull up and dip bars. I was addicted to working out, and it was all I cared about.

Things were going good on the yard. Ken and I had been workout partners for a year and I knew that my time was nearing for classification and that meant that my points would drop and I would be eligible to go to a level two prison. I would try to get closer to my hometown, Oakland. Ken and I were kind of sad because we knew that we would be separated. Ken and I continued to work out together but we both talked about me getting transferred all the time.

I was doing pull ups during afternoon yard which I did every day, and afterwards Ken and I would hit the weight pile at night. Anyways I was doing pull ups when one of my patnas walked over to me and said, "You heard what happened to your boy, Ken huh?"

I frantically asked him what happened and he said, "Big Ken (as everyone on the yard called him) damn near killed this guy in the kitchen. Ken told the guy to stop talking shit to him and the guy didn't shut up so Ken hauled off and broke the guys jaw and nose, so they sent him to the hole!"

I was devastated! I knew Ken was a walking time bomb ever since I was informed that I was up for transfer. Ken used to tell me that he didn't want to be on that yard anymore if I wasn't there. By Ken talking like that all the time, he indicated that he wasn't taking any shit from anybody. I was devastated by Ken being sent to the hole, but I knew that I would be leaving soon anyway so that kind of made the sting less painful.

"Tehachapi"

One week after Big Ken was sent to the hole, I was transferred to Tehachapi State Prison. I was disappointed because I was trying to go to San Quentin State Prison to be closer to Oakland. Tehachapi wasn't that far from Delano, in fact, it was only about an hour drive from there. Tehachapi sat between two mountains and it was a creepy looking place because it seemed as though it were strategically placed so that no one knew its where a bouts. Once at the prison, all the inmates were told the same rules that I had heard at the two prisons I had been to before this one.

Tehachapi was different from the other prisons I had been to because Tehachapi had levels four, two, and one. Unbeknown to me, my points had dropped down to a level one, but I wouldn't find that out for a couple of months.

I was escorted to the cell I was assigned to and by this point I understood that I would be placed in a cell for ten days until I went to classification to determine where I was to be placed. Once again I had to eat half of my food at a time because until I went to classification I couldn't get my property or go to the store. I went back to how I knew to survive without starving.

During my ten day wait, I did one thousand pushups, curls, calve raises, and crunches a day to pass the time. When my ten days were up, I was sent to the level two yard where I thought I was going to be residing for a while. This yard seemed a lot like the streets, as there was a lot of activity going on, and I could tell right off that a lot of those activities were illegal. This yard was like a resort. There were basketball courts, tennis courts, a place to play tennis, a huge weight pile, and even a snack bar. There were some big dudes on the yard but when I came onto it I took the award for biggest dude there, hands down. I was a yard favorite fast and everyone took to me like everywhere else I had been. Everyone wanted to work out with me and I denied all of them until I found out what my living situation would be. Until then, I worked out by myself. There were a few cats from Oakland on the yard and we immediately made a pact with one another that we would stick together. The Muslim brothers on this yard were very soft compared to the Muslims at Delano. The Muslims on the Tehachapi two yard seemed as though they were caught up between gang banging and practicing the religion. I didn't get too involved with that group of characters. I just worked out and read a lot. I didn't even play much chess while being on the level two yard.

One evening while I was sleeping, I was awakened by a guard standing at the foot of my bunk and calling my name.

I immediately woke up, somewhat startled, and said,"Whats up?"

The guard then handed me a paper that said that I was to go to classification the next day.

The next day came fast and I was wondering where I would work and in what building I would be housed in. Once in the classification room, the counselors read off my charges and my points – which were well below level two points – and the counselor said that I would be going to the level one yard before the night was over. I was happy as hell because every inmate on the two yard had dreams of getting to the level one yard. I was told that each inmate had their own key to their cell and it was like the streets on the level one yard. I couldn't wait because I was tired of being around all the dope heads on level two. I said my goodbyes to everyone and I didn't feel any remorse about leaving them because I didn't bond with anyone anyhow.

As I was escorted to level one, I felt a sense of relief. I felt as if I were going home as a free man. As the other inmates and I arrived to the level one yard, we were greeted by all of the inmates that were already there.

I saw one person I knew on that yard and his name was "Bird". He immediately came up to me and asked if I needed anything, and I told him I didn't because I had received all of my property and I had gone to the store while on the level two yard. I was then escorted to a huge gymnasium that was like a college dorm and people were running around like chickens with their heads cut off. It was pure pandemonium in this dorm. I made my bed and talked to my bunky about the do's and don'ts of the dorm area. In the dorm every inmate was given a lock to put on their assigned locker where their property would be in. These locks were vicious weapons that I had seen used multiple times during my stay at the level one yard.

The next day on the yard, I went to the weight pile and I was amazed because it was the first yard I'd seen that had 120 lb. dumbbells. There were machines at this prison that were in gyms on the street. I was in heaven! I let it be known that day that a new sheriff was in town. After five sets of bench press, I took off my shirt and the weight pile went quiet. Everyone started coming up to me and introducing themselves. I felt like a superstar already. Everyone, of course, wanted to work out with me, but I told them to give me a few weeks to get situated on the yard first and find out where I would be working.

Things were going good on the level one yard. The yard had a mediocre Muslim program, but there was this brother there by the name of Zayid who had more knowledge and wisdom than any man I had ever seen in my life. He was not only well versed with the religion of Islam, but he was a realist when it came down to life. We immediately grew a brotherly bond. Zayid ran the mosque on the level one yard. He was the inmate imam, so when the imam from the streets wasn't available, everyone went to Zayid for whatever they needed pertaining to Islam.

After ten days on the level one yard, I was placed to work in the dentist's office as a clerk, which was a job I didn't exactly want because it was interfering with my workout schedule. I had to switch my workout time from the mornings to the evenings and I hated working out in the evenings because I didn't have the same amount of energy at night as I did in the morning. At this point I had no other choice but to try and find another job that suited my schedule.

I worked in the dentist's office for two months and I hated every minute of it because not only was I missing my morning workouts, but the dentist was a shrewd person. He would shoot an inmate up with Novocain but then he wouldn't wait for it to kick in before he would extract the tooth. I saw a lot of men crying in that dentist's chair because of the pain they were experiencing and I prayed that I would never have to get a tooth pulled in jail.

While working in the dentist's office, I had put in for the barber's job, being that I knew how to cut hair, and I had heard that being the barber on the level one yard was the best job an inmate could have. I lucked out and got the job and I was the happiest inmate alive. I not only got the barber job, but I was able to move in with one of my favorite Muslim brothers, Jail, who lived right across from the barbershop. Yes, barbershop! I mean, this barbershop was better than some of the shops I've seen on the streets.

It was me, a Mexican, and white barber working at the shop. I was excited to be able to do something I liked to do while making money doing it, and I was even more excited to be able to get back to my workout schedule.

Life in prison was good, which sounds weird. I would call my mother once a month to reassure her that I was doing well, and she would send me a package every four months which is all the packages that can be received in prison. I would go to the store every month, since I was making a lot of money working in the barbershop, so I had a ton of food. Food is money in prison.

I was so big from working out that the prison system said that they were going to make a rule that the inmates could only work out one hour a day. We were getting too big and the guards were getting man handled when they got in confrontations with inmates. We all prayed that the rule wouldn't get passed because the weight pile was an inmate's only escape from reality, and it helped us pass a lot of time.

I was so big that I looked like I was on steroids and the guards thought I was as well because they would always tell me that they had never seen anyone on the streets as big as me. I was big because I was young, hitting the weights hard, eating a ton of food, drinking a gallon of water a day, getting plenty of rest, and of course because of my genetics. My workout crew and I were the yard's strongest and youngest cats. My one workout partner, Dre, was only 165 lbs but he could bench press

500 lbs. and do whatever I did. He was an extraordinary human being and his strength was unbelievable. I won a lot of money betting on him against other people. My other workout partner, Green Eyes, was a pretty boy that was all most as swole as me. We had a hell of a workout team that everyone on the yard wanted to outdo on the weights. We set the bar high because we not only had bodybuilder physiques, but we were strong as shit too. We were only 21 years old yet we had the bodies of someone that had been in prison 30 years and everyone was trying to catch up with us.

We were working out for six months straight when we all took notice that we were no longer progressing with our bodies or strength, so we decided to cut back from our typical seven days of working out to four days. This would be hard because every day the inmates asked one another what we did on the weight pile that day, so we had to drop our extremist mentality to see if getting rest would make us bigger and stronger.

It was hard at first not working out seven days a week because that was what I was accustomed to doing. After the second week of working out for four days a week though, all of our bodies were bigger and stronger; it was amazing. Our strength had increased so much that there weren't enough weights on the weight pile to accommodate our heavy lifting.

The prison system was talking about dropping the weights down to 165 lbs on the bars, and 75 lb on the dumbbells. This would definitely be a problem because we were so used to going up to 500 lbs on our squats and bench presses. If the prison dropped the weight down, it would be devastating for all of us.

Things were going good on the yard and before I knew it it was time for Ramadan again and I wasn't looking forward to it at all. Zayid had taught me how to read and write Arabic, so I was the second in command to the Muslims on the level one yard. Zayid and I were beginning to compete with each other at that point on who would be the smartest at everything. We had daily debates about everything from religion to politics. These disputes of ours taught me how to be an excellent debater. When Ramadan hit, I did better than last time because I ate a lot more in the morning before the sun rose to sustain me until sunset. I was also able to work out in the mornings right after I ate, so I had my full energy to keep my strength intact.

Ramadan went by faster than I expected and I didn't lose too much weight, just around five pounds, but it wasn't noticeable to anyone but myself. My celly, Jalil, went home so I was in my cell by myself and I hated the idea of getting a new celly but I had no choice. I got two days alone in the cell, which was great, and then I got a celly. He was almost seven foot tall and an ugly motherfucker with big ass African lips. He was cool as hell though and he was a sports fanatic. He would bet on any game that came on, be it baseball, basketball, football, soccer, or hockey. He would bet on it all, and he won 90% of the time.

Right after Jalil went home, everybody started else going home too. I was starting to get to the point where I didn't want to make friends in prison because we would be friends one day and then that friendship would be nonexistent the next. The next friend to go home was Zayid, which really devastated me more than anything else that had happened to me in prison. It felt almost the same as when I lost my brother Archie. Zayid and I had a bond like twin brothers. He had taught me so much stuff that I still incorporate into my life to this day. When Zayid went home, I became the inmate imam on the yard. I held Jummah service when the prisons imam wasn't around, which was practically every Jummah because he would be on the level two and four yards the most.

After a year at Tehachapi, I was ready to get transferred closer to Oakland, so I requested a transfer to San Quentin. After two weeks of submitting my request at classification, my wish had come true and I was granted the transfer to San Quentin.

"San Quentin politics"

The day had come for my transfer and I said my farewells to everyone. I hoped that I was off to a better place where I knew people from the neighborhood I grew up in and who went to the same school as me. Practically every man my age that I grew up with was at San Quentin and so it would be like a big family reunion for me.

The ride to San Quentin was a long ass one and we had to stop at Soledad State Prison for a day lay over. The trip to San Quentin actually took two long ass days. I had eaten so much peanut butter that I was constipated for days after the trip. As the prison bus pulled up to San Quentin, the prison looked like something off a horror movie. It was a gloomy day so that probably made it look worse but that prison really did look like pure hell.

As we pulled up on the yard where all the inmates were, everybody on that prison yard stopped what they were doing to see if they had family members, friends or enemies that were on the bus. While I was being escorted off, I had already seen a ton of people that I knew. Once off the bus the inmates had to stand in a single file line and get naked in front of the guards. They told everyone to lift their balls, and then open their mouth and show them their tongue. They then had us pull our ears back so they could see behind them and once we did all that, the ultimate was to bend over at the waist and cough so the guard could see our asshole contract. All of this was done so the guards were sure each inmate wasn't bringing any drugs or contraband inside the prison. Humiliating, isn't it?

After the strip search, all the inmates were placed in a tiny ass holding cell that was too small for all the people that were in it. Each person was called by a nurse to be given a TB shot (tuberculosis) to make sure that we weren't bringing the disease with us. Afterwards each inmate was given the property of theirs that they were allowed keep, and what they couldn't they had to send home.

When the guard was handing my property to me, he started questioning me extensively, asking me things like, "So what gang are you in? 415 (Kumi) or black guerilla family (BGF)?"

I told him that I wasn't in any gang, that I was a Muslim. He said that he thought I was 415 (Kumi), but I didn't know what he was talking about at that time. However, later on I would know exactly what that guard was talking about. I saw people going to the toilet and removing drugs from their assholes and selling it to the inmates that worked in the processing area. The inmates that worked in processing would come with huge bags of food, hygiene, and tobacco and trade it for the drugs. The inmates that came on the bus with me would sell their shoes for tobacco.

After around five hours of being in that chaotic processing area, the guards finally came and escorted all of the new arrivals (inmates that just had arrived to prison) to the building and cell we would be placed in. This prison was spooky and it reeked of death. I knew that this was where a lot of people were killed, and I respected this fact. I vowed to myself that I wouldn't be one of those casualties and that I would make it out of that place alive.

I was escorted to a building that looked a lot like a castle. Once inside, the guard told me what cell I was assigned to and I went to it. There was another inmate that came on the bus with me that would end up being my cellmate during the classification process. I was in a totally new environment at this prison. I had heard a lot about San Quentin's history and so I knew that I was in for a change from the other prisons I had been to. Once I was settled into the cell, I did my prayers and asked God to watch over me and see to it that I would make it back to society sane and in good health. The first night in San Quentin was hectic. There were people yelling all night about things they heard and things that were happening on the streets. I woke up the next morning groggy and grouchy. I did my prayer and read until it was time for chow. Going to the chow hall was an adventure, even though the chow hall was only 50 yards from the building I was housed in. The reason that 50 yard walk was so adventurous was because all the inmates on San Quentin mainline were all trying to see who we were and figure out if any of us were someone they knew. If they saw someone they knew, they would act like they were glad to see one another in prison.

The people I knew said things to me like, "I thought you went to college," or "What you doing in here?" Those types of statements and questions always irritated the hell out of me because I had made a mistake no different than those that were making the comments. Being in college didn't exempt me from making the wrong decision, but in other people's eyes I was supposed to go to college and the NFL and be successful. Well my cards were dealt differently than that.

The chow hall was heavily secured by the guards. They had their pepper spray cocked and ready for action, but something about San Quentin guards were different from the other guards I had seen in my now three years of being incarcerated. The San Quentin guards seemed like regular people that had a job to do. Most of them didn't abuse their authority; although there were some that did, the majority didn't. There were a lot of black guards at San Quentin, in fact, it seemed as though there were the same amount of black guards as there were white guards. This was totally new to me because I rarely saw black guards at the other prisons I was at. I'm not saying that it made a difference between black or white guards, because some of the black guards were worse than the white guards.

I'll never forget my first breakfast at San Quentin. I had scrambled eggs that were greenish in color, two tortilla shells, beans, salsa, and milk. This was the fourth prison I'd been to, and I began to realize that all of them fed their inmates the same things. I hated this meal, and if I had already had my property I wouldn't have touched that food, but I didn't have my commissary yet so I had to eat that crap as if I enjoyed it. There was a five minute time limit to eat the slop, so there couldn't be a lot of idle chatter while in the chow hall. After eating the slop, all the inmates in the chow hall were escorted back to the buildings we were in.

As I was getting escorted back to my assigned building, I saw a lot of old associates that I knew from school and from the streets. All of them were calling my name, asking what I was doing in jail, and I would just give a dumb founded shrug to a dumb founded question.

The ten days leading up to my classification hearing went by slowly, and I couldn't wait to get out of the building I was in. The cells were smaller than a normal sized bathroom. I mean it, these cells were tiny. When someone had to take a shit in the cell, there had to be a sheet up as a divider so that they could get a little privacy and the other person didn't have to look at them. It was one hell of a way to have to live, but it was the way I would have to live for years to come. At classification I was told that I would be going down to H-unit before I was to be sent to the ranch. (H-unit was a chaotic dorm to live in, and the ranch was like a resort for inmates that didn't have any points). After classification I immediately went to pack my stuff to go to H-unit, and my celly was going to H-unit as well. We both packed our things in excitement to be getting out of that grimy cell we were in. The ten minute walk from north block to H-unit was like being in a circus because of the way all the inmates on mainline were staring at us.

All the inmates had to walk through a metal detector and get a pat down from the guards to make sure that we weren't bringing any illegal contraband to H-unit. Once on the H-unit yard, it was like a world of its own. People were on the basketball courts playing as if they were playing for a million dollars there were guys on the pull up and dip bars trying to get big and buff, and then there were guys running around the track like they were preparing for a marathon. The inmates on the H-unit yard were full of energy like I had never seen before. I didn't know what those dudes were on, but I could see that there was something serious going on in H-unit. The guard escorted all the inmates to a room where we all got our prison uniforms on: jeans, jean jacket, prison blue long sleeve shirt, thermals, socks, towels, tee shirts, and boxers. We were then told what building that each inmate would be assigned to. Once I got to the building, I left everyone and started walking inside. Everyone I knew came and talked to me and told me that if I needed anything to just let them know.

Once in the building I went to my assigned bunk and made the bed and talked to my new bunky about the politics of H-unit. My bunky gave me a rundown of the politics of the yard and there was a lot of foul shit going on there. I wasn't too concerned at the time with the chaos going on in H-unit. I knew that I was classified to go to the ranch in ten days, so I didn't feel the need to get too involved in the politics of the yard. During the ten day wait, I immersed myself into the weight pile on the yard. I was the new head nigga in charge. There were a few cats that had their swole on, but there was no one that could compare to me. Everyone on the yard gravitated towards me because I was the new super swole cat there. Everyone tried to see who I was and what I was all about. Once I let everyone know that I was Muslim, I was then introduced to all the Muslims on the yard. All the Muslims were glad that I was one of them because everyone feared an inmate my size and everyone wanted to have a cat of my nature on their team. In prison, everybody had to be with somebody – be it blacks, whites, Mexicans, Muslims, BGF, Kumi, Norteño, Sureno, Border Brothers, Oakland, San Francisco, or a multitude of other gangs and clicks. The Muslims were glad to claim me as one of their own and they already knew that I was far more advanced than them in the knowledge and wisdom of the religion. I took charge of the Muslim program during my short stay in H-unit. Being in H-unit was hectic because there were so many politics to deal with. On top of that, there were a ton of drugs on the yard and every gang, organization, and click had dope fiends that were dipping in the drug trade. I actually couldn't wait to get sent to the ranch because H-unit was a monster.

My classification day couldn't have come fast enough! In the hearing, I was told that I would be going to the ranch with three years left on my sentence and I was curious to see what the ranch had to offer because I had heard good things about being there. I heard that your family could bring you food from the streets when they came to visit – Food from McDonald's, Kentucky Fried Chicken, or even Pizza Hut. Not only that, but you could walk around freely, you had your own bunk without a bunky, or a cell with whoever you wanted, and you could have your own television.

"The Ranch and Rules"

A few hours after my classification hearing, I was called on the intercom to get my property because I was being moved to the ranch. I told all the Muslims and the other cats I knew that I would see them later and the Muslims were sad to be losing me. Not only was I their leader for the short time that I was with them, but I was also a force of intimidation that kept things in order while I was on that yard.

As I was getting escorted to the ranch, I felt the usual surge of energy that I always got when I was going into an unknown place. The ranch rules were over-the-top. The reason for that was because the prison looked at being on the ranch as a privilege, and therefore one broken rule would get your ass sent back to H-unit or north block. I listened well to all the rules because the last thing I wanted was to leave the ranch, or so I thought.

Once the orientation was over, I was given my assigned bedding. Once I was in the building I was assigned to, I saw that this place was like a convalescence home. It was abnormally quiet and everyone had their headphones on listening to their radio or television. I asked one of the inmates where my bunk was and he told me that I was in the garbage truck cell. This was the cell where all of the guys that worked on the garbage truck were placed. Once inside the cell, I recognized the old bunky I'd had at H-unit, whose name was Frank Nitty. Frank was 415 (Kumi) and he had it tattooed all over his body. He looked like he was 90% white and 10% black. Frank was about 6'6", lean and he was respected by all of the inmates because he carried himself like a gangster. Frank and I were tight like we'd known one another for years. Frank even worked out with me when we were in H-unit. When Frank saw me walking into the cell, he jumped up excitedly and said, "You made it!"

"Yep! I made it! How is it over here?" I said.

Frank told me it was cool but that it could be boring as hell sometimes, and that there were a ton of rules that we had to abide by. Frank told me that I would be working with him and a couple of other guys on the garbage truck, and I asked him how he knew that because I hadn't gotten any paper work about my job assignment.

"If you are in this cell, you will be on that garbage truck with us at 3:00 in the morning!" He said.

"Damn! 3:00 in the morning?" I said.

"Yeah it's kind of cool because when we get off work everybody else is at work, so we get our sleep while everyone is gone, then after chow time we work out!" Frank explained to me.

It sounded as if Frank had a good program going on, so I decided I would map my schedule out like his. The only thing different with my scheduling was that I had to do my five prayers a day, therefore I wouldn't be able to get as much sleep as him and the garbage crew.

It felt like I had just gone to sleep when all of a sudden Frank was telling me to wake up and that it was time to go. I got up and the clock read 2:45 a.m. in the got damn morning. I felt like I was back in Fresno County Jail waking up for chow. I was groggy and grouchy as fuck but I got dressed fast and met the rest of the guys on the garbage truck. When I say garbage truck, I mean it was a real garbage truck, like what they use on the streets. It was freezing outside. It was 1997 and El Niño was on its way to the bay area so the wind was crazy strong. Once Frank showed me how to hold on to the trucks handles we were off.

Frank and I were on one truck and the two other guys were on the other. Our job was to collect all of the garbage off all the prison yards and off the outskirts of the prison as well. The outskirts were where the top administration of the prison lived, so that meant that we were picking up the warden's garbage, as well as other correctional officers that lived on the prison premises. We used to find a lot of contraband picking up the guard's garbage, and of course we kept anything we found that was of value to us. Being on the garbage crew was not my thing though. We had to get the garbage in north block and whenever we got that, there were big ass rats the size of obese cats. These rats were aggressive too. They would jump at you and so we had to be prepared at all times for them trying to attack us. My first day on that truck was one hell of an experience. I had never in my life seen a rat that big and I never wanted to be a garbage man again; that shit was disgusting. After four hours of picking up garbage, we went to the garbage truck garage where Frank and I did some curls with the weights they had there. Afterwards we were allowed to go back to our building at 9:00 a.m. All in all, the day wasn't that bad except for the rats. When we got back to the building we all took turns taking showers. The ranch was cool when it came to showering because there were single showers that you didn't have to share with everybody else. After I took my shower, I was exhausted. I slept from ten am until count time at 4:30 p.m., and I still felt a little fatigued.

The chow hall was small but I guess it was big enough for the amount of people the ranch had. I noticed that a lot of the inmates didn't even eat at the chow hall. Instead, they would eat their own food. The ranch basically had the same food as all the other prisons I'd been to, but the ranch let inmates get seconds if they wanted it. I didn't even like prison food so I definitely didn't want seconds of that slop. Right after I ate, Frank and I went to the ranch weight pile and worked out for an hour and a half. Frank was nowhere near as strong as me but he did the best he could. Afterwards we went and took a shower and got prepared for our 2:45 a.m. wake up call for work.

The next day on the truck was a little more exciting because we found a lot of stuff while picking up the guard's garbage. I know for a fact that the guards intentionally put out stuff in their garbage so that we could retrieve it. On my second day, Frank found a box of wine and I found a shit load of magazines, so it was a good day for us – well, it was good except for the big ass rat that tried to jump on me and Frank at the north block garbage.

After we finished collecting all the garbage for the day, we got dropped off at our building and Frank held the wine tight on the inside of his pants so that the garbage truck driver didn't see it, because the driver definitely would have told on Frank if he'd seen it. Once inside our building, Frank checked out the wine and it was unopened, so I knew that the guard had left that outside his house on purpose. Frank asked me if I wanted some wine and I got offended because he knew that I was a devoted Muslim, so I told him "no" with a sting.

"Alright Farrakhan!" Frank said jokingly.

We both started laughing and Frank got drunk off of his wine after we worked out that night. I read my magazines and we were both happy as hell about our daily treasures.

Things were going pretty good at the ranch. I was running the Muslim services and since it was the month of Ramadan, I was once again doing the fast reluctantly. The guards at the ranch treated the Muslims well, considering we were just inmates to them. Ramadan this year was a lot easier for me because by working on the garbage truck I was up early and able to eat a substantial amount of food. Then after work I was able to sleep until chow time, so Ramadan and my garbage job synched with one another perfectly.

At the end of Ramadan the word was out that a storm called El Niño was set to hit the bay area and the prison. I wasn't too concerned about the storm because San Quentin sat on the ocean and there were harsh storms all the time. Little did I know that El Niño wasn't going to be just any ordinary storm.

Ramadan ended smoothly and things were going good. I had been on the ranch for a little over a month when El Niño hit. The first day of El Niño was nothing I wasn't used to seeing at San Quentin. The garbage crew and I wore thick rain gear and thermals so we kept dry for the most part. However, the second day of El Niño was no joke. The wind seemed as though it were blowing at 100 mph and the rain was going vertical in direction. I had never in my life seen such a storm. The crew and I all vowed that if the storm kept up that velocity until the next morning that we weren't going to go to work because we weren't going to catch pneumonia for anybody. Getting sick in prison was the worst because all the prison would do is give the sick person some ibuprofen and tell them to sleep it off. That's why I vowed never to leave my life in the non-caring hands of a prison. The next day El Niño was still going strong when we were woke up by the garbage truck driver. Frank and I looked at one another and we gave a shake of the head to let one another know that we weren't going to get on the back of that truck while El Niño was causing havoc. One of the garbage truck workers said that he was going because he was a short time from going home and he didn't want to lose any time, so he went and the rest of us refused. By us three refusing, we caused the free men that drove the trucks to not only drive but to have to get their lazy asses out of their trucks and pick up the garbage too.

Frank, E, and I slept all day during the El Niño storm and it seemed as if we were competing on who could snore the loudest. I had thoughts of what would happen on account of us not going to work. I just thought that we would lose a half of day because of it, but oh was I wrong. Count time came and the guard stopped at our cell and called my name along with both Frank and E's. He told us to pack our property because we were getting sent back to h-unit for refusing to go to work. At that point we didn't care because, frankly, we were all tired of the ranch. It was like a slave plantation to us because all we ever did was work and sleep with very little time left over for recreation. Because of our work hours we were always tired.

Frank, E, and I packed our things in what seemed to be excitement to go back to H-unit. I was leery of going back to the drug infested unit, but I was ready for some excitement in my life and I knew that H-unit had plenty of it.

When Frank, E, and I stepped foot back on the H-unit compound, all the inmates that knew us came running up and making jokes like, "We knew yall wouldn't last over there" and "The ranch is for kiss ass people so we knew you would be back!" All the statements were definitely true, because I sure wasn't going to catch pneumonia for anyone.

"The Biggest Union Ever"

Once back at H-unit, I stepped in and took charge over the Muslims again and led them on the same disciplined path I was on. I ran a tight ship and the guards and inmates took notice to how I had the Muslims conducting themselves like they were soldiers in the Army's Special Forces. When I got sent back to H-unit everyone kept telling me that I was no longer the biggest, most cut dude on the yard. Everyone was like, "Big Low is here and he is big as fuck!"

I did my research on this Low character and found out that he was 415 (Kumi), and that he was also a major figure from one of the most respected turfs in San Francisco called Fillmore. After doing my investigation of Low and hearing what I heard about him, I knew that we would either be enemies or the best of friends. After talking to a few people on the yard, I went in my building for count time. During count time everyone had to sit up on their bunks so that the guards knew that each inmate was alive. At the time I was on a bottom bunk but I would switch bunks at count time with my bunky so that I could do a visual check to see who was new in the building. As I scanned the building during count time, I saw Big Low. I saw then how this big motherfucker must have got his name. I mean, I had never seen anybody that came close to my size and cuts until I saw Big Low. It looked like this dude competed in bodybuilding shows, and I was amazed to see that there was another person who had the same drive as I did when it came to sculpting their body. As I was sitting on the top bunk, Big Low and I stared each other down and gave one another a nod of acknowledgement. We were able to tell that we were both kings of this jungle, so we showed one another the upmost respect.

A day had passed since I first saw Big Low and everybody on the yard kept asking me if I had seen him yet. Each time they asked I would tell them that I had, and agree that he was a pretty buff cat. Everybody, of course, asked me in order to get a reaction; they wanted to see if I was intimidated or in shock that someone was actually as swole as I was, but I never said anything negative about Big Low's arrival to the yard. Big Low and I had just finished working out so we were both on the top bunks during count and we both gave each other a nod of respect. At that time I made it up in my mind that I would ease the tension we had with one another, because I could tell that everyone on the yard was trying to put us up against each other. After count time, I walked over to Big Low and we introduced ourselves. I told him that we should work out together to shut everybody up on the yard who was trying to set us up against one another, and he agreed. This was the beginning of a long friendship.

Big Low and I had the entire H-unit compound in an uproar because the two biggest dudes in the history of the department of corrections were now best friends. Everybody was in total fear of us because Big Low had an army of Fillmore and Kumi cats, and I had all the Muslims behind me. Therefore, Big Low and I practically had the whole of San Quentin behind the both of us. The guards, as well as the inmates, were scared as hell about this union.

Big Low and I were able to work out with the weights together for about three months when the news had hit that the weights were getting removed from all California prisons because inmates, such as myself and Big Low, were getting much too big and the prison guards were scared for their lives. This, of course, was some devastating news to all the workout fanatics on the yard. After two weeks of hearing the news, it was official. The prison officials drove huge dump trucks on the yard and they had inmates who worked on the yard crew putting all the weights onto the dump trucks. The inmates that were putting the weights on the dump trucks, of course, were ridiculed by all the workout fanatics that saw this devastating event, but the yard crew inmates didn't have a choice in the matter because if they refused to do it they would be reprimanded by the prison. Big Low and I booed and threw things as the weights were being removed from the yard. It was truly a sad day. I had been preparing myself for this day since I first got word about it one year prior to the weights getting removed. I had my-self a workout plan already prepared that would be just as sufficient as weights. I came up with a workout routine that used people and water bags for weights. I mean, I had an exercise for every body part just as if I had weights. Big Low and I came to love our new routine without conventional weights. I mean, that the guards were so mad at how I had improvised that I actually lost 90 days of my time in San Quentin for having Big Low sit on my shoulders while I was doing squats, true story! Big Low and I didn't care about petty write ups though, especially when it came down to working out. We continued with our workout regimen and we told the prison guards that we weren't going to stop. We said that if it was a problem they could just send us to the hole where we would be able to work out anyway. We made the prison officials feel stupid and they let us continue our workout methods. Big Low and I were getting huge from our new found workout program, and the guards hated it. Pretty soon the rest of the prison started copy-ing our routine and doing it as well. We made a mark in the prison system with our extreme workouts.

Things were going pretty good while I was at H-unit and my moth-er, pops, little brother, cousins, and aunt had visited me while I was at San Quentin. It was the first time in three years that I'd seen my family and of course they couldn't believe how big I'd gotten. I wore a shiny ass bald head at this point. When my family came and visited me, eve-ryone was happy to see me except for Spoiled, who was acting funny and didn't say much to me. I asked my mother what his deal was and she said she didn't know. He looked as if he was mad at the world, and I told my mother that she didn't have to ever bring him to see me again.

It was apparent that my little brother and I would never get along. It is what it is. I never liked him anyway so it didn't matter to me whether I saw him or not.

After that visit I felt sad because I wasn't able to leave with my fam-ily and that's when I realized that I didn't like getting visits as much as I thought I would. When your family goes back to the streets without you, that's when the sadness hits. I didn't like that feeling of being sad because before I started getting visits I never cared about life on the streets, but once I started getting those visits I started getting more concerned with what was going on outside prison. I wanted to go back to the way it was, when my only concern was what was going on behind prison walls. Visits were a distraction to me.

After my first visit with my family, I started thinking about the streets a lot more and I made it a point to tell my mother that she didn't have to come see me again for a while because I had a new job that caused me to work during visiting hours. I had started working at the Muslim chapel as a clerk at this point. The clerk job at the Muslim chapel was gravy and I had a lot of freedom to go about the prison. I gave kutbahs (sermons) at all the buildings in San Quentin, and I was like an icon to all of the inmates because I was so highly versed in Islam – not to mention I was the swolest dude a lot of the inmates had ever seen. After about two months of working at the Muslim chapel, I had decided to type myself up a poem about the conditions of San Quentin prison and how the prison was treating us all wrong. The poem was titled, "Are You Tired of Being Tired?" I'll never be able to forget that poem and I'll tell you why – I typed that poem in the afternoon and when I got to H-unit I had given a copy to a friend of mine, not thinking that he would amplify the poem to be bigger than what it was. The next day I went to the Muslim chapel as I always did, doing my daily chores of cleaning the facility and making sure that everything was in an orderly fashion. As I was sitting in the office typing up a letter, a group of the prison's police task force, also called the "Goon Squad", came rushing in.

The infamous San Quentin Goon Squad came into that office as if I had killed someone. They told me to stand up and put my hands behind my back. I did what I was told and asked them what was going on but they told me they would tell me once they got me down to their office. Once at the office I was nervous but I didn't show it. The head guy of the Goon Squad was a Mexican and he was known for being a bad ass. He started asking me questions like, "What possessed you to write the letter, 'Are you tired of being tired'?" I told him that I didn't know what he was talking about. He and his partner, who was a big, black, planet of the apes looking motherfucker, started laughing. The Mexican Goon Squad then proceeded to show me the letter and pointed out an indention going through the letter "s" all throughout the letter. He told me that every single type writer in the prison had its own distinct finger print, so they knew which office each and every letter typed came from. He asked me again why I typed the letter. I once again told the guard that I didn't know what he was talking about. At that moment, both Goon Squad guards acted like they were mad and banged on the desk and yelled, "Oh! You're going to be a wise ass? O.k. we have a place where you can be a wise ass!"

"The hole"

I thought the hole at San Quentin would be something like a dungeon, where I would be stripped down naked and made to sleep on the cold floor with no sheets or blankets, like I use to see in the movies. As I was escorted by the black Goon Squad guard, he tried to make small talk with me but I didn't say a single word to him. As far as I was concerned, he was my enemy and I wasn't going to give him the satisfaction of hearing my voice. Once we got to the hole, a big ass heavy door like on the Adam's Family was opened by a guard on the inside of the hole and the black Goon Squad guard handed me over to the guard that worked in the hole. I was then placed in a small cage next to some other inmates. As I was in that cage waiting to be housed at a cell, I started getting goose bumps because the black inmates were speaking a language that was foreign to me. I asked one of them in the cage next to me what language it was that he was speaking and he told me it was Swahili. I told him that I had to learn it because I loved learning different languages and in fact, I knew how to read and write Arabic. The guy in the cage next to me introduced himself as "G Man" and asked me where I was from. I told him I was from east Oakland and he said that he was too. G-Man was very friendly and asked a lot of questions. It was abnormal for an inmate to be as friendly and inquisitive as he was. I finally asked G-Man what he was in the hole for and he busted out in a loud ass laugh that startled me. I asked him what was so funny and he told me that he wished he was in the hole, but he went on to tell me that he was on death row instead. My heart started racing when he told me he was on death row. I knew something was different about G Man the moment I met him. When I first looked into G-Man's eyes, I thought to myself, "How does a dark brown cat have light green eyes?" G-man looked spooky! I had never seen a man with a skin complexion like his that had that color eyes. I asked G-Man how long he had been on death row and he told me that he had been on it for eight years.

G-Man found it amusing that I was in such shock over him being on death row for so many years. G Man and I continued to get to know one another and he told me that he'd send me over anything I needed while I was in the hole. I told him I appreciated it, and at that point a guard came and took G-Man back to his cell. After four hours in that cage, a guard came and told me to strip off all my clothes. I had to stand in the cage naked as the guard had me frisk myself and spread my ass cheeks so he could see if I had any drugs or contraband hidden up there. That's, of course, the most humiliating thing done to an inmate in prison. Once I was looked over by the guard, he gave me a yellow jumpsuit – which all the inmates in the hole wore. I was then hand-cuffed and taken to the cell that I would be in for some time.

Once I was in the east block cell, everyone started yelling my cell number and asking where I was from and why I was in the hole. I already knew that the inmates in the hole were on death row like G-Man. The inmates made it a point to find out who each newcomer was that entered the hole because they were anxious to figure out if the person was among their comrades, snitches, enemies, rapist, or rival gang members. I could sense that there was a strong political aspect in east bloc.

Once I told everyone where I was from, what I was in the hole for, and about my affiliation with the Muslims, everyone was at ease. It just so happened that G-Man was two levels above my cell and he heard me talking and called my name.

"Who was that?" I asked.

G-man said, "It's your Patna!"

"What's up G-Man?" I said in response.

He asked me if I needed anything and I told him that I needed a few soups until I went to the store. I asked him if he could also send me some Swahili words so I could start studying them, and G-Man said that he would send them by a guard that he was cool with. I told him thank you and that I would pay him back, but he told me not to worry about it. I knew that G-Man was on death row and he couldn't spare to give anything away, so I vowed I would pay him back plus some. After about an hour in my cell, a guard came by and brought me two brown paper bags – one with about six Top Ramen soups and the other with papers in it. I yelled to G-Man that I had received his package and I thanked him for it. He told me that if I needed anything else to just ask him. G-Man then introduced me to another cat from East Oakland that was on death row named Rob. Rob was from the 700 block in East Oakland and he had also been on death row for eight years. Rob and I grew a brotherly bond that lasted for years.

After I talked to Rob for a while, I started studying the Swahili words that G-Man had given me. I vowed to myself that I would learn all the words at record speed. Of course, it would help that it was all I had to read, so all my energy was easily put into learning the new language.

The first night in the hole was sleepless because there were people that were classified as 5150(crazy) that were in the hole. After the in-mates said a cadence to bring east block to silence, the 5150 people started their irate talking spree. The 5150 people were evidently ex-gangbangers that were called drop outs. These drop outs would say the oaths of whatever gang they had dropped out of out loud and tell all the gang's business for everyone to hear. They would even say the by-laws of the gang they were in, and they would let everyone know who the top ranked officer's in the gang were. East block was total chaos at night and there was nonstop noise that would drive a sane person crazy if they weren't mentally strong enough to handle it. I must say that it had me crazy myself for a while, that is, until I got adjusted to the noise and got used to the madness enough that I could sleep through it.

After a few days in the hole, I was allowed to go outside for a few hours. I was nervous about going to the yard because I didn't know if I would be there with the death row inmates or not. When the guard came to my cell, I was only allowed to be wearing boxers and I could have a tee shirt in my hands. The guards did this procedure so that they could see your body and make sure that you didn't have any weapons on you. There was a little slot in the cell that food was placed in at chow time and I had to turn around so that the guard could handcuff me through that slot. Because of my bodybuilder frame, I had to be restrained with two handcuffs instead of one, so the guards always had to grab an extra pair for me.

Once handcuffed, I was told by the guard to walk out of the cell backwards so that he could grab my wrists and have control of me in case I went crazy or something. As I walked down the corridor to go to the yard, I looked in every cell to see who I knew.

I looked in one cell and saw a pale ass white dude that was having an all out conversation with himself. The guard asked me if I knew who the guy was and I said no.

"That's the night stalker," he told me.

I thought to myself, "Damn, I live right next fucking door to the infamous night stalker!" It was crazy that I had made it to this low of life that I was a neighbor of the night stalker. As I finally reached the area where all the inmates were searched and scanned with the wand to see if they had any metal objects up your ass, I was told to walk down a long ass corridor to the very last yard. While I was walking down the corridor, G-Man saw me and came running to his yard gate. (He was on the death row yard with all the Bay Area and Blood inmates because the two groups were allies in prison.)

"Yo Khalid, what's up bro? You are big as fuck!" G-Man said.

"You know I got to represent Oaktown to the fullest!" I laughed.

G-man told me again to let him know if I needed anything, and I said I would. Rob came up to the gate and introduced himself to me. Like G-Man, Rob told me that if I needed anything to let him know and I thanked him. At this point the guards started rushing me to go to my assigned yard, and as I walked down the corridor that led there, all I could think about was G-Man and Rob. Those dudes looked just like me and here they were waiting to be killed on death row. I felt for those two guys. When I reached my destination, I stood at the gate and waited for the guard in the tower to let me onto the yard. Once the gate was opened, I had to turn around and let the guard take off my handcuffs. When they were off I turned around to a yard mostly filled with Mexicans and blacks. I gave everyone a nod of respect and went over to where the blacks were and introduced myself to everyone. The blacks on the yard were BGF (Black Guerilla Family) and 415 (Kumi). I was the only person on the yard that was only a practicing Muslim.

There were other cats that were Muslim, but their gang came first while they were in the hole. Once everyone was on the yard, lines were formed like we were in the army. Two Mexicans and one black were in the front calling out cadences for all the inmates that were in formation. I was lost; I didn't know what the hell was going on. I just followed what everybody did. The first exercise was to do six count burpees. That's when you drop down and do one pushup, hop back up to your feet, and then hit your stomach before going back down again. This was unlike anything I had ever done before. Of course I had seen guys do these exercises during my stint in prison, but I was the one to build muscle not tear it down. I continued on with the group, but once we did our 25th burrpee I was gasping for air but I knew that I couldn't stop and let the blacks down. I realized that the blacks were in competition with the Mexicans because burpees were known to get mastered by the Mexicans. The blacks wanted to prove that they could do burpees just as good as the Mexicans, so I told myself that I wouldn't stop unless I died.

After the 25th 6 count, a black guy called out, "Now we will be doing 25 8 count burppies, 25 8 count burppies, you got that, you got that?"

The rest of the inmates responded with, "We got that, we got that!" Then the 25 8 count burpees began.

As I was doing the 8 count burpees, I kept asking myself why I was doing this. I'm going to get small doing all of this cardio, I thought, but I refused to listen because I wasn't going to let the blacks or myself down.

After we finished the 25 8 count burpees, one of the Mexicans in the front yelled out, "How do you feel, how do you feel?"

"Good, good!" everyone responded, except for me. I didn't respond because I was too busy trying to suck in some oxygen so that I wouldn't fall out on the yard on my first day, because that would have been too embarrassing.

I just knew that it was going to be over after we did the 25 8 count burpees, but oh was I wrong! Once we finished, one of the Mexicans yelled out, "Now we will be doing 25 10 count burpees, you got that, you got that?"

"We got that, we got that!" We responded.

I, at this time, was seeing stars, but I knew I had to muster up some energy to keep going. I don't know how I managed to continue but I did. After the 25 10 count burpees, I thought I was literally about to die. I could barely breathe. I had never, in all my life, done anything as strenuous as that before. I prayed that we were done doing burpees, but we weren't.

"Now we will be doing 25 12 count, 25 12 count! You got that, you got that?" one of the black guys yelled out.

We responded, "We got that, we got that!"

At this time, I wasn't on earth any longer. I was completely spaced out mentally. I knew for sure that I would have a migraine after all that strenuous exercising. I finished the 25 12 counts with everybody else, but it was pure hell. After we were finished doing the burpees, guys were carrying on like the burpees were just a warm-up exercise for them and some of them even went on to start doing their pull ups and pushups. I didn't know where these dudes got all that damn energy from. After I was done with the burpees, I noticed that my vision was blurry and I knew that that was a sign that I was about to have a migraine. I held my composure until the yard time was over, but I couldn't wait to get off and go back to my cell. Luckily, yard was only three days a week for those of us that were in the hole; however, the death row inmates were allowed to go to the yard every day.

Once back in my cell, I laid down because the migraine was coming on something fierce. Getting a migraine in the hole wasn't cool because there was no silence. The days we had yard were the most quiet because everyone that went was exhausted afterwards, but there were a lot of people that didn't go to the yard and they talked all day every day. I laid on that hard ass bunk and asked God to please stop my head banging migraine. I passed out until I was awakened by a guard with dinner. The guard slid the food through the food slot and I immediately put my food and milk cartons into some bags I had. I went back to sleep after the guard came back to get the tray. We weren't allowed to keep the tray because inmates made weapons out of them if guards forgot to pick them up. I woke up around 2:00 in the morning feeling better, so I ate the food that I had saved, and that's when I learned how to eat cold food, because if I didn't eat it cold I would starve.

The next day after the migraine, I did pushups all day to regain my strength from the day before. I hadn't been to the store yet and I hadn't been given my property either, so I was living off the soups G-Man had given me and the food the prison gave me. I could feel myself losing weight because before I came to the hole I was eating at least four thousand calories a day.

My daily eating regiment before I went to the hole was: five soups, two cups of rice, two cans of tuna, two peanut butter sandwiches, two honey buns, two snickers, and all three meals that the prison gave me. Now that I was in the hole, I was lucky if I consumed 1,500 calories. My body was in shock because of the calorie deficit. It was now well below what it used to be and I knew it wouldn't be long before I started to lose weight at a fast rate. I hoped that I got out of the hole before I shriveled up and lost all my muscle that I had been working so hard for.

The days leading up to the hearing of the write up that I got over my poem, "Are you tired of being tired", were tough because food was my main issue. It felt as though I was always hungry, and I hated that feeling of not eating enough. After 10 days in the hole, the day had come for me to find out my fate. I was escorted by a guard into a room of San Quentin's top officials – being the captain, lieutenant, sergeant, and the two Goon Squad guards that came and got me from the Muslim chapel. As I sat down, my charges were read: escape paraphernalia, threat to the safety of San Quentin prison, and improper use of a prison type writer. After the captain read off my charges he asked me, "How do you plea?"

"Not guilty!" I said firmly.

The captain quickly rebutted that I was most definitely guilty and that I would be spending the next 80 days in the hole. Once my time in the hole was up, I would get reassessed to see if I would be sent back to the mainline or transferred to another prison. I walked out without an expression on my face, but in my mind I wanted to kill every last one of those guards in the room. As I was being escorted back to my cell, everyone asked me what had happened and I told them that I would be in the hole for quite some time. Once I reached my cell, I made up my mind that I would read and work out like a mad man so that when I was released from the hole I would be like a machine.

A week after my hearing I finally made it to the store and it felt like it was Christmas. I got five cases of Top Ramen, some potato chips, a ton of candy bars, a bag of coffee, soap, shower shoes, toothpaste, and some stamps and envelopes to write my mother. I was happy as hell that day, as was everyone else in north block that got their canteen. I had a guard send G-Man the soups he gave me, plus four extra ones. G-Man said I didn't have to do that but I'm a realist. I knew that he needed all of his things and then some. I asked all my other associates if they needed any-thing, and everyone mostly wanted some Top Ramen, because Ramen was like gold in the hole. That was the reason why I bought so many cases, because it was valued so high.

After going to the store I felt like a new man. Since I wasn't starving anymore, I felt like my energy was back up to 100%. I was doing the burpees like a pro and I wasn't getting winded like I did when I first started. I also learned all the Swahili words that G-Man had sent me, so I sent the words back to him and asked him if he had anymore. He said he did and that he would send them by a guard. I was speaking Swahili fluently at that point and so when I spoke to G-Man and Rob, that's all I spoke. This created a domino effect and caused all the blacks and some Mexicans to start studying Swahili too.

East block was a highly political place to be. There were a lot of fights that went on on the yard. The Mexicans were the ones that mainly disci-plined their own, and for a lot of stupid reasons. We blacks rarely had to beat or stab someone, but of course there were some situations that got real ugly. The head black guy, Mwafrika, was the one that ran the ma-chine (burpee routine) and he was set to be transferred soon so every-one was preparing themselves physically in case they were called upon to take his place. I had become the protégé of Mwafrika. I would not only do the machine with everybody else, but I would also do a private machine with Mwafrika. I was a burpee junkie now and everyone knew it. Mwafrika also spoke Swahili fluently so we had a serious bond.

At this point I had been in the hole for an entire month and the Muslim Chaplin had not come to see me at all. I was mortified that he hadn't come to the hole to see if I was alright. My love for Islam started to diminish because the Muslims weren't real to me. They acted like saints but they did the same shit as everyone else in prison, and the Muslim Chaplin not coming to check in on me just solidified in my mind that Muslims were fake. While I was in the hole, my love for 415 (Kumi) grew immensely. They were people that I was used to dealing with. The cats in 415 (Kumi) were themselves and the only thing that some of them tried to do was act tougher than they really were. I knew that I would rather deal with people who were genuine than with people who acted holier than thou but then would go in their cell and shoot heroin in their veins.

I talked to a few of the 415 (Kumi) cats on the yard to get a feel of their organization and what I had heard I liked. It was no different than what I had been doing all my life. The 415 (Kumi) were a brotherhood that took care of one another at all cost. To be in 415 (Kumi), each member had to abide by the by-laws and if they were caught breaking any of them, they would get disciplined. In my eyes, the 415 (Kumi) were no different than being in a college fraternity, because the college fraternity also had by-laws to abide by. After talking with the 415 (Kumi) cats for about a week about their organization, I told them that I was ready to join. They, of course, were happy because I was a force in the prison system that people respected. They knew that I would be a good leader for the not so smart members. During the process of me joining, I had to memorize a multitude of things – which wasn't a problem for me because my mind was sharp from all the Swahili I had been learning and all the books I had been reading. I learned all the information I was given in a single day. The 415(Kumi) cats told me that I was the first member in history to learn all the information as fast as I did. I felt honored and I told them that I would make them proud that they initiated me into their group.

Once I was 415(Kumi), I was given a respect that was unbelievable. I'm not just talking about respect from the inmates, I'm talking about respect from the guards as well. I was already given a lot of respect anyway, because of the way I carried myself, but once everyone knew I was a member of 415 (Kumi) I started getting, "no sir" and "yes sir". It was crazy. I even found out that G-Man and Rob were 415 (Kumi) and so they were excited that I chose to be a part of their organization.

When Mwafrika got transferred, I immediately took over the machine. I thought I was ready to run it but things change when you are in front of all the other guys and calling out cadences. The intensity is full throttle for us in the front leading. All the 415(Kumi) cats thought that I was too big to run the machine, but nobody else wanted to take the responsibility so I told them I'd do it. We started off with the usual six count burpees, then escalated to eight, and then ten. During the middle of us doing the 10 count burpees, one of the Mexicans had to stop because he was winded. One of his gang members came and pushed him out of the way and we continued through the 10 and 12 count burpees. I felt good because it was my first day running the machine and I caused one of the Mexicans to falter. I was on top of the world and all the 415 (Kumi) cats gave me the upmost respect for running the machine. After I got back to my cell that day, I knew that I still had a little ways to go before I would really be considered a master at burpees. I say this because I was still tired after I ran the machine, I just didn't let anyone know it. I knew that Mwafrika didn't so much as break a sweat when he ran the machine and that was the point that I knew I had to get to. I became a master at burpees fast once I started running the machine, because not only did we have the machine when we were on the yard but we also had the machine inside the building in our individual cells on the days we didn't go to the yards.

During my second month in the hole, my mother and pops came to see me. There was a strict "no contact" rule for those visiting in the hole, so that meant that I was separated from my family by Plexiglas and that we had to talk to one another through a telephone. It was terrible but I was happy to see them and to show them that their son was strong as an ox and that nothing would get his spirit down. I talked to my parents about the reason I was in the hole, and I'll never to this day forget what pops told me. He said, "Son, you do what you got to do to make it out of this prison!" I had never heard pops talk like that so it encouraged me a lot.

The visit went good and I told my mother that she didn't have to come visit me anymore while I was in the hole, and she agreed.

As I left the visit with mom and pops, I was placed in a holding cage next to the night stalker. This dude was a serial killer that had a cult of women that came to the prison to visit him. It was crazy how many women followed that dude. As I was in the cage next to him, he was mumbling to himself and doing circles in the cell without stopping. It was totally weird to see this from him. I had never seen someone that looked like him before; I imagined that he must have looked like what demons looked like in pure form. I'll never forget how it felt to be so close to a serial killer. In a strange way, it was kind of exhilarating.

The day of my hearing was here and I was excited because I knew that I didn't get any write ups and that there was a good possibility I would be getting out of the hole. As I was escorted to where the hearing was being held, I said myself a quick prayer to God asking him to grant me freedom from the hole.

Once inside the hearing, I saw one of the lady captains give me a slight smile, so in my mind that was an indication that I would be getting out of the hole. As the captain read off my charges, he said that I had completed my 90 days in the hole for the infraction and that I would be granted to return to the mainline after the hearing. I told all the staff in the hearing thank you for their decision and I was escorted back to my cell. As I was walking back, everybody was asking me what had happened and I told them that I was a free man. They all started cheering for me like I was going back to the streets rather than going back to a different cell. I packed all of my things and gave everyone a farewell. I felt G-Man and Rob's spirit, and I could tell they were sad that I was leaving but I knew that they were used to seeing people come and go, so they knew how to deal with their friends getting out of the hole or transferring to another facility. I told G-Man and Rob that I would stay in touch with them when I went back to the mainline.

"New General"

As I was getting escorted to the mainline, Rob told me not to come back to the hole and I told him I wouldn't, but he knew that being 415 (Kumi) I was likely to come back to the hole on any given day. At the time I didn't realize that, but I would definitely find out soon enough. The word had already hit the mainline that I was a member of the 415 (Kumi) now and that I was no longer practicing the religion of Islam. My Swahili name was Kali, meaning sharp, intelligent, and fierce. I had left the Muslim name Khalid in the hole where my love for Islam stopped. Once I was on the north block mainline, everyone that knew me was cheering and calling my name. The Kumi cats were ecstatic that I was one of their own and when I saw the Muslims I gave them a mean mug.

Once the guard escorted me to north block, I was given my assigned cell. When I got to my new cell there was no one in there at the time but I could tell that whoever was staying in there with me had to be a lifer. There was a television on the lower bunk and a ton of boxes both under the bunk and all lined up on the tiny cell walls. I made my bed up and dozed off for a while until I was awakened by the cell door being unlocked by the guard. It was almost time for count so all the inmates had to report to their cells. I sat up on my bunk waiting to see who my celly was. After about ten minutes of sitting up on my bunk, in came an older, light skinned brother looking to be in his mid-fifties or so.

"What's up O.G.? I'm Kali!" I said.

"Hey youngster! I'm Pops," he greeted me.

I could tell immediately that this O.G. was not just any ordinary inmate at San Quentin, because as soon as he was in the cell all types of cats started coming up and asking him if he was alright or if he needed anything. Pops told them all that he was fine. I could tell that everyone was just coming to the cell to see who I was and to let me know that Pops had a lot of people in his corner.

Pops and I started off with the basic conversation to get a feel of one another and then he asked me the question that everyone asks a new inmate, "Are you affiliated with any group?" he asked. I told Pops that I was Kumi, and he got a frightened look on his face.

"You are huh?" he said nervously.

"Yeah, is there a problem?" I asked.

I immediately took offence to his look and he noticed.

"No there isn't a problem, but I am Kumi as well, so I need to hear that," Pops said.

When he told me that he needed to hear that, I knew exactly what he was talking about. He was referring to the oath that all members had to memorize. I began whispering the oath to Pops and when I was finished he corrected me on a few things that he felt were incorrect., I told Pops that the way I said the oath was the way I was taught how in the hole. He said that it wasn't a problem, but that everyone had their own version of the oath, and he went on to tell me the version that everybody said on the north block mainline and I quickly memorized it instead. I then had to recite the by-laws to him, and he was very impressed with my knowledge of the organization.

When I met Pops, I didn't know that he was one of the top dogs of 415 Kumi. He was actually one of the founders of the organization, so God had put me in the cell with him for a purpose. Pops and I talked until chow time and I could tell that we had an immediate connection.

Whenever our cell bars were unlocked by the guard, there were about 20 dudes waiting for Pops before we could even open our door. He told all the dudes that I was their "love one". Love one is the term that Kumi members use to refer to one another.

"That's cool that he is a love one, but he has to go through the screening process before we wrap arms around him!" The head of the mainline said.

What this meant was that it had to be verified that I was actually a member and that I wasn't just an imposter posing as Kumi to spy on the organization.

I walked to chow basically by myself, that is, until I saw the person that gave me my first gun, my Patna from my block, Ant! When Ant saw me, he took a double look and he called me by my street name, Chuck. I immediately recognized him and walked over to him.

"Ant what's up?" I said.

"Chuck what you doing up in here? I thought you was in college?" he said to me.

I quickly rebutted, "Shit happens, Ant, shit happens."

Ant understood and gave me a smirk. We went to the chow hall reminiscing about the old days when we were running around E Street doing what kids did. Eventually Ant asked me the big question that everyone asked one another.

"Bra, you affiliated with anyone?" he asked me anxiously.

I looked Ant in his eyes and said, "I'm Kumi, bra!"

I saw Ant's eyes get big with excitement and he told me that he was too. It was a good feeling to know that we were a part of the same organization.

Once we got our food, we went and sat down where all the other Kumi cats were sitting. Everybody at the tables looked up at me and asked me where I was going. I told them that I was sitting down with my Patna, Ant. They all said the area was a Kumi area and that only members could sit at those tables.

"I am Kumi!" I said quickly, but they replied, "Well until you are cleared, you can't sit with us."

I said cool and sat at a table across from the Kumi cats instead and Ant came and sat with me. He told me that it was standard procedure that I be cleared first before I could be recognized as a true member and I told him that I understood. Ant and I ate and talked as fast as possible because we only had five minutes to eat our food. Once finished eating, we went to the yard and continued reminiscing and catching up on what each other had been up to.

As Ant and I were talking, one of the Kumi cats came over and said that he needed to holler at me. I told Ant I would talk to him after I dealt with the screening process I knew that I was about to encounter. The Kumi cat and I walked the yard casually as I recited everything I knew about Kumi and its history. The Kumi cat screening me was impressed with all that I knew and once I was done he shook my hand and told me that they were glad to have me on the yard and that they had already heard a lot of good things about me.

I was then escorted by the Kumi cat to all the other Kumi members to be introduced to them. It felt good to be a part of something that I felt was a positive movement for cats from the bay area. While I was being introduced to the Kumi members, I recognized quite a few of them from growing up with them in East Oakland. We all greeted each other with much respect.

The first day of being introduced to the Kumi members went well. I felt like I had made the right decision by being a part of the organization. Pops and I were having a good time as cell mates. We studied a lot about all types of things, varying from history to psychology. Pops was an excellent teacher whom I respected to the upmost. He taught me a lot of things about Kumi and general life.

Word got back to San Quentin that Big Low was on the streets causing a lot of ruckus. I prayed that my old workout partner wouldn't get killed or come back to jail, but the things I heard about him convinced me that he was going to head down one of those two roads.

A few Kumi members and I became extremely close, especially one particular dude from East Oakland named KB. KB had a long ass perm that he got done every two weeks, and he had a few open faced gold teeth that were accentuated by his gold framed prescription Gucci glasses. Everyone treated KB like he was a baller because he carried himself as such. KB and I played chess every day together, and when we weren't playing chess we were just hanging out together. KB and I were the closet to one another besides me and Pops.

Everything on the north block yard was going alright for being in prison, but one day I went to my cell and I was greeted by Pops telling me, "Son, I think that it's time for you to move to another cell." I thought Pops and I were inseparable, but Pops apparently thought otherwise. I took offense immediately.

"Cool," I said, "I'll find another cell immediately."

Pops could tell I was put off by his comment and he explained to me that there weren't any hard feelings between us, but that he felt threatened by the Kumi members and he knew that if a hit was ever made on him that I would have to do it because I was the closet person to him. At the time, I didn't quite understand where Pops was coming from, but I would soon understand why he said what he said to me.

I began looking for a new cell because Pops started acting strange, as if he didn't trust me. At the time I didn't know that there were a lot of internal problems with the Kumi members and I didn't have any rank so I didn't know what was going on with the higher echelon.

I found a cell after two days of looking all around north block. I was fortunate with the cell move because I was able to move into a cell that was empty, which meant that I had seniority. Having seniority meant that I had prison rights to the bottom bunk which was the best to have in the tiny cells, because hopping up and down off the top bunk was the worst. Pops was happy to see me get my new cell and I was happy because I was now the captain of my ship and anyone that entered my cell would have to conform to my rules.

Being in my new cell was cool because I was allowed to be without a celly for a few days, which was like going on a vacation in prison. No celly meant being able to shit without caring about who smells it, farting without having to sit on the toilet, eating without having to ask if the celly wanted some, not having to share the sink, and not being bothered when you don't want to be bothered. Being without a celly lasted for four days and then I was asked by the top dog of Kumi at the time if he could move in with me. I told SB that he could move in with me if he agreed to my cell rules. I ran them down to him: no drugs, no smoking, got to keep cell clean, and respect me and I will respect you. SB agreed to all the conditions of moving into my cell so he moved in with me. SB was about 5'7" with a muscle bound body and he was what I call a shyster. He ran the Kumi car on the yard but he was always making a lot of moves with a lot of the civilians. After moving SB into my cell, I really saw what type of person he was and I didn't like it at all.

After about a month on the mainline, I was given a high ranking position in Kumi. Everybody who was in Kumi longer than me questioned how I was given the position I was given so fast. All the higher ups told the inquisitive members that I was the most qualified for the position and they couldn't refute that because I knew everything about Kumi. Not only that, but I had ran the Muslim car since the beginning of my prison sentence and so I knew how to run an army. All the Kumi cats were impressed with the way I got Kumi running. I didn't mess around and I knew that I would have to show the members that I was serious when it came to getting violent as well. I was awaiting my opportunity to show the Kumi members that I not only gave orders but I would hurt anyone that defied me and those orders. One thing about prison that I learned early on was that the inmates didn't respect anything other than violence. Because of that, I knew that I would have to do something violent to make my mark as a high ranking, feared officer in Kumi.

One day the opportunity presented itself for me to show the members that I didn't just give orders for them to do things but that I would also get down and dirty when I needed to. I was running a drill that Kumi had been doing since its existence. All of the Kumi members would take positions on the yard as if we were getting ready for war. All the members had to keep their eyes on me because I was the officer that would give a signal to attack or retreat. This was just a drill for us to stay prepared for a riot, because anything can happen in the blink of an eye in prison. I gave the signal for everyone to retreat to Kumis's designated meeting place. As everyone made it to the meeting place, I asked where KB was and the Kumi member that was posted with him on their mark. All the members told me that KB didn't see the signal because he was talking and not paying attention to me. Once KB came to the meeting place, I told him that he had violated a by-law and that he had to do 415 pushups as discipline for the violation.

KB looked at me and the other Kumi members and said, "I'm not doing it, and you can send your best!"

When a Kumi member tells other Kumi members to send the best, it means that they are willing to fight whoever is sent at them to fight. Usually when someone said that, we would send three people to beat the defiant members ass and make him get off the yard. After KB said what he did, I responded simply, "KB, just do the pushups because you know that you fucked up. We're trying to show you some brotherly love by just giving you some pushups!"

"I'm not doing it, so send your best!" KB said again. After that, KB walked off like he was the baddest nigga on the earth.

One thing about me is that I am a loyalist that would never go against any rules or laws that I have agreed to uphold. Therefore, I hold everyone up to the same exact standard. I was pissed when KB went against the Kumi car. The officers above me said that they would talk to KB about his actions, and I told them that there wasn't anything to talk about.

"He just disrespected the entire Kumi organization doing what he did, and he said send the best and that's exactly what I'm going to do," I said.

I went on to tell them that I was going to discipline KB myself. Everyone was shocked because they all thought that KB and I were best friends. I told them that Kumi comes before any friendship to me. I told them that I took the oath to uphold Kumi laws at all cost and that was what I was going to do. All the high ranking officers tried to send other members to do the dirty work, but I was adamant about show-ing the Kumi car that I didn't fuck around. I was then given the green light to do the disciplinary action on KB under one condition: That I couldn't let the superiors know that I was given the green light, because KB was brought into Kumi by one of the superiors and he wouldn't approve of the move I was making on KB.

SB and I headed to north block trailing KB to his cell. I knew that KB knew that something was about to go down because of his viola-tion to Kumi. I had seen him looking out the corner of his eyes as we were following him. KB and I lived on the same tier in north block, so I didn't look too suspicious with my attack.

Once I saw KB walk into his cell, I rushed in behind him as SB watched out for the guards. I rushed KB without saying a word. I realized that he was trying to grab a pen to attempt to stab me, but the blows I was putting on him caused him to try and protect his face instead. I got in about 10 punches that had KB semi-unconscious. KB then grabbed me and started trying to poke my eyes out, but I head butted him on the bridge of his nose and he immediately let go. That's when I heard SB say that the police were coming, so I casually walked out of KB's cell. I was on the tier when I heard SB say, "Watch out kali!" I turned around and KB threw a punch that grazed my eye and I immediately started giving power punches that sent him to the ground in an unconscious state. I was worried when I saw KB collapse to the ground because I didn't want to kill him, I just wanted to discipline him. I vowed that I would make it back to the free world, and if I caught a murder in prison then I was never going to get out. SB and I went to our cell and talked about what had happened and he was worried about our superiors coming down on us for the violent act that went down on KB. I reassured SB that he didn't have to worry about my loyalty because I was going to hold my own.

KB was sent to the infirmary and the word spread throughout the entire prison fast. One hour hadn't gone by when two guards came to my cell and told me that the captain of San Quentin wanted to see me. I knew for sure that I was going to the hole once again.

Once I got to the captains office, KB was already sitting there. I looked at him like, you're not all that tough now, and he looked back at me with a look of pity. The captain said that he already knew that this was a Kumi issue. I couldn't understand how the captain knew what happened in less than an hour! It amazed me how fast the prison officials knew why something took place in the prison. The captain then asked the both of us if the situation was resolved and we agreed that it was. The captain then said that if anything transpired between the two of us again that we would be in the hole for a long time. I already knew that KB didn't want to go to the hole because he got a lot of visits and packages and he wasn't the type of person that could handle being away from all the benefits of being on the mainline.

As I left from the captain's office, I knew deep down that the situation wasn't resolved. I knew it was resolved between KB and I, because he knew he was wrong and that he deserved what he got, but I knew that it wasn't over with as far as the head dogs were concerned. When I got back to my cell, it was count time and SB started saying that the superiors had heard about the situation and they were going to come up to our yard and holler at me. Now, in my eyes, when someone in prison says that they are going to come holler at you, it means that there is going to be an act of violence. Therefore, I prepared myself with two prison knives that I had. I told SB that I was going out like a warrior if the top Kumi cats wanted to get into some gangster shit. I had never been jumped in my life, except when Derrick and Darold attempted to jump me as kids, which was nothing compared to getting jumped by grown, muscle bound ass treacherous convicts. I vowed that I wasn't about to get jumped now, so I had two nicely sharpened knives that were awaiting a situation just like this.

SB and I went to chow and I ate my food extremely fast. I didn't have an appetite because I was full of adrenaline, but I knew that I would need some food in me for energy in case I had to deal with a lot of cats in a scuffle. At that point I felt like it was me against Kumi, so I felt like a wild animal just being let out of a cage after months in isolation. When I got to the yard, I saw about 50 Kumi members waiting there for me.

H-unit – which was the dorm living level two yard – had about 60 to 70 Kumi members, which was a lot, and in my eyes most of them came to north block yard to harm me, so I was prepared. All the Kumi members on the yard tensed up when they saw me, so I knew they all knew what was going on. I had on my prison war gear, which consisted of: two jean jackets, jean pants, brown prison boots, Nike gloves, a beanie, and two knives. I was ready for war.

I saw that KB was with the person that not only brought him into Kumi, but also was the highest ranking person on the yard. The person's name was Mike. Mike immediately called me and said that we needed to talk and when he walked towards me I tightened my grip on the knives. Mike saw that I was amped up and he told me that it was cool, I didn't have anything to be alarmed about. I trusted Mike because if he was going to have something done to someone, they would know it because Mike was raw with his delivery and he didn't beat around the bush.

As Mike and I walked the track, his first question to me was, "Kali, who gave you permission to put down that hit?"

"No one, I did that on my own," I said simply.

Mike was the same age as me but he was wise beyond his years. He looked at me and gave a smirk as if he knew the truth. Mike went on to say that I had broken some by-laws and that I would have to run laps around the track as discipline and I said cool. At that time, I didn't realize how close Mike and I would become but that incident started a long lasting friendship between the both of us.

I was relieved that I didn't have to stab any of the Kumi cats, because I truly loved Kumi and its philosophy. I did the laps around the prison track and I did them with pride, feeling like I was the baddest motherfucka on the yard. That was my first and only time that I would get disciplined as a Kumi; after that day my status increased dramatically as well as the respect I got from everyone throughout the California prison system.

After a few months of being on San Quentin's mainline, I was one of Kumi's new top dogs. I called shots and I was given the upmost respect by all the inmates and guards. KB and I were cool again but we didn't have the friendship that we had before the fight. We did still play chess together, but now the chess games were intense because we acted as if we were in a fight again and we didn't want the other to win. Our style of play was about the same, so we were even with our win-lose ratio.

A lot of things went down on the San Quentin yard. On a daily basis there were fights and min-riots. I didn't allow any of the Kumi members to be intoxicated on the yard because anything could happen at any given time. I know you may be thinking, "You didn't let them be intoxicated on the yard? So they could be intoxicated off the yard?" Well, let me tell you, I never even knew what crack looked like until I got to San Quentin. The only difference between prison and the streets was that in prison you couldn't drive and you had a schedule that was hardly ever altered; other than that, prison was just about the same as the streets, including the drugs and alcohol.

There was this one particular day when I had noticed a lot of movement on the yard, and when there was a lot of movement there were usually drug transactions being conducted. I kept seeing a lot of the Kumi members walking frantically so I knew they were up to no good. I even spotted my celly SB in the mix, and SB was the top officer on the yard and even he was up to no good. That just lets you know what type of people were running 415 Kumi.

I continued watching the mischief from afar while the Kumi members remained unaware that I was there watching their every move. I was patiently watching each defiant Kumi member until they were good and high and then I approached them while they sat on the benches fading in-and-out of consciousness from the heroin that they had just snorted.

I walked up on SB and said, "SB, what's up bra, what you doing?"

"Kali, what's up bra, I'm good! What you up too?" SB said, trying desperately to snap out of his intoxicated state of mind.

"You know that you are in violation of the by-laws, right?" I said.

"I know bra I'm tripping!" he responded nervously.

I told SB that he had to move out of the cell with me because I didn't want to share my space with a drug user and I also told him that he would be stripped of his rank as a high ranking officer. He agreed to it all because he knew that I didn't fuck around, and I had all the Kumi members in my corner.

After SB was moved out of my cell and was stripped of his position, I was given his position by the higher-ups and I moved another Kumi member into my cell named Mel. Out of all the Kumi members I've ever met, Mel was definitely one of my favorite. The only thing about Mel I didn't know before I moved him into the cell with me was that he had a pornography addiction. I had never seen anything like it in my entire life. I mean, this dude would ask everybody on the yard if they knew who had fuck books, as they are called in prison. He had stacks of those fucking books and it was one of the few things I didn't like about Mel. I hated those books because I wasn't one to think about sex or have any desire to jack off in jail. I looked at it as a sign of weakness, a big part of the reason being that I was brainwashed into thinking that masturbating made a person weak. I needed all my strength because prison was an unpredictable place that required a person to be at their best at any given moment. Other than Mel's pornography addiction, we were two peas in a pot. We were tighter than most blood brothers.

It had been about six months on the yard and I was holding things together as the top Kumi officer. Things were in order while I was top dog. SB took his ass home, which was good, because he was about to be a victim of Kumi's wrath. He started rebelling before he was released which caused him to get disciplined a numerous amount of times before he got out. Mel was my top officer that consulted with me about the happenings of the yard. Because of my position in Kumi, I tried to be seen as little as possible, which is pretty difficult for a person in prison.

Everything on the San Quentin yard was going as smooth as prison could go, but all smooth things get bumpy in prison. I was about to experience a bumpy ride that I didn't see coming.

When Mel went home, I had the cell all to myself for three days which, like I said before, was like being on vacation. Then I got a celly one evening. He was a tiny fellow and he looked as if he was about 18 years old. I asked him what his name was and he said it was Lil D. Lil D was scared to death when he came into my cell; in fact, I had never seen anyone as frightened as he was.

I asked Lil D what was wrong with him and he said nothing. We made small talk to get to know one another and he started opening up to me because he felt that I was a solid person. Lil D told me that he was from Rich Town (Richmond California) and he might be in a little trouble with one of the top shot callers from Rich Town named Charlie. He told me that he was a witness in Charlie's double murder case and he didn't testify in Charlie's case even though he was put on the stand. He told me that he refused to be a snitch and the district attorney forced him to get on the stand and when he didn't say a word they had to drop charges on Charlie. I told Lil D he did the right thing so why was he worried? Lil D said that he was the only living witness in the case and that he feared that Charlie would do something to him while they were at San Quentin.

I said, "Charlie is here at San Quentin too?"

Lil D said they both came to San Quentin on the same bus. I kind of felt Lil D's pain but he had to deal with his own business.

Lil D and I talked until it was chow time and I was met at my cell by all my Kumi soldiers. When the cell door was unlocked, I saw that Lil D got paranoid but I didn't pay it too much attention. At chow all the Kumi cats were telling me that we had a new comrade on the yard named Charlie and that he just came from beating a double murder case. I was like, damn I got that cat that was on his case in my cell, what a coincidence. After chow, Charlie was screened and I introduced myself to him. I noticed that he had a very rugged type of personality, but I was used to dealing with that with all the Kumi members too. I told Charlie that Lil D was put in my cell and to what extinct was their situation. Charlie told me that he wasn't tripping on Lil D, because he saved him from being on death row.

After a couple of days of Lil D being in the cell with me, he moved out without a warning. I asked him why he was moving and he said that he was moving in with one of his Rich Town Patnas.

I knew that Lil D was uncomfortable living in the cell with me, knowing that Charlie was a part of Kumi with me. I didn't blame him for the move because I knew that it was an awkward situation for him.

During that time Charlie came to the yard, Pops was sent to the hole for not giving the prison officials information they wanted from him. Mike also went home. Therefore, there weren't any strong Kumi members except for myself left on the yard. The other high ranked officer that had more rank than me was a softy and no one respected his judgment so I was on my own in my eyes.

I started seeing KB hanging with Charlie a lot, so I knew that KB was trying to get someone on his side. KB and Charlie started conspiring on my high ranked position.

KB and Charlie went to the softy inquiring about how I was able to hold my position when I hadn't even been Kumi an entire year. Usually people that had my position would have to have been Kumi at least five years, so the high ranking Softy let KB and Charlie get into his head and cause him to doubt whether I was really qualified to hold my position. Softy held a meeting with all the top ranking members, him and I being the highest ranked.

He went on to say that there had been some concerns about me holding the position I had, and about whether or not I had enough experience. I immediately took offence.

"This San Quentin yard has never run this smoothly until I was given the position!" I said. Softy agreed, but he was soft, therefore he let KB and Charlie make him even softer.

"You know what, I step down from that position because that position means nothing to me. I still have all the Kumi members behind me, regardless of what position I have!" I said finally.

"You don't have to step down, it's just a concern!" Softy explained to me.

"I'm stepping down!" I repeated, "Give the position to Charlie or KB and let's see how well the yard runs then."

Softy said that he would just stop all Kumi function until he figured out what to do. "Whatever," I said dismissively, and I walked off, followed by all the Kumi members that were with me. KB and Charlie realized that even if they did get my position, that I had everyone's loyalty.

For two weeks Softy was confused about what to do with assigning people to positions. I wasn't even concerned if Softy ever figured out what to do, because those two weeks without having to make decisions for grown ass men was the best two weeks I'd had at San Quentin. Softy finally decided that I would get my position back, and that Charlie was to be in the position right below me and KB right below him. That was cool with me as long as they did what I told them.

Once everything was in order, KB, Charlie, and I actually became a good team. I think Charlie made the ruckus just to get a high position so he would be able to tell people what to do instead of getting told what to do. Things were running smoothly. I even had a new celly whose name was Bay. Bay was a straight comedian and he was also Kumi like myself. He made my time go by fast because he had a million plus stories to tell. I put Bay in one of the officer's positions because he was a loyalist and he loved Kumi like crazy.

Things were going as well as to be expected when I got word that Big Low was back in San Quentin and that he was causing a ruckus.

All the Kumi cats on the mainline were hoping that Big Low wouldn't come back to the yard, because he was trouble in all their eyes, but I wanted my workout partner back so that we could continue with our training. After two weeks of Big Low being in the reception center, he got into a fight and went to the hole and everybody was for sure that big low he was going to get transferred to another prison.

A month had passed and the word was out that Big Low was on the San Quentin yard and out of the hole. I was happy as hell because I had never been tighter with a person than I was with Big Low. We were like brothers. I saw the look on all the other Lumi member's faces when they heard he was coming to the yard, and they were all shook up.

Chow time came and I went to Big Low's cell because he was on the other side of the building from me. Big Low was super juiced to see me. He told me he heard that I was running the Kumi car now which made him even more juiced, because he had a problem with a lot of the Kumi officers telling him what to do. He was looked at as a rebellious Kumi member to most of the top Kumi officers. I knew Big Low like a brother though and despite him definitely being rough around the edges, he would listen to me. I told him that I would see him when he came to the yard and I headed to chow.

After chow I saw Big Low coming to the yard and he was as big as he was when he went home. Usually convicts that go home and then come back get tremendously smaller than when they left prison because they don't continue working out on the streets. Not Big Low though. If he did lose any size while on the streets, he put it back on fast while he was back in jail.

Big Low and I gave each other a brotherly hug and then we looked over one another to see if the other had lost any muscle size. Big Low said, "Damn, you done got bigger since I was gone, now I got to play catch up!" I told big low that he didn't need to play catch up because he looked huge to me. Big Low and I caught each other up on what's been going on in-and-out of prison. I asked him if it was true that he had been shot and he said it was true and showed me the gunshot wounds. When Big Low showed me the healed wounds, I felt a sense of worry come over me because, in my eyes, if a man gets shot once he is susceptible to getting shot again. I didn't like the fact that Big Low had been shot because he was like a brother to me and I never wanted to see him harmed. It's very complicated for individuals like Big Low and I because everyone fears us because of our physical stature. If we get injured, people start to feel like we are vulnerable to harm just like anyone else, and so the people that used to fear us tend to be the ones cheering for us to get harmed.

Big Low and I talked the entire time we were on the yard and he told me that he would more than likely be going back to H-unit. Big Low liked it in H-unit a lot more than north block because he had more freedom to move around in H-unit. Big Low only had about six months to do before he was discharged from parole.

Big Low and I had gotten about ten days of working out together when he was called to go to H-unit. I saw the look on all the faces of the weak Kumi members that feared him, and it was obvious that they were happy as hell that he was getting sent to H-unit. People feared Big Low because he was unpredictable and would knock anybody out at any given time, friend or foe.

Once Big Low went to H-unit, things on the yard were a lot calmer. It was crazy how one individual could have an entire prison on pins and needles. Things were mellow when Big Low went to H-unit, but things certainly weren't mellow in H-unit where he was moved to. Big Low was in H-unit causing a ruckus. In one month's time, he had already knocked out three guys and most of them were dudes that were from his neighborhood in Fillmore.

Big Low didn't care what gang someone was with. If he had a problem with you, he would confront it with a flying fist. Everyone was scared of Big Low and unfortunately I was the only person that could talk to him and give him my brotherly outlook on things and stop him from being spontaneous. I knew in my heart that he wouldn't last long in H-unit before he was sent back to north block or the hole. Once Big Low was back in San Quentin, my entire energy went into being worried about what he would do next. I knew that many inmates feared him and if inmates were fearful of someone for too long they would conspire to stab or jump the person they feared. I was continuously worried about Big lLow but he thought that no one was bigger or badder than him, and that all the inmates knew they couldn't fuck with him.

A couple of months had passed and Big Low had knocked out so many inmates that I stopped counting. On one particular day, all the Kumi members from H-unit came up to north block to talk to me about him. They said that Big Low and a top Kumi officer had a heated argument at their job so they were going to discipline Big Low. Me, being the most respected Kumi member at San Quentin, pulled my rank and told them that nothing of the sort was going to happen until I got all the details of what took place. I told them to come back to the north block yard at the night time yard with Big Low so we could resolve the issue.

Night time yard came fast, which was typical when there was a chance of violence occurring. All of the 50 plus Kumi members came to the north block yard and Big Low made his grand appearance after everyone was already on the yard. He had his war gear on, which consisted of a beanie hat, thick jean jacket, jean pants, boots, and thick prison gloves. He walked alone like he was a warrior going to war. I saw the look in Big Low's eyes and they had a killer look about them that I was oh so familiar with. I met him half way to the destination that he was set for.

"What's up, bra?" I said.

He immediately went into a heated rave about the fake ass Kumi members who were conspiring against him because he wasn't doing what they wanted him to do. I got his side of the story and I knew that Big Low didn't lie; he told things like they were with no sugar coating about it. After him and I talked, we met up with the Kumi members and Big Low ranted out, "All some fake ass Kumi niggas, nigga! I'll beat all yall asses one-by-one right now!" At that point Big Low took off his jean jacket to expose his buff body. He resembled a peacock when it spreads out its wings to scare off other animals. I mean, when he took off his jacket the entire yard went quiet. Big Low was huge but when he got mad he looked twice the size that he was. He called out each and every one of the Kumi members that were accusing him and none of them stepped to the plate to take him on, which was a sign of cowardice to the Kumi organization.

The Kumi cats in H-unit were talking about jumping Big Low, but they were scared to fight him individually. I looked at all of the

H-unit Kumi officers as weak at that point and I had no more respect for them because they were cowards. Big Low went on to say that he would see them at work the next day and that he was going to make them fight him. The rest of the night was full of tension. Big Low and I talked the entire yard time about what would take place the next day. He had already made up his mind about what he was going to do to the "Kumi suckas."

The next day came and I was waiting on the word that Big Low and the other Kumi members had gotten into a fight, but I never heard anything about it. That night on the yard, Big Low came to talk to me and he said that the coward Kumi niggas didn't even go to work, that they'd rather lose a day off their prison sentence than fight him, which was totally a coward move.

The second day came and I was waiting again for the word that Big Low and the other Kumi members had gotten into a brawl, and once again no word came to me which was very odd because he always did what he said he was going to do.

Big Low came to the north block yard to tell me that the Kumi cowards didn't show up to work for the second day and they should be removed from their position and I agreed. One thing Kumi didn't tolerate was cowardly members and it was evident that these Kumi officers were showing cowardice to the upmost, and I was going to remove them from their position A.S.A.P.

The third day of the Big Low saga continued, and when I got word that he was transferred to north block for undisclosed reasons, I immediately found out what cell he was sent to and paid him a visit. Big Low was making his bed when I got there.

"You made it up here with yo Patna, huh?" I said.

"Yeah them suckas snitched on me to the police saying that I was a threat to other inmates!" Big Low replied.

I was happy that he was in north block with me so that I could monitor his actions. It felt as though Big Low was my younger brother that I had to protect and watch out for, because he was a reactionary and I was a thinker.

Once the inmates in north block found out that Big Low was back, I saw everyone's look of despair, but I was happy that I had my workout partner back.

Since Big Low was back with me, every other prison gang was once again on pins-and-needles, especially since it wasn't only me and Big Low that people had to worry about, we also had big Charlie with us too. We were the swolest cats on the yard and we were all Kumi members so we ran the prison and everyone knew it.

I had been incarcerated for five years and doing time at San Quentin turned out to be a bad decision for me because I lost all my good time. What this meant was that I had to do my entire seven years that I was sentenced to at the prison.

The 85% of the seven years that I was to do had become 100% and left me with having to do time for all my seven years. I lost my good time for getting into fights, like the one with KB (where I lost about 90 days), and getting wrote up for not going to work on days I didn't feel like it, like the time I didn't go to work when I was working on the garbage truck in that deadly El Niño storm.

By that time I was institutionalized anyway and so I didn't care about going to the streets. I had status in a well-respected gang and I was eating when I wanted to eat. That was all that mattered to me at that point in my life. I think when I got to San Quentin that I realized that I was going to do the majority of my sentence because my appeal for my half time was denied, but I didn't care about that anyway.

Things were going smooth as possible on the north block yard. Big Low had knocked out a few inmates and so had I. It seemed like he and I were in competition on who knocked out the most dudes on the yard. Well there's one knock out I'll never forget, which made me a knockout legend in the penal system.

"Prison Ball"

There was a football league that was put together in San Quentin; My Kumi crew and I put together an all-star team with 90% Kumi members and the other 10% were people that wanted to be Kumi. Big Low, Big Charlie and I could take on a team by ourselves; we weren't only massive with muscles but we could all run faster than our smaller counter parts. We had one hell of a team, and we were so good that the prison even went and got a college team to play us. The college team was nervous and I could see it. We were very physical with them and they would try to outsmart us or run trick plays, but what they didn't realize was that I played college football and I knew all the tricks. Big Low and Big Charlie were amazing players in high school so we were dominating the college team and the entire prison was watching and cheering us on. One of the college players had a bad accident when he got hit by one of us and fell into some rocks on the ground. It left a gaping hole in his knee cap and the game was canceled but we still won. Kumi and I had won by 21 points and we were excited and ready to take on the Oakland Raiders now.

After we mauled the college team, the inmates started scouting for the best football players in the prison and they were even holding try-outs in hopes of putting a team together to try and beat us. Finally after a week of practicing, the San Quentin prison team said that they were ready to play us and we accepted their challenge. The word was out that the Kumi team was going to play the so called San Quentin all-stars. Everyone on the yard was hoping that the all-stars would beat us because once again the little people wanted to see the giants fall.

The game started off good. We had the entire prison watching us pounce on the all-stars. On this one particular play, the ball was thrown to the swolest Asian on the yard. The Asian cat had hit one of my comrades pretty hard during a play when we had the ball, so I vowed that I would tear him a new ass hole if he ever got the ball. My chance came sooner than I thought it would. The Asian was thrown the ball on a ten yard hook and as soon as he caught it and had started turning to run, I was there with the hardest hit in the prison systems history.

I laid the poor fella out and I had knocked the wind out of him. I looked at him after I hit him and said, "Now, how did you like that?"

Once I said what I did, I turned to walk back to the huddle and that's when I felt something hit my back. I turned around and the Asian had thrown the ball at me, so I walked over to him already knowing what I was going to do. I asked him why he did what he did, and before he opened his mouth I cracked him in the jaw so hard I thought his head was going to pop off. He was out for the count and I calmly walked away and went to camouflage myself in with all the inmates that were on the yard watching the football game. It hadn't been two minutes when one of the correctional officers came right to where I was and told me to come with him. I had been busted and I knew that I would be going to the hole. The guard escorted me to the captain's office and when I got there the Asian was already waiting outside the office to go in as well. The Asian and I talked while we waited to meet with the captain and he told me that he was set to go to his parole hearing in a few months and that he didn't want this to hurt his chances of getting out of prison. He explained that he had already been in prison for 10 years. I told him that I would just tell them that I had tackled him to the ground and that we weren't fighting. He was thankful for me trying to get him out of this situation. Lifer inmates would do anything to get out of prison. Once in the captain's office, the captain asked me what happened and I told him, "We were playing football and he caught the ball and I tackled him! What did you guys think happened?"

The captain looked at me with a look that told me that he knew I was lying. He gave me a smirk and said simply, "That's not what my guards told me they saw."

"Sir that's what happened, he just tackled me" the Asian chimed in.

The captain didn't know who to believe because the guard that said he saw what happened was in a tower that was far from where the incident took place, so what he saw could have been misjudged. The captain laughed a little and said, "You guys conspired good on this one and I can't do anything with it so make sure nothing else happens after this."

We both said thanks and went our separate ways back to our cells. When I got back, my celly, Bay, asked me if everything was alright and I told him that I got away with it. The guard in the tower couldn't say exactly what he had seen and my story and the Asian's were the same so we didn't even get a write up. Bay said, "Nigga, you hit that boy so hard it sounded like somebody shot a gun. Whatever you do, please don't hit me!" We started laughing and we talked about that incident for days to come.

"Nino Brown"

few months had passed since I had knocked the Asian out on the football field, and now I was working in R&R (the reception center where all the inmates from other prisons were brought in to San Quentin). R&R was the best job to have in San Quentin because it was where all the drugs came in from. Before I started working in R&R, I had never seen crack.

I was a barber in R&R, so when an inmate came to San Quentin and his hair was too long I would cut it to the required length. At this time in prison, no one could have hair longer than three inches. At the time I had dreadlocks and I was one of the first inmates to write the superior courts about it being illegal for the prison to make me cut my hair. I had a good argument under the law of religion. I told them I was a Rastafarian and that it was against my religion to cut my hair. I fought long and hard to keep my dreadlocks but the superior court said that the prison had the right to enforce the hair rule. I didn't care at that point; I was adamant about keeping my hair so I twisted my dreadlocks down to my scalp so that it appeared that I only had three inches of hair. It worked out magnificently.

Working in R&R was great! I was selling cans of tobacco for drugs to sell on the yard. It was very exciting to sell drugs in prison. It was crazy how much the lifers wanted the crack rock. They would sell whatever they had to get it. All I took from them were food and cosmetics, nothing else. When the word got out that I had some crack, the four lifers I dealt with the most would come running to my cell saying that they was getting a package in a few days and they would pay me then. I never gave out credit, so if the person didn't have the items at the time of the transaction I wouldn't give them the crack. I had seen too many problems occur in prison behind drug debts and I refused to have to hurt someone because I trusted them to pay me my money. I never understood how people gave a drug addict something for credit, and I didn't do it in prison or on the streets. Whenever I got crack, which was about three times a week, it was first come first serve with whoever had the money. I, of course, knew that this crack selling thing would not last long because San Quentin was full of snitches who would be quick to tell on me if they were in a bind.

Things were going good at this point in San Quentin. I was making money and I had enough food to feed a small village. Big Low had calmed down on his violent sprees and the Kumi members were all doing what they were supposed to be doing, but I knew that these good times wouldn't last long in San Quentin. Something was bound to happen eventually.

I always followed my intuition, so I ran a military drill to ensure that we would be prepared when the violence struck. The drills were simple and my defense officer was in charge of strategically placing our soldiers where they needed to be so that they could have a clear view of the entire yard in case something drastic happened. The entire object of the drill was to make sure that each soldier looked for the commanding officer to give a signal of attack or retreat. The drill went good but we had the soft Kumi members asking why we were doing them, and insisting that nothing was going to happen on the yard. I immediately shut the Kumi member down and said, "This is prison and anything can happen at any given time. It is my job to make sure that my soldiers are prepared for whatever." There was still mumbling about nothing happening on the yard, but I told them to make sure they were ready when it went down. The main person in doubt was usually the softest one that was going to run when a riot happened.

I knew something was about to happen on the San Quentin yard; I could just feel it in my bones. I knew that God had given me certain gifts and that one of them was knowing and feeling when something good or bad was going to happen. I was never wrong. Word was out that one of Big Lows' patnas from his block had beaten up a Mexican because the Mexican owed him some money. As soon as Big Low found out, we went to his patna's cell and asked him what had happened. His patna told us that he had given the Mexican some weed in agreement that the Mexican was going to pay him on a certain day, however, the Mexican didn't hold up to his end of the bargain and so Big Low's patna whooped his ass. See what I was telling you guys about not trusting someone to pay you later? There was always a problem, and because of this situation that had nothing to do with Kumi members, it would seem as though it was our problem. The Mexicans came to Big Low and me, saying that the Mexican wanted to fight again. We agreed and the Mexican immediately squared off with Big Low's patna, but the Mexican was demolished in a matter of seconds. The Mexican's friends had to pick him up off the floor and take him to his cell. At this time we all knew that this would cause a riot, so Big Low and I went to all the Kumi members and told them that we had to arm ourselves because Big Low's patna just whooped a Mexican that owed him some money. The Mexicans didn't seem like they were too happy about what had happened, so all the Kumi members armed themselves and prepared for the worst. I had a college class to go to at the time, so I gave instructions on what to do if a problem came about.

While I was in class, I distinctly felt that something bad was going to happen at chow time. The class went by fast and after I was released I started walking to the chow hall and I saw that all my Kumi soldiers had already eaten dinner and were waiting for me to eat my food so that we could go to the yard. As I was walking towards my soldiers, I saw a Mexican creeping up behind them and I screamed out, "Watch out behind you!" As soon as I said that, KB tried to run instead of turning to face the Mexican and fight, and so he was stabbed in the upper back. I ran over to help in the fight and knocked out two of the Mexicans fast. One of my soldiers had one Mexican in a full nelson and we continuously beat him until the guards started shooting their rifles from the tower.

After everyone was down on the ground, all the San Quentin guards came running to the scene. Big Low, Big Charlie, Bay, KB and I got as far away from the crime scene as possible. That's when we realized that KB was bleeding badly. We put pressure on the puncture wound in hopes that KB wouldn't have to go to the hospital to get stitches because that would definitely incriminate him as being a part of the riot. The guards went to every inmate to check their body and hands for any signs of being involved in the fight. They came to KB and told him to stand up and take off his jacket. As soon as his jacket was off, the guard looked at his back and saw the puncture wound and all hell broke loose. The guard called other guards and they came running over to where we were and told KB to put his hands behind his back.

The guards then came over to look at all our hands and Big Charlie's hand was bruised up so they took him as well. When the guards looked at the hands of Bay, Big Low and me, we were cleared to go back to our cells. At this point there were only four Kumi members left on the yard: Bay, Big Low, Ant, Big Low's celly, and myself. We talked on the way back to our cells and we told one another to stay on our toes at all times. Deep down, I knew that I was going to go to the hole because I was the shot caller of the Kumi gang, and San Quentin wasn't going to allow me to continue with my reign there. I told Bay that I had a feeling I was going to the hole and he kept saying that if the guards wanted me they would've taken me at the scene. At that point, I knew that Bay wasn't too smart about how the San Quentin staff worked and I began preparing myself to go to the hole despite his doubts. I had some tobacco and I knew that tobacco was like gold in the hole, so I put some of it in one of the fingers of my rubber glove and stuffed it until it couldn't be stuffed anymore. I had never stuffed anything up my ass before, but I knew that if I went to the hole with nothing to barter with that I would literally starve for about a month. As I was getting everything prepared for my possible transfer to the hole, Bay kept telling me that I wasn't going, but I knew better.

"Back to the Hole"

The next morning came and the guards announced that the prison was on lock down pending investigation of the riot that happened; therefore, each ethnic race would go to the chow hall separately. After the very talkative chow meeting between Big Low, Bay, Ant and myself, we went back to our cells. After about one hour in the cell, I heard a guard coming down the tier and I knew there was no reason for him to be walking the tier right after chow time so my heart started racing nervously. The guard stopped at my cell with some plastic bags and called my name. He said that I needed to pack my belongings because I was being sent to the hole for the riot that had happened the day before. The guard told me I had 30 minutes to be ready and I said alright. I had already packed all my things prior to the guard coming anyway because I already knew that I was getting sent to the hole. After the guard left my cell, I heard him at Big Low's cell telling him the same thing he told me. Big Low yelled to me that he was going to the hole and I told him that I was too. Now, the hardest thing in my life was upon me, and that was getting that rubber glove full of tobacco up my ass.

All I could think about was losing my muscle while in the hole and I refused to starve like I did the first time I went there. I greased that glove up and the more I pushed the tighter it seemed like my ass got. This was one of the reasons why I couldn't understand how people got raped in prison, because that asshole tightens up automatically when something is trying to get forced in it. I was sweating trying to get that tobacco up there and after ten minutes of trying I had come to the conclusion that I was going to starve because I couldn't possibly get that shit up my ass. I relaxed for about five minutes and thought about the time I would have to probably do in the hole and I got motivated to try and get that tobacco up my ass again. I greased it down and I tried to relax as much as possible. I slowly pushed that tobacco up my anal canal and once it was in there it was like a vacuum and shot straight up my ass. I was happy as hell because I knew that I wouldn't starve after all.

The guard came to the cell to take me to the hole and I gave Bay a hug and told him to hold it down on the yard because he and Ant were the only ones left, and he said he would. Once outside the cell, the guard told me to put my hands behind my back because he had to handcuff me while I was being escorted to the hole. I saw all the inmates looking out of their cells with a look of happiness because they knew the power of Kumi was no longer going to be there and they were happy because of it. Once I got to the east block hole, it was pure pandemonium. It was so loud from the death row inmates and the inmates that were sent to the hole that it would drive a weak man crazy. As soon as I was placed in the holding cage that I had become so familiar with during my other stint in the hole, one of the death row inmates called my name. I said, "Habari ghani?", which means "what's up" in Swahili. The man was a death row inmate named Frank that I had met on my first stint in the hole.

"What you doing back in here?" he said. I could hear in his voice that he was happy to see me back in the pits of hell with him.

"Oh, you know, a little of this and a little of that!" I responded.

We spoke in Swahili most of the conversation so that people that didn't know Swahili wouldn't know what we were talking about. Frank asked me if I needed anything and I told him that I didn't. The guard then came and handed me my sheets and blankets and put the handcuffs on me to take me to my cell. As I was walking down the tier, I saw some of my Kumi soldiers as well as some of the Mexicans that we had the riot with. All my soldiers that were in the hole started calling my name in an uproar. I jokingly told them all that I had to come to join the party, knowing damn well that I didn't want to be in the hole but I couldn't show them anything but strength. Once my folks on death row, Rob and G-Man, heard people calling my name, they immediately called out my name too.

"We knew you was going to come back and see us!" They shouted.

"You know I had to come back and see you guys, I was missing you!" I replied jokingly. Of course, they knew damn well that I didn't want to be back in there. They asked me if I wanted anything and I told them a few Top Ramen soups to hold me over until I sold the tobacco I had. They said that they would send me some by the guards and I said cool. I asked them if they wanted some of the tobacco I had and they said they did. After I cleaned the nasty ass cell I was in with a ton of disinfectant that I had the guard bring me, I tried to push the tobacco out of my ass and it wasn't moving an inch.

I started talking to my Kumi soldiers about keeping their mouths closed over the tiers about what took place, and I also told them that if they didn't know Swahili that they needed to learn because we would be speaking mostly in the Swahili dialect while we were in the hole. I told Rob to send me down all the Swahili words he had so that I could distribute them amongst our comrades, and he said that he was on it. After receiving the Top Ramen soups and Swahili words from Rob and G-Man, I told the soldiers that I was shutting down for the night to handle business and they all understood. Big Low was about eight cells down from me, so we were able to talk to one another without killing our vocal chords.

I immediately started writing the Swahili words down so that I could distribute them amongst the Kumi soldiers. I was up for hours trying to finish writing all the words, because there had to be about a thousand of them. I finally stopped and tried to get some rest but living in the hole was crazy as hell. Just when you think you are going to get some sleep, some crazy motherfucker starts yelling at the top of his lungs for hours and there's nothing you can do about it. The ones that did all the screaming and yelling were unable to be touched, so they went on with their antics.

I got a few hours of sleep, probably about 3 to be exact, because the first few days in the hole were treacherous. I was definitely sleep deprived when the guard came to my cell early the next with my food – which looked like slop if you asked me. Once the guard saw that it was me, he instantly asked me what I was doing back in the hole.

"You know how the white man does it!" I said, and I gave the black guard a smirk and he smirked back.

I then greeted all my Kumi soldiers with the Swahili greeting,"Njema asabui!", which means "Good morning". It took 10 minutes to greet all the soldiers in the hole. After eating the slop, I finished writing the Swahili words and passed them on to Big Low so he could write them down. Things were chaotic in the hole because there weren't any strong Kumi cats there before us, so I would be setting order.

The days in the hole drug along day-to-day. All there was to do was read, work out, think, and sleep. Fortunately, I had the tobacco to barter with until I went to the store, otherwise I would have starved. I looked out for Big Low, Big Charlie, and a few of the other soldiers, but ultimately I had to conserve what I could for myself because I wasn't going to starve for anyone.

The day finally came when we were all able to go to the yard and get some fresh air. The guards escorted us out one by one in handcuffs with nothing on but our boxers. When Rob and G-Man saw me walking the corridor to go to the Norteño, Kumi, and BGF yard, they went ballistic. They all said that I was huge as hell, and I started to feel like a star with the way they were pumping my head up. I got the same feeling I always got whenever I saw Rob or G-Man; I was overcome with sorrow because I knew that I could have easily been in their shoes on death row and it sent chills throughout my body.

Once on the northern gang yard, the Mexicans that were running the yard showed the intimidation they had towards us on their faces. Big Low, Big Charlie and I looked like silver back gorillas, and better yet we acted like it too. When we got on the gang yard, we shook all the Norteño Mexican's hands to greet them with respect. Once everyone was on the yard, the Norteño began running the machine. I had already told myself that I wasn't doing the machine in the hole this time because I wasn't going to lose all the muscle that I had worked so hard for. Big Low and Big Charlie were right along with me, so Softy did the machine while we watched him.

Once they were done, Big Charlie, Big Low and I began our workout consisting of weighted pushups, where we sat on each other's back with all of our weight so that we could stress our muscles into growth. After pushups we did weighted dips where someone had to pull down on the person doing the dips. Then after the dips we moved on to upside down pushups, which were hell but we still did them weighted by pushing down on the person doing them. After upside down push-ups, we went to side laterals; we did these by holding the arms down just enough to give about 30 pounds of pressure. Then we went to the front raises doing the same pressure method. Then we did reverse laterals for the rear delts by putting pressure on the arms the same way we did for the laterals, the only difference was that the person doing the exercise was bent over as if he had dumbbells in his hand and the person putting the pressure would be standing in front of the exerciser with pressure on the elbows. This workout caused us to have the same effect as if we were in a gym, and the correctional officers hated that we learned how to improvise even though they had taken the weights out of California prisons.

The first day on the yard went good. There weren't any fights or stabbings and we got an amazing workout. I was tired as hell when I got back to the cell, and it wasn't a day where we got to take showers so I was sweaty as hell too. On the days where we weren't able to take showers, the inmates in east block would take bird baths. Bird baths consisted of taking a shower with toilet water, that's right, toilet water. This is the process of a bird bath – I would first get naked in the cell and the thing about getting naked in the cell was that anybody could walk by and see you at any time. If a female correctional officer walked by and didn't like that someone was naked in their cell, they could frame an inmate and say that the inmate was masturbating in front of them. Of course the prison officials would believe the correctional officer over an inmate, which would cause a write up and possibly some lost time. Once naked in the cell, I would lather up some soap with a sock and I would scrub my body as if I were in a shower. Then I would have either a cup or a milk carton to scoop some water into so that I could pour it over my body until all the soap was gone, just like I was in a shower. While rinsing off with the toilet water, there would be a substantial amount of water that would run down the tiers, but an expert bird bather knew how to keep the water to a minimum. After the bird bath, I would have to clean the entire cell because of the excess water on the floor. Bird baths were a difficult process but it was something that had to be done to stay clean or else I would have to wait one to two days before I could take a legitimate shower.

After getting over the first couple of weeks of being in the hole, it started to feel like home. Nothing bothered me about the hole anymore, not after two weeks of living in the noise infested place. As long as I was able to eat when I wanted to I was happy. In fact, Big Low, Big Charlie and I were actually getting bigger in the hole because we weren't participating in doing the burpees. We were all going to the store and spending the maximum amount we could spend which was thirty-five dollars a month. I know it doesn't sound like much but it worked. I would buy four cases of Top Ramen soup, which would be approximately ninety-six soups and cost almost twenty dollars. I made sure I had my soups first and then I would prioritize anything else I needed, such as soap and tooth paste. After I got the hygiene things I needed, I would then buy some things to snack on such as potato chips or candy bars. I made sure I spent my thirty-five dollars wisely. This is where I learned how to manage money to a science.

After all of us 415 Kumi members went to see the prison officials, they told us that they were going to transfer all of us to different prisons to split up the 415 Kumi strong hold at San Quentin. I personally didn't care about getting transferred because I didn't do anything but get into a mass amount of trouble at San Quentin anyway, so I definitely welcomed the change. Out of all of us, Big Low was the most worried because he was supposed to get out in a couple of months and he was concerned that being in the hole with another charge could possibly get him some more time with his parole.

Time started going by fast after we all went to the hearing because we all knew that this may be the last time that we ever see one another again in life, and that definitely turned out to be the case. The 90 days in the hole went by fast, and I think it was the 91st day that I was awakened by an officer at 2:00 a.m. telling me to pack my things because I was being transferred. I asked the officer where I was being transferred too and he said he didn't know. As I packed my things, I told all my fellow Kumi members that I was leaving and everyone said their farewells. Big Low, Big Charlie, Rob, G-Man, KB, and the rest of the crew told me to be safe and hopefully we would meet again under better circumstances. Of course Rob and G-Man jinxed me by saying not to come back when I got out of prison in a couple of years, and when they said that I told them I would definitely try not to, but while I was in prison I saw about 99% of the inmates come back and so I didn't feel exempt.

The correctional officer came back to my cell after about an hour and asked me if I was ready and I said, "Hell yeah." I sent my respects to everyone in east block hole and they sent their respect back. I was actually kind of happy at the time to be moving on to what I was hoping was a better institution where I could finish the last two years of my sentence. Once I got down to the holding where all the other inmates were getting transferred, I found out that I was going to Solano State Prison. Actually I had heard some prison talk about Solano being another drug infested prison that had a lot of 415 Kumi drug abusers, so I already had it in my mind that I was going to have that place running like a boot camp.

"Solano State Prison"

The prison bus ride to Solano took about two hours and I watched the scenery the entire time. It wasn't often that I was able to see normal people in society and all that the free world had to offer. It was an exhilarating ride that had my mind in fantasy land. Once I arrived to Solano, I automatically felt a vibe from the prison that told me there was a lot of evil lurking there, but me, being the leader and strong individual that I am, I was cheering on the good, bad, and ugly.

After I received most of my property, I was escorted to the facility I would be housed in. As we walked to our destination, all the inmates that were in the facility were crowded around us to see if we were their enemies, friends, family, comrades, or religious brothers. I only recognized one person and he was a hot headed Kumi member named Butch. Butch was a short, buff dude that had too much damn energy to be the age he was. I knew Butch from San Quentin and he was always involved in some sort of mischief. When he saw me he came running up to me and said, "What's up, Kali? I heard what went down at San Quentin and I knew some of ya'll would get transferred here." As butch walked with me to the building I was assigned to, I asked him the status of the yard and how the Kumi members were acting.

Butch was a straight forward type of guy and he said, "Kali, you got a lot of work ahead of you because this yard got too many Kumi members getting high on a daily basis!" Butch told it all fast, but what he didn't say was that he was also a part of the madness, but of course he wasn't going to snitch on himself.

As I got to my cell, Butch made a loud laugh and I asked him what was so funny. He said that I wasn't going to want to stay in the cell for long, not with the youngster that was going to be in there with me. I asked him what was wrong with the youngster and Butch said that he was a can short of a six pack. I said that I could straighten out a rattlesnake if I had too.

"Alright," Butch said, "You'll see for yourself."

As the correctional officer opened the cell door, I greeted my new celly. I told him my name is Kali and he said his name was Rafiki. He looked young as hell so we got into the usual greeting conversation new cell mates get into. Where you from? What you in jail for? Are you affiliated in any gangs? Come to find out Rafiki was actually older than me by two years but he looked as if he was about ten years younger than me. Rafiki was mixed with black and Puerto Rican, but he mostly looked Puerto Rican. He was from Berkeley California and, oh yeah, he killed his brother. When Rafiki told me about himself and his situation I didn't pass judgment because I knew the feeling. There was a time in my life that I had considered killing everybody in my house except for my brother Archie, and even he felt my wrath when I stabbed him that one time. I understood Rafiki whole heartedly. After Rafiki and I talked for a while, I took off my jumpsuit top because it was hot in the cell.

"Damn you are big as hell! That's how I want to get, will you help me?" Rafiki said.

I told Rafiki I would teach him everything I knew so that we could get him swole. Rafiki was 5'10' and maybe 140lbs soaking wet.

Prison wasn't a place to be anorexic because you never knew when you would face someone stronger and bigger than you. Being big and strong in prison was a must. The first night in the cell with Rafiki was calm and I thought that he and I would be able to be cell mates for however long we were in Solano. I didn't see any psychological problems the first day of meeting Rafiki, but I would soon find out different.

The next morning came fast and I was excited to be free from the hole and be able to move about like a normal person. Even though I was still in prison, I didn't like to feel like it. Butch met me at my cell when the doors were opened for chow time. He was already full of energy and ready to get in some mischief. I've never been a morning person, so it kind of irked me at how much Butch was ranting so early on in the morning. The good thing about Solano was that chow time was at a normal time of 7:00 a.m. All the other prisons I had been to had breakfast starting at 5:00 or 6:00 a.m., so this was a great change up. As Butch and I were walking to the chow hall, he was giving me the run down on all the Kumi members on the yard and how everything was being run.

Butch said that everybody already knew who I was and that they were a little scared about me coming and enforcing the Kumi laws – which I was going to most definitely do. Once we were in the crowded chow hall, Butch went on and on about how glad he was that a real soldier had come to the yard to get things straight. What I couldn't figure out as he was talking to me was why he didn't get the yard straight before I got there. Butch was a beast in his own right and he would fight whoever he needed to and would even stab somebody if it came down to it. I've seen Butch in action, but I would later on find out why he was unable to change the Kumi member's behavior.

Going to chow with Butch was very entertaining. He was most definitely a talker and a con man to go along with it. He told me that I would be screened by one of the Kumi officers once the yard was opened for the day, which was protocol for all new Kumi members, regardless of their status.

Before I entered the cell with Rafiki after chow, I was told by another inmate that knew him to peek in the cell door window and look at what Rafiki was doing. When I looked in the cell, Rafiki was sitting on his bunk with the television off and laughing as if he were watching a funny comedy on it. I mean, he was cracking up to the point he was crying. I watched him for a while, because I didn't want to believe that Rafiki was looney, but the signs were there telling me otherwise. Once the guard opened the cell door, Rafiki snapped out of the trance he was in.

"What's up, Rafiki?" I asked him.

"Nothing," he responded quickly.

I asked him how he got to the cell so fast and he said that when he went to chow that he put his food in a bag and brought it back to the cell because he didn't like eating around all the other inmates. I told him I understood and I asked him what he was laughing at before I walked in. He said that he was thinking about something that happened on the streets that he thought was funny. I looked at Rafiki and thought to myself, "This is a crazy motherfucka here!"

Once again, I told him I understood, but really I wanted to ask him if he was on psych meds.

An hour after chow, it was time to go to the yard and the cell doors were opened. Once again Butch was there waiting for me. He was like, "You ready bra?" and I responded that I was.

The first thing on my agenda was to go to the receiving building to get the rest of my property. The guard kept my things in order to scan everything and make sure that I didn't bring anything illegal from San Quentin. Once I received my television and the rest of my property, I felt like I was becoming myself again. Butch helped me with my things and I could tell he was scoping out all the food I had the entire time. I kept a close eye on Butch because I knew he was a crook. As I was walking my stuff across the yard, the Kumi officer that did the screenings of all new members walked up to me timidly.

"Hey Kali, when you put your stuff up I have to screen you," he said nervously.

"No problem, brother. I will put this stuff in the cell and I'll be right back!" I replied.

Butch and I took my stuff to the cell but before I went in I looked inside to find Rafiki talking to himself and I knew he had a serious problem at that point. When the cell door opened, Rafiki snapped out of his one-sided conversation and asked me how I was doing. I told him I was great and then pretended as if I hadn't seen anything abnormal. Butch and I decided to put my things under the bunk until I was able to come back to the cell and put all my shit away. Rafiki's eyes were big when he saw all the food I had and I gave him a stern look to let him know that he better not even think about touching my stuff or I would kill him.

Butch and I went back to the yard so that I could let the youngster named Gee screen me. I walked over to where the Kumi cats were and Gee met me before I even reached them and we walked around the track while I recited everything he needed to hear in record time. I could tell that Gee was intimidated by me because he told me that he had heard about me and how I was running shit at San Quentin. We talked a while and then he told me he had to inform his superiors on how the screening went. While Gee went and checked in with his superiors, I figured I would put on a show for the yard and let all the inmates know what a bad motherfucka I was. I went to the pull up bars and did two sets of regular pull-ups. I then went into the muscle-ups and the entire yard went silent as I was doing them. I had my shirt off during this time and everyone was staring at me as if they had never seen a swole motherfucka before. Inmates immediately started asking me questions about working out and about how long it took for me to start doing the muscle-ups. I had the yard in an uproar, even the guards in the towers were taking notice of the swolest cat they had ever seen in their lives. I did a complete workout and Butch jumped in trying to keep up with me but he didn't have the endurance that I had. After I was finished working out, all the Kumi members came and introduced themselves to me one by one. It felt good to be respected and I felt like this yard wasn't as bad as people said it was. I sensed that there were some good Kumi guys here. I knew it was too early to tell what was going on, but I was blessed with a keen sense of judgment of the people around me. After I was greeted by everyone and yard was over with, it was time to go back to the cell until dinner time.

When I got back to the cell, I did my usual peeking in on Rafiki and again he was laughing up a storm with no radio or television on. He was entertaining himself with old thoughts. The cell door was opened and Rafiki snapped out of his frantic laughter and said, "What's up Kali?"

"You alright bra?" I asked him.

"Oh yeah I'm cool. I just been thinking about a lot of funny things that happened in my life!" he said simply.

I decided that this was the time to find out what was really going on with Rafiki. I asked him why he killed his brother and Rafiki told me that his brother bullied him all the time while they were growing up. His brother was a few years older than him and bigger than he was. Rafiki said his brother used to push him around and embarrass him in front of people. Rafiki said that one day he and his brother were at home and his brother started hitting him in front of all the people in their neighborhood, so Rafiki ran off and got a gun that he had stashed away in case he ever needed it. He said once he got the gun, he came back to his house where his brother was outside and Rafiki pointed the gun at him. Rafiki was crying and told his brother that if he ever hit him again that he would kill him. Rafiki said that his brother started laughing and said, "Little bitch, you aint going to kill nobody." and started walking towards him. Rafiki told his brother to stop before he shot him, but his brother kept walking towards him in an aggressive manner. Rafiki pulled the trigger and shot his older brother in the chest three times before running away to a friend's house. Everybody saw what Rafiki had done in broad daylight, so there was no getting out of the situation. The police came and got Rafiki from his friend's house and he ultimately took a deal for ten years for a heat of the moment manslaughter on a family member. I understood Rafiki totally because I had stabbed my brother for trying to bully me once, so I had been in his shoes before.

After a couple of weeks of being at Solano, I got the Kumi members up and running how they were supposed to be running. The top Kumi officers at Solano were drug users that had no respect from the younger Kumi members or the rest of the inmates on the yard. Once everybody saw that a new swole Kumi cat had come to take charge, 415 Kumi had a newfound respect on the yard. I completely took over and I had all the Kumi soldiers behind me. They all feared and respected me for the strength I exuded. Getting the non-drug users in order was simple; it was the drug users that were the problem. Drug users in jail were the worst, especially when they were a part of a gang. The reason being is because 415 Kumi had laws and rules to abide by. One law being that each member had to work out, period. This is where the problem came for drug users because all they wanted to do was get high, not work out. If the Kumi member didn't uphold his obligations there would be hell to pay. Kumi soldiers not working out were a pet peeve of mine because I didn't want weaklings being a part of what I was a part of. I would give out harsh discipline if a Kumi member skipped their workout without having a legitimate excuse. Then you had the drug users that wanted to sleep a lot, and being a part of a gang in prison we had to be prepared to stay awake for days to watch out for enemies.

Drug users would get caught nodding off on heroin, which was the drug of choice for prison drug addicts because it made them forget their problems. Being a Kumi drug addict in prison was tough, because when you had people like me that hated drugs and what they did to people, I was hard on anyone that used them. Once all the Kumi members knew that I was anti-drugs, they tried their best to stay away from me.

Things were running smoothly after I got things in order with the Kumi members. There were a few incidents that I had my henchman Butch to take care of, but I always knew that I was going to have to show my Kumi soldiers and the rest of the inmates on the yard that I put in work as well.

Rafiki and I were still cell mates, but I started to realize that we couldn't be cell mates for much longer. He started trying to get swole like me, and it was cool that he was working-out, but it was the weight gain he had his family sending him that killed me. Our cells were the size of a small walk in closet and when a cell mate had to fart, that person had to sit on the toilet and flush the fart with the high powered toilet that was able to suck whole sheets without clogging. Rafiki was farting so much that he couldn't always make it to the toilet, which would drive me nuts. I told him that he stunk and that if he continued farting like he was we were going to have a problem. I mean, this dude was drinking a ton of milk and drinking those weight gainer shakes like it was going to get him buff in a matter of days. He was seriously trying to get his swole on like his hero Kali, but it just wasn't going to happen as fast as he wanted it to. I knew I inspired people but this was too the extreme and I was getting fed up.

After a few months of being at Solano, the facility was placed on an indefinite lockdown because the northern and southern Mexicans had a major riot amongst themselves. The entire facility was slammed so the guards would bring us our food to our cells. I mean, this was some serious business. While on lockdown, being in the cell with Rafiki for days on end was torture. I mean, when he wasn't farting he was laughing to himself. He had a television and radio but he never turned them on, instead he entertained himself with his past thoughts. I had reached my boiling point after the third day of being on lockdown. Rafiki farted and it smelled so bad that I hopped off my bunk and got in his face and shouted, "If you fart in this cell one more motherfucking time without getting on that god damn toilet, we are going to have problems!" I was actually being brotherly to Rafiki by giving him a warning, because had it been someone I didn't like I would have beaten them senseless in that cell. Rafiki was terrified and said that the fart slipped out of his butt and that he was sorry but he couldn't help it. I looked at him and said sternly, "When this damn lockdown is over with I am moving up out of here!" I could have made him move to a different cell, but like I said, I looked at Rafiki as my little brother and I wasn't going to push my weight around on him.

Rafiki said that he didn't want me to move, but I told him that it would be best for the both of us. Rafiki tried his best to get to that toilet when he had to fart, but it didn't sway my feelings on moving out of the cell with him.

The lockdown lasted an entire week for the blacks and whites but the Mexicans were on lockdown for the remainder of my time on that yard, which was months. Once the cell doors were opened for us to go the yard after the seventh day, I felt like a wild animal being released from a cage. I was full of bottled up energy that I had to release. Of course, I worked out in the cell during the lockdown but working out in the cell didn't compare to the strenuous workouts I did on the yard. Before I went to the yard, I asked the guard (all of them knew me by then) if there were any available black cells open and he said that there were. Come to find out it was a cell that one of my Kumi officers was in and his cell mate had gone home that morning. I told the guard to do the paperwork for me so that I could make the move that day, and he said he would. Once I got to the yard, I felt like I was 10 years old, that's how much energy I had. All the Kumi members met to discuss everything that took place and what the word on the yard was about the riot. The entire yard time was us talking about our security and our preparation for any other riots in the future. After the yard, everyone went back to the buildings they were assigned to and as soon as I stepped foot in building 11, where my cell was, the guard told me to move my things to my new assigned cell. Even though I cared for him, I was happy as hell to leave that nut case Rafiki. He had a sad look on his face as I was packing my things. Inmates get used to having a cell mate that they get along with and meeting a new cellmate sucks, but though I felt for Rafiki, I didn't feel bad enough to stay.

My new cell was only five cells down, so it was easy to move my things to the new cell with my Kumi soldier. The only hard part about my move was having to hook up the two radios I had hooked up to a tape player. I mean, I was in prison, but when those radios were hooked up it sounded like a car with a banging radio system and it had the walls shaking when it was on.

After I was situated in the cell, I finally felt comfortable in my skin. It was nice not having to worry about my cell mate laughing or farting uncontrollably. I felt like I was in heaven at that point. My new celly was one of my Kumi officers and he respected me like an older brother. He was younger than me but he had a life sentence for doing something stupid in the streets of Oakland. He was quiet and laid back and when I told him to jump he asked how high, so this made it all good.

It had been a month since I had moved in with my new celly, "D", and things couldn't have been better for me being in prison. The thing about prison was that it could change in a matter of seconds though, and unfortunately it did, and in a major way.

There were a couple of high ranking Kumi members that didn't like the Palo Alto cats that were on the yard because they were getting all the weed in the prison. They had a female correctional officer bringing it in by the pounds, so they were the most popular cats there. In prison the group that had the most dope to distribute was the most favorite group on the yard.

The Palo Alto cats were all in my building and I hung out with them a lot. Either they were working out with me or we were playing chess together, and ultimately they were good guys. Jealousy was the culprit in Gino and Run rRun's heart and they tried to tell me that they wanted to move on the Palo Alto cats for no reason at all.

I told them that it wasn't going to happen, because they were just jealous of those cats. A week after that conversation, an incident happened where one of the Palo Alto cats said something disrespectful about Kumi to some of the Kumi cat's faces and I was immediately informed about it because I was a porter in my building and I wasn't allowed to go to the night yard that particular night. The word got to me fast that

Bam from Palo Alto said, "Fuck Kumi" and once the yard was closed I approached Bam about what he had said and he apologized. He explained that he didn't mean it the way it was taken, which wasn't true, but he knew that the statement would cause a problem on the yard and so he tried to recant. It was too late though because I had already told myself and every other Kumi member that if there were any more problems between Kumi and Palo Alto that we would attack them. Even though I listened to Bam, I knew that the next morning on the yard it was going to go down on the Palo Alto cats.

All night I mapped out how I would set up my attack squad. I had to figure out which Kumi soldiers I could afford to lose because when things like this went down someone was definitely going to the hole.

The next morning at chow, everything was extremely quiet in the hall. Everybody was always on pins and needles before a riot happened on the prison yard. Inmates would grow silent not knowing what to expect or when to expect it. I informed all Kumi members that when the yard opened all of them were to go to their assigned destination so that we would have the Palo Alto cats surrounded when we attacked them. Yeah, I know, it's crazy that even though these Palo Alto dudes were my patnas that I still had to do them in, but that was just the way prison operated. When the cell doors opened to go to the yard, I was pumped up because I had my plan down to a tee. As I hit the yard, I saw that everyone was at their assigned position, but there was an eerie silence there and that was a red light to the guards because it was usually a sign that something was about to happen. I had Butch and my celly with me; they were like my mini-me henchmen. I walked around the yard and told them the plan and they all felt good about it. I went to the biggest Kumi cat we had on the yard, whose name was big l, and I told him that he had been designated to attack Bam for disrespecting Kumi. I looked him in the eyes to see if I saw any fear there, and though I did, Big l told me that he would handle it.

The plan was for Butch, my celly, Big l and me to walk up to the Palo Alto cats and ask Bam why he said what he did. That was going to be the signal for Big l to start beating up Bam. I asked Big l three times if he was up for the task and he reassured me all three times that he was, but all along I had some doubts in Big l because he seemed soft to me. Like I said, I know a book by its cover when it came down to convicts.

It was a beautiful day outside. Solano was placed right by Sacramento California so the weather was mostly warm all the time. I had never seen Solano as quiet as it was that day. Not only was it quiet, but usually the workout apparatuses were covered with inmates, but there wasn't anyone doing any pull ups, pushups, or anything of the sort. Everybody was standing along the walls with a look on their faces like they knew something was about to happen. As the four of us were putting the finishing touches on the attack, Butch said, "Here they come now!" I looked Big 1 in his eyes and asked him if he was ready, and with a crackling voice he responded that he was. All four of us proceeded to meet the Palo Alto cats and when we got face to face with them I asked Bam, just like I'd planned, why he said what he did about Kumi. I then looked at Big 1 because that was his queue to start fucking Bam up, but he didn't budge. I got into dialogue with Bam and the rest of the Palo Alto cats and we squashed the beef. They walked off and we walked off in a different direction. I was steaming; I couldn't believe that 6'6" 300 lb nigga Big 1 didn't do what he was supposed to do. I walked off with Big 1 and Butch to where the pull up bars were and I asked Big 1 why he didn't take off on Bam like he said he was going to do. As soon as Big 1 started talking, I quickly hit him with a fast upper cut to his jaw and his eyes rolled in his head and he dropped to the ground. On his fall to the ground his head hit the pull up bar and Big 1 was out cold and shaking like a fish out of water. As soon as he hit the ground, Butch, my celly and I quickly walked off before we were identified. Once the guard looked down from the tower above the scene, he immediately hit the alarm and everyone on the yard was told to lay flat on their stomachs. I looked back at Big 1 and he was still shaking. I actually got scared because I thought I may have killed the guy and killing someone in prison carries a life sentence just like killing someone on the streets.

The guards rushed over to see what was wrong with Big 1 and all the inmates said he had a seizure. That's what all inmates say when someone is beaten or badly hurt on a prison yard. The medical staff rushed to give Big 1 medical attention and the ambulance came onto the yard to take him to the hospital. After they took Big 1 off the yard, all the guards at Solano came to assist with the body search that the prison always did when they suspected that an act of violence had occurred. I didn't think I was going to get caught because none of the guards saw what had happened, but I also knew that there were a lot of snitches on Solano's yard. There were so many snitches that Solano had the moniker "Tell-lano".

The guards searched each inmate one at a time and we were on that yard for about three hours after the incident happened. I knew that I got a clean shot on Big l, so my hand shouldn't swell up. When the guard came to check my hands, he saw nothing wrong with them so he told me to sit back down. I was relieved, but I was still worried about getting snitched on.

Once in my cell, I had anxiety because I knew that someone was going to tell on me. I paced the cell, thinking the whole time about going to the hole and starving and losing all the weight I had worked so hard to gain. My celly was called to go to work in the kitchen, so I didn't have anyone to talk to at the time.

I finally laid down and took a nap until I was awakened by the sound of cell doors opening. I looked out the cell window and I didn't see any of the black's cell doors opening, so that meant that the blacks were on lock down until the administration figured out what had happened. Dinner was brought to all the blacks' cells and we were told by the guards that we were on lock down indefinitely. When the guards said indefinitely, you never knew what that meant. I had a ton of nervous energy because I didn't know whether or not the guards would be coming to my cell door. It could happen at any given moment, and it was very stressful waiting on what could be a terrible fate.

The next morning came too damn fast and the blacks were fed in their cells again. I talked my celly's ears off about the situation and he agreed that if I was going to the hole that I would have been sent there already. Luckily my celly played chess, so I beat up on him in chess for a while as we were on lockdown. I watched television and did a workout to relieve myself of the worry I had. When the guard brought our dinner, he told us that we were getting off lockdown the next morning. I was relieved because that meant that I was in the clear. I felt all the way better after hearing that good news.

The doors to the cells opened at 7:00 a.m. and I felt full of energy. I think Solano was the only prison that I felt good at most of the time. I guess it was the clean air in that area of California or something. When my henchmen and I got to the chow hall, we discussed the events that took place and while we were talking, all my new friends at Solano came to me joking around and saying things like, "Whatever you do, please don't hit me!" I felt somewhat bad because I didn't want people to fear me. A scared man was definitely more likely to fight harder, so I was never into making people fear me; I just wanted the upmost respect from my fellow inmates.

When I got to the yard everyone was looking at me with fear in their eyes and I didn't like it. I had the entire yard thinking that I was a good guy, but when they saw the violent side in me – which was good for respect measures – everyone knew that if they had a problem with Kumi that I would attack with an iron fist. This could cause a person to do whatever he had to to protect himself. I greeted everyone on the yard and everyone greeted me in return. I proceeded to go and talk to Run Run and Gino about the situation, and they were always in agreement with me because they knew I made the right decisions all the time.

As I was talking to Gino and Run Run, I saw Big l walking over to where we were at and I met him in his path with aggression, ready to knock him out again. Big l saw the aggression on my face and he said, "I come in peace Kali!"

"What's up bra, you alright, huh?" I said once I realized he wasn't there to fight.

He started smiling and he said that he knew that he screwed up the hit, and that it was because he got cold feet. I told him that I had asked him multiple times if he was ready to handle business and each time he said he was. He kept saying, "I know Kali, I fucked up!" and then he started laughing and said, "Kali you hit me so hard I had a seizure!"

"The good thing is that you are alright," I said. I told him I would talk to him later and he was cleared to go back to his building to get some much needed rest.

I then went back over to Gino and Run Run with butch by my side every step of the way. I told them what Big l said and they all started laughing.

"That nigga is crazy because aint no way I could let yo buff ass get that close to me again and knock me the fuck out!" Run Run laughed, and we all laughed with him.

Dinner came around and I usually just went to the chow hall because that's when pertinent information was divulged about whatever was going on in the prison. I couldn't eat much of the prison food because I still incorporated the Islamic values into my life. Therefore, I couldn't eat hardly any of the meat the prison had because I never knew what was in it, so what I couldn't eat I usually gave to my celly or another Kumi soldier. The only type of meat I ate in prison was chicken, tuna, and oysters.

I had gotten word while we were in the chow hall that Big l had rolled himself off the yard. When an inmate rolls themselves off the yard, that means that they tell the guards, for whatever reason, that they can no longer be there. I didn't realize that I had said some things that had made Big l scared, but when I look back on the conversation we had that morning, I guess I did say some things that would have made a person nervous. When people got to know me they usually got a vibe of sneakiness from me, mainly because I was so calm whenever I talked. On top of that, all the stories that people were generating about me in the prison system, – about me and the way I handled things – were all pretty sneaky. Being sneaky was a tool in my arsenal that I had learned from watching all the gangsters in Oakland. Sneakiness was something they all possessed, and it was a talent I used to my advantage. It was one of my best criminal qualities and I took pride in it.

I was glad that Big l rolled himself off the yard, because of course I wouldn't have been able to trust him after I knocked him out. He knew in his heart that he did the best thing for the both of us.

After my infamous knockout on the yard, everybody that didn't speak to me before spoke to me with much more respect now. I felt like the king of the yard. I was the swolest dude there and I had all my Kumi soldiers doing whatever I told them to. On top of all that, it definitely helped that I was known to knock motherfuckers out. I was a pure threat to all the other prison gangs. I had so much respect on the yard at that point, and with all the Mexicans on lockdown, there weren't too many problems except amongst our own Kumi members.

A couple of months had passed since the infamous knockout and one of my childhood friends, Shawn, came to the yard. Not only was Shawn a childhood friend of mine, but he was also Kumi. I was glad to see Shawn because we were real close growing up. Shawn was about 5'10" and he weighed about 150 lbs. He was skinny as hell and I told him that I was going to put some muscle on his narrow ass. He always told me to not let his size fool me. I hadn't seen Shawn in years, so I didn't know how he was as a person, but I would soon find out.

After a couple of weeks of Shawn being on the yard, the Kumi members and I – along with numerous other inmates – started having a lot of spats with him. Shawn was turning out to be a problem. Not only was Shawn Kumi, but he was also from a reputable neighborhood in Oakland called the 700 block. The 700 block in Oakland was an area known for having some of Oakland's most reputable killers and dope dealers. On Solano yard there were quite a few cats from the 700 block that Shawn hung out with. One guy in particular was also a Kumi member named Mal. Mal was a young dope addict that had to get disciplined a ton of times for his drug usage and his disobedience. I told myself that the next time Mal was involved in some shit that I was going to have him removed from the yard. When a Kumi member is removed from the yard, they suffer a severe beating before they go. I was at my last straw with Mal.

Shawn and Mal grew up together, so they had a weird friendship. Actually, I don't really think I should even call it a friendship. Mal appeared to be jealous of Shawn's demeanor and of all the stuff Shawn was getting, like food and packages. Mal didn't go to the store, nor did he have family sending him anything from the streets, which was a sure sign that no one loved him. Honestly, I could tell why nobody would, judging by his daily actions at Solano. Mal's jealousy came to the surface one night when Shawn received two huge 40lb packages filled will all types of goodies. What happened was that Mal asked Shawn to give him some food from his packages, and Shawn did give Mal some things but apparently it wasn't enough to satisfy him. The next morning while we were all working out on the yard, Mal played hooky while all along he was plotting on Shawn's packages. After working out for an hour, Shawn went into his building (which was an open dorm area that was called the gym). To Shawn's discovery, all his stuff in his locker was gone and someone had shit in one of his brand new shoes (who would do that right?) Shawn came running back to the yard to tell us what had happened, and there was no mystery about who had stolen his things. We all knew that the only person that would do some shit like that was Mal. I sent three of my officers to the gym to get Mal and after 10 minutes he came out chewing on what was probably some of Shawn's food. I didn't beat around the bush.

"Why did you do steal Shawn's stuff? I thought that was your Patna from the block? " I asked him right away.

"That nigga stingy! That's why I did that shit!" Mal responded.

At that point I wanted to stab Mal myself, but at the same time there was something about him that I liked. I didn't know if it was because he did a lot of stupid bold shit or what.

I immediately told Mal that he had to run around the track until the yard was over, and afterwards my officers and I would decide what his fate would be regarding the situation at hand. I had my officers go and take all of Shawn's stuff back from where Mal had hid it – which happened to be in Mal's friend's lockers. He thought he was being slick by putting the stuff in other people's lockers. My officers and I decided it was time for Mal to get a body checking. A body checking was when three Kumi members would beat up the body of a disgruntled member for 10 seconds as a form of discipline. This was sometimes worse than getting hit in the face, especially if you had someone that hit hard. This form of discipline was no joke, since it could possibly break a person's ribs or do all types of other damage to their internal organs.

I told Shawn that he was designated to be a part of the body checking after the yard was over with. At that time Mal would be extremely tired and he would feel the wrath of Kumi if the Kumi members I picked did the body checking right. Yard time was over and I told the Kumi members that I wanted them to go hard on Mal. They all agreed they would, but I felt deep down that those clowns were going to pussy foot around with him. I anticipated all night about what would happen with the body checking on Mal, but I already felt it in my bones that they weren't going to handle business like they were supposed to.

The next morning came around fast and I got word in no time that those clowns didn't get on Mal like they should've. At that point I left the matter alone because if Shawn didn't go hard on the person that disrespected him then why would I worry myself over it? When the yard was opened, I talked to Shawn about what took place though and he told me, out of his own mouth, that he took it easy on Mal because he felt sorry for him.

"You felt sorry for the nigga that stole your property, and used your shoe to shit in?" I said to him, astounded.

Shawn was silent and I went on, "Oh well, that's your Patna so it's all on you!"

At that point Shawn had lost some stripes with me because he was totally disrespected and he actually felt sorry for the person that harshly disrespected him.

After the Shawn incident, things were going smoothly until the prison decided that all the inmates that had less than two years had to move to the gym, and I was one of those people. I hated living in dorm areas because more violence happened there than anywhere else at the prison, because people walked around at all times of the day and night. Not only that, but the gym was full of all sorts of young idiots. I was young too, but I had the mind of a one hundred year old man. I was pissed that I had to move because I had a ton of shit, plus I would possibly lose all the good time I had because fights were on the regular in the gym. Shawn had 10 fights since he had been to Solano for only 90 days, and when he made that statement to me about not under estimating him because he was skinny was absolutely true because Shawn was beating up motherfuckers two times his size.

As soon as I walked into the gym, my Kumi soldiers started cheering for me but I knew they were pissed I was coming in the gym, because they thought I would rain on their parade. Lucky for them, I didn't have any plans on raining on their parade though.

My first night in the gym was tough because I had a top bunk and in the gym in Solano it was a triple bunk with three people so that top bunk was high as hell. If you fell off at night sleeping wild, you could die because it was just that high up. After the first rough night, I immediately made the cat on the bottom bunk a deal he couldn't refuse. I told him I would give him 10 dollars in food to switch bunks and he was all for it. I immediately switched with him and I was even able to tie my television up to the bunk so that I could watch television in private.

When I wanted total privacy, I would hang curtains on both sides of my bunk so that no one could see inside; it was like a cave when I did this. Having the curtains up was the only time I could get some sleep because these wild motherfuckers in the gym paced the floors all fucking night.

My first week in the gym was challenging but I've always been able to adapt to any environment I'm in pretty quickly. To my surprise, I actually started to like the gym because of the freedom to walk around and talk with all the different types of characters that were in there. After a month in there some tension arose though. A black dude had beat up on a Mexican because the Mexican owed him some money, which was pretty much the same type of situation that happened at San Quentin. Now everybody in the gym was on pins and needles and I had all my Kumi soldiers on post. There were 15 of us in the gym at the time, so we had enough soldiers to hold our own, plus I had some swole gangster Kumi cats with me so I wasn't worried about anything at the time. Everybody in the gym knew that we weren't playing with anybody when it came time to get down. I had everyone on post with schedules of sleep and security duty. That was the first time in my life that I didn't go to sleep for 24 hours, and I kept those heavy, hot ass prison boots on the entire time. Because of not taking the shoes off, I had athletes foot for the first time in my life. My toes were split like they were cut with razor blades and I couldn't understand how athlete's foot could happen so damn fast.

Things in the gym were back to normal after the third day, but I was still cautious and I had all my soldiers cautious as well. The Mexicans tended to act like everything was cool and then all of a sudden they would try to do a sneak attack. During the three day lockdown, I only worked out a little because I was so fatigued from not getting my usual 10 hours of sleep a day. I was only getting about three hours of sleep during the situation. During the lockdown I got my first write up at Solano because I was working out in the gym, and the prison officials had a rule that there was to be no working out in the gym. The reason I got the workout was because I had a crew of my Kumi soldiers who

were all swole as shit and the guards were intimidated so they told me that I could no longer work out in the gym. They said I would have to wait until the lockdown was over with and workout on the yard. I straight up told the guard to go tell the warden that I said he might as well send me to the hole, because I'll never stop working out in my entire life, no matter where I'm at.

I think the prison officials made this rule especially for me because they were mad that I looked like a fucking bodybuilder without conventional weights. Instead, my weights were people, books, can goods, water bags, and resistance. The guard did what I told him to do and he told the warden of the prison that I wasn't going to stop working out. A few hours after my meeting with the guard, I was called on the loud speaker to report to the captain's office. I looked at my Kumi soldiers as if I might not see them again, but I didn't give a fuck because I was ready to leave the problematic yard anyways.

Once I entered the captain's office, I was told by him to have a seat. I looked at the captain with fierceness in my eyes. He had a smirk on his face and he went on to say, "So, why won't you do as my guards told you?"

"I will never stop working out, no matter where I'm at. You guys already took all the weights out of the prison and now you're telling me that I can't do pushups and other exercises either?" I replied angrily.

"Look here, the rules are the rules! And you will be given a write up for refusing to comply with them!" The captain said sternly.

"Do what you got to do!" I said, and then I walked out of the office and went back to the gym to tell everybody what had happened. I ended up losing 90 days good time for that write up, but I didn't care because I knew I was doing 100% of my seven year sentence anyhow.

After I got the write up for working out, shit on the yard was going pretty smoothly. I was almost at my one year mark at Solano and I knew that it was about to be time for me to go to classification to see if I would get transferred. In prison, once a year each inmate goes to classification to see if their points dropped, which in turn would result in a transfer if the prison officials saw the need. I didn't care if they transferred me or not at that point, because after living in the gym I was up for any living condition. I don't think it could ever get worse

than the gym because there was no privacy at all. I had to take a shower
with other motherfuckers, and when I fixed something to eat someone
was always begging for some of it. It was a terrible living condition,
even though I made the best of it.

At my classification hearing my points had dropped so I was getting moved to the level two yard. The level two yard was all dorm living, which was similar to the gym. I was cool with that because I heard
that my celly from San Quentin, Pops, was over there so I knew that I
would definitely be the shot caller over there as well.

Two weeks after classification, I was told to pack my things because
I was getting moved to the level two yard. I was sort of happy, but at
the same time sad because I had bonded with a few guys on the yard,
especially Run Run. Even though he did things that I didn't like, Run
Run was the most solid dude out of all the Kumi cats in my eyes; not
to mention our birthday was on the same day. Then there was TuTu,
who was also Kumi and my celly before I got moved to the gym, and
we were super tight because he was a true warrior in my eyes. TuTu and
I continued our bond even after we left prison.

I was sent off by all 25 of the Kumi members that were on the yard. I
told them all that we would meet again on the streets and I took my walk
down the trail to my new journey. It took about 10 minutes to walk to the
new yard that I was going to be housed at. The yard was huge and when I
got to it there weren't any inmates there because it was count time. I was
escorted into the building that would be my new home for the next 10
months I had left of my sentence. The way the building was set up was
entirely different from the gym. It was a lot better because there were
only two people on each bunk and there were about twenty sectioned
off cubicles with four bunks in each, which added up to eight inmates
in each cubicle with a total of 160 people in the building.

Once I reached my assigned bunk, I greeted my new bunky – who
was an older black dude probably in his sixties – and told him my
name. He told me his name was Mr. W and my first impression of him
felt pretty good. I then greeted the rest of the inmates in the cubicle
and we all exchanged names with one another as well. I was glad that
I was in what appeared to be a better situation than the gym on the
other yard.

After the guards did count time and it was cleared, everyone started moving around except for Mr.W, who didn't budge. I could tell that he was somewhat of a grouchy old dude, which didn't bother me at all, because the dorms were set up so that I wouldn't have to talk to him anyway. After count, Mr.W watched his nine inch television – which everyone doing some time had. I wasn't allowed to bring my television because it was a 13 inch TV and it was too big to have at the level two yard, so I actually left it with TuTu on the level three yard. I wasn't concerned with watching television because I spent most of my time working out, reading, and playing chess anyway. I stayed on my bunk when count was cleared to check the scene out and get a feel of what was going on at my new residence. It appeared to me that there were a lot of older guys here than there were on the level three yard. The level two yard was where people that didn't get into trouble and had low points were. The chow hall was about 100 yards from the building I was housed in and I walked there with Mr.W and a few of his old timer friends. I didn't know a single soul in the building I was in, so I was basically trying to feel out how this prison was ran.

The chow hall was small as hell; I mean, we were only given five minutes to eat the food so that the rest of the building could eat as well. One thing I noticed was that not too many inmates ate at the chow hall on this yard. I guess everyone was balling and had their own food. I always kept a lot of my food, but then again I guess I figured I was going to get everything I could out of the prison system, plus I wanted all the calories I could get in order to feed my muscles.

My first day on the new yard, the chow hall had some shit I didn't eat and that was some dry ass enchiladas, beans, menudo, and salsa. I gave that shit away to Mr.W. Once I was done in the chow hall, I went back in the building and fixed myself some Top Ramen with a can of tuna in it. As I ate my food, I watched what was going on and I realized that we had two female guards that were working in the building. All the inmates were flirting with them and trying to get their attention in weird ways, which was funny as hell. I was entertained watching all those clowns trying to get the attention of two ugly ass fat guards. I had been in prison six years and I still didn't find those ugly bitches attractive. As I watched the circus for a while, an announcement went over the intercom that the yard was now open. I jumped off my bunk to go to the yard and as I headed out I ran into one of my childhood friends named Rocky. Rocky grew up with me and played high school football with me. I couldn't believe that Rocky was in jail because he never seemed to be a bad guy. Rocky and I gave one another a brotherly hug and I asked him what he was doing in prison. He told me that he and his friends – who I also knew – did a robbery that went bad. Rocky then went on to say that he heard what had gone down with my case.

We laughed and reminisced for a second before I asked him where the Kumi cats were at. Rocky walked with me outside and pointed to the table where all the Kumi members were meeting at. I told him thanks and that I would holler at him later. I then walked by the table and asked the members where Pops was. All of their eyes got big and they asked me who wanted to know. I told them, "His love one!"

"Oh, you kumi?" They said.

"That's right!" I responded.

"OK, you need to holla at the screening officer right quick!" they said.

Of course I knew the procedure that took place every new place I went, but at this stage in my affiliation with Kumi I kind of felt like I was too big to get screened. I felt like these motherfuckers were supposed to know who I was. Of course I did the screening bullshit though and I recited the shit faster than the dude could hear it. The cat screening me said, "Damn you are tight with your shit!" I told him that I better be tight because I ran every yard I touched. He responded with a simple "OK" but I could see the intimidation in his eyes at that point because he could sense that I was a powerful force in Kumi. After I did the screening, I went and greeted all my new comrades and I looked them each in their eyes as I shook their hands. It was as if I were reading their souls, but really I was looking to see who was real and who wasn't.

As I was explaining to my new comrades about myself, the one and only Pops came outside calling my name. I met him in his tracks and had a smile that went from ear to ear. I was happy to see one of the few cats I had met in prison that I could call a mentor of mine. Pops gave me a brotherly hug and he was happy as hell to see me too. We walked the track and caught up on what had happened to each of us while we were separated.

Pops told me that his case was in the courts and he was hoping to get out of prison soon. Pops had already been in prison 21 years; damn near longer than I had been born. He went on to say that all he did every day is study his case. I ran down to Pops what took place when he left San Quentin and he couldn't believe it.

Pops told me that he was going to put me in charge of the yard, and since he was one of the highest ranking officers in Kumi, he had more authority than practically anybody besides the three other officers that had the same rank as he did. I told him that I didn't want to step on any-one's toes, and so I would be the overseer of the yard instead. Being the overseer consisted of making the final decision on every decision made, so I would have the last word on everything. Pops told me, "You got it!" and he went over to the head officer on the yard and told him my new position. Pops and I talked the duration of the yard time and when it was closed I told him that I would see him the next day. I went back in my building and had a sense of relief that I came to the yard I did. Already I had the ultimate status with no problems, and if Pops wasn't on the yard I would have had to become the top dog by any means necessary.

My first night on the new yard I didn't sleep too well because of being in a new environment. I tossed and turned all fucking night and the bunk that I had squeaked with the slightest movement, so that shit was irritating as hell. After I fell asleep for a few hours, it was time for morning chow which started at about 6:30 a.m. I hated getting up in the mornings and I was always grouchy as fuck when I woke up. I got dressed, washed my face and brushed my teeth, and then went back and sat on my bunk until the building was released for chow – which ended up being 30 minutes later. I had two comrades in the building with me so we walked to chow together and I guess they were grouchy in the morning too because we didn't say too much to each other. After we ate the slop and got our bag lunch, we went back into the building. After chow the yard didn't open for two hours, so most people went to sleep until the yard opened, but the people that had jobs went to work right after chow instead. The building was pretty much empty after chow because most everyone was at work. Even Mr. W was working, whose job was in the optical department making glasses. Working in optical was the best and highest paying job on the level two yard, so Mr. W was proud of himself. I went and sat on my bunk and started reading until I felt my eyes getting heavy, and then I dozed off for a little while until the loud ass intercom went off saying that the yard was open. I jumped off my bunk and made my way to the yard to meet up with the Kumi soldiers and see what was going on. It ended up being about 15 of us and I immediately started asking questions about how the yard was being run, and the top dude in charge ran everything down to me. Everything was run weird to me on the yard. I was told that things were ran like they were because the yard is split up by buildings, so only certain buildings were allowed to the yard on certain days. It was confusing but I caught on in about a week. The prison officials ran this yard in an unorthodox manner that I definitely had to get used to.

I had to show all the inmates that there was a new general in town, so I did my usual two warm up sets of pull-ups to get my blood pumping and then I took my shirt off. You should have seen the look on those inmate's faces when I took off my shirt. You could hear the entire yard mumbling about me. It was an exhilarating feeling to get the respect I did everywhere I went. Everyone on the yard stopped what they were doing to watch me do the muscle-ups. I was like a gymnast on the pull-up bars; I did all types of different pull up variations. I had a fan club on the new yard already. As I was doing the pull ups, one cat in particular came up to me and said, "Damn, you swole mayne!" I looked at him and I could tell that he was no slouch himself and I told him that I could tell that he had his swole on as well.

"Yeah, but I need to get like you!" he said admiringly.

We shook hands and introduced ourselves and I told him that we could work out together if he wanted to do legs. Usually I would deter the weak from working out with me when I told them I did legs, but Mal didn't shy away. Immediately he said, "Hell yeah! I want to get it all!" so I asked Mal what building he was in and he told me building 21, which was the same building I was in as well. I knew this would work out good because on the days we didn't come to the yard we could work out in the building.

After my first day of showing off on the yard, I felt good because I knew everybody would know me and that I would get the upmost respect from everyone. After the yard was closed, everyone rushed in the building to try and get to the showers first. I wasn't the one to rush for anything, so I told one of my comrades that I had the shower after him, which meant that he had to make sure that no one got in that shower before I did.

The cold part about the shower on this yard was that it was right in front of the guard's desk, so the female guards would get a peep show watching us take showers. Everybody took their shower in boxers as a sign of respect to the next man, but some of the perverts in the prison would take their shower without their boxers on. It was funny watching the perverts do their rituals of stroking themselves when the female guards were looking in the shower, especially this one nigga named Frog. Frog was a building porter, so he would take his shower during count time while the female guards were at the desk. This nigga would be damn near jacking off while they watched him, and he didn't even care that practically everybody else in the building could see him. I and everybody else knew that that nigga wasn't right. Later on down the line, we found out that Frog had raped his own daughter and got 12 years for it.

After a few weeks on the level two yard, I started to get comfortable with my surroundings and get over the weirdness that the yard exuded. I was a porter in my building, which was fantastic because I never wanted a kitchen job or one of those early morning jobs. Fortunately, I was always lucky enough to get the job I wanted in prison. I had to have a job that didn't prevent me from getting my workout in. Things were pretty smooth on the yard and it had a lot to do with how the buildings were separated. The only problems on the yard were the Mexicans fighting each other. That would put the entire yard on lockdown for days at a time, but that didn't matter to me because I was a building porter so I was able to roam around all the time.

My workouts with Mal were amazing. We had added two other cats to work out with us, but ultimately it was just me and him because the other cats had jobs that conflicted with our workout schedule. It was good that Mal was also a building porter and we were able to work out when we needed to, even on lockdowns.

Mal got big as fuck working out with me. He had put on about 20 lbs. in 90 days, which was unbelievable. Mal was damn near my size which was crazy. The reason Mal put on so much weight so fast was because he hadn't been doing anything weighted before I came to the yard. He was just doing everything with his body weight. Everything I did was with weight and resistance, so it was just like we had weights. The other inmates thought we were getting steroids in jail and so did the guards. They would search our packages from the streets with the fucking police dogs. It was crazy that everybody thought we were taking drugs just because we were swole as fuck. It was comedy to us and actually we were honored to hear it was going on because it let us know that we were the shit.

Time was flying and I started to get nervous about getting out of prison because I had gotten so used to the daily routine of the prison setting; on top of that, everybody I knew that got out of prison was getting killed or coming back with hefty sentences. I know it sounds weird, but I really didn't care about getting out of prison.

Three weeks before my release date I was enrolled into a pre-release class that taught inmates how to get adjusted back to society and it even let us get our driver's license. Getting my driver's license was my main concern with the class, and I studied my ass off for that test. I ended up passing the test without getting any questions wrong, and I was happy as hell because test always made me nervous.

The pre-release class went by fast and I was down to 10 days before I got out. During the days before my release, Pops and I spent a lot of time together on the yard talking about what I had plans on doing once I got out. I told him that I was going to be a personal trainer and work on becoming a pro bodybuilder. He wished me all the luck in the world because in his 21 years of being in prison he didn't see many convicts survive the mean streets.

Those last few days before I was to be released were the most stressful days while being incarcerated. My mind was all over the place and I definitely didn't want to be a failure and come back to prison like everyone else; however, I knew that there was always the possibility that I would. Most everyone I did time with got out and then came right back. I wrote down all my plans and goals and I promised myself that I would accomplish everything I had written down.

"Freedom Almost"

That precious day came for me to be released, and I was worried because I was what the penal system considered a high risk convict. That meant that there was the possibility that I wouldn't be able to get out of prison on a weekend or a holiday because I was considered a violent convict. It just so happened that the day I was to be released was President's Day, so I knew that there was a 50/50 chance of me not getting out. I had given all my things away to all my comrades and friends, but I told them that if I didn't get out that they had to give me my things back until I did. They all, of course, agreed and I made a lot of people happy because I had seven years' worth of shit to give away and a ton of food. I got cheered on by everyone as I walked out the building at about six in the morning. My heart was racing with excitement. I couldn't believe the feeling I had at that time; it was the best worried feeling I'd had in my life. I walked to R&R where all inmates came in and left out and there were about 12 inmates going home. When I got to R&R, a guard asked me my name and prison number and after I told him he looked at my release papers with a look of concern.

I asked the guard what was wrong and he told me that I may not get out because it was a holiday and I was a high risk convict. The guard said that he was going to call my parole officer to see if I was to be released. All I could think was, "Damn, as soon as it's time for me to get out some bullshit has to happen." I watched the guard talk on the phone in a whispered tone and he hung up expressionless.

He came walking over to me with a serious look on his face and when he reached me he smiled and said, "You are a lucky motherfucker my friend! Your parole officer will be in the office waiting on you to come."

My heart damn near stopped; I thought I was about to have a heart attack or something. The guard brought me the clothes that my mother had sent me, and it was funny to think that she knew what I liked even after all these years. She sent me a clean ass Sean Jean sweat suit and some Nikes. I was probably the happiest man on the earth at that moment. I got dressed with rapid speed and as soon as I was finished the guard escorted all of us out to a van that would either take the inmates to the bus station or outside the prison gates where their family members would be there to pick them up. Of course my mom was there to pick me up. As the van drove outside the prison, I looked back and begged God not to let me ever see a prison again. Once we reached the security gate where the check point was, I saw my mom in a nice long suburban truck. I started smiling ear to ear and I jumped out of that prison van as it was still moving. I went and hugged my mom like I'd never hugged her before. She started to cry and then she managed to pull herself together. I hadn't been in a vehicle except prison buses in seven years.

As my mother was driving, I noticed that I was paranoid because it felt like she was driving too fast, but I didn't say anything because I knew that it was just me tripping. We didn't talk much during the drive because for one I was nervous and two I was sightseeing. My mom asked me if I needed to pick anything up from the store and I said I did, so she said that we would go to Costco. As I rode to the store with my mother it was quiet as I watched the passing cars and the beautiful world that most people took for granted. My mother must have known I was in deep thought and admiration of the scenery because she was just as quiet as I was.

When we got to Costco my mother asked me what I wanted to get and I told her some Top Ramen and tuna. She looked at me, shocked, and said, "Really?" as if I were making some sort of joke. I told her that I didn't know what else to eat and that I was scared to eat regular food that most people ate in society like, KFC, Mcdonalds, and all the other fast food joints. I heard too many stories from the inmates coming back to prison saying how the street food messed up their stomachs for about a week when they got out, so I was leery about eating certain things. My mom and I found the isle with the Top Ramen and I put five cases of it in the basket as if I were shopping in prison, and it almost felt like it because the price of the soup was the same. I felt good getting the cases of soup, just like I used to when I went to the store in prison. My mother sarcastically asked me if that was enough cases and I smiled at her and asked her if she thought I needed more. We then found the isle where the canned goods were, and I immediately went to the spot where the tuna was. I was like a kid at a candy store all excited. I got about 30 cans of tuna and when my mother and I got to the cash register a white dude was standing too close for my comfort and I went off on him.

"Hey dude won't you step back? I don't like people all up on me like that!" I said. The white guy was startled and looked at me fearfully as if I were going to kill him.

"Oh I'm sorry sir I didn't realize I was close to you!" He said apologetically.

"You were entirely too close and I just got out the pen and I ain't with that shit!" I said, frustrated.

The white guy said he was sorry again, probably not knowing what else he could say in that moment. My mom asked me if I was alright and I told her that I didn't like people close to me like that because you never knew what someone would try to do. She looked at me like I was nuts, but she told me she understand anyway, when in fact she didn't understand at all.

My mom and I drove down the block I grew up on and the street seemed extremely congested. It looked like the streets were narrow as hell, but I guess my perception of it was like that because I was used to a wide open prison yard. I told my mother that the street looked narrow to me and she didn't understand what I was talking about; she probably thought I was weird especially after my rant at Costco As I got all the stuff out of the truck to take into the house, I looked around the neighborhood and started reminiscing about when I was a kid playing in the streets there. Even though I went through a lot of stuff growing up in my mom's house, I always had a good time playing outside. As we got in the house, Spoiled was still asleep as if he didn't give a fuck about me getting out. That was already an indicator that he was still a selfish motherfucker, because if he was getting out I would have been there to greet him at the gate, however, I wasn't surprised at all and I didn't even wake him up when I walked in.

The inside of my mom's house seemed as if it was supposed to be for a house of dwarfs. Everything seemed small and it seemed like I could raise my hand and touch the ceiling. I didn't understand why everything seemed so small to me; it was totally weird. After I helped my mom put up all the things we got at Costco, I went into the room that I grew up in. It was the same as when I was a kid but my mom had put in a couple new beds and some furniture. I looked around the room and started fumbling with all the stuff that Spoiled had accumulated over the years I had been gone. There were all types of things that I had no idea about what they were- – like an MP3 player – and there were a ton of CD's and clothes were in every drawer in the room. There were also a ton of tennis shoes, mostly Air Jordan's. I mean, Spoiled had every fucking thing imaginable; it was crazy all the shit he had. My mom came in the room and cleared out a few drawers for me to put my things in once I'd acquired them, because all I had at the moment was some paperwork that I had brought with me from prison. Spoiled finally got up and came into the door way of my room and said a dry ass, "What's up bra, you out of there huh?" I replied, "Yep. I'm out of there!"

"That's cool, I'm bout to take a shower and go take care some business!" He said walking off.

"Cool, I'll talk to you later!" I replied.

I was definitely disappointed in his reaction because I know that if it had been seven year since I'd seen the brother I loved, then I would have been ecstatic to see him and would have greeted him as a brother was supposed to. I got the vibe that something wasn't right in this house though, and I would soon find out what it was.

After I was situated at the house and got the few things I had in order, I went into my mom's room to talk to her and pops. They were asking me what my plans were and I told them that I was going to be a personal trainer and that I was also going to become a stripper. Pops started laughing and he said, "A stripper? Boy you can't dance!"

"I'm about to put these fucking muscles to use and get paid for them!" I said.

We all laughed together but they just didn't know how serious I was about what I'd said. We talked for some hours and I started getting tired at ten o'clock because that was the time my body was used to going to sleep. I told moms and pops that I would see them in the morning.

My first night of sleeping in the free world was great except for having to deal with Spoiled coming in the house around 3:00 a.m. and waking me up. I heard my mother instantly say, "Who is it?" and Spoiled responded, "It's me mom, go to sleep!" I could tell that my mother was always worried about this character and that she was concerned about what he was doing on the streets. I could also tell that I already didn't like this dude because he had no respect for anyone in that house. He didn't care about my mother having to go to work in three hours or about pops either. I was upset with Spoiled's behavior after only being free for about 20 hours.

The morning came fast and when I was awakened by my mother getting ready for work at about 6:00 a.m., I looked around not realizing where I was at. I thought I was still in prison until I was fully awake. My mom told me she would see me after she got off work later and she gave me a kiss on the cheek before leaving out the door. I laid down for a couple more hours trying to soak in the reality of being in the free world, before I finally got up and saw pops cooking some eggs and toast for breakfast. He asked me if I wanted some and I said I did, so after I brushed my teeth and washed my face I went and ate the food pops had cooked for me, and it was good too.

I had gotten so accustomed to eating oatmeal every morning in prison that the change was definitely nice. Pops and I talked for a while until Spoiled came in the kitchen without saying good morning or anything. First thing he asked was where his food was. Pops said that since he was sleeping that he didn't think Spoiled was eating, but then pops told Spoiled that he would cook him some food in a second.

I didn't like what was going on already. I mean, this dude was 19 acting like he was five fucking years old, throwing a tantrum and shit, but what made matters worse was that pops was allowing that bullshit to go on. I immediately told Spoiled not talk to his dad like that and he quickly rebutted that he'd been doing it. That let me know right then and there that my mother and pops had raised a spoiled ass nigga that thought everybody owed him something, and that everyone should cater to him and his needs. I had already taken a dislike to Spoiled in a matter of two days. After pops cooked Spoiled some food, Spoiled came and looked at it and then started complaining and I couldn't take it anymore. I told him to shut his ass up with all that disrespect and pops sort of told me that it was alright. I didn't understand what type of nigga they raised because when Archie and I were growing up, that behavior would have never been allowed. If we had so much as a frown on our faces we would get our asses whopped. I couldn't believe what was going on in moms and pop's house.

After Pops, Spoiled and I ate, we talked for a while but Spoiled acted as if he had some major business to attend and left while Pops and I talked continued talking into the afternoon. I was hungry again at that point so I fixed a spread, which is a famous prison dish that's cherished like a gumbo to prisoners. As I was fixing my spread, pops asked me what the hell I was making and I told him that was was called a "spread".

"What the hell is that?" I said.

I started laughing because pops had a way of saying things that were always amusing. I told him that a spread was Top Ramen and whatever else a person wanted to put in it. I was only adding tuna and Fritos potato chips to mine, with a little sandwich spread as well. After I fixed my spread I asked pops if he wanted to try it and he was like, "Hell naw! You gone head and eat that bullshit, I'm still full from breakfast!" As I was eating my spread in my huge Tupperware, I decided to go outside to see what was happening in the neighborhood. As I ate my food I saw that there was a lot of traffic in the neighborhood and it reminded me of when I was a kid and about all the drug selling that was going on at that time. I was quick to determine what was going on as soon as I caught a glimpse of something. I saw Spoiled riding a bike up and down the streets as if he were patrolling the neighborhood. I knew something was fishy then, because what's grown motherfucker doing riding a bike up and down a street as if he has nothing to do. That's when I noticed the guys at the apartments that I used to love to go to when I was a kid, arguing over whose sale it was when someone approached the apartments. I instantly figured out that there was major dope dealing still going on at the infamous E street apartments. I immediately told myself that I wouldn't come close to those apartments because that would be an instant violation of parole for me and I wasn't going out like that.

As I was gazing down the street from the inside of my mother's yard – which was heavily gated – one of my old neighborhood friends saw me outside and came running down the street towards me.

"What's up with you bra? You made it up out of there huh?" My old friend Ronny said to me.

I replied, "I certainly did bra!"

I asked him where Ant was, because Ronny was Ant's younger brother. Ronny said that Ant would be on the block in any minute. As we were catching up on life, Ronny looked at me as I took a spoon full of my spread and he immediately started laughing and he said, "Bra you're not in prison no more, there is a McDonalds right around the corner!" I told him that I was scared to eat that shit because it would make me sick. Ronny started laughing again and said, "Bra you a fool, you eating a spread on the streets!"

"You damn right! This shit better than McDonalds and I bet you!" I laughed.

Ronny shook his head and then told me how he was glad that I was out of prison and said he would tell Ant that I was out too. I said cool and we shook hands before Ronny went back down to the apartments that he grew up at. I kept eating the rest of my spread, watching all the cars and people that were driving and walking up and down the street. After watching the chaos for about an hour, Ant drove up on me while I was about to take myself back inside the house. He was excited as hell to see me. He hopped out of the car he was driving as if he were ghost riding the whip; I mean, the car was still rolling as he got out of it and he screamed, "My boy is out, my boy is out!"

"What's up, bra?" I said.

"Boy I'm glad to see you home! Damn, what you do like seven years?" He said.

"Yep, seven years exactly!" I replied.

"Damn that was a long time! Oh well, you out now baby and you got to stay out too!" He told me.

I asked Ant what was going on with him and he said that he was about to get an 18 wheeler truck because he just got his truck driving license, so he and his patna were about to go in business together. I told him that I was proud of him and to keep up the positivity. Ant said most definitely, and then he said that when I got the chance I should go to the Muslim service at the Masjid on 82nd and I told him I would think about it. He said cool and that he would holler at me later. It didn't take me long to realize that everyone was moving fast. They would talk about 10 minutes and then be ready to do whatever it was they had to do. It was good seeing Ant and Ronney though. I had a serious bond with Ant because he gave me my first gun, and he was Kumi as well as a Muslim, so we had a lot of things in common.

After Ant left, I went in the house and called an old high school girl-friend named Nicole. Nicole and I were a little more than friends when I was in my senior year of high school, but wasn't ever anything serious. She was two years younger than me and we just hung out sometimes. Corey was messing with her sister in high school at the time, so we used to double date, but I never had sex with Nicole; I wasn't concerned with all that back then. Anyways, I got back in contact with Nicole when her brother came to San Quentin before the riot happened and she gave me her phone number so I could call her. Once I got her phone number, we started corresponding via phone and letters but at the time I had two years left to do in prison and so I didn't engulf myself into something that would distract me from prison life. We corresponded here and there for the remainder of my prison sentence and I called her just to stay on her mind, but again, nothing serious. We said that we were going to get together when I got out and so I called her my second day out. I wanted to spend time with the family first, but since everybody was doing their own thing and didn't seem too concerned with me I decided I had to entertain myself somehow.

I called Nicole and when she heard my voice she asked me when I was getting out. When I told her I was already out, she went ballistic. She said, "You been out and you haven't called me?" I told her that I had just gotten out and she said that she was coming to see me as soon as possible. I freshened up a little and I was actually excited because I hadn't had a conversation with a woman besides my mother and the female guards in a long ass time.

Nicole got to the house as fast as hell. She came from Hayward but it seemed like she was just around the corner. She called me on the house phone to let me know that she was outside and I couldn't wait to see what she looked like now, because it had been over seven years since I'd seen her. I walked outside and saw that she had a little white car, nothing special, and I opened the door and told her to get out so I could see her because it was dark outside and I needed to at least see a woman's silhouette under the moon light. She got out of the car and I gave her a big hug and held her for a while because it was my first time hugging a woman besides my mom in seven years. I immediately became hard as a rock. After we hugged, we got back in the car because I didn't want the police to think we were doing anything illegal, since E Street had police driving down it every 10 minutes. We talked for a while and I told her to drive to the San Leandro marina so we could catch up on one another's lives while we watched the ocean in the moonlight.

We had a lot of catching up to do and I could tell that she was undressing me with her eyes because she couldn't stop saying how big I was now. My attraction to Nicole wasn't all that strong. She was a five out of ten to me. I was still picky as hell, that hadn't changed about me. She was light-brown skinned and a little overweight, which was a definite turn off for me. She had breasts the size of grapefruits and an ass as flat as hell, not to mention she had the head of a Rottweiler. However, I figured a beggar couldn't be choosy, and that was the first interaction I'd had with a female in years, so I was going to make the best out of it. We talked all the way until the police shut down the park area, and then she drove me back to my mom's house and we agreed to hang out again the next day.

As I entered the house, I noticed that my mother was home from work and so we talked for a while. I told her that I had gone for a ride with Nicole from high school, who my mom had met when I was younger. I told my mom that she was alright but that she wasn't really my type. There were a lot of reasons why Nicole wasn't my type, but one of those reasons was that she had a son, which was a definite no-no for me. I had promised myself that I wouldn't deal with any women that had kids because I knew it was a major problem. I had seen too many dudes in prison for getting in a violent situation with their girlfriend's baby daddy, and I refused to be one of those people. My mother listened to me and she understood because she felt the same way even though pops got with her when she already had me and my brother Archie. My mom and I talked a while but we both had to get up early to go and meet my parole officer.

The next morning came fast and I was nervous because going to the parole office was like going to the court house, anything could happen. My mom, Spoiled and I went to see my parole officer. I lived in Oakland but for some odd reason I had to report to the Berkeley sector of parole. I got to the parole office 10 minutes before my time and when I walked in I saw some ex-cons that I had done time with and they all came and greeted me with the upmost respect. My mother was shocked at the respect I got. I had to sign my name on a sheet of paper on a clip board so that my parole officer knew that I was there at the time I was supposed to be And then my mom, Spoiled and I sat there for about 30 minutes before the parole officer called me in his office and my mother came with me inside. The parole officer was a young black dude, maybe 31 or 32 years old. I could tell that he was trying to be an asshole but he didn't have a reason to be one with me because I hadn't done anything wrong.

The parole officer gave me a cup to go and urinate in to make sure that I didn't have any drugs in my system. After that I had to take a picture for him, and he gave me a long drawn out ass speech about the rules of parole. The shit he was saying kind of shook me up because the rules and laws he was conveying to me were just too much shit to cause someone on parole to be sent on the first bus back to San Quentin. I was scared as shit after the parole officer ran everything down to me and my mom. Spoiled had gone and got in the truck so he wasn't hearing all of this. When the parole officer was finally done talking, he told me that he would be coming by the house any day during the week between 6:00 a.m. and 5:00 p.m.

When he told me that I said, "So, I am supposed to wait for you all day until you come?"

He replied, "That's exactly right, sir, because if I come and you're not there that is an automatic violation of your parole."

I told him I would definitely be there when he got there then. No way was I going back to prison for not waiting on the parole officer to show up at my house for a home visit. As my mom and I headed out of his office, he handed my mother a card and told her to contact him if I gave her any problems, and she of course told him thank you.

The next day I waited for the parole officer to come all damn day and I was pissed. It didn't make any sense to me why the parole officer would have me wait all fucking day in the house while I could have been out looking for a fucking job. But I did take advantage of my time waiting on the stupid ass parole officer by going through the yellow pages and calling up all the strip agencies to see which ones were hiring. I started off with the one that had the biggest ad and it was Men of Exotica. I could see that they were the head honchos in the strip business in the bay area. I called them and asked them if they were hiring any dancers at the time and they said they were. They told me to send them some pictures so that they could see if I was someone that they could add to the team. I got their information and told them that I would send them the pictures as soon as possible. I was excited as hell because being a stripper was on my list of things to do. I didn't even call any of the other strip agencies because I was putting all my eggs in this one basket. I knew that if I got with them I was on my way because I heard on the radio when I was in the car with Nicole that Men of Exotica was the hottest male revue in California.

After I talked to Men of Exotica, the doorbell rang and I was hoping that it was that damn parole officer so that I could start my job hunt at some gyms. I went to the door and yelled, "Who is it?" The parole officer responded, "Parole agent!" I opened the door and told him to come in. Before he stepped inside he asked me if I had any dogs and I told him we didn't. He said cool, and asked if we had any outside and again, I told him we didn't. As soon as he stepped in the house he said that the house was nice, and then he immediately asked what my parents did for a living to have such a nice house and cars. He was referring to the cars in the drive way, and I told him that my mother was a nurse and that my pops was a retired business owner that worked in security as a part time job. I didn't understand why he was so shocked at the cars and the nice house we had; he acted like we had a $20 million dollar mansion and a Bugatti in the fucking driveway. It was pissing me off that it was such an issue that we were living like middle class people. I called pops out to meet the asshole to try and divert his mind to see that my parents were law abiding citizens, and that they were not an inkling of the bad person that he saw I was on his paper work.

Pops came out and greeted the parole officer with a stern, "How you doing?" Pops didn't give a damn who the man was, because he was in his house and pops even let it be known that he didn't give a fuck who he was by saying that the parole officer didn't need to knock on the door the way he did.

Before the parole officer rang the doorbell, he knocked on the door like the true police officer he was and pops checked him on it, telling him that the doorbell was right there for him to see and that he didn't need to knock on the door like he was crazy. The parole officer saw that pops wasn't one for the bullshit so he smiled and said, "Yes sir!" Pops then went back into the den to watch television while I took the parole officer on a tour of the house. As I was showing him the house, he ran all the rules of parole to me once again and he even told me some stuff that he didn't tell me in the office. After he cased the house, he told me when my next appointment was and about the parole orientation that I had to go to the following week. He left and I was as relieved as getting out of prison that he was out of my hair until the following month.

When the parole officer left, my mother came home from work early so that we could go and get my first car. As we rode to Aunt Jewel's house in my mother's Mercedes Benz, I watched all the fast movement that I hadn't gotten used to in the few days since I had been back on the streets. I was still nervous riding in the car. I had always been nervous riding with people anyway, even before going to prison; I just never trusted anyone's driving but my own. When we pulled up to Aunt Jewel's house, the car was parked right in front. I looked at it as we pulled up and thought to myself, "Beggers can't be choosy!" I got out of mom's car and went and inspected the car I would be driving. It was a Chevy Cavalier, cherry red, with four doors and no dents. In my mind I knew that this would only be a temporary car, because it wasn't something I could be seen in for long. I still had an image to uphold. I went in Aunt Jewel's house and talked to her and her husband, Julius, who only had one of his legs due to diabetes. They were excited to see me and told me that I had gotten really big. They told me if I needed anything to just let them know, and my mom gave my aunt the $1,500 for the car. I attempted to drive it for the first time in seven years. Moms and pops asked me if I was going to be OK and I told them that driving a car was just like riding a bike; once you learn, you never forget, but what I didn't admit was that once I got into that car I was a nervous wreck.

I was confused for a while on how to adjust the seat, the mirrors, and the rear view mirrors. I was praying that I made it home before it got dark because I didn't know how to turn on the damn head lights. As I made my way to E Street, I was fucking up a lot; I almost even ran a red light. I knew that it would take me a few days to get the hang of driving again. Once I made it home without having an accident or getting a ticket, I felt like I had accomplished something.

I parked the car across the street from the house because our driveway and the side walk in front of our house was full cars belonging to my moms, pops, and Spoiled. I see why the parole officer was looking suspicious about us because we had all those damn cars.

The next day I got up early so that I could go to South Land Mall to take some pictures so that I could send them to the strip agency. I found a place inside the mall that did the type of pictures I needed at a reasonable price. I took the pictures then I walked around the mall until the pictures were ready to be picked up, which was about 45 minutes.

While walking around the mall, I got myself a few outfits and a few pairs of shoes before going back and picking up the pictures. The pictures were cool, nothing to brag home about but enough for what I needed them for. I left the mall and went to 24 Hour Fitness to see if they were hiring. I, of course, had on a tank top to show off my prison muscle that looked like gym muscle. As soon as I walked in 24 Hour Fitness and asked them if they were hiring, they told me to wait a second and then a young white guy came out and shook my hand and informed me that, yes, they were definitely hiring trainers then and that they would love to have me on their team. I was like, "Damn, if this dude only knew that I just got out his pen he probably wouldn't be so anxious to hire me!" But I listened to him and he had me fill out an application for him. I filled it out as if I hadn't been off the streets for seven years of my life. After I filled it out, he said that there was a personal training class that all new employees had to attend to get certified and it started the following week, and he asked if I would be available to start the class. I excitedly told him I would most definitely be able to attend the class. He said good, that he was glad to have me aboard the team.

I couldn't fucking believe what had just happened. I got a fucking job that fast, and here I had thought I was going to get turned down like all those motherfuckers that came back to prison.

I rushed to the house to tell my moms and pop the great news. They were as happy as I was that I had got a job in the first few days of being released from prison. I was also hoping that I would get the gig with Men of Exotica, because that would definitely be the frosting on the cake. I put the pictures in an envelope and took them to the post office to send to the strip club using overnight mail.

My third day out was my birthday, so my mother had a get together with my old friends, Marlon, Corey, Derrick, Darold, Alfreta, Archie's old girlfriend Cynthia, my cousins Erica and Arnetta, and Aunt Fee.

Truthfully, none of them were my friends in my eyes at the time because the only ones that sent me letters were Arnetta and Marlon, who sent me one letter in seven years. I most definitely held a grudge towards most everyone that was there, but I didn't show it outwardly. We all had a good time reminiscing about the old days but I was ready for the new days so I lost interest fast in all the people being there because they were full of shit to me. It only takes 10 minutes to write a funky ass letter to someone and mail it. The most consistent person that wrote me was Arnetta and of course my moms. After a few hours I sent all the people to wherever they were going, which was rude, but I didn't give a rat's ass about anyone's feeling except the people that were there 100% for me while I was incarcerated.

"Stripper Man"

A few days after I sent the pictures off to Men of Exotica, I got a call from them telling me that they would love to have me be a part of the team. I told them thank you, and they explained that I was to meet with them on Saturday at 9:00 p.m., because that would be the night of my first gig at one of the biggest clubs in the bay area called The Sound Factory. It was going to be an all women extravaganza, with over two thousand women and just Men of Exotica and Jon B. I couldn't fucking believe this shit. My first week out and I was already getting in the mix of things. I told moms and pops the great news about me having two jobs in just a few days of being out of prison, and they were happy to see me going down a positive road.

Saturday came fast and I took Marlon with me to see what this stripper shit was all about. I met with the owners of Men of Exotica, Ali and Lori, and they were nice people who I had the upmost respect for because of them giving me a shot to be a stripper. Ali was not only the owner, he was also one of the strippers and I learned a lot from him about the entertainment game. I introduced everyone to Marlon as my brother, which worked because we had a similar look about us and we were never questioned about it. Then Ali introduced me to all of the other dancers he had on the team. I checked all of them out and none of them had the physique I did; the only person that came close to my physique was a mixed dude that called himself Ziac. He had the tightest physique that came close to mine and I could tell that when I shook his hand that even he was intimidated by me. After we pumped our muscles up for 15 minutes, we were all called to the stage one by one and evidently all the women already knew Men of Exotica and its

performers, because they were going crazy when all the dancers went
to the stage.

I was introduced as the new muscle of the team. Ali announced,
"Now ladies, the newest addition to Men of Exotica, 'Mandingo'!" I
came out bouncing my chest and grinding my hips in a sexual manner and the 2,000+ ladies at The Sound Factory went crazy. I couldn't
believe how they reacted to me when I hit the stage. I thought that all
strippers had a physique like mine and so the ladies would be accustomed to someone like me, but I was wrong. The ladies were going so
crazy that they were trying to jump on the stage to get to me, and I
actually pulled one girl up and performed my first trick as a stripper on
her. I laid her down, spread her legs and then did a headstand between
her legs before dropping down in the 69 position. Then I stood up
with her still in the 69 position but standing upright. The crowd of
ladies went crazy when I did that move. I knew at that very moment
that I would be a successful stripper.

After the strip show, I was paid $150 which was amazing to me
because I would have done that shit for free, but here I was getting paid
to show off my body to women. This was the life. Marlon couldn't believe how I had just gotten out of prison and had over 2,000+ women
screaming over me. He was amazed at my dancing skills and how fast
I was making my mark in society. I was on cloud nine after that show.
Ali told me that I did a fantastic job and that we had another show to
do the following weekend. I told him that I would definitely be there.

After the show I knew that I was going to be successful on the streets
because I was already making my mark, and by being a part of Men of
Exotica's team, I would learn about society real fast because the life of
a dancer was nothing but fast.

Monday had come and I had to drive to Pleasanton – which was
about 30 minutes from Oakland without traffic – to start my personal
training class to get certified to start working at 24 Hour Fitness. I was
excited to be given the opportunity to do what I loved to do. The class
started at 8:00 a.m. and it didn't end until 4:00 p.m., which was alright
with me because I had been locked up for years and I was just glad to
finally be able to live amongst civilized people. When the class started,
I made it a point to sit right in front so that I could learn all the in-

formation I needed to learn head on. Most of the students, of course, didn't want to sit in the front of the class because that's usually where the instructors started asking people questions. I wanted to be asked questions and I was training myself not to shy away from any knowledge that was given to me.

Time flies when you're having fun and so the four days of class went by pretty fast. Learning all the aspects of being a personal trainer was fun to me because it was what I wanted to do in life. I passed the test to be a personal trainer with flying colors and I met some cool people while being in the class. I got my certificate for being a certified personal trainer and it felt like I had received my PHD. I was flabbergasted to have completed something positive in the short time period that I had. After the final class, I called my new boss at 24 Hour Fitness and told him that I had passed the test and he told me that he was putting me on the schedule to start on Monday.

Nicole and I were seeing one another a few days out of the week, but with her living with her mom our time together was limited. We mostly hung out on the weekends, and before long Nicole started telling me how I didn't make enough time for her. That's when I knew that what we had wasn't going to last.

My first day working at 24 Hour Fitness was an experience I'll never forget. I was amazed at how the gyms had advanced with their equipment and just the overall seriousness of the business. I loved the atmosphere as if I were born in the gym. Mark, my new boss, showed all of us that had just became certified personal trainers what our daily duties were and how to keep track of all of our clients and their needs. It was fun learning all the things about being a personal trainer, and at the time I could foresee being a trainer for the rest of my life. After Mark showed us everything, he took us to all the employees at the gym and introduced everyone to one another. I saw then that all the employees had a bond with each other that exceeded far beyond just being coworkers. There was a family vibe going on in the gym which I picked up on immediately and I felt comfortable with everyone in the gym right away.

The first day at the gym went by fast once I learned how to handle the job and the clients. I was excited to be given the opportunity to do what I loved to do. I went to my mom's house that night and told her and pops how my day went and they were happy that I was doing the right thing. I noticed that my mom worried a lot about Spoiled, and I didn't like it at all. Spoiled was doing things in the street that my mom knew about but she tried to act like she didn't. I mean, this dude would leave the house at noon and then he wouldn't come home until about 3:00-4:00 the next morning, right before mom was getting up for work. I remember one particular incident that showed me just how crazy my moms and pops were going over the one they raised to be spoiled.

I was in a good sleep when I was awakened by the sound of the alarm beeping throughout the house. I guess my mother didn't hear it, because usually she would yell out, "Who is that?" but this particular morning her room door was almost shut all the way and she didn't say a thing.

The next thing I knew, Spoiled came into my room saying, "Bra, Bra, Bra", in a whisper trying not to wake up moms and pops.

I was startled a little bit and I asked him what was up. He started ranting off, "Bra, I was at Quarter Pounder and this dude was talking shit. I need you to go back up there with me to handle him."

I asked Spoiled who he was with, and he said that he had about six dudes with him.

"So you want me to get out of bed and go get life in prison because someone was talking shit to you while you got six motherfucking dudes with you that could have handled that shit while ya'll was there?" I said, frustrated that he even had the nerve to come ask me for help.

"Them niggas with me soft bra, they ain't gone do shit!" Spoiled whispered.

"Well that's what you get for riding with soft niggas!" I said simply.

"So you ain't going to help me?" he asked.

I looked at him sternly and replied, "Not at all. It's three in the fucking morning and you should have had your ass in the house anyway."

He stormed out of my room mumbling under his breath and my mother must have heard him talking because she asked me what Spoiled was talking about. I told her to go back to bed and not to worry about it, but of course she didn't listen to me and she ran to the front window to see what Spoiled was doing. She saw him drive off with a van of people right behind his car and she yelled to pops to get the gun because someone was following Spoiled and she had to go and help him. This shit was unreal to me, because I couldn't believe that my mom was ready to put in work for her son. Pops got the gun and ran outside to the suburban that my mother had running and I heard them screech off in pursuit of Spoiled and the van that she thought was following him. I laid down and thought to myself that I'd left the frying pan and jumped right into the fire. I mean, prison was less stressful than what was going on with my family on the streets, and here all this shit was happening because of one spoiled ass nigga. Moms, pops, and Spoiled came back into the house after about 15 minutes and I asked her if everything was alright. She told me that she thought that the van behind Spoiled was someone following him but that it was just his friends who were driving behind him. I had to give my mom and pops much respect because they were ready to bust some rounds for their son. Me on the other hand, I wasn't about to go back to prison for a nigga that hadn't even written me a single letter the entire time I was in prison; it just wasn't going to happen.

After the incident with Spoiled, I knew that I had to find myself a place to live as soon as possible because that house was driving me insane with all the drama that was going on there, and all because of one idiot motherfucker.

The second strip show was as good as the first one. This time my fraternity brother Damon came from Los Angeles to see me now that I was out. Damon had graduated Fresno State with a degree in communications. Damon was happy to see me and I was sure that he was going to bring me my things that I'd left in the apartment we shared (when I caught the robbery case), but I was sorely disappointed. I asked him where my sentimental things were, like my class ring and my brother's class ring. He gave me a lame ass excuse about how he had put my stuff in storage and that he didn't know what had happened to it when he moved.

I literally wanted to kill that dude, because if it were him that went to prison I would have guarded his things with my life or even given them to his mother. That goes to show you how hard it is to find loyal people in this world. I held a grudge against Damon from that point on because I felt betrayed by someone that I had risked my life for and yet he couldn't even keep my sentimental property safe while I was gone. After we talked, I drove to San Jose to do the strip show and I brought Damon with me. Damon was acting like he was a fucking saint at that point or something; I mean, he had something to say about every little thing. He even tried to tell me that stripping wasn't godly and that he couldn't understand how I was doing such a thing. This wasn't the same Damon I knew that was fucking all the bitches in college; this dude was definitely not the caliber of guy I wanted to be around. To me, he was a fake, wannabe sanctified motherfucker that I didn't have a desire to ever see again in life after that night was over.

The strip show was off the charts. I mean, I killed it and I noticed that I was getting better and better with each show. I was, of course, learning all the dances and tricks. After the show, I took Damon back to his mother's house in Oakland and I told him bye. I'd never used that word with anyone before but I used it with him because I didn't want to ever see him again. He was too sanctified for me.

My job at 24 Hour Fitness was great. I felt like I was at a club every day, because there were a ton of gorgeous women coming in and out of there on an hourly basis. At the time, I didn't have my personality all the way together because I was still used to just talking when there was a need for it. I wasn't a real conversationalist at the time; I guess being in prison all those years made me kind of introverted and anti-social but I yearned to get rid of my old personality. I used to watch all the other veteran personal trainers and I would envy their charisma. I knew that I would have to come out of my shell so that I could soar as a personal trainer as well as an entertainer.

After I started grooming my personality to be more approachable and more of a people person, I started getting clients left and right. I mean, I was training 12 people a day, which was very taxing on my body, but I was so money hungry that I continued training the clients until I got burned out from it – which was in about a month's time.

While I was training the 12 clients a day, I received the honor of being the number one trainer in the country for 24 Hour Fitness, and I was ecstatic about the award. I was finally getting into the swing of things and it felt good.

Everything was going good at this point but there was just one thing that I had left to do and that was to get myself another car because I was embarrassed driving the Cavalier around. When I had shows to do, I would park the car down the street from wherever I was performing so that the women wouldn't see what I was driving. All the strippers I knew were driving fancy cars and that was how the women rated whether a stripper was good or not, by what he drove. I guess they had the motto that you had to already have money to get their money, so I made sure I didn't let them see what I was driving. I told my mom about the dilemma I had with driving the car and she said that she already knew that the car was an issue from the first day I laid eyes on it.

My mother was a high class woman that raised her kids to be the same way, so she understood. At the time, 5.0 Mustangs were the hottest cars on the street and I told her that I wanted one. Spoiled had one that was all decked out and I liked it so I made it a mission to get myself one as well. I got the Mustang magazine to find out what car lots had them for sale and when I found the one I wanted I took my mother with me to look at it. When my mom and I got to the car lot, there were four nice Mustangs there and I felt like a kid at a candy store. I couldn't figure out which one I wanted the most, so I chose to test drive the one with the least amount of miles on it. With my mother in the passenger seat, I took the mustang for a test drive and I fell in love with all that power it had right away. I mean, I had gotten used to driving a fucking four cylinder to driving the most powerful stock car on the road; it was like day and night.

After driving the car, my mom asked me what I wanted to do and I told her that I wanted it. She immediately told the dealer to get the paperwork, and I couldn't believe that my mom was finally about to do something huge in my life. After the dealer got the paperwork together, after about two hours later I drove my new car home and it was fun. I felt like I had just bought a Rolls Royce or something. For me living in the hood, fresh out of the slammer, I was doing damn well in the three short months I had been home.

Once I got the Mustang I, of course, had to turn the music on in it, and you should have seen all the cats in the neighborhood with their envious looks. They were scared of me but they sure couldn't hide their hate. I mean, these dudes on the block had been selling dope since they were kids and most of them didn't even have a damn car, which was sad. My brother's car was grayish in color and mine was white with the leather peanut butter interior. We had the best cars on the block but boy I'll tell you, the Mustang was a stressful car to have because it was the most sought after car by the car thieves. I used to have nightmares about my car being stolen, so I immediately got a top of the line alarm system installed on it, along with tinted windows. I was on top of the world. I was personal training and stripping, and I was making good money. I was living the life many people only dreamed about.

After I had gotten the Mustang, I started getting a little cocky and I started feeling myself. Nicole and I were barely seeing one another because if I wasn't at the gym training clients, I was out doing strip shows

I called Ali and asked him if he knew someone I could have to mix my music and he had a guy for me that did all of the dancer's music. I made an appointment with the music guy and went and made myself a legit CD for my shows. I didn't realize that it was going to take so long to do the music the way I wanted it. That shit took almost eight hours and I was starting to wonder if the music guy was just stringing me along to get more money. I paid that motherfucker $200 and boy was I pissed. From there on out I learned a better system on how to finish my music faster than I previously did.

Once I had my music the way I wanted it, I had a lot more confidence when I did my shows. I felt like I was the shit at that point, and on top of that, I had bought some clean ass costumes from Ziac. I liked Ziac's style and the fur shit he used to rock. When I asked him where I could buy some of the shit he wore, he told me that he had some costumes that he had never performed in and that were too big for him, so he said I could check them out and see if I wanted to buy any. I went to Ziac's house and he had a shit load of costumes that I was able to take my pick of. I ended up buying three of the costumes from him – the only three that could fit me – and I knew those costumes were about to set me up on a whole different level as an entertainer. I was very appreciative of Ziac for hooking me up with the costumes, even though they didn't come cheap. I didn't care though because I knew that when I stepped into a show wearing the shit I had bought that I would get a lot of money thrown my way. Ziac let me know that if I needed anything else to just ask and he even said that I could go with him to his shows if I wanted to so I could learn the craft more. I told him I would most definitely go with him to his next show.

Money was rolling in at a good pace from my personal training and stripping, so I saved as much of it as I possibly could. Things at the gym were slowing down and I was training about four clients a day, which was peanuts. I got the job during the new year's resolution period where everyone was trying to get in shape, so things started off strong but here it was only three months later and damn near all my clients had stopped training. I didn't understand this at the time but my boss Mark finally explained it to me and I got it. I tried to stay patient with the job, even though I wasn't making the same as I was my first few months at the job. In the midst of my clientele decreasing, I became friends with one of the trainers, Candy Man, and he told me that he was looking for a roommate because his last roommate had up and left him with all the bills. I asked him where the apartment was and you wouldn't believe where he told me he lived. The apartment was down the street from my mother's house, which was perfect. I asked him how much I would have to contribute to the bills and he told me $600 a month, which was also perfect for me. I moved in the next day and even though my mother didn't want me to leave the house, I knew I had to get up out of that lion's den.

Things at the gym started picking back up and I was back to training about six clients a day. I was meeting some unique people while I was working as a trainer; in fact, I had this one client named Angel who let me know that if I ever needed weed or ecstasy pills to give him a call. At the time I was trying not to get involved in any illegal activities, so though I politely told him I would let him know if I did, I had no plans on taking him up on the offer. I had also started training a lot of horny ass women that were trying to get me to sleep with them but I was always afraid of mixing business with pleasure. I didn't want a crazy ass woman that I had screwed to be coming up to my job harassing me at work, so I refused them all. It was weird, because I didn't consider myself a real sexual person at the time, but women found me to be a sex magnate. I didn't understand it, I mean, I was just trying to get rich, and sex was always the last thing on my mind.

Everything was going great with the personal training and the stripping. I was making enough money to do what I needed to do but of course I still wanted more, so I contacted that Angel client of mine and told him that I had some people ready to buy some good weed and ecstasy pills. Angel had me meet him at his house and when I got there I saw that he lived in a guest house off of a huge ass mansion. I went inside and he showed me the weed he had and how he sealed it to keep it fresh.

He had a few pounds of weed in the house and he asked me how much I needed and I told him a few ounces. I hadn't sold weed in this quantity in years, not since I was in college, so I would have to learn the game fast – which wasn't a problem because Spoiled knew how to sell every drug there was. After I got the weed from Angel, I immediately started making calls to all the weed heads on the block. They were all excited and waiting for me to bring the weed so that they could buy some.

When I got to E Street, I sold the weed I had got from Angel and I made a few hundred dollars profit off of it, which was a good day's work for me. The next morning I woke up to the sound of my telephone ringing and one of my patnas called and said that the weed was cool but that it wasn't the fire they were used to. He asked me if I could get something more potent and I told him I would look into it. I called Angel and told him that I had the money for the weed and I needed to talk to him, so he told me to come to his house. I got to his house in no time and I gave him the money that he had fronted me the weed for. I told him what had happened with the cats I sold the weed to, and I asked him if he could get something stronger than what he had and he said that he was waiting on another shipment to come any day. I then told him that I needed some ecstasy pills and he told me that he would have them for me the next day. I told him I would see him when he was ready for me and I left.

I went to the block and told the cats that I was getting some better weed and E-pills (as we called ecstasy pills), and they told me to let them know when I had them. I didn't understand at the time how those dudes on the block didn't have any connections and how none of them had done any time in jail. I guess that's what you call block monsters – motherfuckas that don't leave the block and meet people.

I called up Spoiled and told him that I was about to get some E-Pills, and I asked whether he knew anybody that was looking for them. He told me to just give them to him when I got them and that he would have them all sold in no time. At the time I didn't realize that my little brother was taking E pills, but I used to wonder how the fuck he was so hyper and frantic all the fucking time. Not only that, but he was skinny as hell too. I should have realized what was going on, but I was still naïve to a lot of stuff that was happening on the streets.

The next day I went to 24 Hour Fitness to train my clients and Angel called me and told me that he had the shipment of pills but he was still waiting on the weed, which was cool because I wanted to see if I made a faster profit from the E-Pills anyway. After I trained all of my clients, I went to Angel's house and picked up the pills and they looked like skittles. That was my first time seeing them and I was taken back at how colorful they were. Angel told me that he would give me the pills on the front for $10 each. At the time, pills on the street they were selling for $20-$25 apiece, so I knew I was going to make a good profit.

Once I had the 100 pills that Angel had given me, I immediately called my brother and told him that it was on. I had Blue Dolphins, the most sought after pills on the market at the time.

"You got blue dolphins?" My brother said excitedly.

"Yeah, why?" I said, confused at the significance of it.

"Bra, those thangs are going to sell like crazy! As long as we keep them we will be rich!" He said.

I was glad to hear that because I needed all the money I could get. Once I started selling the E-Pills, things in my life took a turn for the worst. The first thing that happened was me wrecking my new Mustang that I'd only had for about two months.

It was a Friday evening and I had just got my hair twisted. I had dreadlocks at the time and they were down past my shoulders, because I had been growing them for about three years at the time. Anyhow, I had just left the hair shop and I was feeling pretty damn good because my hair was whipped and was about to drive to San Jose to do the strip shows I had lined up. It was 5:00 p.m. rush hour traffic on the 880 freeway, so traffic was stopped almost completely. I was in no rush because I didn't want to wreck the car I loved so much. As the traffic had lifted up, I began driving and I looked down at my radio for a split second to turn up the volume and as soon as soon as I looked back up I realized the traffic had come to an abrupt stop. I slammed on my brakes but it was too late; my Mustang slammed into the back of a young Latino guy's car. My airbag immediately shot out and I was amped up off adrenaline so I jumped out of my car and aggressively asked the guy why he had slammed on his brakes like that. Of course, that was a stupid question, because I was in stop and go traffic and that's what happened in that type of traffic. The young Latino guy started asking me if I saw him and I went into a fit looking at the front of my damn car. I mean, I was only going five miles an hour and I couldn't understand how my fucking car was smashed up the way it was. The front of it was bent up bad. The Latino dude and I exchanged information and once the police officer arrived we gave our information to him as well. Afterwards the officer assessed who was at fault and then we were sent on our way. The highway patrol asked me if I needed a tow truck but I told him no. The car was still running but all the fluid was leaving at a rapid speed.

As I attempted to get my car to my mom's house, it started smoking and I knew that I could possibly fuck up the motor but I had to get my baby home so I continued to the house anyway. Luckily her house wasn't that far from where I had the accident, and when I finally made it to the block, everybody and their momma was outside. As I pulled up to my mom's house, I started hearing all the niggas from the block laughing and cheering because my car was wrecked. I knew that all of them were envious of me and my brother, and so they got off on seeing us fuck up our stuff.

As I got out of the car, I turned to those niggas and told them, "Me wrecking my car ain't nothing, because my shit is going to be better than it was before after I fix it up."

I went in the house and told pops and moms what had happened and they asked me what I was going to do about it. I told them that I was going to get it fixed, painted a different color and have some rims put on it. I had to cancel all my shows in San Jose that night because I wasn't up for doing anything but concentrating on getting my car fixed. I called up Nicole so that I could use her information to get myself a rental car and she rushed over and took me to Enterprise Rental Cars. I got an expensive ass Mustang trying to keep my baller status. That Mustang was entirely out my league price wise. It was $100 a day and for some reason I thought that my car would be ready in about two weeks but oh was I wrong.

After I crashed the Mustang, I kept doing all the activities I was do-ing – personal training, stripping, and selling E-Pills so my money flow was good. I was doing a lot of strip shows at the time and I was getting burnt out with the music I had so I asked the Men of Exotica owner if he knew someone other than the dude I got my last CD made from. The Men of Exotica owner said he knew a stripper cat named Q that had his own studio and he was the best when it came to mixing stripper songs. I had met Q once before, so I knew who he was talking about because Q stripped with Men of Exotica when there were big shows to do. The Men of Exotica owner gave me Q's number and I called him and set a day and time for a studio session.

A couple of days later I went to Q's studio in San Leandro and he had a nice set up. He seemed as if he was a pro in the studio, and to my relief he was entirely different from the white music producer that did my music the last time. I mean, Q knew exactly how to do the music, the intro, and the finale of the CD. I guess with him being a veteran stripper he knew exactly what I wanted. Q and I hit it off and we start-ed talking about the things going on in our lives. I don't know how we got off onto the subject of cocaine, but we did. He started telling me about how his family were big time dope dealers in San Francisco and he could get anything at any time, so I called him on it. I told him that I had a neighborhood where I could move nine ounces easy every day. He looked at me and said, "Come on bra, you can move nine ounces a day?" I told him yeah, with no problem, and Q told me that he was going to hold me to that and call me in a day or so with nine ounces. I thought to myself that the nigga was another one of those talkative ass niggas, the ones that would just talk to get a nigga to like him. After Q was finished making my CD, we shook hands and he said that he was going to call me in a day or so.

The next day came since Q and I had talked about our business venture and he actually called and told me to meet him at the studio. I couldn't believe that that cat was following through on what he said he was going to do. It was kind of weird to me that a nigga would give another nigga nine ounces of coke when he had really only just met him a day before, so this dude was a gambler for real.

I went to meet Q at the studio and when I got there we shook hands and he told me to look in the bag that was on the floor. When I looked in it I saw nine rock solid ounces of crack. He told me that he only wanted $400 for each one, which was lovely for me because ounces were going anywhere from $500-$600 on my block. I was looking at a quick profit and turn around if, in fact, it was some good crack. It had to be good crack for me to sell it to the niggas in my neighborhood because they only bought the best. I grabbed the ounces and told him that I would call him when I was done and he said cool. I was totally shocked at this dude because he didn't know me from Adam and yet he was forking over $3,600 worth of crack, which showed he had major balls.

I immediately took the crack to the neighborhood and the niggas on the block were happy to see some coke coming through because there was a shortage and all of their connections were out at the time. I sold all nine of those ounces in less than 30 minutes, and I sold it to them for $525 a piece because at the time they were paying $600. Needless to say they loved me to death for selling them the dope for less than what they were normally paying. I immediately called up Q and told him that we were going to need some more dope the next day, because the nine was already gone. Q said, "Stop playing bra, you just left the studio not even an hour ago!"

"I told you that I handle business, bra!" I said.

"We going to get rich together!" He said excitedly.

"You damn right we are!" I agreed.

Q and I were rolling for a good few months strong with the coke and we had become like brothers. Q and I were together so much that some broads had the nerve to ask us if we were gay; we were together that damn much. I mean, we went to breakfast every morning, then to the gym, then to the studio to cook and bag the dope, and then we started doing our strip shows together as a package deal to the ladies. We were bringing in mad loot but I knew in my heart that it wasn't going to last for long.

I started getting greedy with everything I was doing; in fact, I even started training clients under the table at 24 Hour Fitness, but the gym management caught onto that fast. I thought I was slick at the time. I would train six clients for the gym, and then I would train six of my own. It was obvious what was going on with me because I went from being the top trainer in the country and in a month's time to being the last ranked trainer in the franchise. The reason I went to the last trainer was because my sales of supplements and training sessions to clients dropped dramatically. The management team watched me one day while I was unaware and they realized that I was training 12 people but that I was only documenting six. I was called into the office after continuing on with that program for a month, and the corporate investigator told me that they knew what I was doing and that I had two options: I could either pay a fine of $500 back to pay for the wages I didn't give 24 Hour Fitness, or I could go fight a civil case in court. As soon as the corporate guy said court my heart started racing and I told him that I would be paying the fine. I was then told that I was no longer an employee with the company, so I packed up my things and told all my co-workers that it was nice knowing them and I left.

The funny thing about the situation was that my roommate, Candy Man, had ran into the same problem like two months before me but here I thought I was being more slick than him; I guess I was wrong.

Once I didn't have a legal job, except for stripping, I actually felt more alive and free because I wasn't on anyone's schedule but my own. Q and I's operation was getting real serious; I was not only selling dope to the cats in my neighborhood, but I was also branching out to San Francisco. San Francisco was kind of unknown territory to me, but there were a ton of 415 Kumi cats there that did what I told them to do.

Two months after I wrecked my Mustang, it was finally ready for me to pick up at the paint shop. I got it painted charcoal grey and I had the rims put on it right after they painted it. I was on top of the world once again. As soon as I picked up my clean ass whip, I drove down the block and once again everybody and their momma was outside and I stopped in front of them all and rolled down the window and said, "How you like me now?" I then started burning rubber until you couldn't see nothing on the street, so I waited for the smoke to clear and once everybody was able to see me again I turned on my knocking ass system with the 4-12 inch woofers and sped off while they all looked with envy in their eyes.

After I got the Mustang out of the shop, I bought a box Chevy – which was another hot car in the bay area at the time – and I sent it to the music shop to get a knocking ass system in it too. When that was done, I sent it to the same paint shop that had painted the Mustang. I was getting the box Chevy painted metallic silver, with tiny flakes in it that made the car look as if it had diamonds sparkling in the light.

I had been out of prison for six months and I loved the way things were going for me. Nicole and I had severed ties because we were on two completely different paths in life. When we severed ties it was done in a hasty manner. I had a telephone in her name and she told me that she was taking it out of her name, but the thing was that that particular phone was generating a lot of money for me, so I couldn't just have her shut it off. Instead I asked her to meet me at Sprint and told her I would transfer the phone to my name and she agreed to meet me.

I pulled up in the parking lot of the Sprint store and I had my music at a deafening volume that caused everyone to turn and see where the loud ass music was coming from. I hadn't seen Nicole since I had got my Mustang out of the shop, so when she turned around and saw that it was me in my clean ass car, she sucked her teeth and walked into the store. Once I got inside, I told her hello but she didn't say anything back. She just told the clerk at the counter that she needed to get my phone out of her name and the clerk took care of it. She stormed out of the store without saying a word to me and that was the very last time I saw her.

Since I was now totally single again, I was on the lookout for a nice young lady that had her shit together, with no kids. Spoiled, of all people, introduced me to a young lady that was far from having her shit together, and had a kid, but at the time I thought I was just having fun.

Monique was her name and she resembled the super model Naomi Cambell. She had a daughter that was about five years old, and Monique's life didn't appear to be in order at all. Monique was a fiery type chick who didn't take shit from anybody, and I mean *anybody*. I guess I was attracted to her ride or die type mentality, but that was about all I liked about her. She did a lot of things that I didn't like for a woman of mine to do. She smoked cigarettes, which I despised, and she smoked weed, which I despised even more. Monique's ambition was all in the wrong places. I mean, I always wanted a working woman that was almost naïve to the street life, but this wasn't the case for Monique. She knew probably more about the streets than I did. I guess that was because she was raised in Sobrante Park, one of the most infamous neighborhoods in the entire bay area. Her family was middle class but the motto in Oakland was, "If you can't beat them, join them!"

The day came when my box Chevy was ready to be picked up and I was one happy camper. I had Spoiled take me to the shop and when I got there I looked at the box Chevy and thought, "These niggas about to really hate me now."

I had already had the music put in it, so now all I had to do was get it lifted in the front how we Oakland boys were doing it at the time. I took it straight to the shop that lifted the cars and it was finished in about five hours, so I had Spoiled take me to pick it up. When I got to the shop, I was thinking, "Yeah, I'm killing them now!" I got in the box Chevy and turned the music up so fucking loud that I was able to be heard from a mile away. I was on top of the world and I'll never forget what I had in the CD player; I had old school Slick Rick's "Hey Young World" – a fucking classic that had more bass than damn near any song ever made. I drove down the block with the Slick Rick song pounding and everybody on the block stopped what they were doing and looked to see who was coming down the street with all that fucking music. Once I got in front of everybody, I put the music on mute and I arrogantly said, "I did it again!" You should have seen the look on their faces. They looked astounded, as if they were thinking "How this nigga only been out for a few months and he got two clean ass cars already?" I turned the music back on and just sat in the middle of the street looking at all of them while the music played. I wasn't trying to show boat my street success to them in a hasty manner, I was just showing them that they could do it too if they set their priorities right and stop blowing their money on shit that didn't matter.

Things were going good; I was on top of the world and I had money and two cars to prove it. I was doing better than people that had never been to jail at all, let alone seven years in jail. I did feel deep within myself that how I was living wasn't going to last though, because I was moving extremely too fast. It's crazy to think that, during that whole time, I didn't drink alcohol or do any drugs. If you had seen my Hyphy energy though you would have thought that I was on some type of substance.

"Buzzard Luck"

My streak of bad luck came about when I lost my job at 24 Hour Fitness and I started selling dope full time on the block. I was what you called a block monster at that time. I would come to the block after I worked out at around 1:00 p.m. and I wouldn't leave until about 4:00-5:00 a.m. I was being totally greedy, but I justified all the hours I put in so that the block would be rolling 24/7, all day every day, and because of my hustle the block was on fire.

I was selling a minimum of four ounces of chopped up crack every day. Off each ounce I sold I would make around $800-$900, so I was making anywhere from $3200-$3600 dollars a day. That's not even counting the ounces that I used to sell to cats on the block, so I was definitely rolling. My life had got fucked up in a matter of days all because a nigga from Brookfield was acting tough.

It was around 10:00 p.m. and my youngster Cam, a few other niggas and I were on the block waiting to sell the rest of the dope we had. One of the broads from the block came down the street screaming that some niggas were beating up Spoiled and Cam's brother Twon. Cam and I grabbed our guns and ran down the street to get whoever was getting on our brothers. When we got down there, my brother wasn't there but Cam's brother Twon was, along with another youngster. They had busted up mouths from being hit by this nigga from Brookfield who came to get revenge for the window of his van getting busted by one of the youngsters on the block. Instead of finding the person who did it, that nigga took it out on whoever was from the block. When the nigga from Brookfield did what he did, there were some other niggas with him and a few of them lived in the neighborhood. Once the situation got figured out, it was out of my hands but I knew that if a nigga pistol whipped me he would definitely feel the wrath of my violence. Anyway, a few days had gone by since the incident had happened and I didn't think anything more about it. Then the news had hit that one of the dudes that was with the nigga from Brookfield lived down the street from the block and he got shot in the head sitting in a car in front of his house.

Two days after the youngster got killed, the word was out that anybody seen on E Street was going to get shot up. I was the only nigga out on the block after the word had hit that it was war against us. On the third day I got word that my little brother had a warrant out for his arrest for the murder of the youngster that got shot. I couldn't believe it because my brother wasn't even in Oakland at the time of the murder; he had to do volunteer work for a ticket at the San Leandro boy's club so I couldn't understand how his name was even implemented in that shit. Once I got word, I called my little brother and told him to meet me at my apartment. Once he arrived, I sat him down and told him that he wasn't turning himself in because the time I turned myself in I didn't see the streets again for seven years. Spoiled was being the hard headed motherfucker he was though, and so he went to the block anyway and 10 minutes hadn't passed before he was apprehended by the Oakland police. My mother said that the police had picked him up on murder charges and that they were searching her house for any evidence they could find. What she told me next had me shook up like crazy. My mother said that while the police were searching the house they saw some pictures of me and started asking her questions. I immediately called my youngsters Cam and Bootsy to see if they wanted to go with me to Reno.

Things were moving too fast so I wanted to get the hell out of dodge for a day or two to think about what was happening. Cam and Bootsy said they would go with me so I picked them up and we headed to Reno to go and gamble.

It took us about four hours to get to Reno and I did a lot of thinking while I was driving the Mustang there. When we arrived, we got us a hotel room that I didn't see again the whole time we were there because I was on one fucking crap table for 12 hours straight. I'm not bullshitting you, I was on that table gambling my ass off. That crap table almost took all my damn money, so I had to fight to get it back. The only thing that took me away from that table was Cam and Bootsy coming down at 10:00 a.m. saying, "We know that you haven't been at this table since we got here?"

"You damn right I been here! Them motherfuckers had my money and I had to get it back!" I said. When we left Reno, I had won $600 and I was happy as hell because I would have been sick if I had lost my damn money. We left the casino and I went and filled up the car and we made our way back to Oakland.

When I got back to Oakland, shit wasn't looking good. Moms and pops were a nervous wreck because their baby boy was about to fight a murder charge, and fighting a murder in Alameda County was hell. I tried to keep moms and pops as calm as possible, but I was also irate about the situation myself at times. My whole problem with the situation was, how in the hell did Spoiled's name get implemented in that shit anyway? I mean, we had proof of where he was at the time of the youngster getting killed. This was a fucked up situation and for the sake of my mother, I was going to do my street investigation.

After getting at niggas about the situation, I came up with a lot of pertinent information. I was going to visit Spoiled while he was at Oakland County Jail. I always told him not to be talking about his case to anyone, because niggas were always looking to snitch on somebody so that they could get out of their situation. I gave Spoiled the do's and the don'ts of the jail shit. After visiting him for almost two months straight, he was transferred to Santa Rita, which was in Dublin California and about 30 minutes from Oakland. When he got transferred to Santa Rita, I went and visited him there too and I was allowed to get all the way down the corridor. That's when I saw 10 deputies walking down the corridor at me and I told Monique and Spoiled's girlfriend that the sheriff was about to come get me and they both said that he wasn't tripping on me. I'm never wrong with my intuition. The next thing I knew the deputies were standing around me and they said, "Let's go!" I walked with them down the corridor and asked them what the problem was, and they told me that I couldn't visit an inmate while I was on parole. They also said that if I wanted them to be real assholes, they could violate my parole for being on the premises. I told them they wouldn't have to worry about me coming up there again, but little did I know that I would see them again, though on different terms.

Things on the streets were very devilish after my brother got locked up. I had become very paranoid and I started carrying my gun everywhere I went. I didn't care if I was at church; my gun was with me at all times. I went to all my brother's court dates and the last court date I went to was his preliminary hearing. At that time the family and I had Spoiled a top of the line expensive ass attorney.

The attorney cost the family $50,000 and if there was a need for private investigators or other specialists there would be additional fees. The preliminary hearing was my last court date I was able to go to, because I got irate in the court room when the eye witness – which was a young girl that was in the car with the youngster when he was killed – said that she saw my brother's nose and that that was how she knew it was him. I went ballistic in that fucking court room; I stood up and told the court that the bitch was lying.

The judge banged the gavel and said, "Order in the court! One more outburst and you will be escorted out of the court room."

Our attorney started questioning the girl and she got real snobby with him, sucking her teeth after every question.

"How did you supposedly see my client when it was in fact dark outside?" our attorney asked her.

With an attitude, the girl replied, "I just did!"

I couldn't help myself. I stood up again and shouted, "Bitch you better stop lying on my brother!" The judge immediately told the bailiff to get me out of there. I walked out talking shit and I waited in the lobby until my mom, pop, and the attorney came out of the hearing. I immediately told the attorney in an aggressive manner that he better make sure my brother beat the case. The attorney looked frightened and said nervously that he would do the best he could. I looked him in the eyes and said, "I'm serious bra!" and at that moment the attorney knew that I wasn't fucking around with him. He looked like a dog who had had his spirit broken as I was talking to him.

Days had turned into months that Spoiled was in jail fighting the murder charge. Spoiled was well taken care of while he was in jail. Everyone knew he was my little brother so they knew not to fuck with him. I continued on with my hustling on the block, but I had become a monster who wasn't one to fuck around with because I carried a lot of anger over everything going on in my life at the time.

Things started turning for the worst fast. I had been out of jail for 11 months and I had become feared in the streets because I had become a no nonsense kind of guy. I kept my gun on me at all times and I regulated how business was being handled in the neighborhood. Everyone was very cautious around me because I was considered unpredictable and they couldn't understand me very well.

It was a good day on the block. I had made a ton of money and I was ready to go enjoy the rest of my night because it was only about 6:00 p.m. and I had sold practically all the dope I had. I asked my youngster Cam if he wanted a ride home because he didn't have his car. He said as soon as he sold his last crack rock he was ready to go. I stood off to the side while Cam made his last sell of the night to a dope fiend we knew from the neighborhood. After Cam sold the fiend his last rock, we proceeded to leave the neighborhood and a van with tinted windows pulled up and the police jumped out of it and told everyone to freeze. I took off running towards my mother's house with a police officer hot on my trail. Derrick and Darold were outside in front of their mother's house and the cop and I zipped by them. I opened my mother's gate and slammed it behind me which gave me a little time to throw the few rocks I still had into the bushes. I then jumped over a few more fences but the fucking police had every place I was running to surrounded. I ended up in the back of the apartments, where I initially ran from, and there were a ton of police waiting on me. They all saw me and told me to get on the ground. Once I did what they told me to, they started hitting me and one of the cops even pulled out his knife and cut off a few of my dreadlocks. He told me to cut that shit off and I was totally infuriated at what had just happened to me. I knew then that after 11 months on the streets, I was on my way back to prison.

"Back Again"

When I got to Oakland jail, it was all new to me because I had never been there before, but jail was jail and I still felt like I was top dog there just like anywhere else. I was a legend in and out of jail, so I got much respect from everybody. Once I went through the procedure of getting searched, I was escorted to a room by myself and I was hand-cuffed to the table so that I couldn't move much. After sitting in that room for about an hour, a black, bald head detective came in and start-ed rambling about my brother's case. This cop was crooked and I could tell. He was saying, "Yeah, I know your brother didn't kill anyone, but he wouldn't tell us who did it so he will be fighting the murder charge!" I didn't say a word; I just listened to him talk about my brother's case as if he were the person framing him. After he talked for a good 15 minutes, he saw I wasn't getting into any dialogue with him so he left out the room. Another cop came in and escorted me to a dorm area. When I got in the dorm area, I knew everybody in the motherfucker. I mean, it was niggas I went to school with and niggas that were in prison with me; it looked like a class reunion or something. Being in Oakland County Jail was no different from any of the other jails I'd been to. Chow was early as fuck, and nasty as fuck. Lunch was in a brown paper bag with dry ass peanut butter sandwiches. Chow at night time was nine times out of ten Mexican food, so there was no difference at all in the penal system's programs. I stayed at the Oakland jail for about four days before I was transferred to Santa Rita jail, which was like a fucking zoo.

The first process at Santa Rita was to give the deputies all of the clothing that I came with and in exchange I was given a yellow, two piece jumpsuit and some jelly sandals. The next thing was to get checked out by the nurse to see if I had any diseases or anything like that. After all that was done, I had to sit around for about eight hours to finally get placed in a housing unit. Once I got escorted to the cell I was going to be housed in, I had never been so happy to get to a hard ass bunk in my life.

I stayed in Santa Rita for about four months fighting the new case I was charged with called "directing traffic". The police wrote up my charges to say that I gave Cam a head nod to sell drugs to one of his informants. I was called the third player in a drug deal. Sounds crazy right? Well, I'm pretty sure the Oakland police just made up this charge to get people off the streets that they didn't want there. After fighting the case for four months, my court appointed lawyer scared my mother into telling her to tell me to take the probation. I didn't want to take no damn probation because I knew that by doing that I would definitely be doomed to be back in prison. As I finally decided to take the deal, I looked at my mother.

"Watch. This is going to turn out to be a bad decision!" I said to her. I then signed the deal and a week later I went to my parole hearing and was given a 10 month parole violation for being a part of a drug deal. I already had four months in, so I only had to do six more months, which I would do standing on my head.

After a month of waiting after my parole hearing, I was called at about 2:00 a.m. to pack my stuff because I was getting transferred to San Quentin. I was happy as hell to be getting out of Santa Rita because that recycled air was killing me.

The ride to San Quentin took about two hours because there was a lot of traffic in the morning rush hour, but I didn't care because I enjoyed looking in people's cars while I was on the journey to the big house. When we finally got to San Quentin, it felt like I was home somehow. I knew all the faces that I was seeing and it was just an environment that I was familiar with. As the prison bus pulled up on the yard, everybody stopped what they were doing and they stared at the bus to see if they could see anyone they knew sitting inside it, even though the windows were tinted pitch black and trying to see in them was pointless. Once the bus stopped, each inmate's name was called and that person had to tell the guard their California Department of

Corrections (CDC) number. Once they got to me, I gave the guard my number (J-62382), and then I proceeded to another guard to do the body search, which was the worst thing about being in prison. After I was done with that process, I went to the nurse to get the tuberculosis shot and then the property room to get my property that I was allowed to have. The guard gave me all my property because he remembered when I worked there. The guard gave me a devilish smirk and said, "Came back to see us huh?" I replied, "Yeah, unfortunately!" After I had my property I went to where the inmates were working and since I knew them I told them to tell my patna Abraham to send me some food. Abraham was a good friend of mine that had a life sentence, and he was an ex-Kumi member that was able to get out of Kumi on an honorable discharge. Abraham was also a nation of Islam Muslim that didn't mess around. He was a slim brother that had a decent amount of muscle packed on his 6'0" frame.

When I got out of prison the first time, I sent Abraham a few packages of things he wanted and from there on out he was a true loyalist to me. A lot of guys would say what they were going to do once they got out of prison, but I was the only one in Abraham's 15 years in prison that did what I said I was going to do.

After all the inmates were processed in the San Quentin data bank, we were then housed. I got sent to west block, which was the holding area for all inmates that were waiting to get transferred or sent to San Quentin's mainline yard. I had never been in west block but I had heard a ton of stories about how it was. West block was everything I heard about it – loud, filthy, crowded, and chaotic. It was like a fucking jungle full of wild ass animals with no sense at all. I had to get prepared mentally for the chaos that was ahead of me living in west block.

As I was getting escorted to my cell, I walked down the first tier and it was like a family reunion once again. People I hadn't seen in years were calling my name and I would stop at their cell and talk to them until the guard would tell me to keep it moving. I'll never forget how I saw one of my closet friends that I'd grown up with on E Street there, my Patna Travis. Travis and I had hung out a few times when I was out, so we were shocked to see one another in San Quentin. When I got to my cell I had a little scrawny celly that started shaking when I walked in.

He was lying on the top bunk, which was his assigned bunk but usually when a person's cellmate left, the person on the top bunk moved down to the lower bunk. In this case I guess the young fella didn't know the prison policies, but he made a wise decision because I would have made him get on the top bunk if it wasn't assigned to him anyhow.

As I was making up the hard ass steal bunk, I introduced myself to the first-timer (A person in prison for the first). He got comfortable after I talked to him for a while. I had to let him know that he didn't have to be scared or timid around me. He started loosening up then and we were able to have decent conversations after that point. As we were talking, some of my Kumi comrades starting coming to my cell to see if I needed anything because the word was out that I was in west block. I talked to my comrades for a while because they were west block porters and they were allowed to walk around all day until the last count time at night. After I talked to them for a while, I found out what was going on in west block and how things were being run as far as Kumi was concerned. After the Kumi cats left, my cellmate and I talked a while until the shutdown was recited. The shutdown was a cadence to get everyone in west block to give respect to those that were going to sleep. The cadence went like this – "West block, west block! The time is now 10:20 we ask for your participation and co-operation in shutting down today's machine. If what you have is not of the upmost importance we ask that you sit on it until the morning. To all my African brothers, njema usiku, to all my brown brothers, buenos noches, and to all the woods and others, a goodnight, chulewa!" Afterwards I read my book until I went to sleep.

Chow time in San Quentin's west block reception center was an early jail time of 6:30 a.m. I was groggy waking up because I didn't sleep well my first night in west block; I could never sleep well when I was in a new environment.

When I got up I woke up my celly and told him to get up too because we were about to be released for chow. I brushed my teeth and washed my face first, and then my celly did the same. After I brushed my teeth and washed my face, I sat on my bunk and it was another 20 minutes before I was released from the cell. I was anxious to see who all I knew that was locked up with me. Going to chow was always an adventure because you never knew what was going to jump off.

As I walked to chow with all the Kumi soldiers that were on my tier, we talked about all the current events of what was going on at the prison, and of course there was tension between the blacks and whites because of a drug deal gone bad, which was the number one cause of prison riots. I was use to that type of situation in prison, so it didn't bother me one bit. I just made sure that we had knives in case a riot broke out with us and the whites. When I got to the chow hall a few guards that knew me started joking with me about my returning to prison. They all said that they thought that they would never see me back because I was different from the rest. I simply told them that shit happens. I reminded them that I was a black man in America living in the ghetto after all and that I was bound to be back in prison eventually. The guards were like, "yeah, we heard it a million times before!" I shrugged my shoulders and continued in the chow hall. West block chow hall was huge and it had two sides to it. The chow hall held at least 500-700 inmates at a time. The food was, of course, the same slop as usual. We had the Mexican special breakfast: eggs, tortilla, salsa, beans, and milk. I rolled the eggs up in the tortilla and ate the two of them in four bites and then I started talking to all the people I knew. After 10 minutes of getting to eat the slop, the guards escorted each row out of the chow hall, and on the way out each person had to grab their sack lunch. As I grabbed my sack lunch, one of the guards shook his head at me and said, "Boy you came back to hang out with us, huh?"

"Naw bitch, I didn't. You ole Uncle Tom ass nigga!" I said. This was, of course, a guard that was affiliated with Kumi as he was one of our mules that brought in whatever we told him to in the prison, be it drugs, alcohol, or tobacco; he did what Kumi told him to do. I snickered at him and he snickered back at me and I walked to west block talking to my Kumi soldiers about the prison politics.

Once back in my cell, I was informed by my comrades that it was our day to go to the yard and take a shower. There were procedures to be up-held being on the yard and taking a shower. There was always a need for security in prison at all times and security is what can make or break a gang in prison, so I was hoping that the Kumi cats that were already in west block before me had everything in order.

I dozed off for a while reading a book on my bunk until I was woke up by the guards yelling over the intercom that it was yard time. It was about two hours after chow time. I jumped off my bunk and made myself a sandwich from my sack lunch because I was starving. That shitty ass breakfast didn't do me any justice. After I fixed myself a sandwich, I walked out of my cell and I was met by my Kumi comrades and we all went to the yard together to meet up with all the other Kumi members.

The west block yard was about the size of a small park. There were only two basketball courts, two huge ass garbage cans, and concrete. I met up with all the Kumi members and they all knew who I was so they didn't even attempt to screen me because I was known as a big honcho now that had put in major work for 415 Kumi, so I was well respected.

I talked with the high ranking officers that were in charge of west block before I had gotten there, and it seemed as though they were running things according to protocol so I didn't have any preservations about how they were handling business. After I talked to the officers and met the Kumi members that I didn't know, I went to get me a workout in. I started off by doing two sets of 50 pushups, then I had one of my comrades sit on my back while I did five sets of twenty. After my last set of pushups, I took off my shirt and the entire yard went quiet and everyone was staring at me in amazement.

I mean, the guards as well as the inmates were in utter shock at how swole I was. For those that didn't know me, it was as if they had seen a ghost and they couldn't stop staring, but fortunately for me I was used to getting stared at. I then started doing up-side-down pushups. I did five sets to failure of these. After that I went to the two garbage cans, which had handles on them that I was able to do dips off of. At this point all the Kumi cats came over to where I was to subconsciously let everyone on the yard know that I was with them. An inmate with huge muscles in prison was highly respected until he did something to lose that respect – such as get his ass whooped, fuck with a punk, or do drugs. I was a king in prison because I whooped ass, called the shots, and was never talked bad about in any shape or form.

After I completed my workout, I walked around the yard so that all the inmates could see that a new general was in town. If anyone wanted some problems with me, I let it be known that they would definitely have them. I caused an uproar on the yard, and then the two hours were up and it was time to get ready to take what I called "a shower in hell".

Taking showers in prison reception centers were the worst and I never looked forward to being amongst other men and transsexuals. I had mastered the art of taking bird baths in my cell, but bird baths would still leave me with an unclean feeling so I would bite the bullet and take a shower every time I was given the opportunity to. Taking a shower as a gang leader was no easy process. I had to be on my guard at all times while I was showering so that rival gangs wouldn't try to ambush me and kill me. Being a gang leader wasn't peaches and cream, because everybody's theory in prison was, "Take the head and the body will follow!" What they meant by that was that if you harmed the top person the soldiers wouldn't know how to function; therefore, there had to always be top notch security on all top ranking officers. I didn't trust hardly anyone, not even many of my own soldiers, so I would assign the people that I felt 80% comfortable with to look out for me. I never put 100% trust in anyone.

The shower in San Quentin reception center was horrid. I made sure that when it was time for me to wash up that I would have one of my soldiers go and designate a shower just for me. I did that so that I could be the first one in and the first one out, because anyone after that was going to be standing in a sea of dirty water that could possibly cause athlete's foot or maybe even gangrene or something. The reason the water rose the way it did was because the drains to the showers couldn't drain fast enough for all the people that were in there, not to mention the hair that would clog up the drain. It was out right disgusting so I had to use my prison power to the fullest to take myself a decent shower. Life in reception center was the worst stage of being in prison. This particular time in the reception center was very hard for me because I had just come from Santa Rita where I ate whenever I got hungry.

In San Quentin's reception center, there was a process to getting to the store. Things had changed dramatically from what it was like the last time I was at San Quentin. I had to be at San Quentin 30 days before I was eligible to go to the store. In the meantime, I had sent word to my good friend Abraham who was a lifer and who had some pull within the institution to go wherever he needed to go. I sent Abraham packages when I was on the streets for this very reason. I guess I knew deep down in my spirit that I would return to prison so I made sure that I took care of the people that I knew could help me if I did. I had gotten word to Abraham that I was back on the yard and that I needed everything until I made it to the store – everything meaning cosmetics and food. After a few days of me sending the message, Abraham came to see me with a huge laundry sack full of shit he knew that I needed. It was weird when I saw Abraham because I was happy to see him regardless of seeing him in prison. He was like an older brother to me and I held him in high respect. Abraham and I talked for a while catching each other up on prison life and street life, then he had to leave for count time. He told me that he would check on me whenever he had the opportunity. We said "chulewa" to one another and he went to his living quarters in north block. My cellmate was in awe of how much power and respect that I had in San Quentin, and I could tell that his curiosity was heightened about the Kumi organization too. Usually inmates that were around me who weren't affiliated with the gang wanted to become Kumi members just by seeing the positive impact I had on people, and of course because of the power I had as well. 95% of the inmates that were my cell-mates eventually became Kumi.

After Abraham brought me all the things I needed, I was in a better place physically, mentally and emotionally because I had food! Without food I was mean and super grouchy. I didn't have compassion for anything or anyone in that state of mind. Abraham bringing me that food did a ton of good for me and the prison occupants.

Once I got the food from Abraham and went to the store to get more food, my time in west block went by fast as hell. Before I knew it I was getting transferred to San Quentin's h- unit, which I wasn't too happy about, because I preferred to be in north block. Beggars couldn't be choosy though so I packed my things, said my goodbyes to everyone that was still in west block, and then I headed to H-unit.

"Hell-unit again"

As I stepped on the H-unit yard I was greeted by my Kumi comrades as if I were the president of the United States. I have to admit, it felt good to be respected the way I was. I went into the assigned dorm that I was housed in and it was like a reunion again. I mean, people that I hadn't seen in years were in that dorm. It was good to see old friends, but then again it was sad because we were all returning through the revolving door of incarceration. Unfortunately, we were proving society to be exactly right about the statistics – that black men in America were either dead or in jail by the age of 25.

My first day of working out in H-unit caused an uproar. Just like everywhere I went and did my thing, people were amazed at my physique and everyone wanted to work out with me. That didn't last long though because I worked every part of my body, especially legs, which hardly anyone in prison wanted to do. I must say, I enjoyed seeing all the guys that started working out with me gradually fall off to the wayside one by one. It gave me a sense of empowerment and made me feel much more superior than the weak individuals that couldn't continue on the journey.

Being in H-unit had its pro's and con's, as do all things in life. There were always drug deals going on and there were always fights because of the drug deals gone bad. The bad part about being Kumi in H-unit was that the prison made it so that anything that went down as far as violence was concerned was immediately blamed on Kumi. We always felt the wrath of any type of violence that went down on the yard.

My 10 month stay at San Quentin went by pretty fast, other than the last month, which went by slow as fuck. The day finally came to be released and I never showed any excitement over it because – living the life that I knew I was going to continue living – there was no need for celebration because I never knew when I would be back. I said my farewells to everyone and told them that I would see them on the streets. Everyone was happy to see me go home but sad that I was leaving them in San Quentin's hell hole. I knew the feeling they had because I would always get that confused feeling when one of my close friends went home.

Of course my mother sent me a top of the line Sean Jean sweat suit with some clean ass Nikes again, while all the other inmates that were being released with me were leaving the prison in prison sweats. I looked at them all and thought to myself, "Ya'll must have burnt your bridges!" They didn't have anybody to send them any fucking clothes, so they had to go home broadcasting that they were just released from prison; now that's fucked up.

"Back at It"

As we approached the front of the prison, I saw Monique waiting for me to come. My heart started pounding with excitement because I knew that I was about to be a semi-free man. I say semi-free because when you're on parole you are almost free until you get off. I jumped out of that van so fast I think it was still going. I hugged Monique for a second but I didn't kiss her because I was leery of what she had been doing while I had been in prison for 10 months. I knew that Monique loved to have sex, so I didn't trust her at all. As we walked to my car I was devastated; it looked nothing like it did when I last saw it. It was dirty as hell and there was a dent on the side rear panel. I wanted to cry and I immediately went into a rant about her not taking care of my car the way she should have. She gave me a lame reason why the car looked like it did and I let it go for that moment. I got in the car and let her drive while I soaked up the free world.

I didn't talk to Monique much on the way to my mother's house. I was trying not to go off on her about my car and my mind was wondering off with thoughts on who she had been screwing while I was gone for almost a year.

My second day on the streets came fast because everyday life on the streets is way faster than slow ass prison life. After eating breakfast I decided to call the only cat I knew who was in my corner – my business partner Q. I hadn't talked to Q but maybe three times while I was in jail for those ten months. I've never been one who liked to talk on the phone, unless it was to talk to my lady or my mother and even with them I kept my conversations brief and to the point. When I called Q he answered his phone the same way he always did, full of energy and enthusiasm.

"What's up bra?" I said when he answered.

"I know this ain't my brother that hasn't called me in months!" he said jokingly.

"Yep! It's your bra!" I replied.

"So when you getting out of there?" he asked me.

"I been out for two days bra!" I laughed.

Q immediately went into a rant on the phone. "How you been out for two days and ain't called me?" he said.

"You know how it is bra, had to relax for a few and get my mind right!" I told him.

"When we putting things back together?" Q hurriedly asked.

I told him that we would talk about everything in person the next day at the gym, because we didn't do any talking on the phone about business. He said cool, and said he would see me at 24 Hour Fitness in San Leandro at our usual gym time of 10:00 a.m. I could hear in Q's voice that he was excited to have his road dog back with him, and I knew that we were going to get a ton of money together this go round because I had got the hook-up on how many ever kilos of cocaine that we could handle.

A month had passed and things were going good. I sold my box Chevy that I loved so much and I sold Monique's Toyota Camry too .I bought her a legend that my cousin was selling and I bought myself a Buick Rivera. Things were looking good and Q and I had us a hell of a program going. We would mostly supply San Francisco with all our dope. I didn't deal with the cats in my neighborhood too often because there were a lot of murders going on and the police were always there.

San Francisco's tenderloin district was a totally different demon from Oakland. I wasn't used to how the dope game was being played there. The drug dealers in that district were loose as a goose. They just made hand-to-hand sells right on the sidewalk without even caring who saw them. It was a fast paced city, and pretty unreal. I had a ton of Kumi members in the tenderloin so I felt secure in knowing what was going on at all times. Unfortunately, most of the Kumi members were on crack or heroin, but I didn't let that stray my love for them. I felt I would help the Kumi members that wanted help, which would later come back to bite me in the ass.

Q and I had things moving well. Q had a dope dealing broad that was like the queen bitch in the tenderloin, so when the word was out that she was outside, all the dope fiends in San Francisco would come and buy all the dope that Q had given her in less than one hour. I'm not talking one or two ounces either; I'm talking nine fucking ounces gone in one fucking hour. It was an incredible sight to watch. I, of course, would give my share of the dope to the Kumi members I thought were trust worthy and to a few females that had taken a liking to me.

A couple of months went by since Q and I had gotten our first kilo and things weren't going so good. The broad that Q had been working with was playing a lot of games with him concerning the dope. One particular time she said that she had been robbed for nine ounces of the dope at her hotel room in Vallejo. Q made her sell dope 24 hours a day until she covered the money she'd presumably lost.

I, of course, knew better, because I'd never trusted the bitch from the beginning. It wasn't long before the broad came up with another lame ass excuse, saying that someone had gone into her hotel room while she was away and taken another nine ounces from her. Once again, Q made her sell dope until she made up the difference for what she'd lost. I saw it as a game she was playing but Q didn't see it that way.

Eventually things got out of control in San Francisco. I had to act out some form of violence practically every day and I felt as if I were being influenced by some sort of demonic spirit. I decided I had to take a break from there and so I went back to my neighborhood. Things were getting better now that the police had calmed down with their hourly harassment.

Being back in the neighborhood had me paranoid at all times because that's where I had my terrible run in with the police that sent me away for the 10 months. Not only was I on parole at the time, but I was on probation as well, so I knew that I was an idiot waiting to go back to jail for being in the same area that landed me in prison to begin with.

Even though I was getting all the coke I could handle, I wasn't seeing the money I knew I was supposed to be bringing in. I was moving at least nine ounces a day but the profit after I sold them was only about $400, which was good to the average citizen but I needed to be moving at least a half of a kilo a day to see the money that I wanted. You see, the thing about being a drug dealer was that as fast as the money came in it also went out; therefore, I knew that I needed to make at least a few thousand dollars a day to live the life I wanted to live from selling coke. It was at that point when I started to realize that the drug game wasn't all that it was cracked up to be.

"You Can't BeSserious"

It started out a good day; I had to get the Riviera out of the shop because the motherfucker was a lemon and it stayed in there more than I drove it. I hated that I bought that car. I was happy as hell when I finally pulled it out of the shop, and I hoped that the Buick dealership had resolved the problem of the car cutting off after only being driven for over 30 minutes. As I drove down E 14th – as it was called before its present name of International Blvd. – I felt like I was on top of the world and things were starting to look up for me. I had about $5,000 on me that I had saved up from my extracurricular activities, so I was definitely happy. I decided to go to the block and see what was going on there, but as soon as I was driving down the street my car shut off. I was mad as hell and vowed to myself that I was just going to sell that piece of shit car because I had just spent $1,200 getting the fucking thing supposedly fixed. I started the car back up and parked in the driveway of a neighbor on the block. I put my money in a hidden spot in the car and I then looked around and I saw one of my youngsters named Bootsy. I asked him what was going on and if there were any dope fiends coming thru and he said that he had just sold two ounces in less than two hours, which was a good day for him.

I then went to my car and popped open the cap on my rims and pulled out an ounce of crack and started selling the rocks. I was almost finished selling the crack when Bootsy and I saw a car driving slowly down the street, so we ducked to the side of the house that we were selling the drugs in front of.

We stayed on the side of the house for a while, and because of it being pitch black outside we couldn't really see anything and we figured we couldn't be seen either. As we stood on the side of the house talking, we noticed what appeared to be a flash light flickering in the darkness. Then we heard, "Police! Come out with your hands up!" I made a mad dash for the fence behind the house we were at and I ended up on the next street over from E Street, which was D Street. I saw Bootsy trying to get over the gate but his pants got stuck and a cop apprehended him and handcuffed him. I was sitting on the porch of one of the neighbors on D Street, helplessly watching Bootsy get arrested, when all of a sudden I saw him trying to throw something from his waistband. To no avail, the gun he had in his waistband just dropped to the ground like the piece of heavy ass steel that it was.

The cop yelled out, "Help! He has a weapon!" and then pushed Bootsy to the ground until backup came to assist. As I sat scrunched over on the steps of people I didn't even know, I heard someone coming to the door to see what was going on outside and I knew that if I were found on their front porch that they would definitely report me to the police. I proceeded to walk outside the gate and act as if I were any ordinary citizen that was walking at night, but my plans were immediately altered when a police officer started running towards me and screaming for me to freeze. The foot chase ensued. I jumped a gate to get back to E Street and I hid in the bed of a truck. All the police were running around the truck until one of them looked inside it.

"Freeze! Police! Get down on your stomach!" He screamed, with his gun drawn point blank range at me.

As I was getting down on my stomach, the entire task force ran up on me and one of the cops hit me hard on the head with his flash light, splitting my head. I then grabbed onto one of the windows of my neighbor Melody's house, which had bars on it, as the police took turns hitting me with their fists and Billy clubs. I refused to let go of the bars on the window out of fear that if I fell to the ground they might kill me. I yelled out as loud as I could for all of the neighbors on E Street to hear so that they would hopefully come to my rescue. After a minute of yelling, Melody and some other neighbors came outside and asked the cops what they were doing to me. The cops told them all to shut up and go back into their houses. Melody told them that she wouldn't go back into her house until they stopped hitting me. The cops were all trying to pry my hands from the bars, and finally one of the cops said that if I let them go they wouldn't hurt me anymore. I released the bars and they all ran me into the ground, still punching me and trying to twist my arm in hopes of breaking it. While all this was going on, the Oakland Police Sergeant had his gun to my head saying, "Act like you're going for a gun so that I can blow your fucking brains out you fucking no good dope dealing son of a bitch!" Melody screamed for them to stop until they finally did and then they handcuffed me and picked me up to me feet. As they pushed me towards the police car, my mom and pops were right there asking them why they beat me the way they did. At the time I didn't know the extent of the police brutality that I had encountered but it must have been bad because my mother was crying asking why they had done that to her son.

I couldn't believe that I was going back to prison, and not only that, but thanks to the Oakland police I had gotten my ass whooped pretty good for the first time in my life. After the police took me to Highland Hospital to get staples in my head from the deadly flash light blow, I was transported to North County Jailhouse. When I got to the jailhouse, I was able to see my face and up until that point I had never seen my own blood. My head and my left eye were swollen like the Elephant Man. My fucking eye was closed and my head was covered with bumps. All I could think about was almost getting killed for a few fucking dollars that I would now have to spend on attorneys and commissary. I also knew that being on probation I could get up to five years in prison, so it was highly concerned with the situation.

My mother and Monique came to see me the next day in North County, and both couldn't stop crying at the sight of my face. I told my mother to get the car and she informed me that she already had that night. I told her where to find my money to hold for me, which I would use to get an attorney with, because this situation was going to need good representation. I was definitely filing a lawsuit against the Oakland Police for brutality. I hated visits dearly, and what made matters worse was having my mother and girlfriend see my face the way it was. It really hurt me that I was putting these people through all this madness. I had only been on the Streets for 90 days and I knew that I would be gone for some time on this one.

After being in Santa Rita for a few days, I asked around to see what attorneys were good with cases like mine and I was referred to an attorney by the name of Anne Belles, the daughter of one hell of a murder case attorney named Robert Belles. I had my mother contact her to see what her rates were and to see if she could represent me.

After Anne came to see me, we decided that she could help me in my case so I gave her a retainer fee of $2,500. She would also file my lawsuit against the crooked Oakland Police, and in this situation I knew that I would get paid because a lot of people had just gotten paid big from the other crooked cops in Oakland that called themselves the "riders". I really didn't care about doing the time; I just wanted to at least get something from it.

My adjustment to Santa Rita was tough because, as usual, the recycled air had me battling with tension headaches practically every day. On top of that, the few items that I did eat in jail were full of sodium, which I wasn't aware of at the time. All the Top Ramen, honey buns, Snickers Bars, potato chips and beef sticks were full of sodium and that was all I consumed every single day, so with all that – on top of the stress and recycled air – I was bound to get headaches.

After a couple of months in Santa Rita, I was scheduled to go to my preliminary hearing to see if the courts had enough evidence to proceed with trying to convict me for resisting arrest and being involved in the sales of narcotics. I was looking at eight years for the charges, but I wasn't worried in the least about it. I knew that I was definitely going to receive a parole and probation violation out of this whole ordeal, but I just wanted to get the least amount of time as possible. Truthfully, I didn't care about doing the time because I felt like jail was the best place for me while I was suing the city of Oakland for police brutality. The reason I say that jail was the best place for me is because the police had killed practically all the young brothers that had gotten money from the "Riders" case, so I preferred to fight from jail so that they wouldn't have a good chance at killing me before I finished my case against them.

As I was escorted into the court room for my preliminary hearing, I immediately saw my mother. She always made sure that she made me and my little brother's court dates. I then saw my attorney Anne Belles looking like she was a she-devil sent by Satan himself. When I said hello to Anne, she immediately went off into an angry fit about my brother "Q" giving her a check that had bounced, and she told me if she didn't receive ten thousand dollars by the day's end that she wasn't going to represent me any longer. I quickly responded by telling her goodbye and that she wasn't doing anything that a fucking public defender couldn't do anyway. Anne immediately addressed the court and said that she was no longer representing me, so the judge set a court date for me to get a court appointed attorney, which was a step above a public defender. My mother was in shock with her mouth moving the words, "What's going on?" I whispered to her that I would call her and inform her of what had happened.

I was mad as hell at this nigga "Q" for giving my attorney a fucking check that bounced, knowing damn well he didn't have the money to begin with. I wanted to kill that nigga. Then I was mad at the fake ass attorney for just taking the money I did give her without her hardly doing shit. I wanted to kill them both. I felt as if I were going to blow my top with hateful rage. All the other inmates and guards knew that they better not say anything to me because I was a walking time bomb.

The day came for the preliminary hearing, which was nerve racking because if the crooked cop didn't show up then the case would be dismissed. Cops usually made it to 99% of court dates, but there was always that 1% chance that they wouldn't and the case would be dropped. I never had such luck as getting a case dropped, but I always wished upon a star that I would.

When I got to the courtroom there was no sign of the police officer and I was getting really antsy because I knew, as well as the court, that if the cop didn't show up then they would have to dismiss my case. The judge then did something I had never seen before, he told me to go and wait in the inmate holding until he figured out what was going on. I knew right then that the judge was giving the cop time to make it to the court proceedings. I waited for about three hours in the holding cell before I was called out by the court's bailiff. My heart was racing because I knew there was a chance for my case to be dismissed. As soon as I walked into the court room, I saw a cop I had never seen in my life. The judge told me to have a seat and I asked my attorney who the police officer was and he said that he was an officer that was present at the time of my arrest. I immediately told the attorney to object because that wasn't the arresting officer that made the police report so how would a cop explain what happened in another cop's police report. Oakland justice system was as crooked as it got and all they wanted to do was get a conviction so they would bend the law by all means necessary. I was basically in a no win situation dealing with Alameda County courtroom.

I knew right then and there that I was doomed. The judge let the officer proceed with reading the other officer's police report as if it were his own. All I could do was shake my head and hope that my attorney would object to some of the nonsense that was being said. After the preliminary proceedings, the judge ranted off that he found reasonable cause to set a trial date for my case, so I knew right then that I would be in for one hell of a fight against the Oakland Police Department. At the time of the hearing I had been in jail for four months and I knew that after filing motions and postponements I would be in Santa Rita for at least 12 months minimum. As I walked out of the courtroom, my attorney told me that he was on the case and he would come to Santa Rita to talk to me. My next court date would be in two months, which was the pre-trial, or what inmates knew as "the court day that a deal would be made by the district".

The two months in Santa Rita were very eventful. I met a guy that had been living down the hall from me named "Crazy D". Crazy D, come to find out, grew up around the corner from me. It was strange to think how Crazy D and I had never spoken until this one particular day. I guess it was because he rarely came out of his cell, but we hit it off as if we were friends for years. Crazy D and I became good friends and I told him about the dilemma I had with a witness in my brother's case that was out right lying about him, saying that he had killed her boyfriend. I explained that my brother was in another city at the time of the murder and Crazy D listened attentively to my situation before suddenly asking me if I wanted the girl dead. He caught me by surprise with what he asked me, but I looked him in the eyes and I knew he was dead serious. I told Crazy D to do what he saw fit. I never thought in a million years that this dude would even pursue the situation when he got out of jail, because people always talk when they are in jail but when they are released they forget all about what they said they were going to do.

A month went by after Crazy D and I had talked about the situation with the lying witness, and the next thing I knew Crazy D was getting called on the loud speaker to be released. He came by my cell and told me that he was going to take care of that situation, and I told him thank you and that I would surely bless him when I was able to. Crazy D left the pod and as I watched him leave I got the feeling that he was going to carry out what he said he was going to do.

A few days had passed since Crazy D had been released and I talked to my mother on the phone. She was hysterical saying that I messed up my brother's case by sending Crazy D over to that girl's house. I asked her how she found out about that and she said that my little brother's attorney called her and said that a guy was arrested for threatening the witness of the case. My mother asked me why I would have someone do that and I told her that I didn't intend for it to happen the way it did. I could tell that she was upset with me and I definitely began to wonder whether I made the right move in doing what I did.

A day after I talked to my mother about the witness situation, I got word that Crazy D was back in the building but on the other side now. I sent a message to him to see if he needed anything and he said he did, so I sent him some food and cosmetic items. A few hours after I sent the stuff to Crazy D, a porter came to my cell with a letter from him. In the letter Crazy D kept saying that he thought I told him that my brother hadn't done the crime. I was getting mad as hell reading the letter because I sensed fear in what he was writing and I became worried about Crazy D saying something to the police that he shouldn't, something which could have gotten me in a world of trouble. I wrote him back a letter letting him know that what I told him about the case was official and that I never would have sent him through there if my brother had committed the crime. I felt betrayed that Crazy D would have even thought that I had lied to him. I felt we had a better report with one another than that. I was on edge worrying about the situation and about whether my family felt that I could be the reason why my brother might get life in prison. I prayed to God that this situation turned out good and my brother would beat this false charge.

The days leading up to my pre-trial were stressful because I not only had to worry about my situation in prison, but I had to worry about my brother's situation as well. I couldn't stop thinking about how I could possibly be the reason for my brother doing a life sentence in prison. I also got charged with attempting to dissuade a witness, so shit was stressful for me at that time. To escape all the chaos in my life, I indulged myself into my workouts and reading. Crazy D and I stopped all communication with one another because the district attorney had the guards on watch out for us. I was having a rough time dealing with all that shit, but I took pride in being a warrior that never buckled under pressure.

My pre-trial hearing was here and I was nervous as shit to hear what the district attorney was offering me. Before I went into the courtroom, my attorney came and talked to me and said that the district attorney was offering me eight years. I laughed at him and asked him if he was serious and he looked at me with a serious look on his face and said, "Yes I am serious!" I told him that I refused the offer and for him to set a trial date for the earliest possible date. He asked me if I was sure that I didn't want the deal, and I gave him a fierce look that said I would kill him if he asked me something so stupid again. He got the picture and left out of the small holding room and went back into the courtroom to tell the district attorney what I said. After about ten minutes my attorney came back and said that the D.A. was now offering five years instead of eight, but I told him I wasn't taking that either and that we could set the trial date as of now. My attorney left once again and after about 15 minutes he came back and said that the district attorney was offering two years on the case and the probation violation ran concurrent. I looked at my attorney and said he had a deal, because I knew that I could have received five years on the probation violation alone. That was the best deal I could have gotten so I jumped all over it.

My attorney left out and I felt relieved to be putting this shit behind me and moving on with my life. I knew at that point that I had around nine months left to do on my sentence after I got the time deducted that I had already done in Santa Rita. I felt good in my spirit about the whole two year deal. My attorney came back and told me that another court date was set for sentencing, which would be in a month. I asked him if we could do the sentencing right now and he left out to ask the judge. I wanted the case to be over with so that I could hit the penitentiary and get my time started. The attorney came back and said that the judge agreed to sentence me right at that moment, and I was happy as hell.

The court bailiff came and removed me from the holding cell and took me in the court room, where the judge immediately started calling out legal codes and asked me if I indeed agreed to the two year sentence.

"Yes your honor!" I said.

I was given a paper to sign with the agreed deal on it and I immediately signed it before the district attorney could switch things up on me the way they did with my first case in Fresno County. The bailiff took the signed paper to the judge and he read off the terms of the deal and said that I would start my sentence as of that moment. I shook the attorney's hand and thanked him for a job well done. I was then escorted to the holding tank with all the other inmates waiting to go back to Santa Rita. I was on cloud nine knowing that I only had around nine months left to do in jail.

When I returned to Santa Rita I had the look of triumph written all over my face and everyone could see it. All the inmates were out for pod time and I immediately told my Kumi comrade who was on the phone that I needed him to get off so I could call someone. He immediately told his loved ones that he had to go and then he handed the phone to me. I called my mother and told her that I took two years, so I would only have to do nine months max. My mother was happy that everything was almost over for me and she asked me about the other charges I was charged with, the ones dealing with the witness situation. I told her that the dissuading witness case was dropped due to lack of evidence, not to mention Crazy D kept it solid. Now I just had to wait for the parole board to come and issue out their time, which wouldn't matter because I knew I would max out on their 12 month max time anyway.

An entire month went by until the parole board came to sentence me to their time. I was sentenced to 12 months, which didn't matter because I was doing 16 months total anyway. Two weeks after the parole hearing, I was called at three o'clock in the morning to bag my things because I was being transferred to San Quentin.

The ride to San Quentin was very familiar to all the other prison bus rides I had been on. I had, after all, been on several bus rides to several prisons, so I was well acquainted with them. As I rode on the Grey Goose to San Quentin, I looked out the window at all the people that were going about their daily lives. They weren't the slightest bit concerned about the inmates that were on the bus going to prison. When I rode the prison buses, I always found myself deep in thought about being a free man in society Time on the bus always went by faster than I wanted it to because it seemed on those rides as if I were still a free man.

Pulling into San Quentin was always the same because the inmates on the mainline yard always stopped whatever they were doing and watched the incoming Grey Goose intently. They stared into the tinted windows as if they had x-ray vision and were able to see through them; already they were searching to see whether or not they had any friends or foes on the inside. As the bus came to an abrupt stop, the militant guards always screamed out orders that could never be understood because of them trying to be overly militant.

As the guard at San Quentin called out my name to check in at the reception center, he looked at me with a smirk and said, "You made it back to us huh big fella?" I smirked back and said, "Yep, they got me back in this shit hole again!" I then went through the process of the prison intake, which I was very familiar with at this point in my life.

The correctional officers working in the reception center were all making cracks at me saying shit like, "Boy we thought you weren't coming back?" or "What happened swole dude, you couldn't handle them streets huh?" And the list goes on. I had to explain myself to a few of the guards that were cool with me because the guards placed bets amongst themselves on whom they thought would be back in a certain time period. I, of course, was the one person that the guards thought would never come back to prison for the third time, and it was shocking to me too because when I was a kid I vowed that I would never go to jail and yet here it was my third time doing real time.

Before I even finished going through the intake process, all the people that knew me at San Quentin were coming to see me at the reception center. It was pure pandemonium. All the Kumi members came to holla at me as well as all my civilian patnas. They all asked me what I needed and I told them the usual: food and cosmetics. My whole concern in jail was to make sure I had food to keep my muscles swole up and cosmetics to keep my ass clean. Before I could even leave the reception center I was loaded up with enough stuff to last me for months and I thanked all of them for looking out for me. I had sent them packages while I was on the streets, so it was almost like I was getting back the stuff I had sent them, crazy huh?

As the C/O (correctional officer) called out everyone's bed assignments, I prayed that I wouldn't be sent to the gym because it was wild as hell there and I knew that if I went in there I would have to keep the Kumi members in line. The guard kept calling out people to go to the gym and sure enough my damn name was called out to go to the gym. I never liked to be around a ton of motherfuckers in a dorm setting because I didn't get along with the low level types of criminals that stayed there or their low level way of thinking.

As soon as I entered the gym, a group of Kumi cats came running calling my name. I was more mad than happy to see those low life bums, but they were my comrades so I had to act like I was happy to see them; I was their leader after all. The Kumi cats grabbed my stuff from me without hesitation and took it to the bunk that I was assigned to. I immediately asked who my bunky was because I had to have the bottom bunk; top Kumi officers couldn't be exposed to harm as easily as civilians could. My comrades went and got the civilian that was on the bottom bunk and he immediately moved his bedding to the top bunk without even questioning as to why he had to move. Civilians gave Kumi the upmost respect because we ran the prisons in northern California and we made sure that all blacks were protected in the advent of racial conflicts.

After I got my bunk and locker in order, I had all the Kumi members come and pay their respects to me so I knew who all my soldiers were that were in the gym with me. There were a total of 25 Kumi members in the gym at the time and that was a hefty amount to be in one place. I felt much more secure once I got the head count of my soldiers; not only were there a lot of them, but I personally knew over half of them and knew that they would kill for me if they had to, or so I thought.

After I talked to all of my soldiers and found out who was in what positions, I mentally took note of how things were being run and I also took note to change some things that I didn't agree with. I got to the gym before the evening count time because all inmates had to be on their bunks while the correctional officers counted every single inmate to make sure that no one had escaped from the prison. After the count was taken, all the inmates were allowed to resume their normal program of watching television, playing table games, talking on the phones, or taking showers. I opted to walk around the gym and see who all were there – how many Mexicans, whites, blacks, and others. I had to get a feel for the environment that I would possibly be in for a few months. Things looked as normal as prison could look. Inmates were running around getting into mischief and most of them were looking to buy drugs to ease their minds from being in prison – total chaos was what it was.

I stayed in the gym at San Quentin for three months and I'd finally gotten comfortable and didn't want to leave but I was put up for transfer to either San Quentin Ranch or Pelican Bay's level one yard. I definitely didn't want to go to Pelican Bay because that was one hell of a bus ride.

I knew deep down that I wasn't going to get the privilege of staying at San Quentin. The prison officials had already paid me a visit and told me that they didn't want me to stay at San Quentin because I was too powerful. When the day for my transfer came I was woke up around one am and told that I was going to Pelican Bay State Prison. All I could do was say, "Damn!" I packed what things that I could and left the things I couldn't take with my Kumi soldiers. All of the Kumi members got off their bunks and sent me off with their farewells. I told them all to take care of themselves and to stay out of as much trouble as humanly possible, which I knew was going to be hard for 90% of those dudes.

A few inmates and I grabbed our property that we were taking with us and took it to the reception center where the correctional officers checked it all to see if we had any illegal things that we were trying to smuggle. After the correctional officer checked my property, he sealed it with tape and put a tag on it with my name and prison number on it.

Once the Grey Goose arrived I was shackled from ankle to wrist and put on the prison bus to Pelican Bay, which was going to be a long ass ride. I had to look forward to 10 hours and four dry ass peanut butter sandwiches on the way. I knew it was going to be rough riding all those damn hours shackled from wrist to ankle, but that was what happened when one didn't honor their freedom.

On the bus ride to Pelican Bay I tried sleeping the entire ride but I was uncomfortable as hell. The seats on the Grey Goose were slabs of metal that caused the ass bone to scream out in shear pain. I was only able to sleep in ten minute increments, which was torture because I would wake up thinking that I'd slept for two or three hours only to find out that I'd just barely closed my eyes. Total torture!

"Pelican Bay"

After 10 grueling hours on that shitty Grey Goose, we made it to the infamous Pelican Bay Prison. As soon as the bus stopped, all the muscles in my muscular body tensed up preparing for whatever the prison had to offer. As soon as all the inmates were off the bus, the wanna-be-tough-correctional officers started screaming commands for all the inmates to go into a holding cell and to remain silent until directly spoken to by an officer. I saw immediately that those correctional officers were going to be just as hardcore as I'd heard they would be. I've never had many altercations with correctional officers because I played by the rules and I never brought unnecessary problems to myself. Don't get me wrong, I've had my fair share of run-ins with the guards in prison, but when I did I was in the right.

My name was called to take the TB shot (tuberculosis injection) and I always dreaded getting it because it was said throughout the prison system that the prison was infecting each inmate with the disease. I was petrified of that damn shot but it was mandatory and if an inmate didn't take it they would get sent to the hole until they decided to comply. After the shot I was finger printed and then issued the property of mine that was allowed by Pelican Bay Prison. I was given most of my property with only a few things being confiscated because they weren't allowed. I was upset of course, but I got over it fast because I knew I couldn't do anything about it. After each inmate was given their property, the correctional officer screamed out where each inmate was to be housed. I was being housed in another gym setting and I hated it. I thought that I was going straight to Pelican Bay's ranch but I had to go through an orientation before I was able to be sent off there – if, in fact, I was even granted to go there by Pelican Bay's higher ups.

The walk to the gym was kind of eerie because it was the infamous prison that was rated the highest in prison murders and violence. I was definitely on edge and hoping that I didn't have to kill anyone and end up in prison for the rest of my life. This was a daily thought of mine the entire time I was in any prison.

Once at the gym, myself and the other inmates were greeted by an inmate that acted as if he was a correctional officer ranting off that he was the person that gave the new inmates the orientation speech. Mr. Talk-a-Lot, as I decided to call him, went on a rant about all the rules of the gym and what the correctional officers liked and didn't like. I mean, this dude would've been one hell of a police officer. He had the posture and the tone down perfectly. It wasn't the first time I'd seen such a spectacle, because at every single prison there were inmates just like this jerk. After Talk-A-Lot gave his 30 minute speech, each inmate was told their bunk number and was able to go and get situated. While I was making my bed a few cats came and hollered at me because they'd gotten word that I was a high ranking Kumi officer. I said what I had to say to the Kumi soldiers and that's when I found out that Talk-A-Lot was also Kumi. I should have figured because Kumi cats were the type to always want to run shit, which was a plus, because we always had first action on everything.

After I said my oath to the Kumi officer that screened all incoming Kumi members, I started asking my typical questions about how things were being run. Getting the info about the happenings on the yard took some time. There were all types of rules and stipulations that were in place in the prison, which I was more than used to by now. After getting the happenings, I assessed if I needed to alter any rules in the gym and I figured I would see how things went for a day or two before I made any decisions. I had the authority to do what I saw fit in any given situation or place that I was in.

The gym sucked because it was a compacted, congested space that had too many damn people in it, and whenever there were too many people in a small space, of course tempers would flare up and there would be physical altercations – which were normal for prison settings.

After my 10 days of being in the gym, I went to my classification hearing to see if I would go to the ranch or if I would have to finish my time in the gym. Of course I was praying I didn't have to finish out my time in the gym, because I needed some room to breathe and not be stuck in that terrible, congested place.

At the classification hearing there were four high ranking prison officials that read off my prison history to determine if I was eligible to go to the ranch or not. Luckily I was found eligible to go to the ranch, which I was happy about but I couldn't let the prison officials know, otherwise they might change their minds. It was set in stone that I would be going to Pelican Bay's ranch in a day or two. At this time I had about nine months to complete my two year sentence, but really I was doing about 16 months because of the back time that I had acquired during my stay at Santa Rita.

The following day came fast and I was called after morning chow to pack my property because I was getting transferred to the ranch. I quickly packed my things and said my farewells to the cats I was cool with that were staying in the gym.

About 10 inmates and I were escorted to the ranch in the rain; it was the winter time so it was raining cats and dogs at the bay, which was what all convicts called Pelican Bay. When I approached the ranch, there wasn't anyone outside at the time. We were escorted to the chapel area where there was another police ass inmate ranting off the instructions and rules of Pelican Bay Ranch. Once again, there were a ton of rules and stipulations that had to be upheld by each inmate and if they weren't, the gym would be the residence to receive disciplinary actions.

There were a lot of weird rules at the ranch, rules like: shirts had to be tucked into the pants while going to the chow hall and hands had to be to the side and not in the pockets while walking to the chow hall. There were a ton more rules that made no sense at all, but if these outlandish rules weren't upheld then your ass would be back in that congested ass gym, and I didn't want to take any part in that fucking gym so I was going to play the game like a seasoned veteran.

Once the rules were explained, each inmate was given their dorm and bunk number that would be where they lived until their respective release date. I went to my dorm and as soon as I walked in, who did I see? I saw my youngster from the block that I had caught the case with the last time I was in jail; it was none other than Cam. I was happy as hell to finally see someone that I knew, and someone that was like family at that.

Life on the ranch was smooth and I worked as the staff barber, which entailed cutting the correctional officers and any other staff member's hair. I had an entire barbershop to myself, along with the shoe shine guy —a young looking older cat that was cool as hell. While working as the staff barber I had a lot of time to read books because not too many of the rednecks working at Pelican Bay took the chance of letting a black inmate barber cut their hair. Of course there were those cheapsters that came and got their hair cut by me because they didn't want to pay to get their haircut in the free world. Once I started getting a few rednecks to trust me cutting their hair though they would get compliments on the haircut and then that would send in a few more correctional officers. At the height of me working at the barbershop I would have to say that I cut about 12-15 heads a week. I loved my prison job because I was away from the strict ass ranch for eight hours a day. Every day after working at the barbershop I would go to the dorm and take myself a nap because I had grueling workouts in the evening after chow.

Since being at the ranch, I was like a celebrity because everyone was amazed at my physique. I had accumulated four workout partners and Cam gave it a shot for a couple of weeks when he fell off and decided that working out wasn't his thing. Once Cam fell off I had two cats working out with me.

Time flew by at the ranch because I stayed entertained by my bunky, Cam, or my workout partners. Not only that, but I had a few Kumi cats that I had to babysit on a daily basis, so that kept me busy as well. There weren't but about 10 Kumi members on the yard with me and those 10 were always involved in some sort of bullshit, so I had to keep an eye on them. I was the highest ranking officer on the yard so I had appointed someone that had the knowledge and wisdom of Kumi to be my commanding officer. Things weren't supposed to reach me unless the commanding officer didn't know what call to make on a situation. I ran a tight ship and I let everyone know that there was a hands on policy if a member violated the by-laws without remorse. Kumi's "hands on policy" was usually enforced when a member did something that was just straight up disrespectful to Kumi, like telling anybody other than a member our business, which surprisingly happened a lot.

Cam went home and my time started flying by; it was flying by so fast because I was getting word that a lot of Kumi members were getting killed. The first person that got killed was KB. If you remember, KB was the Kumi member that I had to discipline for not complying with Kumi rules at San Quentin. KB got killed two months after he got out of jail because the word was that he was trying to take over a neighborhood that had already had some cats on it who were doing their thing. A youngster that KB had called himself smashing on chased KB down and killed him right on a main city street in East Oakland.

The next person to get killed was Big Charlie. Big Charlie was in Fresno California for a motorcycle extravaganza and one of his enemies from Richmond California saw him and gunned Big Charlie down. Big Charlie was on the streets for close to a year before he was killed. After hearing all the violence that was taking place on the streets, I was leery about getting out again because I didn't want to have to kill a nigga or get killed. My time had arrived for me to get out and I must say that I was nervous about the streets but I had to go face those cruel streets of Oakland eventually.

"Dope Man"

The ride from Pelican Bay was long as hell but I enjoyed all the scenery while being on the bus for eight hours. I didn't sleep much because my adrenaline was pumping and I was anxious to put all the game I acquired in Pelican Bay to some good use. After eight long hours, I finally made it to the West Oakland Greyhound Station. I stretched my back as I go off the bus and then looked around anxiously for my mother. Once I got inside the bus station, I saw her and pops waiting for me and smiling like crazy when they saw me. They looked me up and down and my mother said that I looked like a superstar because I had gotten so big.

My first few days on the streets were all the same. In those first days I had to report to the parole office and go to a parolee meeting where the Oakland Police tried to scare us into not doing any more crimes.

Two days after I got out, Monique got word and came to my mother's house to try and reconcile. I was mad as shit that Monique had fallen off while I was in prison, but I figured I would use her until I got on top and then leave her like a bad habit.

Monique was living with a crazy, light skinned broad that lived in Hayward California in some nice apartment complexes. We had a small ass room but we made the best out of it. I wasn't the type to be in a person's face I didn't know, so I was real anti-social with her roommate because I never wanted a bitch to think that I liked them or I was making a pass at them in any form or fashion.

My first weekend home, Monique, her daughter and I went to the movies in Union City CA. I didn't want to go where a lot of niggas were because I didn't get along with niggas. I preferred to go where the whites were because they respected the muscle, while the blacks were just intimidated by it. We had a good time watching the movie and as we were leaving someone yelled out my name and I turned around to see Q walking towards me. I wasn't happy to see him and I'd actually had plans on doing something to him for having my attorney withdraw from my case. Q walked up with a look of pity on his face and he said, "Bra, why you didn't call me when you got out?" I told him that I wasn't going to fuck with him anymore because he wasn't a loyalist like me. I told him that I never would have played with his life the way he did with mine. Q started telling me how sorry he was for fucking up with giving the attorney the money, and that he wanted us to sit down and talk about what was on my mind. I got his cell phone number and I told him I would call him.

The day after seeing Q at the movies I gave him a call and he told me to meet him at the new studio in West Oakland.

"You got the studio in West Oakland?" I asked.

He told me that it wasn't what I thought, that the studio was a safe place in a building full of top heavy metal and rap artists, so I agreed that I would meet him there.

When I got to the studio I must say that it was a very professional spot. In order to get in the building there was a security key that was needed to enter. Q came and opened the door and he showed me around the building and I loved it. There was a spot that food was cooked and served and there was even a cannabis club in there; I didn't smoke but it was cool that it was in there nonetheless. After Q showed me the entire place, we went inside the studio and it was magnificent. I must say that there were a lot of Q's ways I didn't like, but the fella sure knew how to put a studio together. He started off by telling me he was sorry for fucking up with the attorney and I accepted his apology. Then we went straight into our plans to get money. Q told me that he owed our connection almost $30,000 because of losses he took in dealing with the broad that was selling his dope. I was shocked that Q owed that much money to our connection. As soon as he told me that he owed that amount I put it in my mind that I was going to have to kill him, because I'm the one that brought Q in with the connect in the first place and he had faltered. Q and I finished talking but I had to call my connection as soon as possible because I had to find out how they were thinking.

After I left the studio, I called the connection and he told me to meet him in Hayward at a fish spot. My connect was also one of my Kumi comrades so we had more than a business relationship, we also had a political relationship.

I got to the fish spot first so I went in and ordered some fish and right when I was finishing my order my connect came in and said, "Whats up, folks?" The connect and I sat down and he told me everything that was going on with him and Q. After the connect told me about Q, I asked him if he wanted him killed and the connect said, hell no, that he would never get paid from a dead man. I was glad to hear that because I didn't want to kill Q, but if it was going to take some heat off me I would've ended Q's life. The connect told me that he was trying to get Q to buy a house so that he could pull out the equity and pay him back with interest. I said that was a damn good idea.

My second week out, Q and I started going to the gym in San Leandro at 24 Hour Fitness. My first week back in the gym was hell because that shit I did in prison didn't add up to the dead weight in the gym. I knew that it would take me about a month to get my strength back to normal so I hit the weights like there was no tomorrow. My strength and muscle fullness came back fast because of the real street food and the real weights.

I started going to San Francisco to see what was going on out there in the tenderloin district where all the low lives of the bay area frequented to buy their drugs. The tenderloin was saturated with Kumi members that were straight scumbags on dope and weren't any good to anyone. Once the word was out that I was in the tenderloin, all the Kumi cats in San Francisco came to meet up with me to see if I was going to bring a mass amount of drugs for them to sell. I held a mini meeting and found out all the happenings in the district and the report I got was anything but good. I told all the Kumi cats that I was going to set up shop in the tenderloin and whoever wanted to get rich with me could do so as long as they were loyal, as well as prepared for punishment if one became un-loyal. The Kumi cats that had faith in themselves told me they wanted to fuck with me, but the weak Kumi cats that knew that they would falter didn't take the offer.

I didn't want to sell dope but my money was getting low and I didn't know when my new found pimp life would start seeing some money, so I had to do something to bring in some cash and cocaine was the first accessible way to do it.

I talked to Monique about her selling dope for me and she was hesitant but then she didn't want another broad to sell my dope, so she agreed to do it. I was thinking about all the money I would make with Monique selling the dope instead of getting a fucking dope fiend to do it, who I would probably have to kill over a few hundred dollars.

The next day after talking to Monique about her selling my dope, we set out to San Francisco to make a ton of money. I could tell that Monique was nervous about going to San Francisco with me but I reassured her that she didn't have anything to worry about.

After parking the Lexus I gave Monique simple instructions on how to sell the dope and told her that I would be right by her at all times so she wouldn't have anything to worry about. Monique was still nervous but we made our way to sell the dope we had to sell. I stayed off to the side while Monique sold the crack. I watched everything and everybody making sure that nothing happened to Monique because I needed all the money.

Monique was a natural at selling dope. I was shocked at how fast she sold all the drugs; I hadn't seen anything like it before. As we were leaving, one of the top dope dealing broads in the tenderloin walked past me and Monique and said, "Ya'll ain't the only ones getting money out here!" I went off on that bitch, telling her to watch when I came around the corner in my sparkling ass Lexus and then to tell me who was getting the money!

I hurried up to the car and told Monique to hurry up. When she got in the car I drove around the corner where everybody sold dope on Sixth Street and I had all the windows rolled down and the sun roof opened. I pulled up on the dope broad and said to her, "Now what you was saying about who ain't getting all the money, well bitch if you ain't riding like this than you ain't getting money!"

We ranted off shit to one another until I said, "Bitch, you ain't getting money and you ugly!" That seemed to strike a nerve. I saw the broad had a water bottle in her hand but I didn't think anything of it until she threw the whole bottle inside the Lexus and got it all on Monique because she was on the passenger side where the crazy dope selling broad was. Monique's black velour sweat suit immediately turned colors and that was when I realized that it was bleach that the bitch had thrown. I was glad that the shit wasn't acid. Not much of the bleach got on my interior. I told Monique to get out of the car and whoop that bitch's ass. Monique was hesitant at first but she got out of the car and her and the dope selling broad went toe to toe throwing punches. Monique got the best of the broad and knocked her to the ground and got on top of her until people started pulling Monique off of her. Dope broad got off the ground and ran into a store where she thought she was safe because she knew the Arab owners of it.

When I got to the entrance of the store, two Arabs were standing in the front as if they weren't letting me in. I immediately told them to move and they said no, so I slammed one of the Arabs and pushed the other one to the ground. I told Monique to go get the dope broad. As Monique tried to get her, the bitch started throwing canned goods at us, but Monique didn't let that stop her pursuit. Monique finally chased dope broad down and whooped her some more until I heard somebody call my name and say that the police were coming. I immediately told Monique that we had to bounce up out of there. She stopped whooping the broad and we high stepped it to the still running, sparkling Lexus. We got in and smashed across the bridge to Oakland.

Our ride to Oakland Monique kept saying that she could've gone to jail and I kept saying that she didn't go and that's all that counts. Monique said that she was never going to sell dope again because she had a daughter to worry about. I told her I understood but I was going to get broads to sell dope for me and she said she didn't care what I did in San Francisco. I took all of what Monique had to say and dissected it and came to the conclusion that she didn't care about me at that point. I lost all respect for her because I felt like we had made our mark and she shouldn't have been a coward and bailed out. But you can't make a person sell dope for you so I let it go with Monique.

After the fight in San Fran I stayed away for a few days to let things cool down because I was getting calls that people thought that Monique and I had jumped the dope broad, but I told every last one of them motherfuckers that the bitch was a motherfucking liar, and in fact my bitch whooped her ass all by herself.

"Ecstasy"

The following weekend after the fight in San Fran, I went to Antioch to meet up with my old cellmate Tutu. Tutu was a stand-up guy that was always on the prowl for a come up. He was famous in Pittsburg and Antioch because he was a bad acting motherfucker. I loved Tutu's style because he was raw and uncut. Tutu and I decided that we were going to go to the seafood festival and before I came to Antioch I went and bought 20 ecstasy pills from one of my comrades in Oakland. I had never taken an ecstasy pill in my life at that point. What made me curious about ecstasy was all the talk with the youngsters about how this drug was the best drug on the planet. They would say shit like, "On an E-pill you will talk like a fucking beast!" "Ecstasy has a motherfucka felling way too good, you touch yourself and that shit feels good!" and "Ecstasy gives you mad energy and you will fuck the hell out a bitch on ecstasy!" All these attributes of ecstasy were right up my alley, so I decided to give the drug a try.

I went and picked up Tutu and as we walked around the festival people couldn't keep their eyes off of us. Finally we gave them all what they wanted and took off our shirts to really show off our prison made muscle because we were all fresh from doing bids. An hour had passed and I told Tutu that I didn't feel anything from the ecstasy pill I had taken so he said to take another one because my muscle mass might make it hard to get high. I popped another one and we walked around the festival having a good time but another 30 minutes had passed and I still didn't feel anything. Out of nowhere some police walked up on us and told us that we needed to put our shirts back on. Tutu immediately responded, "You haven't told all these white boys to put on their shirts, so why you sweating us?" The young cops looked like they were looking for some action on this hot ass day. Tutu kept arguing with them, telling them that he would whoop both their asses. I was shocked because the Oakland Police would have shot a motherfucker for talking to them like Tutu was. I told tTutu that we needed to go and that they were just hating on the muscles. I was able to calm Tutu down and we left the festival

At that point I had taken three ecstasy pills and I was feeling the best I had ever felt in my life. I had a ton of energy, I felt great, and I was talking a lot more than my usual self. Ecstasy had all the attributes that the youngsters told me about and I was on cloud nine. I loved my new found drug. For the first time in my life, I stayed up for four days straight doing some of the wildest shit I had ever done in my life. Ecstasy had definitely changed my life.

I got back on my grind in the tenderloin but I knew that I wasn't going to see the money I wanted by selling crack. I knew that pimping was going to get me the cash I needed, without having to worry about the police all day every day. I had it in my mind that I was going to be a pimp so I started sweating every hoe I came across. I would chant, "You ready to go to the top girl? Come fuck with a real motherfucker that is going to treat you like the queen that you are!" You had to talk a lot to be a pimp so I talked a lot. I had sweated at least a hundred hoes before I got a bite.

"Pimping Ain't Easy"

'll never forget the night I got chosen by the first official prostitute that I had on Swole-Pimping Team. All my workers had sold all of the dope I'd given them and I was heading out of San Francisco, since it was around three o'clock in the morning. As I told all the drug dealers on the block that I would see them the next day, a thick broad that I had seen a few times asked me if I was leaving and whether or not I could give her a ride to her house. I told her that I was indeed leaving and I didn't mind giving her a ride home.

When we got to my car, her eyes got big and she asked me, "Is this your car?"

"Yes, do you like it?" I replied.

The bitch acted like she had hit the lottery or something. We got in the Lexus and I drove off and we started talking. We started the conversation by asking for one another's name, and then I asked her what she was doing down in the tenderloin. She said that she was trying to make a few dollars and I asked her how? That's when she told me she was selling a little dope but that wasn't what she was good at; I asked her what it was that she was good at and she told me that she made most of her money being a prostitute but she couldn't find a solid dude to team up with. I looked up to the pimp god and said thank you.

I picked up Mocha (my new prostitute) the next day to let her sell some of my dope and she did it with no problems. The only reason I had her selling dope instead of pussy was because I still had dope that needed to be sold. I could tell that Mocha didn't like selling drugs because she wasn't getting a lot of sales. I finally asked her after two hours of being in the Tenderloin one day what the problem was and asked her why she hadn't finished selling the dope yet? The bitch outright said, "I'm not a drug dealer, I am a prostitute, and I told you that!" I said OK and then asked her to give me the remainder of the dope. I explained to her that we were going to get her cleaned up and that I would take her to the hoe track. With an attitude the bitch was like, "Thank you because I told you when I met you how I got money!"

"We are going to get you all fixed up and get you some hoe gear and I will put you on the track," I reassured her.

My first day on the track was like an action packed movie. I picked up Mocha and took her to get a new outfit because the one she had on was whack. I spent almost $200 on the bitch and she hadn't even come with a choosing fee so I was pissed. She needed an outfit, hair done, and nails done. I could already tell why there weren't many wealthy pimps because a hoe was expensive to maintain. After I got the bitch geared up to set her down on the track, I ran my pimp rules to her.

"Look here, don't look at a black motherfucker because they will think you are choosing and kidnap your ass! If you get stopped by the police, under no circumstances are you to say my name and if you go to jail I will have someone other than myself to come and bail you out. Don't call me until you have $200," I said. Everything was in order and I told Mocha that I would be driving around until she was done and she said ok.

After I set the bitch down on the hoe stroll, I felt like I was a real pimp at that moment. I had my first hoe and she should be able to bring in some major dough because she was a nice looking hoe. After I set the bitch down on E 14th (International Blvd), I drove around and took care of some business. In about one hour I got a call from Mocha saying that a nigga was trying to kidnap her and I needed to hurry up and get there. I checked my 40 cal. to make sure all the hollow point bullets were intact because I never underestimated Oakland's mean streets. I got to E 14th in record time and as I drove down the track I saw Mocha in the hands of a big black nigga. This nigga was about 6' 5" and had a shiny bald head. When I pulled up the bitch started trying to break free out of the niggas grasp. I rolled down my window with my trigger finger on the trigger of the 40. Cal and I said, "Bra, that's my bitch so un-hands her!"

"I'm going to let the bitch go this time but if I see her again I'm going to have her." The nigga said.

Mocha got in the car and I told the nigga, "This bitch is under Kumi guidelines, nigga, so you best not put a hand on her again!"

The nigga said something that a motherfucker never came close to saying to my face. The big nigga said, "I don't give a damn what guidelines the bitch is under and if I see her I'm going to have her!"

My damn top blew off my head. I pointed the gun out the window and when the nigga saw I had a pistol he started running and I started shooting. I wasn't shooting to kill the nigga, so I shot in the air, but the bitch didn't know that. Right after I unloaded the entire clip I said to the bitch," "See? I don't fuck around. I will protect you as long as you stay loyal!" The bitch was far from scared; she actually had a look of empowerment on her face knowing she had a real gangster as her pimp.

The next few nights of putting the bitch on different hoe strolls other than Oakland was not prosperous. The bitch was only bringing in about $200 a night, and in profit I was only making about $80 because I had to feed the bitch, clothe her, house her, and put gas in the Lexus. At that point I realized that a hoe was actually getting more from the pimp than the pimp was getting from a hoe. I was starting to question this new career choice of mine.

After the few days that the bitch wasn't producing as I knew she could, I went on a mad hunt for some more hoes because this one wasn't getting any real money. I was sweating every hoe I saw and I finally got a bite.

I took my potential new hoe, Ree, to a rinky dink Asian restaurant that she thought was something special and I screened the bitch thoroughly and found out that she had been hoeing for over 20 years and her first pimp was her father.

Ree told me that every pimp she had beat her and I told her that I wasn't into putting my hands on anyone, especially a woman. This was when she showed a sign of relief. I told her that we needed to team up and get some real money together. Ree told me that she didn't do hard drugs but I could tell she was lying. She told me that she only drank from time to time, but every time i saw her in the tenderloins she used to be pissy drunk where people would have to carry her off, so I knew exactly what I was getting myself into. This bitch emptied her pockets of all the money she had and gave it to me and said that she was choosing me.

I counted the money as she talked and it ended up being $300, which was cool because all of my patnas told me that a real hoe would come with a choosing fee, so I gladly accepted. Ree wanted to prove herself to me so she hit the track the same night and brought me another $500 at the end of the night. I felt like I had struck gold. I made $800 profit and didn't have to do shit. I decided if pimping was like that then I was going to pimp the rest of my life.

I had been out of prison for a few months at that point and things were moving extremely too fast. I was losing weight from drinking and popping pills. I was missing workouts more than I ever had. My money was alright but once again even though Ree would make $500 a day, I had to put about $250 towards daily necessities. It was still better than selling dope though, and I knew that I wouldn't see real pimp money unless I had at least three money getting hoes.

Ree was still making her $500 a night, which was cool, but I needed more. Since I didn't want to sell dope, I decided to start selling the dope dealer's dope at a cheap price, which was consistent money.

I'll never forget the night I lost Ree. I went to the San Francisco Bart Station to pick up Cam because he was going to hang with me. I had gotten wind of a lick and I wanted him to come with me as an intimidating force. When I got Cam, I immediately gave him a pill and told him that San Francisco was a different world from Oakland. Cam was with me the entire night and I had done one pickup from Ree of $300. I told her to make sure that she called me every hour on the hour and she agreed that she would. It was great having a seasoned hoe because I didn't have to babysit the bitch like I did with the young hoes.

After I got the money from her, Cam and I went to a few clubs and had ourselves some drinks and were having a ball. After the last club we went to, it was about three o'clock in the morning and I hadn't heard from Ree in about four hours so I was worried as hell because I couldn't afford to lose a $500 a night hoe. Cam and I went to the room I had gotten for the bitch at Holiday Inn and we waited for her until the both of us dosed off and fell asleep. At around five o'clock in the morning my phone rang and it was Ree.

"Bitch, where have you been? I been worried sick about your ass!" I said.

Ree said that she fell asleep at her trick's house and that she was sorry for having me worried. I told the bitch to hurry up and get to the room because she deserved a smacking for having me worried. The phone hung up and I knew at that moment that I had lost the hoe.

Two weeks had passed and I hadn't heard anything from the bitch and my pockets were once again getting low. I kept getting hoes that would stay with me for a couple of weeks and then they would go on to the next nigga. All my hoes would end up going to the dope fiends – the so called "pimps" that would do dope with the bitches to keep them. Even though I popped pills I didn't consider it a hardcore drug like heroin, crack or speed; that left all the hoes I had feeling insecure because they usually got high off dope and since I didn't do it they would leave and find a dope fiend that let them get high whenever they wanted to. I ran a tight ship where the bitches couldn't do any drugs or drink until they brought their daily quota. Things weren't getting better for me at all; I was out of control at that point. Q and I still worked out together but I just knew that he wasn't cut from the same cloth as me and so I kind of stayed away from him. I had started selling dope again but things were crazy because every day I had to act out some form of violence. The tenderloin had turned me into a careless monster. I knew that something bad was going to happen soon; I always had an intuition that was unreal. I was committing violent acts on the workers I had that would run off with my money. That was the thing about dope fiends in the tenderloin district. You'd give them some dope to sell and as soon as you took your eyes off of them they would be in an alley smoking it all up. I mean, at that point I had whooped every worker I had and there were at least 20 of those motherfuckers. It had gotten so bad that I just started pistol whipping motherfuckers that fucked off my money. I knew my time on the streets would be short lived at that point.

Since the word was out that I was hot, I decided to stay away from the tenderloins for a couple of days so that my name would simmer down in the streets. Word getting around about me meant that the police were going to be on my trail, so I had to watch my back. I went to the strip club to relax and have a drink and that's when I got a call from one of my comrades, Dre. Dre was a hustler like me and he also got his money selling dope and sending prostitutes to get money for him; on top of that he was Kumi and from Oakland, so he and I had a lot in common.

Dre called me while I was in the strip club and said that he wanted to talk to me in person and that he was in the tenderloin. I was reluctant to go to the tenderloin, but I went against my better judgment and left the strip club to go and meet up with Dre. I intentionally parked my car far away from the tenderloin so that the police wouldn't detect me because they seemed to always know where everyone in the tenderloin district was.

I walked down to meet Dre in an area that was right in the open for everybody possible to snitch on me, and that's exactly what happened. Dre and I had been talking for about 15 minutes when all of a sudden I heard screeching tires and looked up to find what appeared to be all the San Francisco police force surrounding us.

I was a little tipsy from some alcohol I had at the strip club, so I found the whole ordeal humorous. These police rolled up on us like we were terrorist or some shit. I put my hands on a wall and luckily I knew that I didn't have anything on me at the time; I kept my gun in the car, which was good, otherwise I would've been done for. As the police walked behind me while I had my hands on the wall, I asked, "What's going on officers? We can't talk on a public street anymore?" A female cop told me to shut up and I laughed and told her sarcastically that I wanted her to search me.

"Recidivism"

All of us in the area were searched and they found some dope on a dope fiend nigga that I went to junior high school with. The police immediately accused me of having the nigga selling dope for me, but I told the police that I didn't even know the nigga and asked why they were coming down so hard on me. Dre and a few other cats were released at the police station, but I was on parole so they were going to violate my parole for being in a drug invested area. Shit everywhere in the bay area was a drug area, so I knew that it was all a ploy to get me off the streets. I was mad as fuck about that bullshit but I knew that the day was coming so I was able to digest it a little better because I'd already known my fate beforehand.

When the police told me I was charged with directing traffic and being in a drug area while on parole, all I could do was laugh. One of the arresting cops came and told me that someone had called them and told them I was down there with a gun. The first person to pop in my head was the dope selling bitch. As soon as I was about to get processed to get housed in San Francisco's County Jail, a cop came to my cell and dangled my car keys and said that they knew where my car was and that they were going to search it. I was scared shitless at that point because I had the gun and some drugs hidden in a spot somewhere in the car.

I was escorted to the dorm I was being housed in and as I looked around I realized I didn't like the looks of the jail at all. I immediately asked where the Kumi phone was and I was directed to it.

I got on the phone and called Q and told him where my car was parked and asked him to go get it before the police did. I then called my mother to let her know what was going on. They were all shook up because they knew that I could possibly be gone for a whole year, because being a violent criminal I was given flat time on my violations. Truthfully, I was happy to be in jail because I was out of control and I felt like a demon on the streets.

Being in San Francisco County Jail was terrible. They had dorms that housed about six inmates in each room. There were only two showers that all the inmates had access to. There was one television that brought about a fight every night, and there was a water pot that niggas used as a weapon to throw hot water on each other if there was a fight. I knew I only had to stay in San Francisco County for 10 days max because the district attorney didn't pick up a case on me so I would just have to deal with parole. Luckily the police didn't find anything in my car and my mother had Darold go get it from San Francisco and take it to her house, so that was a relief.

My 10 days had passed and I was called early in the morning to go to San Quentin and I was happy as hell to get out of San Francisco County Jail.

The word traveled fast that I was back at San Quentin and all the Kumi members that knew me came to talk to me while I was at the reception center getting booked into the prison. All the Kumi cats, as well as patnas from the streets, came to see if I needed anything and I told them that I didn't but for them to find Abraham to tell him that I needed some food and cosmetics. They got on it immediately. It was, of course, embarrassing to be back in prison, but I just blamed the white man for my misfortunes and that made me feel better about myself and my predicament.

It took what seemed like forever for the prison staff to send the inmates to their housing unit. I learned to have patience when I was in San Quentin's hole the few times I had been there. After being at San Quentin for eight hours, the correctional officer finally called out everyone's name and told them where they were being housed. I was called to go to west block building, which was where inmates were that didn't have a life sentence. I had been to west block before and I hated the filth, the showers, and the noise that reeked throughout the section on a daily basis.

As I walked into west block, it seemed like the same people were in San Quentin that I saw the last time I was there. Truthfully it was sad that we put ourselves in the same position time and time again, but it was what it was. Everyone was calling my name from their cells and I would stop and talk until the guard prompted me to go inside the designated cell I was given

Time in west block was slow because I didn't get my food from Abraham for about three weeks, so I knew that I had lost a few pounds. I was unable to go to the store until a week after I got the food from Abraham, and at that point I had too much food but I took full advantage of me being stocked up.

A couple of days after I went to the store I, along with a ton of other inmates, were called on the prison intercom to be moved to the gym. I hated living in dorm settings but I figured that it would break up the time I had to do, and at that point I had 60 days left.

When I got to the gym, all my Kumi comrades and old associates came running to me as if they were glad that I was back in prison. I knew that the gym was chaotic because of what I had heard while I was in west block, so I knew that I would have to change a lot of things up while I was there. As I made up my bunk, I was bombarded by what seemed to be one thousand people that came and talked to me. It was crazy because inmates were always happy to see their associates in jail, which was always weird to me. I finished putting my stuff away and I called an immediate Kumi meeting.

After I told the commanding officer that was in the gym that I was calling a meeting with all the Kumi members, he got to it and all the Kumi comrades were standing at attention waiting for me to come. Once at the back of the gym, I started the meeting by reciting the Kumi oath. I then recited the first by-law and everybody followed suit until we said all of the by-laws. I did this to see who knew their shit and who didn't, and there were a lot of cats lacking knowledge in what they should have known. I then went over all the rules in the gym and how I was implementing a strict program of working out and staying alert at all times. The gym was able to go from easy going to all out riots in a matter of seconds, so I took pride in making sure that all my Kumi comrades made it to the streets alive. After the hour long meeting, I told everybody to resume their normal program and we went our separate ways.

Time in the gym went by fast because there were always a lot of things going on – things like drug deals, people getting tattooed, fights, and people drunk from drinking prison made alcohol. There was always a lot of action, which was good for doing time. I had a crew of six cats that worked out with me. A lot of the inmates couldn't hang with my workout so each day someone would drop off from the crew and another inmate would give it a try, only resulting in the same thing. My workouts were grueling. I worked out every day, except Sunday, which was my rest day. Most cats dropped from my workout crew because they weren't used to being as sore as they were. My crew and I were all swole, me being the biggest of course.

Things were going good in the gym for a while, but something always changed the easy going dynamic of the gym. This time it was my actions that did the changing of the gym. Day after day Kumi members were coming to tell me that a member named D was breaking a lot of the by-laws because he was associating himself with a BGF (black guerilla family) member. BGF was Kumi's adversary because Kumi was a gang that began as a means to stand up to the BGF. The BGF were extorting a lot of black cats from the bay area, so that's how Kumi was birthed. Me, being the top dog at the prison, I wasn't even supposed to be told of minute situations such as D fraternizing with the enemy. The Kumi officers I had in charge of the gym didn't seem as if they could come up with a solution for the problem though, so I stepped in to talk to D. D and I had somewhat of a friendship, not only in jail, but in the streets where we did a lot of business transactions together.

I figured I would detonate the situation and talk to D with diplomacy and tact. I talked to him about how his fellow Kumi members felt about him fraternizing with the enemy, but D brought up a valid point to me. He asked if a Kumi member had family members that were BGF, would he not be allowed to hang out with them? I told D that he was absolutely right, because personally I didn't care who hung out with who, as long as each member did their daily obligations. I told him that he could continue to hang out with whoever he wanted to and I left the situation alone.

A few days after D and I had talked, I did start to get uneasy about him fraternizing with a known Kumi hater. Now if this were D's relative, then all Kumi members would have understood, but the BGF cat that D hung out with he'd just met while being in the gym, so that was a problem. I watched D for a few days to see how he was doing with his daily program, but I noticed he didn't do his daily obligation to Kumi one particular day so I disciplined him with doing some burpees. All Kumi members hated burpees because they wreaked havoc on the cardiovascular system, so when a Kumi member was told that they had to do them, they would express their dislike. D did his burpees without any whining though, so I gave him a word of encouragement after he was done. D understood why he was disciplined and he admitted his wrong doing. After D got disciplined, I started to dislike him because he didn't have the love for Kumi that the rest of the members did.

There was this one particular morning when chow time was delayed for unknown reasons. I had recently decided to stop drinking coffee because I didn't like being dependent on anything that gave me headaches if I didn't have it, so that was the first day I decided to stop drinking it. I knew that I already woke up grouchy and that not having my morning coffee for that first day was going to be hell on the head. All the Kumi members and I went to breakfast and D sat with the BGF cat at the BGF table. All of my Kumi comrades looked at D with dismay and D just rolled his eyes as if he didn't care what we thought about him. I was steaming because I felt like he was mocking Kumi.

My Kumi officers and I talked about us eventually having to do something about the D situation, which meant that we were planning an act of violence against him. After breakfast we all returned to the gym and by this time my head was pounding from caffeine withdrawals, but I saw D and I called him to come and talk to me anyway. As D and I talked, he had a look on his face as if he were trying to ignore what I had to say.

"D, you looking like you got a problem or something." I said in my overly aggressive voice.

D kept the stupid look on his face and said, "If I had a problem ya'll would know!"

As soon as D said the last word know, I gave him a quick left hook to the jaw, which had knocked him off his feet, and then I sent him to the ground with an uppercut. That's when my Kumi comrades yelled out that the police were coming, so I went and sat on my bunk as if I hadn't done anything wrong. When the police came to the back of the gym where the commotion happened, D had already woke up and went to the bathroom to clean up the blood that was all over him.

I told all my Kumi comrades that I wanted D out of the gym as soon as possible, because I couldn't have one of my victims sleeping in the same place as me. I told all 20 of the Kumi cats to keep an eye on the nigga in case he tried to do some kamikaze shit, because I knew that he knew that I was sending some Kumi members to remove him from the gym.

About an hour after the incident, I was sitting on my bunk talking to 20 Kumi members about what was going to take place with D, and something told me to look up. I saw D about 20 yards away from me with something in his hand, and as soon as I looked up I felt something hit me in the head and I immediately started chasing after him. At the time I didn't know what had happened, and my head was bleeding profusely but I didn't care. I continued to chase D but the bitch nigga ran to the police and three correctional officers guarded him from me. At that time the correctional officers had already sounded off the alarm, so I knew that I wouldn't be able to get to the bitch nigga at that point.

"I'll see you on the streets bitch nigga!" I said and I meant it. I vowed to myself that I was going to kill D the next time I saw him because he was now an enemy that I had to demolish.

My head had to get 10 stitches and I was mad as hell because I had to get shaved where the laceration was. At the time I thought D had a lock in a sock but later on down the line I got word that he threw the lock at me. After I got stitched up I was taken to east block hole. Once in the hole I kept my presence unknown so that I could hear what was being said. D was already in the hole before I got there. I knew that he talked like a bitch, so I listened on as he told people why he was in the hole. I stayed quiet for a few days until I went to the shower, and at that time I saw that D was only about eight cells away from mine on the same tier as me. As I walked past his cell, I paused and looked inside and just gave him an evil stare. D looked like he had seen a ghost.

Days went by slow in the hole until I was able to go to the store. Fortunately for me, I was able to get some Top Ramen from Rob – who was on death row – and those few soups helped me to get past the hunger pangs until I was able to buy some food of my own.

The three weeks waiting to go to the store was hell, but when I was finally able to go, I was happy as a child going to McDonalds. At that point of the incident I had under 40 days to complete my 90 day parole violation, but this incident with D had the probability of causing me to catch some extra time on my sentence so I was worried about not getting out when I was supposed to. Technically I could have received a parole violation for what was called a "mutual combat" between D and me.

During my time in the hole, I once again played chess with other inmates where we yelled the numbers out loud for the opponent to move the pieces. I know you may be confused, but the way chess was played in the hole was actually clever. I had to make chess pieces out of toilet paper and then I would make a board either on the metal slab bunk or on a piece of cardboard. After the board was made, I would put the pieces on the board and whoever I was playing against would pick white or black, then we would get to calling out numbers where the pieces were to be placed on the board. Playing chess, reading, and working out were past the time.

The noise level was worse than the other times I had been in the hole and reason being was because the drop-outs were 10 times what they used to be. People were tired of the gangs they were in so they removed themselves from them. It took me about a week to get used to the noise level; it was so noisy that a lot of inmates went crazy because of it. Most of the death row inmates were now on the side of east block that had all death row inmates and not inmates that were just in the hole. The only person that stayed on the loud side was "Rob". I didn't understand how Rob was able to stay on that wild side, but he looked at all the noise as a way to escape his death row sentence.

The day of my release came and I didn't hear my name called in the morning so I figured that I would have to stay in the hole for an extended stay in San Quentin's east block. I proceeded with my daily routine of working out, playing chess, and reading. I took a nap until

I was awakened by a guard clanking his keys on my cell bars to let me know that chow was being served. It was the same ole shit being fed to me that I had been eating during my stay in the hole. This particular day it was two dry ass burritos, corn, salsa, and apple sauce. Actually, this meal was my favorite because of the burritos. I ate both burritos and I was satisfied so I started reading a book. One hour had passed and a guard came over the loud ass intercom in east block and said, "The following inmates are getting released, so pack your shit and get out of here and don't come back!" Three names were called and I lost all hope in getting out, and then all of a sudden I heard my name called and I couldn't believe it; I was getting out of the infamous San Quentin once again. This was the best time ever of being released from prison because I was getting un-institutionalized, and not only that but I had a lot of money waiting for me on the streets, and having money definitely changed a person's mentality.

I wasn't happy to be getting out yet because San Quentin was known for making mistakes about inmates getting out when they were supposed to get out. Once I finished the process of leaving San Quentin, then it became a reality that I was getting out. I was then told to get in the prison van, which drove all inmates to the front of the prison if they had someone picking them up or to the bus station if they didn't. Unfortunately, I didn't have anyone picking me up this time because I didn't know my actual release date.

"It Don't Stop"

The prison van drove me and three other inmates to the Marin California Bus Station and there I got on a bus to the Vallejo Bart Station. During the ride I visualized what I was going to do once I was a semi-free man. The Bart ride from Vallejo to Oakland was fast, and once at the Oakland Bart Station I took a cab to my mother's house because that's where my car was.

When I reached my mother's house, I rang the doorbell like I was a crazy person because I knew that it would piss pops off, and it did, at least until he saw who it was at the door. Pops opened the door and paused for a minute then he said, "Damn son, you out of there huh?"

"I sure ain't escaped from San Quentin!" I joked.

We laughed and then I walked inside the house that was, at the moment, just occupied by pops, since everyone else was gone. I took myself a shower and ate some fried chicken that pops had just finished and boy was it good. Pops and I sat and talked until I heard the front gate close, which signaled that my mother coming home from work. As she pulled her car in the driveway, I stood on the porch and she had to wipe her eyes as if she couldn't believe it was me. I hugged my mother and told her that I missed her and we went back inside the house. I was taking this time to bond with moms and pops before I started my crazy and wild life again. I knew that I would be running around like a chicken with my head cut off in just a matter of a couple of days.

A couple of weeks on the streets and things were going slow for me because I didn't want to sell dope so I took my time and got my thoughts together for a few weeks. During that time period Big Low and I had reunited and we were back to working out like we did inside prison. This time around we also had Big Low's cousin Big Shawn working out with us too. Big Shawn was 6'6" and about 350 lbs at least. He wanted to strip off the fat from his huge body, so we took him under our wings. My strength took about three weeks to get back to what I was lifting before I did the 90 days in San Quentin. I was feeling good, and things were looking up.

Since I didn't want to sell dope any longer I decided that I would give stripping another shot until something else came along that I could make more money from. I got myself some new cards made and I got with three different stripper companies; as soon as I got with the agencies I was busy as hell. Big Low, Shawn and I worked out five days a week and we were all looking damn good.

I was making a cool amount of money at the time from stripping and selling a little ecstasy on the side, so I was without any worries; however, I wanted to make more money so I asked around for some heroin to sell and I finally hooked up with my Patna Flo in San Francisco. Flo was a legend in San Francisco because he used to be one of the biggest dope dealers there, but now he just sold a little shit here and there to keep himself afloat.

I was out for about six months and things were going pretty good. I reconnected with one of my Kumi comrades named Dog. Dog had two kids and he was broke as a joke so he wanted me to help him get money. At first I tested Dog with a little ecstasy and once he brought all the money back to me I knew I could put some of my trust in him. I kept Dog stocked up with whatever drug he thought he could move fast.

I'll never forget the day that changed my outlook about Dog. I was supposed to meet Flo and I decided to take Dog with me, which was the wrong thing to do. When I picked up Dog he was real jittery and I couldn't figure out what was wrong with the cat. I finally asked him if he was high and he said no. As I drove from Oakland to San Francisco, Dog kept asking me if he could see my gun so that he could rob somebody for some money. I told that nigga that I didn't have my gun on me, even though of course I had it, but I wasn't going to tell a nigga that, especially a nigga I barely trusted. The entire ride across the Bay

Bridge that nigga Dog kept talking in his desperate tone about needing some money, and I knew that something fishy was going on with that cat. When I got to Flo's spot, Flo pulled me to the side and asked me if the nigga Dog was cool. I told Flo that the nigga was cool but I made sure not to let Dog see the transaction that Flo and I were going to make.

It was about 6:00 p.m. and the sun was still out when I drove from San Francisco back to Oakland and at no time did I tell Dog that I had any drugs or gun on me. As I drove Dog to the entrance of his apartment complex, a police officer who had arrested me two times prior drove past me and we made eye contact. I then sped up and told Dog to hurry up and get out, and when I think back it seemed as though the nigga was trying to stall me. I pulled off on him while he was still closing the door. I hit the gas and tried to get to the freeway. I saw a ton of cop cars closing in on me in my rear view mirror. All the cars behind me got over to let the cop cars pass and as I got over to do the same a cop car tried to block me in and that's when I realized that the police were after me. I didn't understand why the police were after me, but I wasn't about to give myself to them while I had a gun and dope in the car. I put the pedal to the metal and the Lexus shot off like a rocket. I had what looked like the whole police force after me and I didn't know why. That was the first time that I'd ever heard my brother Archie talk to me, and it may sound weird but he told me that I had to get away and I listened to him.

I sped up the 73rd hill and when I got to the freeway I had great distance away from the police so I threw out the heroin on the freeway and the gun was in my hider spot – which was in the trunk, so I couldn't have gotten the gun out of the car.

I had that Lexus doing 140 mph on the freeway. It was all like a dream because my path was clear. There were a lot of cars on the freeway but for some odd reason no cars got in the way of my high speed pursuit. I decided to get off on the exit closest to Lisa's apartment so I could try to make it to her spot. Once I got off the freeway I came to some lights, which were all red for me but I ran them anyway and almost got smashed by a car in the process. The car was coming right for me so I hit the gas and just barely escaped from getting killed. I then hit some corners and I jumped out of the car and ran through back yards until I got to Lisa's house. By the time I got to her apartment, I was exhausted because I had jumped fences and ran through people's back yards to get there. The entire time the police helicopter had on the spot light and they were having a mad search for me, but I refused to let the coppers take me down. When I got to Lisa's I banged on the front door like a mad man and she ran to the door asking who was there. I told her it was me and she opened the door and asked me what was wrong. I told her that I had just bee in a high speed chase with the Oakland Police and I needed her to go to where my car was at to see if it was still there or if the police had found it and taken it. Lisa hurried out the door and she went to see about the Lexus. While Lisa was gone I was the most paranoid I had ever been in my life and I was pacing the floor trying to figure out what had happened. Lisa came back to the apartment and said that the police were hiding out around the car to see if I was coming back for it.

I decided to see if my mother could get the car back. My mother, being a loyalist, didn't think twice about going to get the car, and I was worried the entire day about her trying to retrieve it. Finally my phone rang and it was my mother. I got a surge of nervousness because I just knew that she was going to tell me that the police were going to confiscate it. I answered the phone and I heard a sense of happiness in my mother's tone.

"Well son, I got the car, but we are going to put the car up until this thing blows over," she said.

I was happy as hell that my Lexus was out of jail. Moms and pops took the car to my Aunt Donna's house and put it in her garage. I felt good about my car being out of jail but I was sad that it had to just sit up and collect dust, but it was either drive the car and go to jail or let the car stay hidden until the shit blew over.

I went three months without my car and I was anxious to get in it, so I called up my mother and told her that I was ready to get my car from Aunt Donna's house.

"Son, as soon as you get in that car the police is going to take your ass to jail!" My mother tried to tell me. I didn't want to hear anything she was saying though, so I went to her house and we ended up getting in a heated argument about the car. I got irate, and that's when moms and pops both said, "Go ahead and get the damn car then, but don't say we didn't tell you so about that hot ass car."

"Freedom Isn't My Friend"

Being in my car was the best feeling ever. I went out every night to a club, bar, or whatever. I had the Lexus out from hiding and I was going to show the car to Big Low's sister to see if she wanted to buy it. When I showed the car to Big Low's sister, I got apprehensive about selling it, and I mean, Big Low's sister wanted that car bad. I told her to let me think the whole thing over and I would get back to her, but I didn't want to really sell the car.

There's one day I'll never forget because it was such a beautiful and productive day. I got an amazing workout with Big Low and Big Shawn, and then I went to my mother's house and took a shower because I was getting ready to go party. After I'd taken my shower, I popped myself a naked lady (E-Pill) to get me going and then I ate a little food and headed out the door. The feeling I remember having that day was surreal; I mean, I was floating on cloud nine. I felt in my spirit that that day was too good to be true. I got in the Lexus and turned up my 4 -12 inch woofers and felt the surge of the beat flow through my body. As I pulled from the curb, I didn't see a soul in sight on E Street. I turned left on Elmhurst Street and then took a right on C Street, and out of nowhere cop cars bombarded my car like I had just killed 10 police officers.

All the cops had their guns pointed at me and they told me to take the car keys out of the ignition, to drop them on the ground and to keep my hands where they could see them. I was a little nervous because I had about 20 ecstasy pills on me and I had tucked them in between my butt cheeks as soon as I noticed the police. The police took me out of the car and searched me. As they searched me I could feel the baggie of pills sliding down my pants. I knew that I couldn't let those police find my pills because it would have been an entirely different charge from what I was going to jail for. After I was searched, the police put me in the cop car and that's when I asked them what was going on.

"What is all this about?" I said, acting genuinely confused.

"You know why you're going to jail, Kali!" The asshole cop answered.

When I still acted confused, the cop continued, "You remember that high speed chase you did on the 73rd hill? Well now it's time to do your time for that!"

I played dumb and replied that I didn't know what they were talking about, and that my car was stolen. The two cops in the car started laughing like two crazed lunatics.

Asshole cop said, "We know that was you, so you can lie all you want but guess what, you're going to jail to do your time for the high speed chase and also for the gun that was found inside the car!"

At that point I went mute and didn't talk anymore that night. I knew in my spirit that I was going to do some real time on those charges.

Downtown at the county jail I was being stared at by the inmates and police because I was wearing a tank top, so everyone was amazed at how swole I was. I didn't talk to anyone about anything. I was placed in a cell by myself and that was when the stress came and I thought of all the time that I might possibly have to do for my crimes. The cell was one of the biggest cells I'd ever seen. There was a toilet, sink and a hard ass concrete slab that was supposed to be a bed. I was given a thin ass sheet and that was it. I tried to go to sleep but stress kept me up pacing the floor and looking out the thin window at the infamous Mexican restaurant, Mexi Cali Rose. I saw people going in and out of there and everyone seemed to be having fun, which just added to my stress because I wished I were in the free world like them.

The ride to Santa Rita was depressing because I wanted to be on the streets rather than heading to prison. Seeing everybody driving about their business was very depressing. I thought about how much time I would be faced with. I knew that a gun alone could be 10 years, and the high speed chase would be one to three years. Being in the life of crime I knew how much time every charge carried. I was stressed to the max and I think all the other inmates knew that I was in a crazy state of mind, so no one said anything to me on the bus.

When I got to the assigned cell I was given, the door popped open and I looked inside before I went in it to see what caliber of person I would be sharing the cell with. I was a top gang leader and I couldn't be cellmates with a snitch, rapist or punk. Before I walked inside, I spoke to the cat in the cell and said,"Whats good bra?"

The cat looked as if he could be a skinny brother of mine, and he replied with, "Alright how you doing, bra?"

I could tell by a simple greeting how an individual was and he seemed to be solid. I made up my bunk as my new cellmate and I got to know one another. He was from San Francisco, the same block as Big Low, so we already had a lot in common because San Francisco was my second home.

At pod time my celly, Shawn, introduced all the blacks to me that didn't know me and I saw right off that there were a lot of wanna be gangster youngsters in that pod. After I made my rounds getting to know everyone, I went and got on the Kumi phone. There weren't any Kumi members in the pod at the time, so I had the phone to myself.

I had been in the pod for about a month when two young black cats from Berkeley came in. Right after them two white boys came in the pod too, so it was evident that these four individuals were being sent to the pod for an unforeseen reason that usually wasn't a good thing. After the four individuals were in the pod for about two hours, we were called to eat dinner and that's when everybody in the pod found out that the two white boys had a fight with the two Berkeley cats. I asked the Berkeley youngsters in the pod how they were going to handle the matter and everybody seemed hesitant about retaliating on the white boys. I pulled their card and said, "Ya'll just gone let some woods get on ya'll Berkeley folks like that?"

That's when one of the Berkeley cats that thought he was tough said, "I will handle those white boys in the morning!" but I knew by the tone of his voice that he was soft as cotton balls.

After dinner there was no pod time because I just knew that the Santa Rita guards put those white boys and the youngsters in the same pod for some excitement.

The whole night after the youngsters and the white boys were sent to the pod, I told Shawn that the soft ass Berkeley cats weren't going to do anything, so I was going to get on the white boys myself. Shawn said that he was with me on the attack. I planned to be the first person to finish eating my breakfast and I would catch the white boys at the right time to pounce on them.

The morning came fast and it was weird because I wasn't nervous or anything. Usually I would get a few butterflies when I got violent but this time was totally different as I was calm as still waters. When the cell doors were opened at 5:00 a.m., I hurried to the first floor to visualize my attack. I was the first person to get my food and everyone knew that I was about to do something because of the way I moved. I sat down at my designated table with Shawn and we discussed the attack and Shawn said he was going to follow suit after I attacked the white boys first. I ate the slop in record speed and then I watched the white boys to see if they felt the tension, and though I could tell that they were nervous, their nervousness just fueled my anger. Once I saw the white boys getting up from their table to put their trays up, I also got up and met the white boys at the spot to put our breakfast trays away. As soon as I set my tray down I side stepped to where the tallest white boy was and I hit him with a right uppercut and he was knocked out on his feet. I was so fast that before the knocked out white boy hit the ground I had pounced on the other white boy and I didn't stop hitting him until the police came running in the pod and tackled me.

"What's wrong with you, why did you do this?" The guards kept saying to me.

"Ya'll know why! Ya'll probably had a bet on the entire set up!" I yelled.

I was amped to the 10th power and my adrenaline had me feeling like I was on 10 ecstasy pills. I was placed in a holding cage until the head honcho of Santa Rita was able to come and investigate the melee. I looked out of the small window to see what was going on and I saw a lot of movement. I saw the white boys on gurneys getting rushed to the hospital and I was somewhat nervous when I saw them getting wheeled out by paramedics because I knew that if they were severely hurt I had a chance at catching another case in Santa Rita. I started pacing the tiny cell out of nervousness. I knew that my hands were deadly weapons but damn I didn't realize the damage I had done on those white boys. After a couple of hours a guard finally came to the cell I was in and asked me questions through the tiny window.

"Why did you beat up the white boys like that? How many times did you hit them? Did you do this to retaliate because of what they did to the young black youngster?" The guard asked, drilling me with questions.

I played dumb during the questioning and just shrugged my shoulders after every one the guard asked. After a couple more hours in the tiny cell, I was let out to go and pack my things because I was being sent to another building. As I packed my things I told my cellmate Shawn that it was good meeting him and that I hoped that his case turned out how he wanted it to. We gave each other a fist pound and I was off to the other building I was being housed at.

Once I reached the new building I was being housed in, I saw that there weren't any inmates out of their cells, which was an immediate red flag for me because that usually meant that there wasn't a lot of pod time jumping off. As I walked to my assigned cell, I heard people banging on their cell doors calling my name and I saw two of my youngsters from E Street that were fighting murder cases. I yelled to them that I would holler at them when we came out for pod time. When I reached my cell, I once again looked inside before the door was opened to see how the person inside was living, but the cell was empty and I was ecstatic about not having a celly. I went inside and unpacked all my property, and then I cleaned the cell thoroughly using a makeshift towel. I had the inmate porter to bring me some disinfectant so I could wipe down everything in the cell because you never knew who had been in there before you. After I cleaned the cell thoroughly, I laid down on the hard metal bunk and read a book until I fell asleep.

Days in the new pod went by fast, because everybody was fighting a case that had everybody scared to death. My two youngsters were convicted of first degree murder and attempted murder so they both received 50 years to life and got transferred to San Quentin. A lot of inmates were happy when the youngsters were gone from the pod because they exuded stress every single day. I can't say that I was happy for the youngsters to be gone from the pod, but things were at peace when they left.

My case wasn't looking too good in my favor. The district attorney went all the way up to 10 years on my case, which was crazy because there was no evidence against me. The only thing the district attorney had was the crooked cop's testimony and that was a lie. Now, the good thing I had going in my favor with the case was that the courts would be able to see that this particular Oakland police officer had a vendetta against me, or at least I prayed that the judge would see that and take it into consideration.

Time in Santa Rita slowed down on me after six fucked up months in jail. I was dealing with a ton of bullshit in my pod.

My court date came and the courts assigned me another attorney. I had a good man to man talk with that attorney and I told him that if he wasn't going to work for me full heartedly then he would need to remove himself from my case, because this was my life and I wasn't going to let anyone fuck it over. The new attorney vowed that he would do everything in his power to get me exonerated from the case. I felt better hearing the new attorney say that, but I was still apprehensive because I knew that the court system did what they wanted to do. I was given a court date for another month, so by the time I went back to court it was going to be eight and a half months served in stinking ass Santa Rita.

Time was going by pretty fast in Santa Rita because everyone was leaving the prison or going home. At that point I had a celly named Mike-G. Now, Mike-G was the first celly I'd ever had that was fluent in knowledge like me and he was an all out hustler that knew how to talk very well.

The time came for me to start my trial and I was nervous as hell because things usually didn't go right for me when dealing with the penal system. After three hours of waiting in the holding tank, I was called to go to court by the bailiff. When I left, all the other inmates wished me luck and I knew that God and luck was exactly what I needed to come out with a victory against Alameda County. Once outside the courtroom, I was told to wait again, and this time I waited outside of the courtroom for two hours. I was grouchy as hell by that point and whenever I saw a bailiff I asked them what was going on with court for me and all the bailiffs would say was that they didn't know what was going on. After the third hour of waiting outside the courtroom, a bailiff came and got me and said that I didn't have to go inside of the courtroom at all. When I asked him why, he said that my attorney was going to come and talk to me in a few minutes.

I was in total confusion because the Alameda courts always had some type of illegal court proceedings going on, which was nine times out of ten not in the favor of the defendant.

I was escorted back to the holding tank and all the inmates were asking me what happened and I told them that I was about to get railroaded because I wasn't even allowed to go inside my own trial. Everybody just shook their heads and said, "That's Alameda County for you, they do what the hell they want to do!" After one hour of sitting in the holding tank, I was called to meet with my attorney. I walked out of the holding tank knowing that something was about to transpire with my attorney. I was first to reach the tiny visiting cell that had a telephone and stool, and Plexiglas to separate the inmate from the free person coming to see them. After waiting in the tiny cell for 30 minutes, the attorney finally came and immediately picked up the phone.

"I have some good news for you!" He said excitedly.

"Oh yeah! They are dropping my case?" I said hopefully.

"It's not that good!" The attorney laughed, but then he continued, "This is what's on the table for you. You can either take the gun charge or the high-speed chase for a 16 month sentence, and you've already been incarcerated for 10 months so you would be getting out any day if you were to take the deal today!"

I asked the attorney, "What would you do if you were in this situation?"

"I would take the deal for the high speed chase because I wouldn't want another gun charge, since you already have one prior!" He told me.

With that said, I told the attorney that I would take the 16 months for the high speed chase.

Two weeks after I was sentenced, I was called early in the morning to pack my things because I was being transferred to San Quentin. I was in disbelief because I thought that I was going to spend the rest of my time in Santa Rita, because I thought that my time was officially over, but oh was I wrong! I packed my things and told everybody in the pod that I was going to San Quentin.

"Once Again"

I got on the prison bus knowing that I was going to have to go to the hole at San Quentin, because the last time I was there I had paroled from the hole. Policy was that if you paroled from the hole you had to go back to the hole because the situation hadn't been resolved. I dreaded the thought of having to go back to the hole because I knew that I would definitely starve until I went to the store or I was able to get word to Abraham or someone else on the mainline to send me some food.

Once I arrived to the dreary looking San Quentin, I was escorted to a cage by myself so that the correctional officers knew that I was going to the hole. I saw a lot of lifer inmates that I knew that were working in the reception center, and I made sure that I told every single person I knew to let Abraham know that I was going to the hole and for him to send me some food. I didn't get any word back from anyone that Abraham had received my message, so I knew that I was going to starve for a while.

My 10th day in the hole was when I went to classification and found out that I was being released from the hole and able to go to west block. I was happy as hell to get out of there; I knew that I had lost a good 10-15 pounds while I was in the hole because I was eating far less than I was at Santa Rita.

Once in west block it was like I was in a totally different world, I mean, it was total chaos. People were everywhere running back and forth to cells talking to their friends and making transactions. People that knew me came running to me asking me all the questions that inmates always asked. They asked me what I was in jail for, how long I was in jail for, and whether or not I had any tobacco on me. The word was out fast that I was in west block and everybody and their mammas were coming to talk to me as if I were a Hollywood celebrity. It felt good to receive all the respect I was given because respect was everything in prison and if you didn't have it you definitely wouldn't make it.

My first day in west block was chaotic because everybody was coming to talk to me and letting me know what had been transpiring the last couple of months in west block. There was a lot of shit going on. A week before I came to west block, there was a riot with the black and white inmates so there was a lot of tension in San Quentin. I got word that the Kumi soldiers handled their business in the riot. As I walked to the chow hall, I was surrounded by 10 Kumi soldiers that had already got word that I was in east block so they knew to give me security. I walked to the chow hall talking to Mike-G and I found out that he had become Kumi and he had talked himself into the top position –Of course I knew he wasn't qualified for it because he had only been Kumi for a month.

After 10 days in west block I went to classification and found out that I was going to get out in a few weeks. I was happy and mad at the same time, because the date I thought I was getting out on was wrong Turns out I was getting out two weeks later than I had calculated. I was told by the administration that I would more than likely be paroling from west block, which was cool with me at that point; I had gone to the store so I had plenty of food to eat.

The weeks leading to my release went by too damn slow for me. Three weeks seemed like three years and I was getting antsy as hell. I found myself snapping at people over nothing and disciplining Kumi members for the slightest infraction; everyone could tell that I was getting the short time fever, and everybody knew that people with short time fever weren't to be messed with.

My mother sent me a letter letting me know that my little brother was released from prison after doing five years on a five year term. I was glad to hear that my brother made it out of prison in one piece, because he was getting in a lot of fights while he was incarcerated.

The day of my release finally came and I was high on life when I heard my name called over the prison's intercom, informing me that I was paroling. I didn't have many things to pack so I just took my paperwork and ran out of west block, saying my farewells quickly. Once I got to the reception center, I realized that I was finally getting out of jail after doing 13 months. My mother, and my freshly out of prison little brother Spoiled, came to pick me up. As my mother drove away from the prison, I looked back at San Quentin and vowed that I was never going back, and that was the first time I had ever uttered those words.

"Got To Get It Right"

On the 580 freeway heading back to Oakland, I gazed out of the car window and visualized living a prosperous life and putting prison life far behind me. I knew that I had it in me to be successful, but I just didn't know how exactly I was going to do it because by that time ex-cons had messed it up to where other ex-cons weren't being hired for jobs. Even the gyms weren't hiring a person with a criminal record. I planned on starting my own personal training business and maybe do a little stripping to bring in some money. I definitely didn't want to sell dope anymore and I didn't make a ton of money from pimping, so I was going to forget about that as well.

For a couple of weeks I tried to find my way in society and boy was it tough. Every door I knocked on I got no answer. I finally decided to try and get a job at Bally's Gym in San Leandro Ca. I felt like this was my last resort at getting a job. The day I went into Bally's to inquire about a personal training job, I was told that the gym was hiring trainers so I needed to fill out the application and talk with the fitness manager. I filled out the application and then I went to talk to the fitness manager. He was all for me coming to be a trainer at Bally's Gym. It sounded all good to know that I was wanted as a trainer at the gym, but in the back of my mind I knew that I had another obstacle in front of me and that was the criminal background check that all businesses did at that point in the world. I was told by the fitness manager that I would be contacted after he reviewed my application and did the background check. I got the chills when he mentioned the background check because I knew that it was going to be the reason that I didn't get hired.

A few days after filling out the application to work at Bally's Gym, I saw the fitness manager and reluctantly asked him about me being hired. I said, "Hey buddy how are you?" He replied that he was great and that he had some great news for me. I had goose bumps all over because I knew that I'd been hired and I couldn't have been more grateful.

"Everything went through and you are hired as a trainer if you still want the job!" The manager told me.

"Hell yeah I want the job! When do I start?" I said. He told me that I could start whenever I wanted to and I immediately said, "How's tomorrow?" He told me that tomorrow would be great, the sooner the better!

"I'll see you tomorrow then, and thank you very much for the opportunity!" I told him.

I was pumped after I got the news and I went and told my family and friends. They were happy for me, because they knew that if an ex-con didn't get a job in a month's time of his release then he would resort back to the only way he knew how to get money.

My days working at Bally's Gym went by slowly because it was a slow time of the year as far as personal training went. During the summer months a lot of people were on vacation and traveling so that meant less money for personal trainers. I just walked around the gym and talked to members trying to make some new clients. I had a few clients but it just wasn't cutting it. Something had to change before I reverted back to the streets for money.

After a few weeks working at Bally's in San Leandro CA, my boss came to me and asked me if I wanted to transfer with him to the Bally's Gym in San Ramon CA. I wasn't hesitant at all with my decision; I told him with lightning speed that I would definitely transfer with him. I knew that the gym in San Ramon had more financial opportunity than San Leandro. The trainers made a lot more money per client in San Ramon as well. The decision was made that I was going to San Ramon with my boss the beginning of the next week.

My first day at San Ramon Bally's was very exciting for me. After I met all the staff I was taken through another orientation by my manager that I had transferred with and he went over the pricing of personal training sessions, which were $40 more than what I made in San Le-andro, so I was excited about that. My boss informed me that at this particular gym there were a lot of rich people that had been asking the facility when they were going to be getting some bodybuilder trainers at the San Ramon Bally's, which was perfect for me because I was the only buff trainer at the gym. After my orientation I was escorted around the gym to learn where everything was, which wasn't as much as the San Leandro gym so it was a breeze for me to learn the facility. After the orientation it was time for lunch so I went to a sandwich café with my boss and he treated me to lunch, which was awesome for me because my money was low and gas to San Ramon was going to take a lot of my money if I didn't start making some real cash. My boss and I ate at one of those fancy sandwich spots where they cut your meat right in front of you and make the bread from scratch right where you can see them behind the counter.

I was on top of the world after my first day in San Ramon. I saw myself getting financially stable from working at the high class gym and all my family members were proud that I was giving the legit lifestyle a chance again.

My second day of working in San Ramon was very eventful, as I talked to a lot of the gym's members and got a better feel of the facility. I trained a few people on my second day and I felt that things were going to work out great in San Ramon. During break time my boss asked me if all the information on my application was correct, and of course I told him that everything was correct. My antennas went up because it was weird that my boss was asking me about my application after he had already hired me. I was kind of leery about why he asked me that, so I asked him about it. He told me that the general manager was just updating all the new employees' information, which sounded highly fishy to me. I went on with my fulfilling day and trained a few more people, and then by the end of my work day I was approached by a beautiful lady saying that she wanted for me to be her personal trainer. I asked her if she was training with anybody at the present time and she told me that she was but that she trained with all the trainers to get a variety of fitness tips. I told the beautiful lady that I would love to train her, so I gave her one of my business cards – that was unrelated to Bally's Gym – and after saying goodbye we went our separate ways.

I then went to the second floor of the gym to get my duffle bag that had my things in it, and as soon as I reached the staircase walking down the stairs I was met by one of the trainers and he said, "Did you give my client this card?" I responded that yes, I had, and asked him why he was asking.

"Well, this is not a Bally's card, therefore you can't give them to members of the gym!" he said. I told him no problem and took my card back and put it in my pocket before leaving the gym.

I went home after my second day of working in San Ramon and I had a gut feeling that something was wrong. I replayed the incident at Bally's over and over again concerning the staff and how they made such a huge deal out of me giving my card to a member, so it had me pondering on what was to come.

I went to work the next day and as soon as I walked in the door it felt like everybody was looking at me with a strange look. I walked upstairs to the second floor where the personal trainer's office was and I was greeted by my boss. He had a look of turmoil on his face. I asked him what was wrong, but deep down I already knew.

"Why didn't you tell me that you were convicted of a felony?" He asked me.

I asked him whether I would've got hired if I didn't, and he told me that there was a chance that I could've been hired with a felony.

"Come on, there is no way you would've hired me if I put I had a felony," I said, looking at him seriously.

"Kali, I am sorry but I have to let you go, on the premises that you lied on your application," boss man said regretfully.

"Well thanks for the opportunity and I hope I didn't make you look bad!" I told him, and I truly meant it.

"I wish I could keep you, but my higher ups made the call!" he said.

I told him not to worry about it and that I understood his position on the matter. I left the gym that day mad at the world. I kept asking God why I couldn't keep a legit legal job. I was frustrated to the tenth degree, and as soon as I left that gym my heart turned black with anger and rage. I knew then that I was about to relapse into the life of crime.

"Crime Relapse"

After getting fired from the gym, I was mad at the world and I didn't know what I was going to do for money, so the first thing that came to my mind was robbery. I made some calls to some of my comrades and one of my road dogs was ready to go do some dirt with me because he was short on his rent. I went and picked up my road dog and we popped us a pill and had a little drink, then we decided that we were going to rob some drug dealers out on the streets.

The next day I had remorse for what I had done to get the measly few hundred dollars I did, so I went to church with moms and pops. While I was at the church I felt as if the pastor were talking directly to me and I knew that God was upset with me for the wrong turn that I had made once again in my life.

The pastor designated a time in the service for anyone who wanted to repent of their sins to God, to come to the front of the church and ask Him for forgiveness. By this time I was crying like a baby and I walked to the front of the church with head held down in shame for what I had become. I begged God to accept my repentance. After the church service my mother asked me why I was so emotional and I told her that I had done some things that I wasn't proud of and that I was repenting for it. She said that she understood and left the matter alone.

After going to repent for my sins at church, I went to a barbershop on 91st and International to talk to the owner about him letting me work there as a barber. The owner, Tre, turned me down not once, but twice.

I was back to hustling for two months straight and I was tired of worrying about police and niggas so I decided to go back to the barbershop for a third time. I had never sweated a job like this in my life, but I knew that the open chair at the barbershop was for me. When I got to the shop I saw an old friend that sold the shop to Tre named Fred. Fred used to cut my hair when I was in junior high, because my brother Archie started taking me to Fred's make-shift barbershop at his parent's house in the garage. Fred was the best barber I had ever been to and he was cheaper than barbershops. When Fred saw me he called me by my birth name, Chuck, and he was excited as hell to see me. We talked for a while and he told me he was cutting hair in Oakland on the weekends because he moved to Las Vegas after he sold the shop to Tre. I had let Fred cut my hair while I talked to him and Tre about letting me work at the shop. Fred said that it would be a good thing if Tre let me work there and after Fred finished cutting my hair he told Tre that I was a good dude and that I was definitely worthy of working in the shop with him. Ultimately Tre took what Fred said to heart and asked me when I was ready to start work. I told him ASAP, so Tre told me to come to work the following Monday. I was excited as hell because this was my out from the streets. I thanked Tre and Fred for giving me the opportunity and I told Tre that he wouldn't be sorry for hiring me.

"Let's Do It"

After getting hired by Tre to work at the barbershop, I went and bought myself all the utensils I needed to work there. I also went and got my cousin Bobby's barber license and had it altered so that my name was on the license instead of his. You had to be crafty in this world to make it, and crafty I was.

Monday came and I was excited as ever to be starting a new career that I could finally be happy with myself for doing. I parked outside the barbershop and waited on Tre for about an hour before he finally pulled up and said that he was sorry but a lot of shit was going on with him at the moment. I told him not to worry about it because I would've waited all day if I needed to. Tre and I hit it off good our first day in the shop together. He was a natural comedian and not only that but he was a pimp, or as he preferred to call himself, a "Mack". Tre talked about macking on a hoe all day every day, and crowds of people got their haircut from Tre just to hear him talk. He took at least an hour on a person's head, which was far too long, but his clientele loved to be around him so time wasn't an issue. This worked out great for me because it left room for me to cut three people to his one.

It was my third week at the barbershop and I was making consistent money. It was slow at the shop my first week, because a lot of people in the neighborhood didn't get their hair cut by Tre due to the fact that he took so long. Once people found out that there was another barber in the shop that barely talked and gave amazing haircuts, the people started rolling in. I must say that the third week was a charm. I was making a good $200 dollars a day, which was good money to me and I didn't have to worry about the police; it was simply great.

My fourth week at the barbershop I went and bought myself a pearl white Cadillac with low miles on it and boy was it a beauty. I think seeing Tre's Cadillac made me want a caddy (as we called them) as well. I put the Lexus up for sale because the Lexus dealership was trying to charge me $5,000 to work on it and I told them hell no, that I could go buy a car with that, and that's exactly what I did.

My caddy was pearl white and Tre's caddy was a pearly silver color, and his was a different style from mine. I had a two door and Tre had a four door. We started calling ourselves the caddy boys.

After a few months things were rolling at the shop and I was making about $1,000 a week at that point, so things were looking up. I had decided to put some 22" rims on the caddy, because Tre had got his caddy out of the shop and boy was it a beautiful car, so he inspired me to step my car game up too.

It was in April of 2007 that I was introduced to the woman of my dreams by one of Tre's customers who brought her son to the barbershop to get his haircut by Tre. I was always talking mess about what type of woman that I had to have and how she had to look, so Tiff told me that she had someone for me. I told her to show me a picture of what the woman she had in mind looked like and boy when I saw that picture of my future wife I was immediately blown away. She was the most beautiful woman I had ever seen. After I was shown the picture, I told Tre's customer to call her, which she did. When I was put on the phone with the beautiful lady I immediately went into my suave talk. Dvyne was her name and she wasn't budging when I talked to her; she told me that she wasn't dating at the time because she had a lot going on in her life, but I wasn't giving up that easily. I quickly responded with, "Is it alright if I send you a picture of myself?" Dvyne told me that I could send her a picture if I wanted, so I sent her one of my modeling pictures I had just taken like a week before meeting her. It was a picture of me holding a beach towel over my crotch area, and I was glistening like a shiny Hershey kiss. From that point on we were inseparable.

I'll never forget the first date my future wife and I had together; it was definitely a surreal experience. We met at The Elephant Bar in Emeryville CA. I had been to this particular Elephant Bar a few times before, so it was a place that I was familiar with and I felt comfortable going to meet that beautiful lady of mine there. I was already high off alcohol and from a pill I'd taken before I arrived to The Elephant Bar, so I pulled into the parking lot with my music blasting and acting like a common street punk with a nice car. As I drove around looking for a place to park, I saw the beautiful lady I was meeting and I got overly excited. After I finally found a place to park the caddy (Cadillac), I went and greeted Dvyne and I showered her with compliments and I could tell that I had her blushing like crazy. We sat at a table and I continued to tell Dvyne how beautiful she was and how I was ready to marry her after meeting her for the first night.

We talked for about five minutes and a young lady with a short haircut came to our table and said hello to Dvyne. Dvyne said hello and told me that the girl was her friend Roz. I said hello to Roz and me, being on ecstasy and some alcohol, I was known to say the wildest things to people. It hadn't been an entire minute that Roz had sat down with us and that's when the outbursts came. I said, "Roz, do you know that you look like you could be Prince's sister?"

Roz looked at me with a look pure hate and said, "What is that supposed to mean?"

"Oh it was a compliment! I didn't mean to offend you or anything!" I said sincerely.

I could tell that Dvyne was tickled but that Roz wasn't tickled at all; in fact, she was definitely offended by the comment. Dvyne and I continued talking and getting to know one another and we were having a good time but Roz was ready to leave after I offended her the way I did. Dvyne and I kept talking for about 45 minutes while Roz was still sitting at the table with a mean look on her face. After I was done with my drink, I told the waitress that we were ready to go and for her to bring us our tab. At that point Dvyne shocked me by saying that she was paying for the drinks. I was floored that a woman so beautiful would offer to pay for my drink. Dvyne had already showed me that she was a classy lady, and I was definitely smitten by her. I knew that this was going to be my future wife, and I was spending a lot of time with her.

We went out practically every night during our courting. I was never the one to pressure or even insinuate about have sex; I was always one to just go with the flow of things because I was never a pussy hound. I was always focused on getting successful in life and I could tell that I was something totally new to Dvyne. I made her laugh when she didn't want to and I always said things she had never heard before, so she was very intrigued with me as I was with her.

I could tell that Dvyne was going through some trying times in her life, due to her recent divorce and her insatiable desire to get back to Los Angeles. Dvyne definitely had a lot on her mind, so when I was with her I tried to free her mind from all of her troubles.

One night Dvyne and I had gone out to dinner and afterwards she said that she wanted me to go with her somewhere. I didn't ask her where, I just went with her because I trusted her in a way that I had never allowed myself to trust anyone before. Dvyne drove me to a house in West Oakland which I had passed many times in my lifetime. When we got inside the house, Dvyne called out, "Brother, I'm home!" All of a sudden I heard the floor screeching as if a five hundred pound beast were running and my eyes opened with excitement to see who the person was that was causing the ground to shake under my feet. That's when I saw a light skinned, heavy set guy enter the room. He was a weird looking, baby faced fella who immediately ran to Dvyne and kissed her on the lips. I was in shock for a second and in my mind I thought to myself, "I knew that this was too good to be true. There's no way that I found the most beautiful woman I had ever seen in my life and that she would come baggage free!"

"Kali, this is my brother, Kente. Kente, this is Kali!" She said introducing us. At that point I was relieved to know that the man was her brother, but I still found myself confused by their relationship.

"Nice to meet you, how are doing?" I said to him. I could tell immediately that something wasn't normal about her brother because he kept staring at Dvyne without blinking. I didn't know if incest was going on or what, but I was totally confused because I had never before encountered a situation as the one I had encountered in that moment. While my mind was trying desperately to process what was taking place, I heard footsteps that were far from normal.

All I could hear was, clunk, clunk, clunk, and clunk! My eyes opened with excitement once again and then out came a white man that looked as though he was supposed to be a part of the Adam's Family or something.

"This is my father, Daniel." She said.

When Dvyne said that, my head jerked as if in shock and Dvyne looked at me to see how I was reacting to all this weird information. I played everything off as if things were totally normal and I talked with both Daniel and Kente. Kente went off on a tirade about every old school song there was. He was like a computer when it came to old school music and movies. I could tell that he was highly intelligent in a weird type of way.

I hung out with Dvyne and her weird family for a while before eventually I told her that I had to leave and that I would see her the next day. We hugged and I went about my business. When I left Dvyne's house, I tried to process what had happened while I was there and I weighed the pros with the cons of the situation, trying to figure out if I could deal with Dvyne's weird family.

Dvyne and I were infatuated with one another. We were together every single day and I was falling in love with this woman fast. Dvyne was the first woman I can honestly say that I was not only infatuated with, but who I was ready to be with for the rest of my life. Dvyne had all the qualities that I wanted in a woman. She was gorgeous beyond description, she was heavily versed in the bible, she was a praying woman, she was loyal to her family, and she had strong morals and principles that I praised her for; not only that, but the love making was the best I had ever encountered in my life. I knew I was going to make her my wife.

Things were going great with Dvyne and I, and I got to understand more about her family and what her life was about. I never knew about autism until I met Dvyne's brother, Kente. It was something foreign to me until that point. I knew that Dvyne was an aspiring singer that already had some amazing songs recorded, and her desire was to get to Los Angeles to be a big star. Dvyne and I had the same outlook on life, which was rare to find in someone, especially in Oakland. We were learning more and more about one another on a daily basis, and the only conflict we had was her problem with my long hustling hours. Dvyne wanted to take up a lot of my money making time, which was causing us to bump heads because hustling was what I did and I wasn't going to let anyone stop that.

"Resurrection of a Demon"

It was the month of July and things were too good to be true. Tre and I were doing great at the barbershop and I had a few side hustles selling whatever I got my hands on. A lot of people started coming to the barbershop because they could hear Tre and I talk about everything from pimping to hustling and we were well liked by everyone that came to know us.

Everybody in the area thought that Tre and I were doing very well financially, and we started to get a lot of unknown people coming to the barbershop but we thought nothing of it. I was still in the pimp game a little, and I had a couple of raggedy hoes at the time that were more of a problem than they were an asset. I had a raggedy black broad that had gold hair and weighed about 90 pounds. The only reason I had these problematic hoes was because they each brought me about $200 a day. I would've stopped pimping but that extra $400 a day was nice to get for not having to do much.

Tre and I were the talk of Oakland because we were doing our thing in and out of the barbershop; however, what we didn't know was that we were being talked about so much that it was making a lot of people jealous, and jealousy was the root of evil in Oakland CA.

There's one day that I'll never be able to forget for the rest of my life. It was a beautiful day and the sky was clear and I felt so good that it was actually scary. I got to the barbershop around nine am so I cleaned up the shop a little before it got too busy. After I cut a few heads, Tre strolled in and the fun began. I had received a call from one of my Kumi comrades that he wanted to buy the pistol grip shotgun that I had for sale, so I told him to come by as soon as possible before it got too busy. At 1:00 p.m. my comrade came to get the shotgun, which I had inside a duffle bag.

A couple of hours had passed and the barbershop was half full. Tre's father was there and a few friends from the neighborhood were there too. We were having a good old time, when suddenly I looked up and saw two masked men pushing a female inside the barbershop. I quickly went to the back of the shop because I knew that a serious situation was about to take place if motherfuckers had on masks and were carrying what looked like some big ass guns.

As I nervously listened from the back of the barbershop, I heard a dude say, "Pull everything out your pockets and if you try to leave something in your pockets you will be killed!"

I was thinking, "Damn, I can't let my people get done like this and not do anything about it."

I thought that the situation might have been directed at me, because there had been a few killings in my neighborhood and I figured that those cats were there for me. I came from the back of the barbershop and said, "What's going on?" The masked men immediately told me to get on the ground and take everything out of my pockets, just like they had done to the others.

I could clearly see that the masked man had a shotgun pointed at Tre, his father and the two females. The masked man that told me to get on the ground had an Uzi pointed at me, and I could tell that these cats were experienced at robbing people because of how they moved and how they were in sync with one another. The masked man on Tre looked through Tre's wallet and said, "This all the money you got? I thought you were a pimp?" Right then and there I knew that those people must have been someone that had known or heard about Tre; I just hoped that they weren't real killers because if they were we were all going to be dead. Luckily once all the robbers got what they came for, they left out the door. A few seconds after they left I ran outside to see if I could see what type of car they were getting in, but I was a second too late because I didn't see anyone except the nosy ass neighbors looking dumb founded. I was so mad I thought that my fucking head was going to explode. Everyone was a suspect at that moment. I became paranoid and I thought everyone on the planet had had something to do with the robbery.

I vowed that I would find out who robbed us and that they would feel my wrath, simple as that. Tre was as mad as I was and so we decided we were going to be partners in crime at that point to find out who had the guts to come and do that to us. I had never been robbed in my life, so my ego was bruised and I had to fix my bruised ego in whatever way I possibly could. My sole mission after that was to find out who robbed us, which I knew would be simple to do because I had Kumi comrades all over the Bay Area who always had info on whatever had happened in the Bay, good or bad.

The morning after the barbershop was robbed I went to the shop with two guns in my waistband and opened up as if nothing even happened. I kept the door locked until I finished cleaning up the shop from the previous day's commotion, and once I finished cleaning up I checked to see if my guns were ready to be fired with no problems. The day was uneventful; there were just noisy ass people trying to get information on what had happened the day before. Tre and I made a pact that we wouldn't even speak on the situation to outsiders.

My second day at the shop I was even more paranoid because I had been questioning a lot of people about the incident and I knew that if I had asked anyone that knew the perps that it would get back to them. In Oakland California, the rule of thumb was to kill your enemy before they could kill you, so I tried to stay quiet about the situation as much as humanly possible.

A couple of hours after I was at the barbershop, a Kumi comrade of mine came to see me. He was from the 800 block of East Oakland and he had a lot of respect for me for trying to change my life and be a working man. As I started cutting his hair he said, "Big bra, I know who did the robbery!" I immediately stopped cutting his hair and I turned the barber chair so that I could look him in the eyes.

"Who was it, bra?" I asked him earnestly.

"It was those niggas back there on the dead end block. I heard them bragging about it," my Kumi comrade told me.

When Tre pulled up to the barbershop later, I was standing outside with my hand on my pistol waiting for him, and as soon as he saw the look on my face he knew that something was going on.

"What's up bra?" He asked me as we walked back inside the barbershop. Once we were inside I told him that I knew who did the robbery and Tre stopped in his tracks, a look of excitement plastered across his face.

"Who?" He asked happily.

I said, "It was the niggas back there on the dead end block!"

"I knew it was those niggas because they are affiliated with that nigga I don't like," Tre said.

The rest of the day Tre and I premeditated how we would get our revenge, and we came up with a master plan. Tre and I went and did what all gangsters did when they were wronged. I never felt bad about doing things to people that wronged me because I was a respectful person that minded my own business, but when someone got in my business then I gave them what they deserved.

The day after the retaliation I stayed home with Dvyne getting my thoughts together about what my life was going to be like after the barbershop ordeal. I knew that working there was over for me because I wasn't going to be a sitting duck to where people knew where I was all day every day. I had to go invisible for a while because I knew that the violent tirade I went on was going to make me some enemies, and I wasn't going to give anyone easy access at killing me.

I decided at that point to lay low with my girlfriend Dvyne in West Oakland. I stayed in the house for a few days until the day Tre's baby son was born and I went to see him. It was a blessing for Tre and me to see his son being born because the past few days had been crazy for us. I had a deep appreciation for life after being there with Tre and his newborn child.

A few days after Tre's son was born, Dvyne's grandmother passed away, so there was a lot of chaos going on in my life at that time; not to mention we were living in the house with Dvyne's autistic brother, who wanted attention like a newborn baby. It was very stressful dealing with Dvyne's family. If it wasn't her brother, it was her mother causing

Dvyne huge amounts of stress. I had to get away from the madness before I busted a pipe.

Dvyne told me that she owned a duplex house converted into an apartment complex in East Oakland, so I had her take me to look at it. After seeing the place I asked her why we couldn't just move in and rent out the other apartments. I saw Dvyne's eyes widen as if a light bulb had come on in her head.

"I didn't even think of that. That is the best idea ever!" she said excitedly.

Dvyne and I went home to pack all of our things and we were out of her brother's house so quickly it would've made your head spin. Dvyne already had furniture at the house in East Oakland, so it wasn't too bad of a move because all we had to pack up were our clothes.

After a couple of days at the new place on Foothill, I started to feel as if it was home. We weren't stressed out by her mother or her brother. We had room to breathe and it was very peaceful in the area we now lived in. I was back to hustling on the streets selling whatever I could get my hands on and half-heartedly pimping a couple of hoes.

The barbershop chaos had died down for me because I no longer worked there. I knew what I had done and I wasn't going to let anyone get a stripe off of me. Tre was still at the barbershop because that was his only means of income and he said he wasn't going to let anybody stop his income from coming in. I had Tre's back to the fullest, and if I even heard that someone was looking at Tre crazy I was going to shoot first and not even worry about asking questions later.

After about a month of living on Foothill my money started to get low so I decided that I had to start getting back into hustling. I had a raggedy black hoe that would bring in about $200 a day, which wasn't shit after I had to pay for her room and board. Luckily I didn't have to pay for rent during that time because of Dvyne owning the place we lived in. I did everything from cutting my patna's hair at their houses to personal training. I had my hands in everything.

I had become a treacherous criminal once again and I blamed it on the barbershop robbery. I was now riding around with guns galore and I started looking for all the people that had pissed me off.

Luckily I kept working out, which always allowed me to get a clear mind set of my life and where I was going. Big Low and I were working out together again and he had just gotten out of the federal half way house so he was doing well for himself. He had a supportive girlfriend that made sure he had everything he needed and wanted; not to mention he had gotten his license to drive big rigs, so he was doing great for himself and I was proud of the positive path he was on.

I always told Big Low about all the things I was involved in and he would tell me that I needed to be cool and that I should get my license to drive big rigs like him. I didn't like to drive so that was out of the question for me. I knew that I had to find something to do as a career choice though because I knew that hustling wasn't going to last for long; nothing ever lasted long in the realm of negativity.

Big Low and I were back to pumping that iron like we did in San Quentin. We were on a five day a week regiment, but because Big Low worked a lot of long hours he would miss days here and there. I was like a robot so I never missed a day of working out.

I finally got my act together and started living as best as I possibly could. I still had to hustle but I chose not to hustle the way I used to, the type of hustling that caused me to be a violent fool. I chose to stick to selling ecstasy pills and personal training. I had also made a conscious decision that I was going to start competing in bodybuilding because I felt that bodybuilding was going to be my only way out of ghetto ass Oakland.

December 2007 was a crazy month for me and it started off on Christmas Eve when I usually would have had all my holiday shopping done, but I still had to get Dvyne a few things.

I was cool with my little brother's step kids, so I decided to take them to the mall with me. One was around 14 years old and the other was about 17 years old. I thought the two of those niggas were some little gangsters because they always talked gangster shit, so I was letting them hang out with me to see how they acted in public. I decided to go to Southland Mall in Hayward. I'd never, in my life, had one problem at a shopping mall, so I never even worried about running into problems there.

When I got to the mall I was high from an ecstasy pill and some gin I had been drinking. I was cool though; nobody ever knew when I was high because my high was always fighting the high. I walked around the mall for about 45 minutes and eventually I found the things I wanted to get for Dvyne and so the two youngsters and I left. I was putting all the bags inside the car, when something came over me and I had a feeling I needed to go back in the mall. To this day, I don't know why I went back in there.

As the two youngsters and I got inside the mall, again I was high as hell and I was feeling fantastic. I had just started stripping again so I was passing out my business cards to women; not being rude or anything like that, just passing out my cards and trying to get some business. After I'd passed out about 10 of my cards, I saw a tall cat walking towards me and he had a tough guy look on his face.

"Here's your card. You gave it to my sister and she is too young!" he said aggressively.

Now, maybe I would have accepted what he said, but it was how he said it; he said it as if he were going to whoop my ass or something, and it infuriated me. I casually put my arm around the 6'0" tall cat, which was an old school move that a person was never supposed to let another man do. I walked with the cat and asked him where he was from.

"I from Oakland, you heard of Brookfield nigga!" he said.

"I'm from 98th and E Street nigga, and we don't get down like that from East Oakland!" I said.

At that point I released his neck, pulled back and caught that boy with a right hook on his chin. I hit him so hard that my fist went through his jaw. I knew right away that I had broken it because I heard it crack and then I started my non-stop assault of power punches to his face. I had knocked him into a store and I was on top of him talking to him with every punch.

"You ain't from Oakland nigga! Out here playing with a gangster and you getting your ass murdered!" I shouted down at him as I continued to brutally punch him.

Oh I was talking a ton of shit! I was so pumped up that I'd never realized that he had some patnas with him and that they were hitting me on the back of my head but I never felt a thing. The only thing that stopped me from punching that cat was the Hayward Police, who had come and pulled me from on top of that nigga. I didn't realize that my little brother's step-sons had left and didn't throw a single punch. The police escorted me to a police car that was outside the shopping mall and I just knew that I was going to jail on a probation and parole violation.

The police asked me what had happened and I said that I didn't remember anything.

"Oh you don't huh?" they said doubtfully, "Well I guess you'll be spending Christmas in jail buddy!"

I was mad as shit at myself for even going back in that damn mall. I sat in the police car knowing that my fate was not going to be good that Christmas.

As I awaited my fate, one of the officers came back to the car and said, "Well this is your lucky day, mister! The fella you beat to a pulp was a big youngster, only 17 years old, and he told us exactly what happened and he was definitely in the wrong, so we are going to let you go with no repercussions!"

I said "thanks" and I went to find my car. I realized as I walked through the now empty mall parking lot that my car was nowhere to be found. My mind started racing all over the place, because I didn't know where my damn car was. I started walking to find a telephone because my cell phone was gone, when a sharp pain started surging through my ankle and I looked down to find that it had swollen up the size of a cantaloupe. I knew that I must have twisted it when I punched the youngster the first time, and then I tasted blood on my lip and realized that I had a deep gash on my lip too, which I knew was going to need stitches. I figured that the youngster's friends must have hit me in the lip, because I knew that the youngster didn't get in a single punch.

After walking on my twisted ankle for about a half of a mile, I finally reached a gas station that had a pay phone. Since I didn't have any change on me, I had to call collect and so I ended up calling my mom's house. Pops answered the phone and immediately asked me if I was in jail and I said, "Hell naw I ain't in jail, why did you think that?"

"Your brother said you were in jail!" Pops told me.

"Well I'm not in jail, so have Dvyne come and pick me up at the gas station by Southland Mall!" I told him.

Pops said he was about to call my mother's cell phone because she was with Dvyne at my brother's house getting my car from him.

After waiting outside with a cut lip and swollen ankle for about 20 minutes, Dvyne pulled up in the caddy with my mother in the passenger's seat. I hobbled to the car and got inside and my mom and Dvyne started with the barrage of questions.

I asked Dvyne how she got my car and she told me that my brother had driven it to his house.

"How did he get the car? He wasn't at the mall." I asked, confused.

Dvyne told me that he was at the mall, and that he saw me fighting and didn't do a thing for fear of getting a parole violation. I was fucking pissed and I told Dvyne to take me to that nigga's house.

We dropped my mother off at her house and went to visit my cowardly brother. I was ready to kill everybody inside that house at that point. As soon as I walked inside, I told the two youngsters that they were straight up little bitches for not helping me. Then I went at my brother and told him that he was a bitch too, and that his bitch with the 10 kids was a bitch, and that I would kill everything in that fucking house right at that moment. Everybody knew I had done some recent shootings so they were scared shitless.

I got my stuff from my coward brother and it took everything in me not to kill those motherfuckers in that house. Dvyne and I sped off in the caddy and I had to go to Highland Hospital Emergency Room.

After my lip was stitched up and the x-rays showed that I had a sprained ankle, I was released from the hospital about 10 hours later. It was about 6:00 a.m. on Christmas day when I finally got home, and I immediately went to sleep, though the throbbing ankle didn't let me sleep much.

"Living In West Oakland"

After the holiday fiasco of violence, things were getting better in my life. I had taken on a few personal training clients, I was back to stripping, and I was wanted throughout America by modeling photographers and by women wanting me to do strip shows for birthdays and bachelorette parties. I was in high demand and I was traveling quite a bit at that point – from Los Angeles, Las Vegas, and as far as New York. I was getting around and all because of my physique. I was also preparing myself to do my first bodybuilding show in May 2009 in Los Angeles California.

The place on Foothill that Dvyne and I were living in had gone into foreclosure so we did cash for keys and then moved with Kente to West Oakland, which I didn't want to do but we didn't have any other options at the time.

Living in West Oakland was definitely a challenge for me because there were a ton of niggas that were always outside selling dope and acting a fool, and I knew that my day would come when I would have to let everyone know that I wasn't the one to be fucked with.

Wherever I lived I made it a point to never get familiar with the neighbors because in Oakland if the hood niggas thought you were weak then they would try you, so I went everywhere with my mean mug on and the 40 cal with slugs in my waistband. Because of that, those niggas stayed their distance from me and my family.

Living with Kente was pure hell. I remember telling Dvyne that living with her autistic brother was worse than being in prison. I mean, this dude would wake up at the crack of dawn and start his daily tirade.

You have to remember that this dude was 320 pounds and when he walked around upstairs it sounded like the floor was going to cave in on top of us. Kente and Daniel were early birds and they would be talking at 4:00 a.m. as if it were noon. Dvyne and I would regularly have to tell them to keep down the noise.

My financial status was climbing because I was now shipping thousands of ecstasy pills out of the state. I was making at least $3,000 a week but I always knew that it wouldn't last long because hustling narcotics never lasted for a long time. I rode the wave as long as possible and I made sure to save as much money as I could. My stripping days were over at that point because I was only in the stripping game to be able to pay my bills, and once I started bringing in a ton of cash weekly I had no need to strip any longer.

"Big Low and Bodybuilding"

I had been living in West Oakland for six months and tragedy hit home hard. Big Low had been in a shootout in East Oakland and the doctors were saying that he was possibly going to be paralyzed for the rest of his life. I was saddened by the recent turn of events that took place with Big Low, as I knew this would be devastating to his life.

I went to visit Big Low when he was admitted to the facility for rehabilitation in San Leandro California, called Fairmont Hospital. This wasn't my first time visiting that hospital because I used to visit my friend and comrade Shawn when he was paralyzed from a bad car accident. I hated that hospital because it was where a lot of young people were who had been paralyzed due to getting shot in the streets. Big Low was my closet friend at that time in my life and I was very hurt by the situation he was in. My first day going to see him was very emotional for the both of us.

Big Low was always a tough guy, but this was the first day that I had ever seen him show some emotions. Big Low was very down on himself saying that he wasn't going to live as a paraplegic, and that he didn't want to live anymore. I had to be emotionally strong because I knew that Big Low had to hear a lot of encouragement. I couldn't imagine what it would be like to be in his shoes. I stayed there with him for a few hours, trying to ease his mind as much as I could. When I left from visiting with Big Low, I was an emotional wreck; visiting him was mentally, emotionally, and physically draining.

I continued to visit him every day and I pushed him outside in the wheelchair so that he could get fresh air. Big Low was very friendly with all the other patients that were in the hospital as well. I went with him to his physical therapy sessions, which were very tough for him in the beginning, because Big Low was still carrying a ton of muscle. He was weighing about 240 lbs. but since he had no feeling in his legs they were extra heavy and he didn't have a lot of upper body strength at the time to get himself in and out of the wheelchair. Big Low was very frustrated with himself and his situation, and I encouraged him that he would walk again but he always went off what the doctors said, which was that he was never going to walk again.

A month after Big Low's accident, I had one of my childhood friends go with me to see him. My childhood friend was also paralyzed, so I wanted him to talk to Big Low about the formalities of being paralyzed and what he needed to learn while being paralyzed. When my childhood friend, DJ, and I got to Big Low's room, it was evident that he was depressed. DJ snapped Big Low out of his depression and gave him a lot of pertinent advice. At the time Big Low was unable to get himself in and out of his wheelchair, so DJ showed him how and Big Low caught on fast. He learned how to move his body within 15 minutes. DJ had been a great help to Big Low's progress, because DJ had been paralyzed for eight years and so he knew a lot of things that Big Low didn't.

Big Low progressed fast and in order to go home he had to show his physical therapist that he could get in and out of bed and in and out of the wheelchair. Big Low was allowed to go home after three months in the hospital. He was released from Fairmont Hospital and into the care of his girlfriend that stayed in an apartment that only had rooms that were upstairs. That meant that Big Low's bed had to be downstairs in the living room. It was terrible seeing my best friend in that terrible situation. He was quickly sinking into a state of depression and there wasn't anything that I or anyone else could do about it.

Big Low needed two in home care providers so I agreed to be one of them. He would be getting a huge back pay from the state because he had been getting care since his being paralyzed. Big Low had me and his aunt as his in-home care providers and I was coming daily to his apartment to do whatever he needed me to do. I mostly drove him in his car to Fairmont Hospital on the days that he had therapy because there wasn't anyone else strong enough to help Big Low do a lot of things, besides me, so I was his go to guy.

After a few months of being Big Low's in-home care provider, I noticed that I was getting emotionally drained because of his depression and the way he was always talking about dying and killing himself. I was definitely losing myself in Big Low's situation and I knew that I wasn't going to stay going on like this for long.

Another tragic thing happened in November of 2008, when Dvyne was four months pregnant and she was working as in-home care provider for an elderly lady. Dvyne had been over working herself and she ended up having a miscarriage. It was a truly sad point in both of our lives because we had planned on having our first baby together. I had to be there for Dvyne emotionally, which I was used to doing at that point because I had been helping a lot of other people emotionally too, but now it was my girlfriend who needed me and I had to keep as emotionally strong as possible. Tragedy after tragedy was taking place and I just couldn't understand where life was taking me at the time

Dvyne and I knew that our only way out of crime ridden Oakland was to move to Los Angeles once she won her lawsuit against the crooked real estate broker. I, of course, had some money saved but it was hardly enough to move to a city like Hollywood, so we were praying daily for God to make a way for us to be able to move to the city of dreams.

After the miscarriage, Dvyne was depressed and she started putting on quite a bit of weight. I was eating up everything because I was preparing to have my bodybuilding debut in several months and Dvyne was eating right along with me. I saw her gaining weight and I would strategically say something to her about it but she would always say that she wasn't gaining that much weight, and so I would drop it until the next right time.

2009 came around and I had made a lot of plans for the New Year. Dvyne and I were going to get to Los Angeles by any means necessary. I was all out focused on the upcoming bodybuilding shows starting in May and I planned on doing about five shows during the summer of that year. I knew I had what it took to be a top bodybuilder, but I didn't know if the judges would think the same thing. I put a ton of pressure on myself studying the scientific parts of bodybuilding day in and day out. I had to learn everything myself because the few bodybuilders that were in Oakland didn't help out other up and coming bodybuilders one bit, so Google was my best friend and coach.

The months were going by fast leading up to the start of my body-building career and I was always on edge because of the pressure that I was putting on myself. It was very stressful because I knew that body-building was about knowledge and I knew that I didn't have all the knowledge that I needed to have and not having a mentor to teach me the game was definitely a handicap.

In February of 2009, I had to start the crazy bodybuilder's diet to prepare for the start of my bodybuilding career. I was super cranky at that point and it was putting a strain on the relationship between Dvyne and me. I explained to her that I needed her to hang in there with me while I was dieting and for her to be emotionally supportive while I was going through the foreign process I was going through to get into contest shape.

My diet preparing for the bodybuilding shows was fairly basic and monotonous, but monotony was normal for me. This was my diet: (meal 1: 1 cup oatmeal: 8 eggs) (meal 2: rice (1 cup) chicken meal) (meal 3: same as 2) (meal 4: rice(1 cup) 2 beef patties) (meal 5: same as 4) (meal 6: rice(1 cup) 2 tilapia fillets)

I ate the same meals for months without any deviation, and if I tried to eat anything different I would get sick, so I couldn't deviate even if I wanted too.

In April of 2009, Dvyne and I flew into the Burbank California Airport and rented ourselves a car for the three days we would be in Los Angeles. Dvyne and I had been bickering a lot because of my short tem-per and my bossiness, so we were butting heads like crazy by that time. Once we got in our rental car and got to the hotel, we got into another argument and I doubted whether I should have even brought Dvyne because she was stressing me out more than anything. It wasn't good to stress before a bodybuilding show because your body would make crazy unwanted hormonal changes.

Finally the day came when I was about to step up on a bodybuild-ing stage for the first time. I was backstage with the other competitors assessing my competition, and I didn't see anyone except another big ass black dude named Sergeant, who would later end up giving me a problem for the overall title. I thought I was the biggest dude at the show until I saw that mammoth of a man.

At that point in my life I was still somewhat ghetto and mean, so I didn't talk to many people or even speak to them. Everybody at a body-building show has a mean look on their face for whatever reason. I had my mean look on because I didn't feel good and of course because I was nervous. Once I started oiling up my body to go on stage, a lot of people started coming over and talking to me, saying things like, "You know you are going to win this show right?" I stayed humbled and acted like I didn't know what all the other competitors were seeing in me that I didn't see in myself. Deep down I knew that I was going to win my weight category, but I also knew that I would have to deal with that big nigga Sergeant for the overall title.

The time had come when I would find out if all my studying was going to pay off. The top five heavyweights were called individually to do their posing routine. I saw that Dvyne and a few other friends were in the audience cheering me on. I did my posing routine to gladiator music and I felt confident in everything I did. After all the heavyweights did their posing routines, all five of us were called out to find out the first place winner.

As I and another competitor stood as the last two on stage, it seemed as though time had stopped and the announcer called out the second place winner and it wasn't my name. I jumped for joy as I took first place at my very first bodybuilding show. I was ecstatic that all my home-work had paid off. I heard Dvyne and my friends screaming my name and I held up my trophy so all could see me.

The show wasn't over for me because even though I had won my weight category, I still had to go up against all the other first place win-ners to see who would be the Orange County overall winner. Back on stage I had to pose against all the other first place winners and I felt confident because the word was out that the overall winner was going to be between Sergeant and me. Sergeant and I battled on stage. We were posing hard against one another and it was exhausting but I wouldn't let anyone know that I was tired.

After the pose off, the announcer said, "Orange County's overall winner is – Sergeant!" I shook Sergeant's hand politely and walked off the stage.

I was definitely disappointed that I hadn't been the overall winner, but I was happy at the same time because I had won first place in my weight category. I learned a lot from the Orange County show and I knew that I had more studies to do because when I saw the pictures I wasn't satisfied with how I looked. I had a couple of weeks to make some corrections to my body before I was to do the Contra Costa Bodybuilding Show in Hayward California.

Preparing for the Contra Costa Bodybuilding Show was much more stressful for me because I knew that I was in my back yard and that I had to do well. After the Orange County show, I knew that I had to learn the science of removing all water from under my skin so that I could achieve what bodybuilders called "the dry and grainy look". I was studying day-in-day-out about the science of bodybuilding and I thought that the more cardio I did then the drier and grainier I would get but I was sadly mistaken.

The day before the Contra Costa bodybuilding show, Dvyne and I went and got ourselves a hotel room close to Chabot College in Hayward California. I could have just driven to the bodybuilding show from my house in West Oakland – which was about a 20 minute drive – but I didn't want any stress getting to the show, as stress was definitely not good before a competition.

After Dvyne and I got settled into the hotel room, I relaxed the rest of the day and did the necessary scientific protocols to rid my body of the water that lay between the skin.

I had a real dilemma on my hands, because ever since I'd done the Orange County show, I noticed that my ankles were holding a lot of water and I thought that it would go away because of the cardio I was doing but here it was, the day before the bodybuilding show, and my ankles were still engorged with water. I knew something was terribly wrong, but I hoped that the water would be gone before I stepped on the stage.

The night before the competition I couldn't sleep at all and I noticed that this happened at the Orange County show as well. It was nervousness and anxiety all in one. I tried to force myself to sleep, because I was on my second day of drinking no water and that water I had in the refrigerator was calling my name.

The morning finally came and I was wide awake at 5:00 a.m. I got dressed while Dvyne was sound asleep and I went to the nearest restaurant and had the typical meal that bodybuilders ate the day of competition – pancakes, eggs, and steak. After I ate the meal I gained some energy and my body looked much better. I felt good but I noticed that my ankles were still swollen and now there was no definition in my calves because of all the fluid that had built up there; I definitely knew something was wrong with my body at that point. When I got to the weigh in for the competition, I saw a lot of the same competitors that were at the Orange County show and once they saw me they would shake their heads and say, "You came here too?"

I would reply," "Yep, I got to learn all I can learn about my body and the only way to do that is to compete!"

As everybody weighed in, I didn't see any serious threats to me. It didn't appear that Sergeant was there so I wasn't worried the least bit. I felt as if this show was mine and I was going to be the overall champion; not to mention I weighed in as a super-heavy weight at this show. I didn't understand how I was super heavy at the time, since I was doing a ton of cardio and I had depleted to zero carbs before the show, so I knew something was wrong.

During the pre-judging show, I was placed in the middle of all the super-heavy weights, which usually meant that the person in the middle was clearly the winner of that weight class, but the judges would sometimes surprise the competitors and change their minds on who the winner was. I never got excited before I heard the judges say I was the winner, even if everybody at the show told me that I was going to be the winner of the show.

After the pre-judging I went and ate with Dvyne and a host of other family and friends at Sizzlers. We had a good time and everybody was telling me that I was clearly the winner of the bodybuilding show, but I knew how these shows worked and I worried that they might jinx me with their compliments, so I didn't get too excited.

The night show came and once I was called out as the first place heavyweight winner, I just knew that I was going to be the overall winner of the show. After I received my first place trophy, I had to stay on the stage to compete against all the other first place competitors.

I got word that I was going to have to battle it out with the heavy-weight winner because he was dry and grainy, but he had tiny legs so I figured I could pull off the overall win. The heavyweight and I battled as if we were at war. I was clearly bigger than him but he was in better condition than me. I had people in the crowd screaming my name and it truly felt good.

After the pose down, all the competitors shook one another's hands and told one another good job. Then the announcer came on the mi-crophone and said," "The 2009 overall Contra Costa winner is – Mr. Rick Figoni!" I didn't show any sign of disappointment. I just shook Rick's hand and told him good job. I walked off the stage and grabbed my first place trophy and thought about what I had done wrong to not win the overall title. I knew that I had to do more research on getting dry and grainy because Rick had the shit down to a science.

The show didn't end until midnight and I was so exhausted and upset that I didn't even say bye to my family. I went straight back to my hotel room and just drank about a half a gallon of water before going to sleep. The next morning when I woke up I noticed that my ankles and calves were worse than they were the day before. I could press my calve area and it would leave an indention in the area that I pressed. Dvyne saw my ankles and said that we needed to go to the hospital but I told her that I was going to be alright. I got on my scale that I always took with me to bodybuilding shows and I saw that I had gained 12 pounds just by drinking a half gallon of water. I didn't know what was going on but I definitely had to find out because I knew that it wasn't good at all. Since I was in contest shape, I decided that I was going to do the California bodybuilding show in Culver City CA.

I knew that I had to get the grainy look that Rick had and it was simple as that. I studied like a mad man and learned that I needed to take certain fat burners to get the grainy, dry look. I started taking them right after the Contra Costa show because the California bodybuilding show was only 14 days away. I noticed my body transforming immediately and I started getting the dry grainy look that I knew I needed to win the shows. I was, of course, still learning through trial and error about this bodybuilding thing, and it was complicated to learn without a scientist on deck.

The California bodybuilding show I decided to go to by myself because Dvyne and I weren't seeing eye to eye at the time. When I got to the Lax Airport, I rented a car and found my way to the hotel I was staying at. Once I was settled in at the hotel, I went and got myself the things I would need for the competition. I went to the grocery store and bought a bag of potatoes and some cooked whole chickens. I learned through my extensive studies that eating potatoes would help me to get the super dry grainy look I was trying to achieve.

The California bodybuilding show was the first show that I actually abused the diuretic called lasix. I was willing to do whatever it took to win the overall title and I stopped drinking water the day before the competition.

My body was transforming on an hourly basis. I was happy with what I was seeing and I knew that it was the best I had looked at any of the other shows I'd been to. I stayed in the hotel and ate all day and night without drinking any water. I was looking the best I had ever looked and I was excited. I was the most veiny I had ever been; I was so veiny that it was actually scary. I didn't see any water build up on my calves and ankle area so I was even more happy about that.

The next morning came and I didn't sleep much so it was almost as if I didn't get any sleep at all but when I got up at 6:00 a.m. I looked at myself in the mirror and I was amazed at how my body looked. Veins were places I had never seen them before and my abs were so cut it looked as if I didn't have any skin on my muscles. I knew I was going to win this show as it was going to be my best showing.

When I got to the weigh-ins, the first person I noticed was Rick and then Sergeant. I was actually happy to see them because I had brought an entirely new physique and I was a heavy-weight for this show so I, Rick and Sergeant would get to battle it out once again. When I got on the scale to weight with the heavy-weights, everybody was asking me if I was a heavy-weight or a super-heavy and I answered with a smirk that I was a heavy-weight. I saw the grim look on everyone's face when I told them that.

At the pre-judging, Rick was put in the middle, I was on the right side of him and this other black competitor with the biggest legs I'd ever seen on an amateur competitor was on the left side of Rick. I didn't think anything of not being in the center because I knew that the judges would do things other than the norm at these shows.

I felt confident after the pre-judging that I was the winner. I analyzed my competitors and I didn't feel threatened at all. Rick had tiny legs but his conditioning was amazing and Sergeant looked like crap so I just knew this was my show to win. I went back to my hotel room after the pre-judging and ate a ton of food to fill out my muscles even more than they were filled before and I was looking fantastic.

The time had finally come to see who the winner of the heavy-weight class was going to be. I was confident as I stood on stage with the other four competitors.

As Rick, Big Legs, and I stood on stage, the announcer called out, "In third place we have –Kali Muscle!"

I looked around for a second in shock and when I realized that my name was called, I went to get my trophy and then I shook the two remaining competitors' hands. Big Legs was called for second place and then Rick was the first place winner again. My mind starting thinking about all types of negative things. I was thinking to myself that that show was straight politics at its best. I felt that Big Legs should have won first place over Rick, but evidently there was something going on beyond my comprehension. After the heavy-weight class was done, I packed my things and left the building as fast as I could.

That was the most upset I had ever been at a competition because I knew that the shit was definitely rigged up. I had left before I even found out who the over-all winner would be. I figured that it would have been Sergeant, but I was wrong again because Sergeant was placed second in the super-heavy. Rick had won the Mr. California title and I was madder than words could ever express. I was so mad about losing that I went to Denny's and ate food and drank fruit drinks until I was about to bust. That was the first time in my life that I had actually drank or ate anything until I was sick. I had gained about 15 pounds from that junk. I looked terrible the next morning when I woke up. I felt defeated and bamboozled at the 2009 California bodybuilding show;

I knew that I had to bring a physique that was farfetched in order to win an overall title.

Once I was back in Oakland I decided that I was going to do the San Jose bodybuilding show, which was in seven weeks. I had to learn more about my body and figure out how to get the excess water off of it, but I didn't know how to do that at that point. I had seven weeks to learn what I could about the art of bodybuilding. It seemed as though I learned something different every day that I researched. Bodybuilding was definitely a complicated sport because the only way a competitor could win was to know the scientific aspect of the sport. I knew that I had more muscle than all of the competitors I came across, but I had a lot to learn about the art of getting the body in competition condition.

I had to give Dvyne a lot of credit for dealing with me during this complicated time in my life as I tried to find my way in the sport of bodybuilding.

The next bodybuilding competition I did was the San Jose body-building show in San Jose California. I was doing this show to prepare myself for the biggest show of the year, the USA's in Las Vegas, Nevada. The USA bodybuilding show was the bodybuilding show that the top three overall winners received their pro cards, which was every amateur bodybuilders dream to do.

I was named the 2009 San Jose bodybuilding show heavy-weight winner, but I was denied again of the overall title. I didn't know what to do to win an overall title. I was more upset than the California body-building show because this dude that won the overall didn't have a cut in sight. Once I saw what was going on, I knew it was politics. My fire to compete in bodybuilding was getting extinguished by that point. I decided I would go to the USA bodybuilding show in Las Vegas to see where I stood against the top bodybuilders in the country.

The USA bodybuilding show was 10 days from the San Jose body-building show. I was in great shape so 10 days was perfect for me to do what I needed to do in order to get my body in better condition than it was in. I weighed 220 pounds at the San Jose bodybuilding show and I looked great. After the San Jose show, something told me that I needed to drop down to a light-heavy weight, and if I did that then that meant I had to be 198 pounds at weigh in at the USA bodybuilding show. As soon as I got home from the San Jose show, I started doing cardio more than ever to drop the 22 extra pounds within the 10 day deadline.

I knew the ten days would fly by so I did everything from two cardio sessions a day, to getting in the tanning bed every day, to sitting in the sauna. The first 10 pounds came off fast but that last 12 pounds was hell to get off. I wasn't consuming any carbohydrates the last seven days before the bodybuilding show and the extra pounds still weren't coming off.

The day came when Dvyne and I had to go to the Oakland Airport, and I was still about five pounds overweight but I knew that by the time I reached Las Vegas that the diuretics I was on would shed off the pounds I needed off. As Dvyne and I went to the passenger gate, we were told that we wouldn't be able to get on the next flight because we had buddy passes and the flight was already booked. Two more flights came after the first one we missed and we were getting short on time because the weigh-in was over at 8:00 p.m. The next flight that was leaving was set to land in Las Vegas at 7:00 p.m., and I prayed that two seats were available for Dvyne and me because if I missed that flight I was going to miss the entire competition. Luckily the next flight had two available seats for us and I knew that God had made a way for me to do this bodybuilding show.

When we landed in Las Vegas, Dvyne, being Dvyne, wanted to get a limousine to the hotel so we rode in a stretch limo to the Cancun resort. After we checked in at the resort, I checked to see if I'd dropped the extra pounds and I hadn't so I went to the resort's gym and got on the bike to do some cardio to hopefully drop the two extra pounds that I was having a problem getting rid of. When the time came for me to weigh-in, Dvyne and I went to the hotel that was hosting the USA bodybuilding show. When I got to where all the competitors were, I was overwhelmed with all the competition. I didn't know how I would do at the biggest show of the year. There were some huge motherfuckers at that show and I became mad at myself for burning up a lot of my muscle trying to come down to a weight that I hadn't been since I was a teenager. When I got on the scale, I was 198 on the nose. I felt like I had already won just by getting down to that weight. Right after I was finished weighing in, I went and ordered all types of food to fill up my deflated muscles. I felt the energy surging through my body as I ate the high carb, high fat food.

Once Dvyne and I were back to the Cancun, we went and hung out by the pool and enjoyed the summer heat. I was unable to drink any water so I was looking like I was about to die from dehydration. I'd never seen myself look so sickly. It was kind of scary. My cheek bones were protruding out of my face and I was so dehydrated that my eyelids were sticking to my eyes; all of this for the sake of trying to become a pro bodybuilder. I ate the rest of the night, trying to fill up my deflated muscles, but I didn't yet fully understand the science of filling back up my muscles so my body wasn't gaining the muscle size back the way I hoped it would.

The morning of the show I looked at myself and I wasn't happy at what I saw in the mirror. I had lost all my leg size to the point my legs looked like stilts. I was very disappointed in myself for losing all my muscle size on the account of what was implanted in my mind about going to the light heavy weight class.

When I got to the bodybuilding show and saw my competition, I knew that I would be lucky to be in the top 15 because most of the light-heavy weight competitors were way shorter than me with thick legs and here I was way taller than most of the light-heavies with small legs. I looked at this competition as a learning experience for the years to come.

I ended up being in 11th place, which was good for how I had fucked up so badly. I had beat some guys that I thought for sure were going to beat me. One thing for certain was that I was peeled to the bone, literally.

I had a photo shoot the next day with a company called Strength-net, so I couldn't party too hard because they were paying me $600 so I had to be professional and come to the shoot sober.

The shoot went great with Strengthnet; it was a simple video of me working-out and talking smack. It was good for entertainment. I learned a tremendous amount doing the USA bodybuilding show. The main thing I learned was that I had to learn the science of the bodybuilding sport. I could tell that I didn't know the things that the top competitors knew so I would have to step up my knowledge of science.

I was glad that I was finished doing the bodybuilding shows but now I knew that I had a lot of work and research to do in order for me to become a pro bodybuilder in the future. My studies started immediately after I got back home from Las Vegas.

Everything was going good for me financially. I was still shipping the ecstasy pills out of state, so I was definitely making good money. I was also training a few people here and there, so life was definitely looking up for me, but I had a gut feeling that things weren't going to be going good for too much longer.

After my last bodybuilding show in July, I found out through extensive studying that I had to do things differently than how I had been doing things before. The first thing was that I needed to incorporate two days of leg training into my regiment. The second thing was that I had to increase my repetitions on all of my exercises to 15-20 repetitions per exercise. Thirdly, I had to start eating more food. I came to see that the sport of bodybuilding was a very complicated sport, but I was up for the challenge.

Things were getting shaky with the ecstasy business and I knew that it was going to be over with very soon, so I started saving every bit of money I could. I stopped shopping for clothes every week and I slowed down on me and Dvyne going out for dinner as much as we were. I still had a few personal-training clients, but they were always shaky. You never knew as a personal trainer when the client was getting short on money until they told you that they couldn't afford to train any longer. The personal training business was an unstable career choice for sure.

Months were going by fast and I had proposed to Dvyne while we were at the Oracle Coliseum at a gospel sing off competition. The ring I'd bought her wasn't what she expected and I could tell by the way she took a double take of it. I wasn't familiar with the typical proposal and marriage stuff, so I thought that I did a pretty good job. After seeing Dvyne's reaction to the ring though, I felt kind of bad, but I said to myself, "Oh well! If she didn't like it then that's her problem; I did the best that I could!" Plus, I still had to buy another ring for the wedding and I was far from rich so everything I did counted in a major way.

Christmas 2009 had come and I made it a point to do all of my Christmas shopping before everybody else so that I wouldn't get into any other altercations during the holiday season. I never liked the holidays because it seemed as though all the holidays did was have people spend all their money on trying to make other people happy. Not only that, but there were all sorts of family feuds that took place during the season too.

After the Christmas dinners were over, I went home and got on the computer to do my daily research of bodybuilding. As I was deep into my studies I heard the front door open and in came Dvyne smiling.

"What's up baby?" I asked curiously.

Dvyne was excited and told me that she wanted me to meet someone and I, hating to meet new people, asked with obvious attitude who it was. Not only did I dislike meeting new people, but I disliked it even more when I wasn't informed beforehand. As soon as Dvyne finished her introduction, in came a nigga as dark as me and he was clearly an older man trying to dress like a youngster.

Before I could say, "Who is this?" Dvyne said, "This is my father, Michael!" I reluctantly shook the man's hand because I already knew enough about him to know I didn't like him. Anytime I heard him talking to Dvyne, he was always trying to make her give him money so I didn't have much respect for him. I knew from the get go that he was a dope head that always tried to take what he could from whoever fell prey, so my defenses were up and I let him know through my stern demeanor that I didn't like him and never would.

I asked Dvyne why she brought him to our house. Dvyne said that she was going to let him stay upstairs with Kente and Daniel because he was sick and needed somewhere to go. I immediately threw an irate fit.

"Why you bringing a fucking dope head to our house, knowing that I got my business I do and not to mention all the money I got in the house? I don't trust him and I don't want him living here, period!" I shouted angrily.

Dvyne started to talk and I hopped in my truck and took a ride to clear my mind. When I got back to the house Dvyne and her father were gone.

I called Dvyne's mother first and asked her if she knew about the decision that Dvyne had made without anyone's approval and Dvyne's mother said she didn't know at the time but that she was about to call her about it. I was so mad it felt as though my fucking head was going to explode. I called Dvyne and told her how I felt about the situation and she started telling me some bullshit that her conman father had told her about him being sick possibly dying soon. Dvyne said that she was going to help her father no matter what

"Alright don't expect me to say shit to the dude because he's a fucking dope fiend and you will see the real him soon enough! He's never done anything for you in your life, you even told me that he stole your mother's money when they were together, and now what makes you think that he won't steal from you?" I said irately.

I was overly mad so I had to calm myself before I busted a blood vessel. I didn't know what it was about Dvyne and her mother, but they thought that they could save the world by letting people live with them, despite the fact that all the people did was fuck them over, time and time again.

2010 came around fast and Dvyne had settled out of court for one of her real estate lawsuits for $10,000, so she was waiting for that as well as a settlement for her disability claim she had put in because of her bad back. We were expecting a few lump sum amounts and we had decided that we were going to get married as well as move to Los Angeles when the money came.

At the beginning of 2010, a new law came out about felons not being able to be in-home care providers so I immediately told Big Low that he needed to get someone else to be his in-home care provider. I was looking for an out because I didn't want to see Big Low like that any longer; it was not only depressing but it was also draining my spirit hearing him be so miserable all the time. After the in-home care was transferred over to Big Low's person of choice, I stopped communicating with him all together because I felt that it was best for the both of us. If you ask me why, all I can tell you is that my heart and spirit needed a rest.

The year was flying by and I was still personal-training, shipping pills, and also preparing to do some bodybuilding shows. Dvyne's brother Kente was as belligerent as ever. That dude would get off work at the YMCA every single day and come home and start his rant of crying, stomping, and screaming. Kente was definitely getting out of control. He had hit Dvyne, her mother, Daniel, Dvyne's father (Mike), and Dvyne's step-father, and I would always rough him up when he did so. The thing was that if I wasn't around he would try to harm them all, but when I was around he would act like an angel, most of the time that is.

One morning around 5:00 a.m., Kente came downstairs to our house knocking on our door, being belligerent, and I told him to take his ass to his house and shut up. Kente kept knocking on our door as if I didn't say anything to him, so I got dressed.

Dvyne knew something bad was about to happen so she got up as well. When I went to the door that Kente was banging on, I opened the screen door with force and it hit Kente in the face. As he was falling backwards I grabbed him and slammed him on the iron gate that enclosed the house. I ran Kente into the gate and I saw blood squirt out from his head.

I remained calm and said, "See what you made me do? Now we got to take you to the damn hospital!"

Kente was crying at that point and Dvyne grabbed him and brought him into our house to try and stop the bleeding; all the while Kente was talking a ton of shit and I told him to shut his mouth or I would whoop his ass some more. Kente tried to swing at me and I hit him with a two piece combo.

"No! This is my brother! Please don't hurt him!" Dvyne screamed.

"Well you better get that lunatic out of my face before I really do something terrible to him!" I threatened.

After the incident with Kente, I got the upmost respect from him. He knew after that night that I was not one to fuck around with and it was sad that I had to hurt him for him to figure that out, but violence was the only thing Kente respected. If Kente didn't have fear of a person he wouldn't respect them.

By the time March came around I was full swing into my diet preparing for my first bodybuilding show of the year. I had learned a lot of things that I'ddone wrong the previous bodybuilding year, so I felt that 2010 was going to be my year to do well in bodybuilding. Since I was dieting, I also got Kente and Dvyne on an exercise and diet program. Both of them were dropping weight fast as I had them both on a low carbohydrate, high protein diet that consisted of a ½ cup of oatmeal in the morning and baked chicken and veggies the rest of the day. This was a wonder program for Kente because he was losing a minimum of 10 pounds a week and Dvyne was also losing weight fast. She had gotten up to 180 pounds, which was very unacceptable and she knew it. We knew that we were heading to Los Angeles soon so that was her motivation to lose the excess weight.

While I was preparing for the May bodybuilding show, the family and I found out that the house we were living in was being foreclosed on and the family decided that we were going to try and buy it. I didn't agree with their decision to do that because the house was in a terrible neighborhood and it wasn't somewhere that you would want your family to live.

My wife and her mother had an accountant that did the paperwork to try and purchase the house, but it didn't go through. The next step was for me to try and purchase the house with my credit. I knew that we weren't meant to get that house because it had far too many problems. After my credit and income was unable to purchase the house, it eventually went to the auction. I had $15,000 saved up and I had agreed to put $10,000 up for the house at the auction.

Dvyne, her mom, the accountant and I went to the auction to learn that the house had been taking back by its rightful owner, the bank. This house situation was truly stressing me and the entire family out. The family knew that we had to make something happen, and fast.

Things weren't going good with my mom and me at the time because my mother had confronted Dvyne about telling my brother's new girlfriend that the family didn't have a lot of money. Dvyne didn't say that to talk down on the family, she said it to the girl because the girl seemed like a gold digger trying to come up off of my brother. That conversation with Dvyne and my brother's girlfriend caused my mother and me not to talk for seven months. Whatever was connected with my younger brother, my mother always believed it, whether it was true or false. That was something I had experienced with her all my life, and that's why we were never as close as a mother and son should have been.

Right before the incident with Dvyne and my mother, I had bought myself a beautiful truck with some of the money I had made from selling pills. I had given the truck I was driving before back to my mother to ensure that there were no ties when we disconnected for the lengthy amount of time we did.

After the bank had gotten the house back, they immediately put it on the market to be bought and people started coming by trying to see it. I would scare off every potential buyer because I knew that there was a possibility that if, in fact, someone bought the house, that they would want me and my family out of it in a certain time period. That's why I did everything in my power to hold onto the house as long as we could, at least until we figured out our next move.

I had a beautiful pit bull named Zuri that was about nine months old at the time. I'd gotten her when she was only six weeks and she had grown up to be one of the most beautiful dogs I'd ever seen; however, Zuri had a discipline problem that I didn't know how to deal with. I spent all day, every day with Zuri, playing with her and training her to the best of my ability. Zuri was actually a good dog, aside from the fact that she was overly hyper when I took her outside and that she would get mad when made her go to her bed that was in the front room of the house.

Zuri was becoming very destructive and she always knew when she did something wrong because she would squat to the ground and crawl to her bed. Every time Zuri did that, she had either shit on the floor somewhere in the house or she had chewed up something. Dvyne was getting fed up with Zuri's behavior and I was as well. I knew that I would have to get Zuri some training soon or else she was going to grow up and be uncontrollable.

The bodybuilding show had come fast and I had done all the necessary things to prepare myself for the show. I did all the crazy things like: carb depletion, diuretics, stopped drinking water, tanning, posing, cardio, and carb load. Bodybuilding was an intensely complicated sport where everything had to be perfect to look perfect. Even stress levels have to be perfect or the body wouldn't respond to the things that were being implemented for the perfect physique.

I had the same year as the previous year in the bodybuilding competitions. I took first place in my weight category at every competition but I didn't win a single overall title.

Hustling pills came to a screeching halt because I had sent the pills out of state and the cat I was sending them to, who was supposed to be one of the only trust worthy Kumi comrades I had, supposedly sent the money in some gloves in a box but the money never came. When I received the box that the $10,000 was supposed to be in, I opened it to find that there wasn't anything inside it except for an empty pair of gardening gloves. I just knew that that cat couldn't possibly have fucked me over, because if he did I was going to fly to where he was and blow his fucking brains out.

After calling the Kumi cat a few times to figure out what we were going to do about the situation, he stopped answering his telephone – something he never did in the entire two years we had been in business together. Once the unanswered calls started happening, I knew that he was guilty of charge, and I made a pact with myself that if I ever came across that cat again there would be major problems, because I had never been bamboozled like that my entire life, especially for such a large amount. I not only wanted to find this cat and kill him, but I wanted to find his family as well. I had done some unspeakable things for $10,000 in my life, so this was very serious to me and my ego.

Before the pill hustle was ruined, I had saved about $15,000, which would have been $25,000 if I would have received my $10,000. At that point I wasn't making the money I was used to making so consistently, so I had to put a halt on all the unnecessary spending I was doing. I had a total of about $3,000 a month in bills, including food. Dvyne wasn't working at the time so I had to foot the bill, which was draining my savings super fast. I knew that if I didn't start making money that I would be broke by July, the month of the bodybuilding show. Things weren't looking good at the moment but I knew that we were waiting on some money to come, so I wasn't overly worried.

July came fast and just as I had predicted, I was down to about $2,000 and I was a bottle of stress waiting to explode. Just in the nick of time, Dvyne received a portion of her settlement with the real estate case and her disability case so we decided it was time for us to get married. Our marriage wasn't the typical wedding. Dvyne and I went to the gym together and it was Dvyne's first time ever going to the gym with me. After our workout we decided to go to the courthouse and get married.

Dvyne called her step-father and told him that we needed him to come and be a witness, because we were going to get married at the courthouse. Dvyne's step-father showed up and we went ahead with our proceeding of becoming husband and wife.

As Dvyne and I stood face to face, and the lady facilitating the proceeding started saying the matrimony stuff, I felt my eyes watering up because this was the first woman that I had every connection with. I saw Dvyne's eyes watering as well. I said what I felt at the moment, as did she. We were both happy as ever and it felt as though I was on cloud nine. Dvyne was now my wife and I wanted to be everything she ever dreamed of in a man.

Right after our courthouse wedding, Dvyne made plans to have us a wedding reception at the Claremont hotel, which was a very prestigious hotel in the bay area. Dvyne got everything together within three days. She had invited everybody she wanted because I didn't care who was there. Dvyne even invited my mother, who I hadn't talked to in months. Dvyne invited our closet family and friends. We had a total of 20 people there and the only person I invited was my closet friend Tre.

The day came for the reception and everything went smoothly as Dvyne and I had gotten us, as well as her mother and step-father, a room at the Claremont so that we could be right there when everyone else left. It was like we were starting our honeymoon there.

The reception was one of the best times for me and Dvyne, because we had everybody there that we cared most about. My mother and I's encounter was sort of awkward, as we hadn't spoken in over six months – something we had never done before. Dvyne had her father Mike there and he was looking the best I had ever seen him. Mike was decked out in a nice suit and he was acting like a normal human being. Kente was there and he was about to start with his usual irate tactics but I saw him before he started and I told Mike to get him out of there before there was a problem, so Mike took Kente outside and talked some sense into him. Kente was known to mess up a party, as he had done so many times before. Dvyne had invited my cousin, baby cousin and her mother, who I was happy to see. Dvyne also had her cousins there and even her accountant, who was a friend of her family but who I never liked because he was a shady wannabe minister and I knew they were undercover dope heads.

The night went well and I even recited a poem for Dvyne and then I did a skit to get everybody laughing. The wedding reception was a total success and I was happy that Dvyne was happy. The next morning she and I got massages and got pampered at the Claremont hotel before we got ready for our trip to Las Vegas for the bodybuilding show.

I went to the USA bodybuilding show just like I did in 2009, but this year I was a heavy-weight and I took 13th place because I still didn't grasp the science of drying my body out to look like a bodybuilder was expected to look. I was content with myself but I knew that I had to do a lot more studying if I expected to become a pro bodybuilder.

Dvyne and I were in limbo about what we were going to do with our dog Zuri, because we weren't sure if we could take her to the place we were moving to in Los Angeles. Zuri made things simple for us because she started doing some evil things, like taking poops when she was mad and tearing up things around the house. Zuri had become possessive over me and she wanted all my attention at all times and if I didn't do what she wanted she would do something evil out of spite. The straw that finally broke the camel's back happened one early morning, around one am, when I told Zuri to go to her bed and she looked at me with an evil look and reluctantly did as she was told. I was awakened around four am by the horrid smell of shit. I hopped out of bed and Dvyne was awakened as well and I starting sniffing as did Dvyne. I went into Zuri's room only to find out that she had shit all in her bed. Zuri was looking at me with evilness and I immediately grabbed her crate and drug it outside so that I could clean it and her, but that's when Dvyne came out and proclaimed that she had had enough.

"It's time to get rid of her because I am tired of her evil ass!" Dvyne said furiously.

After I sprayed Zuri and her crate clean, I put the crate on the back of the truck and drove Zuri to the SPCA so that she could be adopted by a family that wanted a beautiful pit bull and who had the time to give her the proper disciplinary adjustments she needed. She was a great dog, and in the right hands she was going to be a great pet. I was actually sad when Zuri was gone and I missed her like crazy but I knew that my life was about to take another turn and hopefully for the best.

During the month of August something very dramatic happened at the house. Dvyne's mother was over and she had left her purse upstairs where Dvyne's father Mike was. When she realized she left it, she said she needed to go upstairs and get it before Mike saw it. Dvyne's mother rushed upstairs to get her purse and she realized that she had $40 missing from her wallet and that Mike was long gone. Dvyne called her father's phone to no avail for hours until his phone battery was dead. All I kept saying was, "I told ya'll not to have that dope fiend nigga at this house, but no; ya'll want to save the fucking world!"

After hours of trying to call the dope fiend nigga's phone, Dvyne and I finally decided to lie down at about one am. I knew that the dope fiend nigga would try to come back and go upstairs when he thought everybody was asleep, but I told myself that if I heard one single noise, I was going to go upstairs.

I dozed off but I was sleeping lightly because I knew that Mike would try and come back to the house. Sure enough, I heard the front gate make the clicking noise it made when someone opened it. I immediately hopped out of bed and got dressed in my infamous red outfit I wore around the house. As I got dressed, I didn't say a word to Dvyne but she got dressed as well because she knew something was up. I grabbed my 40 cal. pistol and rushed upstairs. I saw that the nigga had left the front gate open because he knew that it would alarm me if I heard it, but unfortunately for him I heard it anyway. As I walked up the stairs I saw that Mike had left the front door open too, so I wouldn't hear it close. When I opened the door with my gun brandished, I saw the dope fiend nigga getting his stanking ass in the bed and I stopped him in his tracks

"What you doing nigga?" I said to him.

He was startled because he didn't hear me come in the house. Mike started stuttering and I screamed at him, "I should kill yo bitch ass right here, right now nigga! The only reason I ain't is because of your daughter!"

Mike tried to say that he didn't take the money, but that just pissed me off even more and I started to shoot him right then. I wanted to kill him but I knew that I would be told on so I had to play it smart.

I waived the gun at the nigga and told him that he was no longer welcome at our place of residence and it was time for him go before things got ugly. I had to do everything in my power not to do something to the thief. Mike acted as if he was being wronged by being put out. He had this mad look on his face and I was ready to shoot him right in his ugly ass face. As I escorted the nigga out of the house and closed the gate, I saw him lingering down the street and I came out the gate and asked him if there was a problem. Mike tried to look as if he was mad and I told the nigga that he better leave before he got found. Mike was from the streets, so he knew exactly what I was talking about.

Once that Mike character was gone from the house, things were a little more calm, but of course Kente kept some chaos going one way or another. Things were going crazy in Oakland at the time and we knew that it was our time to leave, so we were in preparation of leaving the corrupted city.

Dvyne received the monetary portion of her lawsuit that she had been waiting on for the past six months, all to find out that her lawyer wasn't going to his office and that he didn't know that the check had been sitting in the damn office for months. Once Dvyne deposited the check, she started making calls to Los Angeles to get us set up at an apartment to live in and start our new life away from all the madness in Oakland.

"Hood to Hollywood"

The day had come for me and Dvyne to move and we were ecstatic to be leaving all the chaos of Oakland. We rented a U-Haul truck to put our clothes in and all the other miscellaneous things we needed. We didn't need to take our furniture because the place we were going to be staying was already furnished. After I loaded up all of our things at 3:00 a.m., Dvyne, Dvyne's father-in-law, Dvyne's brother Kente and I had set out for our drive to the city of dreams.

The ride to Los Angeles took six hours because the U-Haul that Dvyne's father-in-law was driving – with Dvyne's Mercedes Benz on the trailer – was hell getting up the steep hills. To make matters worse, the damn U-Haul was a gas guzzler and we had to make about three gas stops.

I'll never forget the moment that I saw the sign on the road reading: "Now entering Los Angeles County". I had never felt so free in my life. I didn't even feel that free when I was released from prison after the multiple times I had been there. It felt as though a huge weight were removed from off my back. I knew that something great was going to take place in Los Angeles, I just felt it in my soul.

Once we arrived to the Oakwood apartments I unloaded all of our things into the two bedroom, spacious apartment that my wife and I would call home. As I, Kente and my father-in-law unloaded the trucks, Dvyne put the things up where she wanted them to go. We were done unpacking in about three hours. It was hard work but it was exhilarating at the same time knowing that we were going to be residing where stars were made.

After all the clothes and dishes were put up, we all cleaned up, relaxed and soaked in the beautiful atmosphere. I felt as though I'd finally
found a place that I could call home. I was mentally free and I felt that
this was going to be the place for my wife and I to raise our children
and be a successful, powerful couple.

After a few days, our father-in-law and Kente went home and our
quest for success had started. Dvyne started her quest by hiring her past
publicist, Eugenia, to get her back into the mainstream Hollywood. I
decided that I was going to help my wife reach her dream while I was also
going to fight for my dream of becoming a professional bodybuilder. I
knew that my wife was going to skyrocket to stardom and I was going to
be her biggest fan and supporter. I started by researching the things that
I knew would be pertinent to the success of her singing career. I started
Dvyne a YouTube page and I got her Facebook and Twitter accounts
up and running, as well as got her a great amount of followers in a short
period of time. I was putting in mad work for my wife's career to be
successful while I continued working out and preparing my body for
the next time I stepped up on the bodybuilding stage – which wasn't
even on my mind at the time, so I just focused on Dvyne.

A few days after being in Los Angeles, Dvyne and I did a photo-
shoot with one of Los Angeles' top photographers. His pictures turned
out alright, but nothing to brag home about.

After a week of being in Los Angeles I saw that Dvyne was spending
a lot of money on things that were frivolous to our success at that particular time. She and I got into a lot of arguments over her carelessness with
spending money. We only came to Los Angeles with about $20,000, give
or take, and the apartment we were staying in was a ridiculous price of
$2,700 a month. Dvyne ended up getting a place so pricey that there was
an argument between us about her getting an apartment that cost more
than a mortgage on a million dollar home. Dvyne, being Dvyne, told
me that she wanted a room for when her family came to Los Angeles,
but I immediately told her that she was making a huge mistake trying
to live up to something that she and our bank account weren't prepared
for. Not only was our rent outrageous, but Dvyne was also paying Eugenia $2,000 a month. At that rate we would be broke in about three
and a half months, period. I told Dvyne that she was going about

everything wrong. She, being the stubborn person she was, kept saying that something was going to come through financially for us before the money ran out. Dvyne was always referring to the lawsuit that she was still fighting against the crooked china man that bamboozled her out of money for a fixer upper raggedy ass house. Dvyne had a good case against the china man, but her black real estate attorney was a piece of shit that did things as a black attorney would do – ridiculously unorthodox.

I wasn't familiar with real estate law, but being that I dealt with criminal law a huge portion of my life i knew that Dvyne's attorney was taking entirely too much time getting the case in the courtroom in front of the judge. I knew from firsthand experience dealing with criminal cases that the defendant would prolong a case as long as possible so that unforeseen things could transpire in the case that would ultimately help the defendant, especially when dealing in a case that was for monetary gain. If, in fact, too much time was dragged along, the person being sued could transfer money and do what they needed to do legally or illegally to save themselves from paying out a hefty settlement.

The end of our first week in Los Angeles, I saw that I was going to have to do something to bring in money because Dvyne definitely wasn't a master of knowing how to deal with finances. My first attempt at bringing in money was me going down to Gold's Gym in Hollywood to see if they were hiring any trainers. Fortunately they were hiring, so I filled out an application and turned it in and I was told to come back for my first of three interviews to see if I would be working at their facility.

I was always pessimistic when it came to working in a structured environment because I knew that, first of all, most places did background checks and that would knock me out of the box; second of all, people were intimidated by me because I had the persona of a no-nonsense guy, which was daunting; and thirdly, you just didn't see many black faces at these places, so I always went in with preconceived thoughts in my mind.

I went to the first and second interviews and they acted as if they were all for hiring me at the gym. The third interview I was told that they were going to do a background check and they would go from there. Once I heard background check, I definitely knew that my chances of working there were slim to none. After a few days of not hearing from the gym manager, I went to Gold's to see what the end result was going to be. When I walked into the gym, I walked into the manager's office that before had acted so eager to hire me and I said, "Hello there!" as friendly as I could.

The manager looked up as if he was startled and he said, "Hey Kali, I just got word that we are on a hiring freeze here in Hollywood, but the Gold's in Marina Del Rey said that they have an opening there for you!"

Not being familiar with Southern California too much, I asked him how far that was from the location we were at, and he said about 45 minutes. I immediately told him thanks for the opportunity and I walked out feeling the defeat I always felt when I tried to work at fitness facilities. I knew that the manager was trying to sell me a ton of bullshit, but many have tried to sell it to me before and I never fell for it, I knew the real.

After being turned down at the Gold's gym, I had to come up with another way of making money and I needed to come up with something fast because I didn't want my mind reverting back to things that my mind reverted back to when I was financially challenged. I immediately got on the computer and started doing research on being an actor. I came across a list of places and websites that I had to sign up with in order to get started with acting. I figured, why not! I had tried robbing, selling dope, pimping, gun for hire, stripping, barbering, bodybuilding, personal-training, and modeling, so I might as well try acting now. The internet told me that I needed to start off by signing up with central casting to be listed for background work, so Dvyne and I went down to central casting and waited amongst hundreds of other individuals trying to get in the acting game.

After a long day of signing papers and taking pictures at central casting, we finally left after about four hours of pandemonium and I felt as though this was going to be the beginning of a new Kali Muscle.

I was adamant at that point about getting into the acting game because I just wasn't seeing anyone muscular on television anymore and it bothered me. After I signed up with central casting, I then signed up with Actors Access and LA Casting, and I saw why aspiring actors didn't make it a lot of the times in the business because everything cost in Hollywood. To place my pictures on those sites I had to fork out some real cash, but I felt in my soul that it would be well worth it. I also put my wife's picture and resume on the sites I had mine on but I knew that the pictures she took were too sexy, which was a no-no for a black woman in the acting business. I told Dvyne that her pictures were too sexy but she told me she knew what she was doing because she'd been in Los Angeles way before me.

I had seen on the internet that Craigslist was also a place that actors got jobs, so I went on there and I typed in bodybuilder and what did you know, there were people looking for bodybuilders so I submitted to a music video and a host of other things.

The next day after I submitted to the Craigslist jobs, I got a phone call saying that the music video submission I did wanted me to come in for an audition. I screamed to Dvyne that I had my first audition and she was as excited as I was. Dvyne was my everything, even though we butt heads at times we had a relationship that was nothing short of amazing, and we supported one another to the fullest.

"Gangster Turned Actor"

When I got to the audition, I greeted the secretary at the door and everyone was friendly in a way I had never experienced before. It was weird to me coming from Oakland, a city where people barely smiled at me, and then coming here and having white folks calling me sir and smiling at me. It was totally odd to me but I was like, what the hell, and I greeted them with just as much personality as they greeted me.

After waiting for about 10 minutes, I was called into a room and a fella walked in behind me and he looked very familiar so I said, "Hello, you look very familiar."

He and the secretary looked at one another and smirked, and the familiar looking guy said, "You will figure it out!"

I was then told to remove my shirt and I stripped out of it with no problems, as it was something I was very used to. I was then instructed to say, "No! You're not on the list!" and so I said it like I meant it.

"Great! You will hear from my secretary!" The familiar looking fella said to me.

I thanked him and walked out of the room. I felt pretty good about myself at that point because I had a feeling that he liked me enough to give me the job. As I walked out behind the secretary, she announced to me that I got the job and I couldn't help but smile from ear to ear. That was my first stint as an actor and I couldn't have been more excited. I immediately called Dvyne and said I got the job.

"Dang, your first audition and you get it, now that's crazy!" she told me enthusiastically.

I was on top of the world and I had a great feeling about my move from Oakland to Hollywood.

The next morning I had to be on the set at 9:00 a.m. and I was excited to now call myself an actor doing my first gig. When I walked up to the set, I was greeted with a lot of smiles and hellos, which was still kind of weird to me but I greeted them all back with the same tenacity. I was told to go to the wardrobe trailer, so I did that and I was given a skimpy pair of briefs and a bow tie, which reminded me of my stripper days.

I was quite comfortable in my own skin and I loved to show the world the body I had worked on for so many years. After I got dressed I came and sat on a bench where all the other talent was and all the females were going crazy saying stuff like, "So do you guys know who is directing the music video?" A lot of the people seemed to know as much as I did because I heard quite a few people asking who.

The ding bat broad answered, "Freaking Matthew McConaughey! Like, oh my God I'm going to faint!"

The shit was hilarious and I couldn't remember what movie I remembered him from but I called my wife and told her that Matthew McConaughey was the guy that I auditioned for. The phone went silent.

"Dvyne, you there?" I asked. My fucking wife was stuttering and shit and I asked her if she was alright. Finally she caught her breath and she blurted out to make sure I got a picture with him. I told Dvyne that I wasn't into all that picture taking shit, and that I was as much of a celebrity as Matthew.

"Yeah whatever, just don't come home without a picture!" she insisted.

Being from Oakland it was instilled in me not to trip over another human being because of their position in life, and not only that but I had had a bad experience with the first celebrity I'd met in my life when I was a kid in Oakland, so it was against my religion to speak to a celebrity again.

The first day on my first Hollywood production was a long ass day, but I had fun. The day ended off with me being in a bow tie and

Speedos on Hollywood Blvd while cars were driving by honking asking to take pictures with me. It was cold as hell outside, so I had to do pushups to stay warm.

The day ended after me being on set for over 12 hours and I definitely found a new respect for actors after that because I saw that it was no walk in the park. Once I got dressed I caught Matthew taking pictures with some of the talent so I reluctantly asked him if I could take a picture with him and he made a joke and said, "What you think I'm going to say no to you?"

Everybody laughed, and then Matthew and I took a picture showing our biceps; it was epic and I had an entirely different outlook on celebrities at that point.

I got home and Dvyne immediately asked me where her picture was and I played like I didn't get it and she threw a child tantrum!

"I'm just playing with your ass, here it is!" I said. Dvyne grabbed my phone and looked at the picture and I saw her knees buckle.

"Damn girl you alright?" I laughed. I don't know what it was about Matthew but all the ladies loved him, no matter the race either.

The next day came and I had to go to Venice Beach to shoot the second half of the music video. It was my first time at Venice Beach since I had moved to Los Angeles and it was a whole other world for sure. A ton of weird people were there that I wasn't used to seeing in the Bay Area, unless I went to Fisherman Wharf in San Francisco, where there were weirdo's dancing and singing for money while painted all silver. Fisherman Wharf didn't have shit on Venice beach, it was for real creepy motherfucka.

The shoot went well, but it was taxing on my body as I had to do a ton of squats in order to get the perfect shot that Matthews's production team was adamant about getting. After several grueling hours, we were finally finished and we were wrapped and I went and gave Matthew a handshake and told him that I hoped to work with him in the future, to which he replied, "Likewise!"

Right after the music video, I started going on a lot of auditions and I even went on an audition for a top notch commercial agency that I ended up signing with called Venture IAB.

I also signed with a couple of theatrical agents, unexclusive, which means that they didn't have a signed agreement so I was able to work with other agents. I went and met with one of the most talked about agents in Los Angeles named MZA.

I was skeptical about MZA because the reviews on the internet were terrible to say the least. I went against what all the reviews were saying and I went and met with Mr. Zanuck and he seemed like a business man, so I didn't see someone that really cared. Mr.Zanuck gave me some paperwork with acting classes and photographers. He said that he wanted me to take photos and take a class. I left his office not feeling right about something, so when I got home I Googled what an aspiring actor should look out for and everything Mr. Zanuck did was listed on the red flag notice. I figured I could use some professional pictures and I could take an acting class, so I went to an amazing commercial instructor named Daphne Kirby. Mrs. Kirby was amazing; I learned a lot from her about how to stand while doing an audition and how to speak being in front of the camera. I felt that Mrs. Kirby's class gave me the tools I needed to be the great commercial actor that I am.

I then went and did another photo shoot with a young guy that was pretty good. He captured some of my headshots that I used for quite a few years. I felt like I was on my way to being the next hot thing in Hollywood.

Things were looking good as far as the acting thing was concerned, but I wasn't seeing the revenue that I needed to continue to pay the high ass rent that we were paying. I knew that I was going to have to eventually get another source of income because our funds that we came to Los Angeles with were just about gone. We were fighting a lawsuit for a bad real estate deal and it was also taxing on our money because my wife was back and forth to Oakland to go to court dates.

After two months in Los Angeles, Dvyne's publicist became too much to pay for, as we were paying her $2,000 per month to do what publicists do, but Dvyne's publicist was only getting us into c-list functions that had the bottom of the barrel actors and entertainers. I could see very fast that we were going nowhere fast with the publicist. I saw that we had wasted over $4,000 to go to a few red carpets and a couple of internet radio stations that didn't even have a following. We had to let our publicist Eugenia go but she understood our position and she still let us know when red carpet events were taking place in case we wanted to go.

My money was at an alltime low so I started to panic as I always did when money was low. The devil got in my head and was telling me to just go do a quick robbery or something, and I had to fight off the thoughts like a crackhead had to fight off the thoughts of smoking crack while they were in rehab.

I knew I had a purpose on this earth to do great things, but not being able to take care of my wife like I knew I was supposed to bothered the hell out of me. I thought of all the things I could do to make money and I remembered that I had my fake barber license, so I decided I was going to put that thing to use. I went on Craigslist and searched for barbershops that were hiring and I saw a few that caught my eye. I told Dvyne what my plan of action was and she agreed with me as she usually did.

The first barbershop I went to was called Bolt Barbers and it wasn't going to open for a week as it was a new location that the owner was opening. I went in and introduced myself and my wife, and then I looked around the place and I knew that it was somewhere that I would love to work. I could tell that the owner was investing a lot of money into the barbershop because he had wood grain floors, ping pong machines, and he served beer and sodas. It was definitely a first class establishment. I did a quick interview with the manager and he told me that I had to bring in someone and cut their hair the following week when the place was up and running fully.

The following week I had a friend of mine that I met on the set of "Mr. Sunshine", whose name was Thai, and I got him to let me cut his hair. Thai was an aspiring actor himself and we became friends in the struggle of being a newbie actor. I cut Thai's hair to a tee. He was happy and Bolt Barbers' manager was impressed. He told me that I could start the next day. I was happy as hell because in Oakland when I was in the shop with Tre I was making at least $1,000 a week, so I was expecting the same thing in Hollywood.

After a few days of working at the shop, the owner and I had hit it off good and he wanted me to go with him to get some of his money back from a guy that he had made an investment with. Of course I knew that Matt, the owner of Bolt Barbers, wanted me to be his muscle and scare the guy, and I had no problem with it as long as he threw me a bone.

I rode with Matt about 40 minutes outside Los Angeles and when we arrived to the place where the guy was that owed Matt the money, he tricked the guy into letting us inside his store. When we were buzzed into the store, the guy's eyes got big and Matt went into a rant about the guy not holding up his side of the bargain. The guy was scared as hell staring at me as Matt was telling the guy that he was going to have to hand over some goods to compensate him for his lost money. The guy started stuttering, saying that he could give Matt some of his products to compensate him for his loss. Matt agreed and we started loading Matt's truck with some bullshit that you get at the dollar store like oxidizers that didn't do shit.

After going on the mission with Matt, I thought he was an alright guy but I saw that he was an asshole too, and I started to despise him.

Bolt Barbers on Melrose was slow as hell and I was barely making $300 a week, and for a man whose rent was $2,700, that was nothing. Fortunately I was making money in the acting business as well, but it still wasn't enough to pay all my bills with no problems.

I had started going on a lot of auditions and booking commercials and Bolt Barbers' owner and manager started saying little shit about my career taking off. I knew working at Bolts wasn't going to last long because I could see that the hate was beginning. I guess they thought that cutting hair at Bolts was the only thing someone was to do.

After a couple of months of working at the Melrose barbershop, I saw that I was drowning so I told Matt that I wasn't making enough money and that I needed to work at the downtown Los Angeles location. The shop downtown was like a crack house in the 1980's with non-stop traffic. The barbers downtown were making a boat load of money, with each barber bringing in that $1,000 a week that I used to bringing in when I was in Oakland with Trae. Matt agreed to me working at the downtown shop two days out of the week, which was great for me because I had heard from all the other barbers that I could easily make $300 a day working there, so I was pumped.

My schedule got hectic because I was going to a ton of auditions and I was booking most of the jobs I went out for. It was becoming a real hassle to work at the shop and I knew that my time was coming for me to leave. Working at the downtown shop was annoying as hell because the customers would go on Yelp and leave crazy reviews if they received a haircut that they didn't like. I received a bad review, which every single barber in that shop had got at least once a week. Cutting white people's hair was easy for me because they weren't as critical about their haircut as black people were, plus the white people left hefty tips, unlike the blacks, so I actually preferred to cut white people hair. The word had gotten around that a black was cutting hair at Bolts downtown and a slew of young blacks started coming to the shop for me to cut their hair. It was getting monotonous as hell for me. The only thing that motivated me to continue to cut hair was the money to take care of my wife. I definitely wasn't one of those people that loved to cut hair, nor was it my passion.

"Chaotic Christmas"

Christmas 2010 was upon me and my money was at an all-time low. I didn't want to do anything other than stay in Los Angeles and work on making money. My wife kept hinting around to me that we needed to go to Oakland and celebrate the holidays with our family. I was totally against it. I had a love hate relationship with Oakland, because of all the negative things that had transpired during my life while living in that crazy city. During that time, I didn't want to spend upwards of three hundred dollars to drive to and from the Bay Area. On top of all that, I was having nightmares about me being in Oakland and having to shoot someone, so I was totally against going back there any time in my near future.

My wife kept pestering me to go to Oakland, because both of our mothers were saying that everything was going to be just fine.

Going against my better judgment, as well as intuition, I drove to Oakland with my wife. The ride there was chaotic, because my wife's mother was calling while we were on the freeway with total chaos. I was on the verge of turning around at that point and going back to Los Angeles, but once again I went against my gut feeling.

We arrived to Oakland on the gloomy eve of Christmas, and I felt like I was battling a demonic force, just by seeing the evil looking people with their angry stares. I had brought my gun with me just in case something jumped off.

Dvyne and I went to our fully furnished house in West Oakland, which her brother Kente and godfather Daniel still lived in. When we were finished unpacking our bags, we went to talk to both Kente and Daniel until later that night.

When Christmas arrived, I was reluctant to go to my mother's house. I wasn't on good terms with her or my brother at the time, because of an argument we had had before my departure to Los Angeles. Dvyne and I decided to go to her mother's house to celebrate the festive time of year instead.

My mother-in-law was the best cook I had ever known. I felt like I was in heaven whenever I ate her cooking, and I was always stuffed with good, rich food. I didn't want to leave from my mother-in-law's house, but my wife had talked to my own mother, who wanted us to stop by to get our Christmas gifts that she had for us. We decided that we would go over there to take my mother and Wallace their gifts as well.

When Dvyne and I got to my mother's house, I didn't feel at ease because she and my brother were making snide remarks. It began with my mother telling my wife that we were coming into her house with that Hollywood stuff, which was supposed to be a put down to people in the ghetto. I didn't hear when my mother said it, but my brother said the same thing to me a while after my mother said it to my wife. On my laptop computer, I showed the rest of the family my accomplishments since being in Los Angeles. My brother made the comment again that I was with that Hollywood shit now.

It was the second time that I'd gone off on him and said, "You damn right I'm with that Hollywood shit, what you doing to get rich nigga? Your mother and father bought you everything you got! You ain't did shit on your own!"

That's when Wallace (Pops) butted in. "Hey, that's enough, let's enjoy this time together without the bickering!" he said.

I looked at my wife and she gave me a nod, hinting that we should leave, but even though I knew I should, my ego wouldn't let me.

A few more negative comments were made by my brother regarding my wife's makeup products, and I immediately checked him on that and I saw my wife was ready to leave but I still didn't want to. Thinking back on it, I may have wanted there to be an altercation deep down inside, because of my hatred towards the family that catered to my brother.

Pops tried to ease the tension by bringing out some of his best whiskey, and he did a toast to me and my brother saying how happy he was that we were out of jail and on a positive path. We all did a toast and I felt good after Pops gave his speech, because that was the first time I'd heard him sounding so prophetic.

About 15 minutes after Pops gave the toast, everybody got on the subject of Real Estate, and my little brother was talking like he knew how to capitalize off the Real Estate market. He was saying that he was going to get a house and pull the equity out and get a host of apartment complexes to rent out. Nothing he said was sitting well with me, so I challenged him on what he was talking about. At that point another heated argument ensued between us, and at that moment both Pops and Moms tried to calm me and my drunken brother down, all to no avail. Things had gotten out of control at that point, and my brother was asking my wife and me where our Maybach was, since we were supposed to be Hollywood stars. That provoked my wife to get loud, and in turn my mother got loud too. It was total chaos and I was going to show them who the crazy one was in the family.

As the argument continued, my wife casually took food out to the truck so that we could leave, but my brother was acting tough with his chest all pumped up, so I was going to show him who the real gangster in the family was.

While my wife was putting all our food and gifts in the truck, I went to the truck and grabbed my 40. caliber gun. My brother was ranting off like he was tough and so I shot several times into the air and the family started screaming. That's when I went over to my brother and put the smoking barrel to his head. My mother and Pops stood right next to their son while I had the gun on his head, pleading with me not to kill their son. At that moment I was having an outer body experience. My life flashed before my eyes because I knew that if I pulled the trigger that I was going to be in prison for the remainder of my natural life.

As I held the gun to my brother's head, I told my mother and Pops, "I will kill your golden child right now! I will blow this nigga brains out right now!"

While I was saying all types of devilish things to my parents, my brother was screaming continuously at me, "Do it nigga, blow my brains out! I don't care!"

"Baby, the police are coming!" my wife said, and I snapped out of my killing trance and I got in my truck and drove back to West Oakland.

After I left the chaotic situation, all I could think about was killing my brother. I thought of all types of ways to kill him, without anyone realizing it was me. I wanted to hurt my parents for the love that they showed towards him. I kept thinking that I had to kill him, because in the streets if you pulled a gun on a nigga it was a must that you killed him, otherwise he had the opportunity to get revenge.

I was fighting a lot of thoughts that night, but my wife assured me that we had a successful life waiting on us in Los Angeles.

"I told you something bad was going to happen when we came to Oakland!" was all I could keep telling her. I only blamed myself, because I knew deep down that I wasn't supposed to go to Oakland, but reflecting on the situation now, maybe it was written for that to happen.

The day after the chaotic Christmas, my wife and I drove back to Los Angeles and as soon as I saw the huge sign that read, "Now entering Los Angeles County," I got goose bumps just like I did the first time we entered L.A. County. I felt deep down that great things were going to happen once I had broken free from my past.

As soon as I returned to Los Angeles, I called my mother and had the most intense conversation I'd ever had with her in my life. In that conversation, I told her that I hated her son and that the only reason I didn't kill him was because I didn't want to spend the rest of my life in prison. My mother kept blaming me for the situation that happened, which was what she always did. In her eyes her baby son could do no wrong.

After the heated argument my mother and I had, we didn't talk to one another again for months, which was just fine with me. My brother tried to call me but I didn't answer, so he texted me saying that he was sorry, and that he didn't even remember what had taken place because he was drunk. I couldn't accept his apology, because whenever

I was around him he took me to another place mentally. I almost blew his brains out, and that wasn't someone I wanted to have any ties with. The main reason I was upset was because I was ready to sell my soul to the devil for this dude many times in my life and he took all I did for him for granted. My heart was hurt, so I made a wise decision to just remove myself from that situation with my so called family.

"Struggling Actor"

By February 2011 I felt like my acting career was taking off but I still wasn't seeing enough money to take care of my wife comfortably; it was a total struggle and doing wrong was on my mind daily.

The all-star 2011 was hosted in Los Angeles and everybody from everywhere was coming there; it was total chaos. I worked at an all-star red carpet event and it was raining and cold as hell. I had on a thermal under my Bolt's shirt and I was still cold as hell, so I just knew that I was going to get sick.

Damn if I wasn't right. I got sick and my damn wife was in Oakland dealing with that damn real estate case so I was dealing with one of the worst colds I'd ever had in my life. I still had to work though; I couldn't let a cold stop me from working, even though I felt like shit.

My wife came back home to find out that our publicist Eugenia was in the hospital because she had a cold that had progressed into pneumonia and it wasn't looking good for her. Dvyne and I were very worried about her.

A few weeks had passed and our beautiful Eugenia had passed away. Dvyne and I were devastated, and Dvyne was in a state of disbelief over Eugenia's passing. Dvyne and Eugenia were very close, so I tried to console Dvyne as much as possible during that terrible time.

The funeral came and Dvyne's mom came to Los Angeles to go to the funeral with us. The funeral wasn't a typical funeral because Eugenia's husband was a Muslim, so it was a Muslim type funeral. It was very sad and I even shed some tears myself because I had spent a lot of time with Eugenia and I had mad love for her. Dvyne held up pretty good at the funeral. After the burial everybody went to a restaurant around the corner from the burial site. Everyone at the restaurant was jolly and sad at the same time but we made the best out of a terrible situation and mingled amongst one another.

"In High Demand"

I started to book a lot of commercials and low budget movies. It seemed that if someone needed a buff black dude in Hollywood then I was called. It was great to know that I was finally making a living at something that I had fun doing and I got medical benefits doing it.

I had been booked to do Wonder Woman and I was going to be working on it for an entire week. This was my ticket into the actor union SAG. I was excited that I was going to be able to be in the actors union as fast as I was. It sometimes took actors years to become a part of the union. After Wonder Woman was done I booked another job on a movie called "White T" where I was going to play a bouncer. I was definitely on a roll and the haters at Bolt Barbers weren't happy with me being gone so much, but I didn't give a damn because I was on my way to stardom.

Things were being said when I would come to work at the barbershop and the manager even told me that the auditions would have to slow down if I planned on working at Bolts. I laughed at the manager in his face and told him that when I had an audition to go to then I was going.

This one particular day I went into the downtown shop to work and I had cut a few people's hair when Matt called the shop phone and told me that it was time for us to part ways. I replied with a simple, "No problem!"

I packed up my barber utensils and all the other barbers asked me what was going on and I told them that I had just been fired. Everyone that worked in the shop had been fired before, so they just thought that

I would leave and be back the next day, but that wasn't me. It was over and it was funny because my wife said that I wasn't going to be at the shop that long anyhow.

Leaving the barbershop was the best thing ever. I had my freedom again and I could do the things I needed to do during the day to further my acting career. I did take on a few personal training clients to supplement the money I wasn't making at the shop any longer. I also booked my first national commercial with Old Navy. Getting the Old Navy commercial was a dream come true because I had heard that an actor could make a shit load of money from national commercials, ranging from $10,000 to $100,000, so I was happy as hell.

Doing the Old Navy commercial was fun and I was glad that I had a lot of experience doing a lot of other commercials before that one. Commercials were easy as long as the actor followed great directions. The commercial shoot took about 10 hours and I didn't give a damn because I could have stayed there all night for that good commercial money.

The real estate case that Dvyne and I had been fighting for the past four years had come to an end and it wasn't good. The fucking attorney we had let too many things happen that made things good for the crook we were suing. The main thing the idiot attorney did was let too much time lapse so the crook was able to move money around and make it look like he was broke. We only ended up getting around $10,000 for four years of endless work and countless trips back to Oakland to go to court dates. In actuality we lost because my wife was always stressing over the case and all the plane tickets.

One day coming back from the gym I saw a paper on our apartment door and I thought it was another eviction notice as I had become accustomed to seeing them there. It was weird because we would always come up with $2,700 somehow; it had to be God because there was no other explanation for it. As I read the paper it said that the rent was going up $600, making the rent $3,300 for a two bedroom. The Oakwood apartments had lost their damn mind if they thought I was going to pay $3,300 for an apartment. Shit, in Oakland that was enough for four months of rent. Los Angeles was killing me with the rent and I wasn't going to live in no ghetto where I had a tendency to do something stupid to someone.

Dvyne and I decided to move into a one bedroom as we should have been doing from the jump. There was no reason for us to even be in a two bedroom when the rent was an arm and a leg. Anyhow, we moved into a nice huge one bedroom that I actually liked just as much as the two bedroom.

Things were going good and then my Old Navy commercial aired all over the nation and everyone was calling my wife because I changed my phone number so often that no old associates had my phone number. People were on Facebook trying to contact me in any way they could. It was kind of overwhelming when the commercial started and I got leery about being famous because I knew a lot would probably come along with fame if all I did was act in a single commercial and people were going crazy the way they were. I could only imagine what would happen when the huge shit jumped off.

The commercial had been running for two weeks and I got a call from my commercial agent and he was asking me if I did porn before. I told him I didn't but I did take pictures and there was possibly a solo video of me when I had my stint as a model. My agent said that Old Navy was informed that I was a porn star and a gay porn star at that, so they wanted to hear from me on what my position was on the accusation. I told my agent once again that I had never done porn, but there were pictures and possibly a video or two floating around of me. I told my agent that I knew that Old Navy wasn't tripping off me when they were trying to hire a famous person that had an actual porn tape on the market and the entire galaxy knew about it. My agent agreed with me and the situation was resolved. That situation showed me a lot about the ethics of Hollywood and how my past would make me or break me. I was definitely scared of being famous at that point but acting was the only way that I felt I was going to be able to get rich how I wanted to get rich.

After I did the Old Navy commercial I got booked for a ton of other commercials. I did a national commercial that bodybuilders hated me for, but go ahead and ask me if I gave a damn. I did a Planet Fitness commercial that had a comedic undertone making fun of bodybuilders. I've never been one to care what any human being thought of me because I was doing something legal, first and foremost, and secondly I had to pay my damn bills.

After I shot the Planet Fitness commercial I decided that I needed to have my umbilical hernia fixed because it was preventing me from winning bodybuilding shows and I was always having to take off my shirt at auditions. I was always self -conscious about my ugly hernia, so I went and got the surgery and I must say that I had never been in that much pain in my life. Dvyne had to take care of me for about a week because I couldn't get in and out of the bed by myself; the pain was crazy. After the seventh day I started to get more mobility back and I was able to get in and out of bed without my wife's help. By day 10 I was feeling 90% better. I was real hesitant about taking off the bandage so I waited until my follow up with the doctor. Unfortunately, at the time I didn't have medical so I had to go to the county hospital and have the procedure done and when I went to have my follow up and the nurse took off the bandage, I saw that a knot was still on the side of my stomach. I asked the nurse why the knot was still there and she said that the doctor didn't fix the knot because it was a cosmetic job and the doctor didn't do cosmetic jobs. I was fucking pissed and I knew that I was going to have to have another surgery to fix my damn stomach.

When that Planet Fitness commercial came on television, all over the internet there were blogs talking negatively about me and I would just laugh because I knew that none of the internet warriors would say the shit they were saying on the internet to my face.

I responded to a few posts I saw that were filled with lies about me, but I didn't get overly involved in the internet talk about the infamous Kali Muscle. People were curious as to how I was on television so much when I wasn't even a pro bodybuilder. Hollywood didn't care what your title was though, they just wanted to see if you were what they were looking for, for their project.

I started to get bitter about the bodybuilding community. I was following Arnold's footsteps by having an acting career and the fake, holier than thou bodybuilders were acting as if they were perfect human beings that wouldn't have done the television stuff I did if they had the opportunity. I loved the sport of bodybuilding and sculpting my body, but I didn't like the bodybuilders in the sport who acted as if they were saints when I knew they weren't. None of them were saints, I'm here to tell you. It was a trip because when the Planet Fitness commercial started airing, two game shows I did came on all in the same day. I was on the game shows "Fear Factor" and "Who's Still Standing". The blogs went crazy on the internet and the jealous ass bodybuilders couldn't disguise their hate for me. I was hot, and when I say hot, I mean hot. People were seeing me every time they turned on their television.

After my stomach had healed, I decided that I was going to do a few bodybuilding shows to see how the bodybuilding judges were going to see me in the sport, especially since I had my hernia semi fixed. Since my legs were my lagging body part, I worked them twice a week to get them bigger. I was trying everything imaginable to get my legs big. I was having terrible knee issues because of the frequency at which I was working them out.

Everything was on point but my cash flow, which had been hurting ever since I started doing everything legally. Dvyne wasn't feeling well. She was having a lot of back pain and so she was taking Norco Vicodein for about two years at that point. I wanted her to get off that shit because I knew that if you took anything for that long that it had to be harming the internal organs. I would mention her pain medicine usage to her and she would get offended and it would turn into us being mad at one another for five whole minutes, but then after that we would be back talking as if nothing ever happened.

In April of 2012 I had decided to do my first bodybuilding show of the year and redeem myself from the Los Angeles bodybuilding show I had done in July 2011 – where I placed second to someone that I knew I had beat. Bodybuilding was a subjective sport, so you needed to completely annihilate your opponent in order to give the judges no other choice but to grant the best body the win. I was frustrated with bodybuilding after I took second place at that show, because I had become accustomed to at least winning first place in my weight category, so I had to redeem myself in 2012.

I trained like a mad man for the entire time after my hernia surgery. I had brought up my legs some but I still wanted them a lot bigger; I was going to dominate with the weapons I had. Each year that I'd competed in bodybuilding, I found flaws in the previous year's diet plan so I would revamp it every year. This particular time I was preparing myself for the Grand Prix Classic so I was going to try and do a mild diuretic instead of the harsh stuff that sucked the life out of me all the times before. On top of that, I was going to do a mad carb up process of about 1,000 grams of carbs for three days. The Grand Prix bodybuilding show came fast and I did everything I was supposed to do to win so I felt in my soul that I was going to.

I dominated at the show and I just knew that I was going to be the overall winner because a million people were saying that I would win, hands down. Again though, I wouldn't feed into everyone's thoughts of me winning because that was a jinx to a bodybuilder.

The night show came and I did a standard but exciting posing routine that got me a standing ovation. I never got cocky at a bodybuilding show and acted as if I had won the overall before I did, because you never really knew what was going to happen when dealing with the bodybuilding judges.

The first place winners of each weight category stood in front of the judges doing the symmetry round and then the pose down. I knew I was bigger than everyone by a long shot, but there were a few people with better condition than me. After the pose down, we all waited as Lonnie Teper announced the winner and, unfortunately, it wasn't me. Lonnie announced that the winner was a little Latino guy – whose name I forgot – and the winner looked around as if a joke were being played on him. He wasn't alone; everybody else looked confused too. I shook the overall winner's hand and walked off the stage without showing my disbelief.

After the grand prix bodybuilding show, I decided it was time for me to get in touch with one of the top people in the NPC bodybuilding federation to find out what the hell I needed to do to win a fucking show. I contacted one of the judges and he told me that I had to bring up my legs some more, but mainly I had to be more conditioned.

I decided I was going to do the Contra Costa bodybuilding show in Hayward California a few weeks after the Grand Prix, that way I would still be on my diet and cardio and come into the Contra Costa ripped to the bone. I had to win the overall in front of my home town so I put all my energy into preparing for the Contra Costa.

I went to the extreme preparing for the Contra Costa. I stopped drinking water for two days and then I did a crap load. Once your body had no more water, you were supposed to eat a shit load of sugary and salty foods to harden and fill out the muscles.

As I drove to Oakland by myself going to do the bodybuilding show, I was cramping from not drinking water and taking water pills. It was a tough drive because my body was going through a lot of changes. When I made it to the Bay Area I stopped by In-N-Out Burgers and got around four hamburgers and two orders of fries. I never even ate hamburger and fries when I wasn't getting ready for shows. I hoped that my body wouldn't have a bad reaction to the beef, because every time I ate beef I had a weird feeling.

"Winners Circle"

When I got to the weigh-ins early Saturday morning, everybody's eyes got big once they saw me because, not only was I a celebrity, but I was known for being one of the biggest bodybuilders in the amateur ranks, so people got scared when they saw that I was competing. A few of the competitors even asked me if I had a client competing and I told them no, that I was competing, and I could see all the air leave out of their lungs.

I relaxed outside in the sun as I awaited my turn to go on the stage and it felt good to get back to doing the show because it was taking place in my back yard and I knew practically everyone there. I talked a lot, which was good because it passed the time and helped me not to dwell on the situation at hand.

For the pre-judging I was called to the middle, which usually meant that I was the winner but like I said before, you just never knew. After I did my mandatory poses, I was feeling good and felt as though I was finally the winner because the rest of the competition wasn't ready for me. All the competitors came and congratulated me before the show was even over, which I hated because that was a jinx.

The night show came and all my friends were there and I rocked the audience with my posing routine and got a standing ovation. Afterwards all the class winners came out to battle for the overall winner title and I didn't see anyone that was giving me a run for my money except a youngster that had some big ass legs. As I stood on the stage awaiting Lonnie Teper's announcement, my heart was racing.

"The 2012 Contra Costa overall winner is," Lonnie began, and then he paused for dramatic emphasis before continuing, "Kali Muscle!"

I couldn't help it; I jumped up and shouted with joy. I was happy as hell because it was my first overall title, but thinking about my next show, Mr. California, kind of brought me off my high. The California bodybuilding show was the show I wanted to win the most. I wanted to be able to say that I was Mr. California, which was the title I had been dreaming of since I started competing in bodybuilding.

Mr. California bodybuilding show came fast, as it was only two weeks after the Contra Costa. This show was crazy hyped up by competitors and fans. The word was out that a white competitor was projected to win the overall title. This was the first show that I had butterflies over because of all the hype.

At the weigh-ins for the California bodybuilding show I watched everybody as they got on the scale to weigh-in. I didn't see any threats to me other than my Patna Khanjo, who was the closest thing that would stand on stage next to me and even his condition wasn't close to mine. The white guy that everybody had hyped up looked way off, as his body looked deformed without any cuts or separation. I had a feeling that this show was mine.

At pre-judging I was placed in the middle of the heavy-weights, which usually meant the winner but of course I never counted my eggs before they hatched. After the pre-judging everybody once again came and congratulated me telling me that it was my show to win. I thanked everyone for their kind words but I didn't let it get to my head. It was evident that Khanjo had beaten the white boy, as there were only going to be two super-heavy weights. I figured that it would be Khanjo and me battling for the title because the rest of the competition wasn't looking good at all.

The night show came and I did my same dramatic posing routine and got the crowd to their feet. As the top five of the heavy-weights were called to the stage to find out what place they took, I got anxiety because I wanted to be Mr. California so badly. Once the announcer called the second place winner, I threw up my hands and yelled out in victory. I looked at the judges and bowed to them in thanks.

Khanjo was named the super-heavy weight 1st place winner, and then all the class winners had to come to the stage to do comparisons to see who Mr.California would be. We did the symmetry poses, then the mandatory poses, then the pose down. I was dripping with sweat when we were done, and I tried not to show that I was exhausted but I was. As we stood on that stage, all I could think about was being Mr. California, and to my surprise the announcer called out my name as the winner of the title.

I jumped up and screamed, "It's about time, yeah!"

I shook Khanjo's hand and Mr. Lindsay came to the stage to hand me the overall title sword. I shook Mr. Lindsay's hand and told him thank you. I was happier than I had ever been in my life because I felt like I'd finally accomplished a goal in my life.

Winning the Mr. California title was amazing and I thought that my phone would be ringing off the hook but there was nothing. I had booked a commercial for Geico so I quickly got over winning the Mr. California title because I was about to be the featured person in a huge insurance company commercial; it didn't get any better than that for an upcoming actor.

For the Geico commercial I beat out all the bodybuilders on the west and east coast, so I was once again the talk of all the internet blogs. Geico flew me in first class to New York and had me in an alright hotel suite. When I got off the airplane, I felt weird and I didn't know what was wrong with me. I did have that damn air blowing in my face on the plane because it was so damn hot, so I figured that was the problem.

After I checked into the hotel, I went and put all my stuff in the room and then I walked to the nearest market and bought myself some chicken breast, rice, and some other junk I needed. I had started drying out my body again by not drinking water so I was really feeling like crap. After I came from the store I cooked some rice and chicken. I was feeling worse by the minute; it felt as if I were catching a cold. I had a full two days before the shoot so I just stayed in the hotel room, other than a couple of times when I went out to get something to eat.

The morning of the shoot I was feeling a little better than I had for the past two days, which was a blessing because I was feeling like pure crap for two whole days. At eight am a van for the Geico commercial came and picked me up at the hotel and we drove for about five minutes to the location in Manhattan where we shot the commercial.

I filled out the contract and tax paperwork and then I got dressed in my skimpy shorts and awaited the producers and directors to say they were ready for me.

After being in New York for two and a half days, the shoot was over within 30 minutes and the directors were amazed at how fast we got the shots we needed. They were happy I was easily directed. I told everyone thank you and I took a cab to my hotel and awaited the next morning to get back to Los Angeles where my wife was moving our things to another apartment in Burbank California. The Oakwood apartments were just too damn expensive for me and I needed some breathing room in a place that didn't cost as much.

As I was about to board the airplane at JFK Airport, my commercial agent called me to see if I could make an audition at 2:00 p.m. I told him that I was set to be back in Los Angeles at 1:00 p.m. so I would definitely try and make it.

I slept almost the entire flight back to Los Angeles because I knew that I had my work cut out for me once I got off that plane. After the airplane had landed and I got my bag, a chauffeur was waiting on me with a billboard in his hand that had my name on it; I must say that made me feel as important as ever.

I told the driver that I needed him to take me to Sunset where my audition was and I got there 10 minutes early so I was able to go over the lines for the commercial. It was for the role of a bouncer at a high profile club. I usually didn't book bouncer jobs, because I wasn't the ideal height of a Hollywood type bouncer, but I did the audition anyway and my wife came to pick me up afterwards.

I was happy as hell to see my wife, but I could tell that she was irritated with the moving she was doing so we kept our conversation to a minimal. When we got to our old apartment I loaded all the stuff left into the back of my truck, and we were almost able to get everything in the truck which was great. There were only a few odds and ends left in the apartment, which I told Dvyne I would pick up the next day.

The move wasn't that bad because we didn't have any furniture to move, plus Dvyne had got a few Mexicans at the U-Haul place to move most of the stuff for us. I was done getting everything into the new apartment in an hour. Dvyne and I had the apartment situated in a few hours. The bed I had bought before I left for New York was sent by the furniture store but we were still waiting on the rest of our furniture for the living room, which would arrive in a day or two whenever the furniture store received it from the distributor.

Our new place at the Avalon was nice; it had a fitness room that had enough equipment in it for me to train my personal-training clients. All was good except a neighbor that lived on the second floor that had a fucking tapping problem that would get on my damn nerves and I would bang the broom on the ceiling to let him know to shut his ass up.

While I was preparing to do the USA bodybuilding show in Las Vegas in July, bad things started happening. Dvyne was in crazy pain and we had to take her to get an X-ray because we thought that something was wrong with her back. As we awaited the results, Dvyne and I started examining the x-ray and we saw something that resembled a baby in her uterus. We suspected Dvyne to be pregnant and it even looked like she might have twins. We were getting excited and Dvyne started telling people that she thought she was pregnant, which I was totally against because we didn't know for sure what was going on; we were only speculating. A few days had passed and we got a call from the doctor office telling us that Dvyne needed to go see a specialist as soon as possible, because there was a tumor inside her stomach. We were a nervous wreck.

We went to see an amazing doctor and he was straight to the point. He told us that there was a tumor that was growing rapidly inside her stomach and it could be cancer, and he also said that Dvyne had a fluid pack that needed to be removed as well, possibly an ovary. I was in shock and I listened but when he started speculating about cancer I cut him off and said, "You don't know that for sure, now do you?" The doctor said Dvyne was too young for the tumor to actually be cancerous, but there were always special cases. I had to hold Dvyne because she got teary eyed and I tried to console her. The doctor told us to go get all her blood work done now and he scheduled the surgery for Monday, which was three days away.

When Dvyne and I went to go check in to get her blood work done, I had to walk out of the waiting area because I started crying nonstop. I just couldn't understand how such a beautiful woman had to go through such a dramatic thing. I tried to gather myself but every time I thought I was done crying, I would start back up again. I finally wiped my eyes and went back into the waiting area with Dvyne and she could tell I had been crying because my eyes were blood shot red.

After the blood test we went home and things seemed like a dream. I tried my best to console my wife as best as I could under the circumstances. Dvyne's mother was getting on the next flight to Burbank CA. to help us deal with this tragedy. Dvyne's mom flew in to the Burbank airport and I went and picked her up and we talked as we always did but she saw the worry in my eyes and I could see it in hers as well. I took her to the house to see her daughter and they hugged as soon as they saw one another.

Dvyne and her mom went to the grocery store and when they returned I thought they had bought one of everything there. As I walked in all the groceries, I asked Dvyne where all the stuff was going because they had bought a ton of it and we didn't normally eat those things.

After putting up the food, Dvyne's mother did what she did best, and that was cook. Dvyne's mom was the best cook I personally knew; she was no joke, and she cooked all types of dishes and sweets to go along with it.

The weekend awaiting the surgery was nerve racking; we all had anxiety but we dealt with it by trying to keep one another's mind off the situation. I tried to focus on preparing for the USA bodybuilding show, even though I wasn't sure I wouldbe able to still do it after my wife's surgery.

The day had come and Dvyne wasn't able to eat for 24 hours and she had to drink some nasty shit, so she was fatigued going into the surgery.

Dvyne kept dozing in and out of sleep, and her mom was so nervous she couldn't stop eating all the snacks she had packed in her large purse. We were all getting antsy and Dvyne was saying that she had a terrible headache and she felt like she had to throw up. I could hear her stomach growling and I felt bad for her. My wife was going through it, and I couldn't do anything about it.

The worst part of the ordeal was when the "sharp shooter" came in the room to put the IV in Dvyne's arm. Nurses were all saying she was the best at putting in IV's, but now that I think about it, I think they were just making fun of her by calling her the sharp shooter. The sharp shooter had Dvyne grimacing in pain because she couldn't find my wife's damn vein and it was pissing me off. After 10 minutes of trying, the IV finally started to drip fluids. The experience started off as a total nightmare and I sure hoped that everything else went smoothly.

Five hours later Dvyne was finally wheeled in to go into surgery and Dr. Friedman came in to talk to us. Dvyne's mom and I were attentive but Dvyne was delirious so she couldn't really comprehend what was going on.

Dr. Friedman left the room to get ready for surgery and then a nurse came in the room reading off of a paper saying that Dvyne's right ovary would be removed. I cut the nurse off before she could even finish her sentence, and I told her to be quiet because I didn't want Dvyne to hear all that before surgery.

After the surgery I got to see my wife and she was high as hell and was slurring to the nurse, "You see my buff, fine ass husband? He buff ain't he?" The nurse just started giggling and I said, "Damn girl you high as hell" but I couldn't help but laugh uncontrollably as I said it. I was just so happy that Dvyne made it out of surgery and she was cracking jokes. I felt relieved to know that my wife was still with me. After a few minutes I went and got mom so she could see her daughter.

When the drugs wore off, Dvyne was put into another room until she was able to urinate. I fed her some crackers and let her drink some apple juice. After an hour Dvyne was able to use the restroom and that was our queue to leave so we got her dressed, which was hard as ever because she was in so much pain that it was crazy. After we finally got Dvyne dressed we put her in a wheelchair and took her home.

I continued my preparation for the USA bodybuilding show, just in case I was able to do it. Dvyne was getting better by the day and it was looking like I would possibly be able to do the show.

Dvyne's mom went back to Oakland so Dvyne and I had the house to ourselves once again. I would do my daily workout and then I would take care of her the rest of the day. Dvyne's pain level was getting better so I decided that I would be able to do the USA bodybuilding show that was in a few days. I could tell that Dvyne wasn't happy about me leaving her after only one week of her getting surgery, but she told me that she would be alright. I was in a messed up place because I didn't want my wife to think that I was choosing a bodybuilding show over her.

The day came for me to drive to Las Vegas for the USA bodybuilding show and I was sad that I was leaving my wife but I had to do the show. My Patna Khanjo rode with me to Las Vegas and we made it there in three hours. Once I put my things up I made a beeline to the grocery store to get all the crap I needed to dry out for the show. It was about 6:00 p.m. and 110 degrees outside. After I went grocery shopping I went back to the resort and put everything up and prepared the food I needed. I then called my wife and talked to her until I turned in for the night.

Thursday was always weigh-ins for the USA and that's where everybody got to see their competition. I saw a ton of people I knew and it was actually like a reunion of the bodybuilders. A lot of bodybuilders acted like they had sticks up their ass and those were the ones that I wanted to do something to. Everybody had seen me on television doing my thing but no one except the top officials gave me props; of course, I didn't expect any props from those broke ass hating bodybuilders anyway.

After the weigh-ins I decided that I was going to go and get in a sauna to suck out any fluids under my skin. I was definitely on point and I was probably over-killing with the sauna but this show was all about the conditioning and I was going to bring it any cost.

Friday came fast, the day of prejudging, and I was pumped and nervous at the same time. This year's USA bodybuilding show was anyone's to win. There wasn't anyone there that was a favorite to win this year, so that definitely gave me hope.

While I was backstage I observed all the competitors and I didn't see anyone that caught my eye. I walked around with the confidence of a winner, as well as of a representative of the sport of bodybuilding all over the nation; everyone knew who Kali Muscle was at that time.

Pre-judging came and I was in a calm state during my mandatory poses. I hit each pose with enthusiasm and confidence. I felt good and this was the first show that I didn't cramp at, because of the loading process I did with the junk food.

After the mandatory poses, the judges called out the people that would place in the top five, my name not being one of them. I was pissed but I held my composure and kept a tiny smile on my face. The second set of five competitors was called out and I was in that line-up. I hit my poses as if I were still the winner, even though I knew that I would be in the top 10.

When the pre-judging was over I went back to the Cancun Resort and called Dvyne to tell her what the outcome was going to be. I rested in the room all day and all night because I didn't have the energy to do anything; not to mention I was upset with the politics of bodybuilding, even though I loved the sport with all my being. I just wanted to get it all over with so I could go be with my wife.

The finals were on Saturday evening and by that time my water intake was still almost nothing. That was the third day of no water so I felt like crap. I questioned myself if this wanting to be a pro body-builder was even worth it.

Finals went by fast because everyone's name was called out and we were allowed to hit our favorite pose and then we were all directed off the stage. As the competitors left the stage, we were told whether or not we made it to the top five, which would be the ones doing their posing routine. As I walked off the stage, the guy with the clip board said "no", meaning I hadn't made it to the top five. I asked him what place I was in and he told me that I made it to ninth place. I said I would be happy to just make it in single digits and that's what I did so I was no longer upset; it was what it was.

After the show I went back to the Cancun Resort and called Dvyne and told her what place I took.

"Oh well, just come home!" she said.

I told Dvyne that I would be there early the next day, and she was happy because she was lonely and still in pain so I realized I definitely needed to get home to my wife.

When the bodybuilding show was over, it was back home to my wife and a host of bills. The rent was due and I didn't have the total amount so I came back to a stressful situation. Rent was still killing me, as I could never get ahead because of the high rent and all the other bills I had. The commercial checks came every so often and when they came I had to distribute the money on past bills, so I had to come up with a solution to my financial struggles.

God always came through for me and yet again I went to the mailbox and, what do you know, a check. It was enough to pay my rent and save a few dollars for the next month's rent. God always came through when he was needed the most.

Since the first hernia surgery wasn't complete, I decided that I would go and have my stomach repaired to perfection. I went to a good doctor that was unsure at first if I should even worry about the knot on the side of my belly button. I told the doctor that the knot was a distraction in bodybuilding as well as acting. The Dr. understood where I was coming from and set me up for surgery.

The surgery went well. It wasn't as painful as the first surgery and it didn't take long to heal. Right after I got the surgery, the Geico commercial started airing around the country and it was crazy because people I hadn't talked to in years were trying to Facebook me and get my phone number. The bodybuilders were mad as hell that I did yet another commercial. I couldn't help but read certain things about me that people put on their blogs and forums. I would usually respond to some things that were potentially damaging to my career or to someone starting rumors about me that weren't true. This Geico commercial was huge and it made people take notice of me. This was a new level of fame that I had reached and there was a lot that came with it – haters and nut riders both. I was all over the television again because I had three commercials airing at the same time and it felt good to see myself on the TV when I turned it on. The only problem was that I didn't feel like the money was adding up to the fame. It seemed to me that I was supposed to be well off financially but I wasn't. When checks came they went right back out on bills and I couldn't understand why I wasn't stacking money. I knew that I was taking care of my wife because she wasn't bringing in any money, but damn it didn't make any sense to have three commercials airing and not have the money to show for it. I prayed that things would change.

Things improved in my life after the Geico commercial aired. I did a lot more commercials, television shows, and movies. You can go on imdb.com and see my work.

In May of 2013 I became a partner with a young genius named Arash Baboo that did a short documentary on my life called, *Monster: The Kali Muscle Story*. It was a huge success bringing in over three million views in two days on YouTube. It was amazing and it opened a ton of doors. I launched my foundation, Xcon to Icon, to help the youth and people that had rough lives but who were ready to change and become productive, positive pillars of the community. I also invented an energy drink called Hyphy Mud that took the world by storm.

My mom and I's relationship at the completion of my book was the best it has been in my entire life. I haven't talked to my little brother at the completion of this book since the incident that happened during Christmas of 2010. Who knows, maybe in the future my brother and I will be able to be cordial to one another, but truthfully I don't care because my life has been great not dealing with him and his spoiled ways.

My wife's makeup line started to take off and, of course, I am still acting and sculpting my body into the most perfect body I can make it into. We have also started our own non-profit organization for adult autism and now we are going to work on having children and leaving a legacy.

Conclusion

I wrote this book personally to share my story so that you, the reader, could and would get empowered beyond empowerment. It doesn't matter whether or not you've been told that you won't amount to anything in life, or whether you're an ex-con that is trying to stay positive and do things in a legal manner. This book is for you to see and understand that you can be successful in life if you choose to do so.

Success is hard work and something you have to strive consistently for. It won't be handed to you without any resistance. Work hard to prove the naysayers wrong and make your family proud to say that you are a part of them.

JUST SAY NO TO FAILURE!!!!!!!!